THE MUSIC OF
ELLIOTT CARTER

David Schiff

EULENBURG BOOKS · LONDON
DA CAPO PRESS · NEW YORK

The permission of various publishers to reproduce poems and extracts as itemized below is
gratefully acknowledged.

Farrar, Straus and Giroux Inc
Elizabeth Bishop: 'Anaphora', 'Argument', 'Sandpiper', 'Insomnia', 'A View of The
Capitol from the Library of Congress', and 'O Breath' from *Elizabeth Bishop: The Complete
Poems*. Copyright © 1945, 1947, 1949, 1951, 1962 by Elizabeth Bishop. Copyright renewed
© 1974, 1979 by Elizabeth Bishop.

Farrar, Straus and Giroux Inc, and Faber and Faber Ltd
Robert Lowell: extracts from 'Myopia: A Night' from *For The Union Dead*. Copyright ©
1956, 1960, 1961, 1962, 1963, 1964 by Robert Lowell.
_____ 'Words for Hart Crane' from *Life Studies* (Selected Poems). Copyright © 1956, 1959 by
Robert Lowell.

Horizon Press
Edwin Denby: 'Daily life is wonderfully full of things to see . . .' from *Dancers, Buildings
and People in the Streets*. Copyright © 1965 by permission of the publishers, Horizon Press,
New York.

Alfred A. Knopf Inc, and Faber and Faber Ltd
Wallace Stevens: extracts from 'Notes Toward A Supreme Fiction' and 'The Poems of our
Climate' from *The Collected Poems of Wallace Stevens*. Copyright 1954 by Wallace Stevens.

Liveright Publishing Corporation
Hart Crane: extracts from 'The Bridge', 'The Broken Tower', and 'The Return' from *The
Complete Poems and Selected Letters and Prose of Hart Crane*, edited by Brom Weber.
Copyright 1933, © 1958 and 1966 by Liveright Publishing Corporation, New York.

Princeton University Press
St John Perse: extracts from *Winds*, trans. Hugh Chisholm, Jr, Bollingen Series 34.
Copyright 1953 by Princeton University Press.

The New York Review of Books
Charles Rosen: extract from an essay in *The New York Review of Books*. Copyright © 1973
Nyrev Inc.

Viking Penguin Inc
John Ashbery: 'Syringa' from *Houseboat Days*. Copyright © 1977 by John Ashbery.

The author gratefully acknowledges the permission of the Trust Under the Will of Igor
Stravinsky and of Robert Craft to reprint the conversations between Igor Stravinsky and
Robert Craft about Elliott Carter, on pages 226-7, from *Dialogues and a Diary* by Igor
Stravinsky and Robert Craft. Copyright © 1963 Igor Stravinsky, Robert Craft.

Contents

to
Helen and Elliott Carter

List of Plates

Elliott Carter at home, 1965

Front cover
Between pages 160 and 161

Glossary

semibreve	=	whole note	=	𝅝
minim	=	half note	=	𝅗𝅥
crotchet	=	quarter note	=	♩
quaver	=	eighth note	=	♪
semiquaver	=	sixteenth note	=	𝅘𝅥𝅯
demisemiquaver	=	thirty-second note	=	𝅘𝅥𝅰
hemidemisemiquaver	=	sixty-fourth note	=	𝅘𝅥𝅱
bar	=	measure		
semitone	=	half-step		

Foreword

This book is a study of Elliott Carter's music from his earliest surviving student efforts to his latest work. It is intended as a guide for listeners, performers and composers. Although the book is not a biography—that would have demanded a different scope and emphasis—I have tried as much as possible to view the music from the perspective of the composer's development and also to relate Carter's compositional techniques to those non-musical arts with which he has been deeply involved.

I wrote the book during a period when I was also studying composition with Elliott Carter at the Juilliard School. For the better part of three years I met him at least once a week to discuss my music, his music, the music we were both hearing and thinking about; I remember in particular his detailed, penetrating reactions to the first performance of *Lulu* by the 'Met' that occurred during this time. I have been privileged therefore not only to be able to get to know his music and writings, but also to know the man, and to be in close contact with the on-the-spot workings of his musical mind—for Carter is as intensely and spontaneously critical of his students' music as he is of his own. I was also able to study the letters and sketches in the Special Collections of the Research Library of the Performing Arts at Lincoln Center, and have spoken to performers of Carter's music and to many of his friends.

Nevertheless, this book is neither an oral history, nor a collection of documents. It is *my* perspective on Carter's music. Where the composer and I have occasionally differed I have indicated his viewpoint, but the book should be read as an outsider's interpretation of the music and the composer is in no way responsible for any errors of judgement or fact that may appear.

A monograph can easily begin to appear monomaniacal, and the reader will often react by demanding more balance. Arthur Berger in his fine book on Aaron Copland anticipated this problem with words that I would apply to my book as well:

> It is generally considered a virtue in a book on a creative personality to balance favourable comment against unfavourable. This is thought to make for an honest report, while anything approaching eulogy is suspiciously viewed as the expression of a fanatic or as a form of paid publicity. It should therefore be said that the effort spent in analysing . . . scores so closely would seem hardly worthwhile were it not for a conviction

of their very great quality. The still greater effort to put these analyses into words would be pointless were it not a matter of primary concern to acquaint others with music that has aroused in me such strong feelings.[1]

I would augment this statement only by explaining the absence of any attempt to 'place' Carter among contemporary composers. This I have avoided primarily because it tends to treat other composers superficially. Little is gained by facile comparisons based on chronology or national character, and very often those artists who in retrospect seem to have had the most in common have been viewed as diametric opposites during their lifetimes. If Carter is to be compared with other composers of his generation, I think the most enlightening contrasts might be drawn with Wolpe, Gerhard or Lutoslawski, all of whose careers resemble his to a certain extent. But if Carter's development is some day to be placed in relation to that of other artists of our time it would seem more interesting to cross artistic barriers and link his work to that of Louis Kahn, Willem de Kooning, or Robert Lowell.

[1]Arthur Berger: *Aaron Copland* (New York: Oxford University Press, 1953) p. v

Acknowledgements

Although the literature on Carter is not large and critical acceptance was slow in coming, he was fortunate to have several early advocates who not only admired his music but also understood it. I am very much indebted to the pioneering articles by Richard Franko Goldman, William Glock and Abraham Skulsky; to Wilfred Mellers's *Music in a New Found Land*, and to more recent writings of Bayan Northcott, Kurt Stone, Robert P. Morgan, and Charles Rosen. Three books proved indispensable aids to my study of the music: Allen Edwards's book of stimulating conversations with Carter, *Flawed Words and Stubborn Sounds; The Writings of Elliott Carter*, meticulously selected and edited by Else Stone and Kurt Stone; and last but not least, the catalogue of the exhibit honouring the composer on his 65th birthday by the Music Division of the New York Public Library, *Elliott Carter, Sketches and Scores in Manuscript*, which was prepared by Richard Jackson, Head of the Americana Collection of the Music Division of the New York Public Library, assisted by Pamela S. Berlin and John Shepard.

Writing this book proved to be an unalloyed pleasure, not only because of the musical riches I was able to discover, but also because of the many people who helped me along the way. Helen and Elliott Carter were unstinting in their time, assistance, advice and encouragement; I can only begin to thank them for all their warmth and generosity. Charles Rosen not only offered me what seems in retrospect to have been a crucial bit of editorial advice but also gave me a place to work, without which the book would not have been possible. Paul Jacobs, Richard Hennessy and Allen Edwards kindly read parts of the book in draft and offered many helpful suggestions. Minna Lederman Daniel provided me with vivid accounts of the composer's early career, and was an enormous help in putting my large task in perspective.

I am much indebted to the staff of the Music Division of the New York Library. For many months the Research Library of the Performing Arts at Lincoln Center was my home away from home, and I always received the greatest possible co-operation and help. In particular I wish to thank John Shepard for all his assistance in tracking down Carteriana at the library, and for preparing the bibliography.

Many performers shared their knowledge of the music with me and helped me to see it from a performer's point of view. I am grateful to Ursula Oppens,

Robert Mann, John Graham, Barbara Martin, Karen Lindquist and Marvin
Wolfthal for their assistance. I would also like to thank Yehudi Wyner who
lent me tapes of performances by himself and his wife Susan Davenny Wyner,
and of an extended and probing interview he had done with Carter for
Canadian radio.

Phyllis Birnbaum was of great help in researching the performances of
Philoctetes and *Mostellaria* by the Harvard Classical Society. Ellen Taaffe
Zwilich was a constant source of good sense and the driving spirit behind the
festival of Carter's music held in New York in 1978, which made it possible for
me to hear works in live performance.

Richard Goodman read and closely criticized two complete drafts of the
book. Without his keen literary judgement the book might easily have lost all
sense of focus and direction.

The intelligent and enthusiastic understanding of Carter's music by British
musicians and music-lovers, was a great inspiration to me. I am especially
thankful to Simon Emmerson, Bayan Northcott, Brigitte Schiffer, Tim
Souster, Maureen Beedle and Julian Mitchell Dawson for their assistance,
and to Peter Maxwell Davies for letting me attend his classes at Dartington
Summer School of Music.

I have been most fortunate to have Sir William Glock as my editor. Not
only has he been a long-time champion of the cause of contemporary music,
but as an editor he has been both patient and precise. Knowing that my
writings would be closely and sensitively read made my job immeasurably
easier.

My family has been a great source of strength throughout the writing of this
book. My parents, Jack and Lillian Schiff, encouraged, advised and assisted
me every step of the way. My wife Judy filled my life with the joy necessary to
sustain this project.

David Schiff

1

An Overview:
Family, Education, Creative Method

Elliott Carter makes music out of simultaneous oppositions. A piano accelerates to a flickering tremolo as a harpsichord slows to silence. Second violin and viola, half of a quartet, sound cold, mechanical pulses, while first violin and cello, the remaining duo, play with intense expressive passion. Two, three or four orchestras superimpose clashing, unrelated sounds. A bass lyrically declaims classical Greek against a mezzo-soprano's American patter. These surface oppositions point to profound structural and aesthetic polarities. The music is often Apollonian and Dionysian at the same time. This is not because different aspects of the music belong to one of these categories or the other, as when we say that Brahms's melodies are romantic and his structures classical, but because every aspect of the composition articulates opposed values. The music is often at once highly structured *and* improvisatory; fragmented, yet unbroken.

Carter has an appetite for opposites. He is not interested in reconciling them, as a romantic composer would be; nor does he choose to ignore them. He delights in them. Highly charged contrasts provoke his imagination, inspiring patterns of unprecedented complexity, as when two webs of plucked tones mesh in a dizzying, hallucinatory gauze.

Carter's taste for opposition manifests itself throughout his musical life, from his boyhood through his education and onwards through the slow process of creative self-discovery. His precocious love of music set him against the values of his family, a conflict that became exacerbated through the years. On his father's side he is descended from Chittenango, New York, farmers—although like another New Yorker, Henry James, Carter is often mistaken for a 'New Englander' by Europeans because of his manners and culture. His grandfather Eli C. Carter ran away from home at the age of fourteen, and lying about his age, joined the Union Army. After the Civil War he became a successful lace importer in New York City. He and his wife Marion Levy (of Polish Jewish background) lived a grand life of Baedeker travel, conspicuous consumption of minimal culture. They were not Boston Brahmins or even New York Grandees after all. The family business was business. Eli Carter's son, Elliott Cook Carter, Sr., was trained at an early age to negotiate with the lace makers of Flanders and Switzerland even though the effects of polio made trans-Atlantic business trips painful. Eventually the son dutifully bought out his father's share of the company—to Eli Carter's advantage. These experiences gave the composer's father a less rapacious sense of business values. He was an idealist and pacifist with socialist sympathies. His wife, Florence Chambers, came from a modest Brooklyn family of Ulster Irish descent. Early in the composer's life his father showed him the scarred battle-fields of the First War as a moral lesson; when he died he left the company to its employees. His sympathies did not extend to musical composition.

Elliott Cook Carter, Jr., was born on 11 December, 1908. The family lived on 95th Street on Manhattan's West Side, then a prosperously middle class area, though not fashionable. The young boy was groomed for the third generation of lace importing, learning to speak French before he could read English. (This purely mercantile linguistic training later blossomed into a virtuoso command of languages and literatures.) The boy had other interests. Before he could read he was able to identify and sing all the music in the family's record collection, an accomplishment which the *New York Times* found fit to print but which did not impress the family. Carter had to beg his parents for piano lessons.

When a composer grows up in a cultured musical family he tends to be conservative. The family presents him with the classics of music, takes him to concerts, gives him the best of teachers, prepares him to enter the musical establishment. The young composer is rewarded for imitating the classics, an activity which is often confused with composition. When the family lacks musical culture, however, a young composer can develop without the prejudices of the past. Particularly in American society, where the past is apparently so unimportant and history scarcely seems to exist, it is far more natural for a young composer to be attracted to the latest thing. And if the latest thing offends the parents, so much the better.

At a very early age Carter decided that he only liked *modern* music. Mozart, Beethoven, Wagner had no interest for him. The family's yearly business trips to Europe allowed him to purchase new scores unavailable in New York—his favourite composers were Scriabin and Stravinsky. Carter says that hearing *The Rite of Spring* made him want to become a composer. But when he bought a piano roll of Stravinsky's ballet his parents sold their player piano, and familial warfare was declared.

Fortunately, Clifton Furness, the music teacher at the Horace Mann School, where Carter studied from 1920-26, shared his student's interests and recognized his talent. He took him to avant-garde concerts in Greenwich Village, introducing him to Katherine Ruth Heyman, a theosophist who played Scriabin and Schoenberg, and, in 1924, to Charles Ives. By the age of sixteen, Carter was already cultivating a life style that was the antithesis of his parents'. The Village of the '20s was much like today's Soho: it was the centre of a bohemian counter-culture based on advanced artistic ideas and a free life-style—free at least by comparison with American Prohibition Era values. The world of advanced art, opposed to the genteel artistic entertainment of the rich, did exist in American society, but only in a cultural ghetto, an enclave of self-conscious spirituality surrounded by a continent of Babbittry.

Carter's youthful musical interests are shown by the repertory of works he performed on the piano with Clifton Furness. This entire list that follows was offered for a concert in Hartford, Connecticut, in 1928. The composer no longer remembers what (apart from the Schoenberg pieces) he actually played from this very adventurous offering:[1]

Program

Wednesday Evening, December Twelfth, at Eight-thirty o-clock

At the Home of

Mr. and Mrs. Charles A. Goodwin, 84 Scarborough Street

played by

Clifton Joseph Furness and Elliott C. Carter

Part I

Sacre du Printemps	Stravinski
Concerto (mechanical piano roll)	Stravinski
Le Boeuf sur le Toit	Milhaud
Six Piano Pieces	Schoenberg
Sonate a Quatre Mains	Poulenc

Part II

Puppezetti (mechanical piano)	Casella
Impressioni dal Vero	Malipiero
American Dance	Henry F. Gilbert
"Thoreau", from Sonata "Concord, 1840-1860"	Charles E. Ives

Part III

Parades	Satie
Larghissimo, from Piano Concerto	Stravinski
Nusch-Nuschi Dances	Hindemith
Ballet Mechanique (mechanical piano)	George Antheil

Despite his musical interests and accomplishments, it was a forgone familial conclusion that Carter would attend Harvard, not then known for its music department. Charles Ives wrote the following letter of recommendation:

Carter strikes me as rather an exceptional boy. He has an instinctive interest in literature and especially music that is somewhat unusual. He writes well—an essay in his school paper—'Symbolism in Art'—shows an interesting mind. I don't know him intimately, but his teacher in Horace Mann School, Mr Clifton J. Furness, and a friend of mine, always speaks well of him—that he's a boy of good character and does well in his studies. I

15

am sure his reliability, industry, and sense of honour are what they should be—also his sense of humour which you do not ask me about. (WEC 331)[2]

Put off by the conservatism of the music professors, Carter studied English, philosophy, mathematics and classics at Harvard, taking theory courses and oboe lessons at the Longy School, and spending one summer in Tunisia transcribing Arab music for the Baron Rudolphe d'Erlanger. Perhaps the family thought they had reduced their son's musical interests to a hobby, but after graduation Carter returned to Harvard to get a Master's degree in music. (Gustav Holst, then a visiting Professor at Harvard, advised Carter that free counterpoint was more interesting than strict imitation—a lesson well learned.) In 1932, on the advice of Walter Piston who had recently joined the Harvard faculty, Carter went to study with Nadia Boulanger in Paris. His father promptly cut his allowance to five hundred dollars a year. The punishment involved sacrifices if not squalor—Carter says his teeth never recovered from those years of neglect. The family, whose fortunes do not seem to have suffered in the Depression, further reduced Carter's allowance after his return to the States in 1935. Friends of the composer say that his parents never attended concerts of his music. His father died in 1955; his mother in 1970.

In 1939 Carter married Helen Frost-Jones. A sculptor and art critic, active in the WPA[3], she had pursued a course of artistic rebellion parallel to her husband's. Friends from that time also say she was known as one of the wittiest women in New York—as she still is. Their son David was born in 1943.

Although he performed as a pianist, oboist, singer and conductor in his early years, Carter does not enjoy performing and he stopped when he could afford to. Like most American composers he has taught in universities. Unlike most, he has taught Greek, philosophy and mathematics as well as music, and devoted much serious thought to the teaching of music as a liberal art to non-musicians. As a teacher of composition, Carter shows no interest in the systematic development of skills; he leaves that to the pedagogues and theorists. Instead, he is an open, frank, kindly but ruthless critic of his students' pieces, making the same demands on them as he does on himself, though never imposing his own style or even discussing the techniques of his music. Every detail of the student's music is questioned and focused so that it achieves precisely what the student intended but could not realize. The main question is 'where is this going?', and the student who cannot answer had better rethink the conception. Lessons are largely silent. Carter hears the student's music as he reads through the score. Then he begins: 'That's no way to start a piece. Much too crude. It won't be effective that way. May I suggest. . . .' The student soon has a clear idea of the piece he was attempting to write.

Since the mid-fifties Carter has composed most of his music in Waccabuc, about forty miles north of New York City. The simple, grey clapboard house stands on a wooded hill overlooking a long lake in which the Carters swim every day when the weather permits. Considering its proximity to New York, the setting is surprisingly rural. Deer can often be seen in the woods, and the loudest noise is the dawn chorus or the evening cricket recital—except at weekends when speedboats and water skiers take over the lake. Around the house Carter tends a rose garden and a herb garden, and relaxes by playing Bach on a clavichord given to him by Paul Jacobs. But most of the time he withdraws to his studio above the garage, about 100 yards from the house. The furnishings there are simple: a Steinway upright, a large desk with electric pencil sharpeners and erasers, dozens of coloured pencils, walls of scores, books and records. A hanging chart shows the spatial alignment for polyrhythmic combinations. On one wall are photographs of Varèse, Wolpe, Schoenberg, Dallapiccola, Stravinsky and Ives.

[II]

There have been two traditions of advanced music in this century. One is the experimental tradition, beginning perhaps with Satie, then developing in early revolutionary Russia and the United States. Experimental composers have sought a total break with the European musical past. They have been interested in using sound *per se*, sound stripped of its cultural history, and in breaking down the barriers between music and the other arts. Rejecting the central European tradition, the experimental movement has flourished in the provinces where the tradition was weakest: New York in the 1920s was such a place. The other line of advanced music developed in the capitals: Vienna, Paris, Berlin. It is the line of High Modernism. This movement produced works such as Schoenberg's Third Quartet and Bartok's Fourth, Webern's Symphony and Stravinsky's *Apollon Musagète*. Although these pieces once seemed stylistically antagonistic, they now appear to share progressive concerns more profound than the merely stylistic elements of neo-classicism, folklorism or serialism. The High Modernist composers sought an autonomous, non-referential musical language. If the goal of the experimental composers was transcendence, the goal of High Modernism was immanence. Carter's mature style emerged from a profound consideration of the liberated sound-world of New York's experimental avant-garde and the non-representational discourse pursued by the High Modernist masters in Europe. He is one of the few composers (Wolpe was another) who has been able to draw on both these traditions. His musical education centred on representative figures of each movement: Charles Ives and Nadia Boulanger.

New York in the '20s was the centre of an active musical avant-garde to which the young Carter was strongly attracted (see the article 'Expressionism and American Music' in WEC). He heard performances of Ives, Varèse, Ruggles, Cowell, Rudhyar, Ornstein and others. The impact of this music on Carter has remained so great that the term 'post-avant-garde', though awkward, accurately locates him both musically and historically. The polyrhythms of Scriabin (who had not yet gone out of fashion in New York), Varèse's exploration of percussion, and many of the rhythmic and intervallic procedures proposed in Henry Cowell's *New Musical Resources* were

17

eventually to become essential elements of Carter's style.[4] But Ives's influence was to be the most personal and pervasive.

Carter's relationship with Ives can be traced through many of the articles collected in WEC.[5] Their personal acquaintance lasted from 1924 until Carter's departure for Europe in 1932. The difference in age and, even more, the differences in attitudes and values which separated them made a continued friendship difficult. Ives had chosen the life of a businessman, perhaps as a response to the demeaning social position of his bandmaster father, whom he revered. With a conscious contempt for a society that treated music either as cheap entertainment for the ignorant or refined amusement for the rich, Ives nevertheless identified with the very attitudes that had stigmatized his father's career. Already at Yale, Ives chose a life of gentlemanly social activity and intellectual sloth which shocked his father. Later Ives cloaked this betrayal in the transparent garments of transcendental idealism, claiming that the business world was more democratic than the world of culture. This claim seemed valid, because Ives accepted the definition of culture given by the American society of his time; he was unable to imagine an alternative to it, except in the democratic vistas of his music. The music itself, most of it never completed and left in a state of chaotic disarray, was often crippled by Ives's inability to connect it to a musical community in which it could be realized.[6]

By contrast with Ives, the young Carter was rebelling against his family's business values. He sought out the bohemian community of Greenwich Village as an alternative to his family's bourgeois lifestyle. Ives's defence of business must have struck Carter as naively old-fashioned (see Aaron Copland's sharp reaction to Ives's politics in *Modern Music*[7]), but Ives's destructive ambivalence towards his own music was far more upsetting. The emotional force that Ives's own confusion exerted on Carter was demonstrated when in 1946 Carter undertook the job of sorting out Ives's manuscripts to prepare performing editions. He found himself temperamentally incapable of piecing together the barely legible fragments of Ives's imagination. For Carter this was not a simple job of editing, it was a confrontation with the massive evidence of a tragic career with which he still strongly identified. (Though he left the editorial task to others, Carter was nevertheless instrumental in bringing *The Unanswered Question*, *Central Park in the Dark*, and the Fourth Symphony to performance.)

His differences with Ives first surfaced in a review of the *Concord* Sonata that appeared in *Modern Music* in 1939 (see WEC). It is a balanced review, warmly portraying Ives's personality and sensitive to the strengths and weaknesses of the Sonata. Its negative thrust was aimed at the pre-concert publicity surrounding John Kirkpatrick's second performance. After years of ignoring Ives, the press suddenly hailed him as a great American original— but before hearing the music. The very critics who created the event were dismayed by what they heard there. Carter, who by that time had known Ives's music for fifteen years, found himself in the difficult position of having to puncture a publicity bubble and at the same time do justice to the music, about which he now had mixed feelings. That he failed to accomplish the latter task haunted him both in his subsequent relations with the Ives family, and also in his own evolving sense of a creative mission. It would be another decade before Carter could come to terms with Ives's creative legacy and use it in developing his own idiom.

What was Ives's legacy to Carter? Their works rarely sound similar; Carter never quotes hymn tunes, ragtimes or football marches. Ives's exploration of polyrhythms and the superimposition of contrasted materials[8] has been powerfully suggestive to Carter but the expressive uses to which the two men put these techniques are widely different. Ives's music at its best is magically photographic, Carter's is passionately philosophical. To name moments of resemblance—the seventh variation of the Variations for Orchestra and *The Unanswered Question*, or the second movement of the Piano Concerto and *The Fourth of July*—is also to indicate how widely distant are the two composers' expressive worlds. From Ives, however, Carter received something more basic than effects or techniques—he received a critical attitude. Ives's most damning criticism of music was that it was too simple:

> Often he would poke fun, sit down at the piano to play from memory bits of a piece just heard, like *Daphnis and Chloe* or the *Sacre*, taking off the Ravel major seventh chords and obvious rhythms, or the primitive repeated dissonances of Stravinsky, and calling them 'too easy'. 'Anyone can do that' he would say playing *My Country 'Tis of Thee*, the right hand in one key and the left hand in another. (WEC 48)

Any student of Carter's will recognize how closely Ives's criticisms of the latest European music parallel Carter's own comments as a teacher: too crude, too primitive, too simple-minded, are his inescapable scourges. For both composers any music that is reducible to a few easily imitated tricks fails to achieve the full potential of musical expression. Music has to have the complexity of natural phenomena—or of cities. And it has to be as intellectually challenging as the best poetry or philosophy.

Ives's critical attitude must have seemed overwhelming in its demands to a young composer, but it struck home. It shaped Carter's outlook on contemporary music, on his own music and even on Ives's music. Indeed the 1939 article criticizes the *Concord* Sonata for falling short of Ives's own intentions, in relying on an aesthetic 'too naive to express serious thought'. (The *Concord* Sonata with its rambling structure, patchwork quotations, post-Franckian thematic transformations and relatively simple textures combines all those aspects of Ives that Carter has never been drawn to; Carter's Piano Sonata owes nothing to it.) Although Ives had allied himself with the New York avant-garde, his demanding critique of new music prepared Carter to search for a more sophisticated musical language than that proposed in *New Musical Resources*. Carter soon realised that he would have to make direct contact with European modernism.

As Charles Rosen has noted,[9] Nadia Boulanger was Stravinsky's pedagogic surrogate. The Russian master did not teach, but his latest works were previewed for Boulanger's students: Carter heard *Perséphone* and *Duo Concertant*[10] at these privileged sessions. Many Americans hoped to use Boulanger's teachings to master a modern idiom quickly and launch successful careers when they got home as Aaron Copland and Walter Piston had done. Carter's experience was different. Although he composed much music with Boulanger, he destroyed it all. His main interest was the rigorous study of counterpoint. He credits Boulanger with making him a contrapuntal composer, no small compliment from the composer of the Third Quartet. Unlike most of his contemporaries Carter was aware of Boulanger's limited range and judgements as a teacher of composition—particularly her espousal of the Stravinskian aesthetic—but he also understood her vast resources as a pedagogue of musical technique at its purest; she was always able to seize on the minutest detail of a counterpoint exercise and relate it to a chorus from *Così* or the B Minor Mass. Carter did not need Mlle Boulanger as an introduction to modernism[11]—he had already assimilated most of the new music in the '20s. Instead he used his years in Paris to relate the advanced music he knew to the basic contrapuntal traditions of Western music in the pursuit of a non-referential musical discourse. The main vehicle for these contrapuntal traditions was choral music. Carter has said that the Bach cantatas were the central musical experience of his Paris years; he read through nearly all of them in weekly sessions conducted by Mlle Boulanger. Carter also sang in a chorus led by Henri Expert and later conducted his own chorus, making performing editions of Pérotin, Dunstable, Dufay and Gabrieli.[12] These experiences were to lead to the remarkably assured choral works of the late '30s.

Carter's relationship with Boulanger was as ambivalent as that with Ives, though less emotional. Boulanger appreciated his manners and culture but not his compositional ability. (On hearing the First Quartet in 1953 she said to him, 'I never thought you would write anything like this!') Few of Carter's contemporaries understood the use he made of her instruction. He was not interested in learning the Parisian modernist style because he perceived that modernism transcended style—note his early appreciation of Berg's Violin Concerto and Bartok's *Music for Strings, Percussion and Celesta*, both beyond the Boulanger pale (wec 8, 16). Furthermore, the daily news of growing Nazi barbarism that he heard from the many refugees arriving in Paris led Carter to question the relevance of neo-classicism—'a masquerade in a bomb shelter'. Carter was seeking not the mannerisms of style but the resources of structure. Counterpoint, both in the abstracted form of exercises and the realized form of the early choral masterworks, provided a model of self-sufficient musical design. In species counterpoint there is no harmonic modulation or thematic development, little rhythmic interest and no colour; there is nothing but arching lines of pure musical motion. Carter's later music, for all its innovations of rhythm and colour, depends on the mastery of contrapuntal writing he attained in Paris; the techniques of early polyphony are fundamental to his music. And through the study of the older masters the inner workings of new music became clear to him as well. Carter's early works, while rarely Stravinskian, show a sure grasp of Stravinsky's compositional innovations. His youthful enthusiasms were now supplemented by technical understanding. After Paris he could begin to compose.

[III]

It was out of the many contradictory forces he was experiencing that Carter chose to make his music. Every work would be a 'crisis in my life'. The conflicting claims of a mechanized society and individual freedom, of order and disorder, European tradition and American innovation, would not be obstacles to creation but would become the subject of creation. Each work would be a summation of opposites, and each new work would be a fresh start, a new crisis.

It took many years to develop a musical language capable of serving Carter's expressive intentions. The mature idiom only emerged fully in the First String Quartet of 1951—written fifteen years after Carter's return from Paris. The First Quartet was not as radical a departure as it has sometimes seemed. It rests on the achievement of the previous works: some of them, particularly *Heart Not So Heavy As Mine* and the Piano Sonata, already reflect the whole of Carter's creative personality. Others seem distracted by issues that became irrelevant to his expressive needs. The populism of the finale of Symphony No. 1 or the restrained tone of the Wind Quintet proved to be detours from Carter's developmental path.

Carter composes three kinds of music: discards, studies, and masterpieces. There are surprisingly few minor works or occasional pieces. Throughout his creative life he has thrown out works that were merely facile. In the early years the casualty list included an opera, two string quartets and a symphony; later the pile of rejects consisted of thousands of pages of sketches for each major composition. (As we examined those for the Brass Quintet, Carter said to me, 'To look at all these you'd think I didn't have any idea how to compose music!') Occasionally the sketches have turned into published compositional studies, such as the *Eight Etudes* for woodwind quartet or the timpani pieces. Other studies Carter has saved for his own compositional use: the Harmony Book, a kind of atlas for his harmonic universe, or the many charts of polyrhythmic relationships developed since the First Quartet.

Carter's scrupulous compositional habits serve the demands of his expressive vision. Very often he will compose seven or eight different versions of a particular event, until it achieves the proper dramatic resonance. Often too he begins by sketching the point of greatest tension in a work, so that all the music can emanate from it—as the Double Concerto ripples outwards from the gong crash at the beginning of the Coda. New projects are chosen for fresh challenges. The string quartets were deliberately spaced a decade apart so that they would not live off the previous work's idiom. Perhaps surprisingly, Carter finds the most perplexing challenges in writing for conventional instrumental combinations. He told me once that the Duo took years of struggle because he wanted it to be unlike any older work for violin and piano, and had to establish a totally new relation between the two instruments. Carter consciously avoids facile innovation spawned by special effects—contact mikes, tape loops—choosing instead more rigorous and dangerous paths to new visions. As he said to me during the composition of *Syringa*, 'I'm setting John Ashbery's poem because it will force me to do

21

things I've never done before'. He said it with an eager tone of creative delight.

Notes to Part 1

1. From the archives of the Wadsworth Atheneum, Hartford, Connecticut, provided by Donald Harris
2. *The Writings of Elliott Carter,* compiled, edited and annotated by Else and Kurt Stone (Bloomington: Indiana University Press, 1977). All further references to this book will be indicated by WEC followed by page number.
3. WPA – *Works Progress Administration*, a New Deal measure, giving work to artists
4. Cowell's suggestions for associating different divisions of the beat with different intervals, though crudely realized in his book, certainly anticipate the tempo and interval relationships of Carter's music. Carter's copies of Scriabin's études and of *The Rite of Spring* are covered with detailed analyses of their polyrhythmic structures that he made during his student days. His acquaintance with Varèse also dates from the '20s. Varèse conducted *To Music* and was present when the New York Philharmonic read the Symphony No. 1, though these works are hardly Varèsian. In 1952, when Boulez made his first visit to New York, Carter introduced him to Varèse. A talk Carter gave on Varèse on 29 October 1975 for the ORTF (in French) is collected (in English) in *The New Worlds of Edgard Varèse*, A Symposium, ed. Sherman van Solkema (New York: Institute for Studies in American Music, 1979)
5. See 'The Case of Mr Ives', 'Ives Today: His Vision and Challenge', 'An American Destiny', 'The Rhythmic Basis of American Music', 'Shop Talk by an American Composer', 'Charles Ives Remembered', 'Music Criticism', 'Brass Quintet', and 'Documents of a Friendship with Charles Ives'.
6. My description of Ives's personality owes much to Frank Rossiter, *Charles Ives and His America* (New York: Liveright, 1975)
7. Aaron Copland: 'One Hundred and Fourteen Songs', in *Modern Music*, XI no. 2 (Jan.-Feb. 1934) pp. 59–64
8. The Fourth Symphony, *Three Places in New England, The Fourth of July, Central Park in the Dark,* and *The Unanswered Question* were works that particularly fascinated Carter, especially for their polyrhythmic, stratified textures
9. Charles Rosen: *Arnold Schoenberg* (New York: Viking, 1975) p. 72
10. Almost certainly the works Stravinsky wrote around the time Carter was in Paris, particularly *Symphony of Psalms,* Duo Concertant, *Perséphone* and the Concerto for Two Solo Pianos made a profound impression on Carter—especially since Mlle Boulanger had her students memorize these pieces. The abstract discourse and rhythmic structure in the first movement of the Concerto certainly point to Carter's later music; there are even a few 'tempo modulations' though Stravinsky had explored that area already in *Les Noces* and *Symphonies of Wind Instruments.* Stravinsky's works of the late '30s and early '40s, whose neo-classicism was more stylized and quotational, had less appeal for Carter. The Symphony in Three Movements, which in many ways takes up the thread both from the Russian period and from the more abstract neo-classical works, is a Carter favourite, however. Because of their mutual friendship with Nicholas Nabokov, Carter saw Stravinsky quite often, and they attended many concerts together. Most memorable, however, were the post-concert post-mortems—even in the late '60s a performance of *Siegfried* was followed by anti-Wagner diatribes lasting well into the early morning.
11. Her taste at that time reportedly ran strongly to Sauguet and Poulenc, composers hardly likely to interest Carter even then, though of course she always kept abreast of the latest developments, however unsympathetic she may have found them. Carter recalls finding her at a rehearsal of the Berg *Three Pieces for Orchestra* in the early '60s. She had obviously studied the score closely, but told Carter: 'This is terrible—just like the music my students used to write in the '20s!' '
12. Carter gave these transcriptions to Noah Greenberg, founder of the New York Pro Musica, when Greenberg was copying parts for the First Quartet

2

Musical Time: Rhythm and Form

Any technical or aesthetic consideration of music must *start* with the matter of time. The basic problem has always been that analysts of music tend to treat its elements as static rather than as what they are—that is, *transitive* steps from one formation in time to another. All the materials of music have to be considered in relation to their projection in time, and by time, of course, I mean not visually measured 'clock-time' but the medium through which (or way in which) we perceive, understand, and experience events. Music deals with this experiential kind of time and its vocabulary must be organized by a musical syntax that takes direct account of, and thus can play on, the listener's time sense. . . . (FW 90)[1]

Carter's rhythmic and formal discoveries spring from his fascination with the phenomenon of musical time, and his dissatisfaction with the simple approach to it in much twentieth-century music. Indeed his thinking about musical time has been influenced less by recent music than by the novels of Joyce, Proust and Mann, the poetry of Hart Crane and St John Perse, the films of Eisenstein and Cocteau. These artists created time-worlds in which simultaneity is at least as important as the linear succession of events. Carter's preoccupation with the two temporal dimensions of simultaneity and succession have led him to invoke the analogy of a 'time-screen' on which music is projected. The time-screen 'is considered to be a stretch of the measurable time of practical life, while the music itself may be incorporating another kind of time'. (WEC 344) Musical time for Carter is contrapuntal and relative: it is superimposed on the random experiences of everyday life and the measured time of clocks, which, taken together, define the borders of our experience of time. Events seem random only when we are not thinking about time; as soon as they are placed in a temporal framework we relate them, even causally. Clocks turn time into space, simplifying time 'to the point of leaving out the most interesting aspect of time, namely the appearance of passage'. (Suzanne Langer, quoted by Carter, WEC 345) A performer approaches a piece of music (at least at first) from the standpoint of measured time, time measured by musical notation; the listener perceives the music in terms of the illusionistic, experiential time which the music, like a novel or a movie, projects on 'real' time. The music can seem stretched out or compressed in time, it can seem to move forwards or backwards, while its measurable real time moves steadily forward.

Musical time creates a counterpoint between measured time and illusionistic time, just as a painting creates a counterpoint between the flat pattern of paint on a canvas and the illusion of depth. In Carter's music, as in Hofmann's or Pollock's paintings, the conflict between these basic types of perception is no longer resolved by a traditional hierarchical formula of metre or perspective. Rather, every composition discovers new structural and expressive possibilities in the complexity of temporal experience. The interplay of real and illusionistic time generates the surface rhythms of each work and determines the nature of a work's structural rhythms and formal processes.

Rhythm

. . . I was preoccupied with the time-memory patterns of music, with rethinking the rhythmic means of what had begun to seem a very limited routine used in most contemporary and older Western music. I had taken up again an interest in Indian *talas*, the 'tempi' of Balinese gamelans (especially the accelerating *Gangsar* and *Rangkep*), and studied the newer recordings of African music, that of the Watusi in particular. At the same time, the music of the *quattrocento*, of Scriabin, Ives and the techniques described in Henry Cowell's *New Musical Resources* also furnished me with many ideas. The result was a way of evolving rhythms and rhythmic continuities sometimes called 'metric modulation', worked out during the composition of the Cello Sonata (1948). (WEC 270)

Sources

In the late 1940s, Carter developed a new rhythmic language, breaking sharply with the main tradition of Western music. Whereas Schoenberg traced the 'progressive' element in his rhythms to Mozart and Brahms, Carter turned instead to non-Western and pre-tonal rhythmic systems. All of his sources share two features that distinguish them from European tonal music: their rhythmic polyphony is not associated with tonal harmony nor is it derived from regular metre.

The disappearance of metre has been the most important development in the rhythmic language of twentieth-century music. By metre I do not mean the merely notational device of dividing up music into bars—this is a symptom of metre too often confused with metre itself. Musical metre is the hierarchical, regular organization of musical pulses. It is both quantitative and qualitative. In a waltz, for instance, there is an unchanging sequence of three beats: a strong downbeat, a weak beat, and an upbeat that prepares for the next downbeat and so is the most tense and expressive. Whether this pattern is confirmed or denied by other aspects of the music, it is always present. Metre came to dominate European music at the same time as tonality—in the Absolutist seventeenth century—and both function as *dieux cachés* in the music, invisibly controlling every moment. Later, freer extensions of both metre and tonality were generalizations of the rigorous musical control epitomized in that most typical of seventeenth-century forms, the chaconne.

The breakdown of metre accompanied the rise of chromaticism and modality in the late nineteenth century. It can be heard in the shifting accents of Tristan's delirium, and in the floating syncopations of the *Liebesnacht*. Already in Debussy's music the opposition of downbeat and upbeat had been so weakened that it could only appear through assertion; without the literal repetition of rhythmic patterns *Pelléas* would often seem to have no metre at all. The final break with metre appeared contemporaneously with atonality, and in two different forms. The changing accents of *Le Sacre* abolished the upbeat. The listener hears a stream of pulses inflected by irregularly placed downbeat accents. Whatever the scheme may be for their arrangement, these accents are never prepared by the swelling upbeat of metric music. (The *Danse Sacrale* reverses this situation, because it is a sequence of irregular upbeats which the final chord fails to resolve.) Stravinsky replaced metre with pulse-rate; pulse is the rhythmic constant and the basis for his rhythmic counterpoint. In Webern's Bagatelles, by contrast, the downbeat was abolished. Although notated in terms of a metre the music hovers around the beats and nowhere articulates a hierarchy of pulses. Webern replaced metre with a liberated rubato; his rhythms are pure expressive gestures freed from any sense of a regular pulse.

Carter has extended and combined both of these tendencies. His rhythmic language stems from the opposition of metric pulse representing clock time and a-metric rubato which creates an illusion of more subjective temporal experience. This opposition is shown in the opening of the Cello Sonata (Ex. 1). Note that in this passage the piano does not articulate a ¼ metre. The

Ex. 1 (♩ = 112)

Cello Sonata

25

staccato pulses must be evenly accented; their ticking is inflected only by the irregularly voiced chords. The cello never coincides with the piano's pulses, but it is not syncopated. Its line must be played not as a series of syncopated off-beats but as an independent rubato shape which irregularly speeds up and slows down. The piano's pulses are not an accompaniment or background for the cello. The two instruments are equally important. The superimposition of their contrasted rhythmic shapes creates an overall texture whose manifold relationships emerge as the piece evolves.

Cross-pulses and Tempo modulation

In tonal music metre serves a large-scale structural role.[2] Small groups of beats, bars, are themselves grouped in hierarchical patterns, phrases, organized around structural downbeats. Without metre such grand rhythmic organization became difficult; Stravinsky had to rely on ostinati, and Webern had to reduce his time-scale drastically to compensate for this loss. While some recent composers reacted to this problem by abandoning strictly notated rhythm and replacing it by a more-or-less random sense of eventuation, Carter has developed a new kind of rhythmic design. The basic structural element of his rhythm is the cross-pulse. At almost any point at least two pulse speeds are articulated.[3] The proportions of speeds between pulses are chosen so that the pulses will rarely coincide. Because coincidence of two pulses would create regular metre, Carter's music articulates proportions of 15:8 or 20:21 instead of the simple proportions of 2:1 or 3:1 found in tonal music. He further suppresses the appearance of metre through the irregular accentuation of each pulse stream. He thus replaces the rigid grid of metre with the complex but ordered interference patterns of two or more constant pulse speeds.

A cross-pulse is not inherently interesting; after a while its repeated cycles become merely mechanical. To avoid such monotony Carter frequently alters the overlap of pulses. Different speeds appear as others fade out, so that the overall tempo of the music fluctuates rapidly. The notational means for achieving this effect is known as 'metrical modulation'.[4] This term is slightly misleading, because the metre does not really change—since there is no metre. Carter now prefers 'tempo modulation'. Tempo modulation is not new. Very often in older music there is a ratio indicated between tempi, such as 'new crotchet equals preceding dotted minim' ($\mathit{d.} = \mathit{d}$). Carter merely extended this practice to achieve his flexible web of cross-pulses. A passage from the Third Quartet can illustrate Carter's practice (Ex. 2, bars 116-127):

Ex. 2

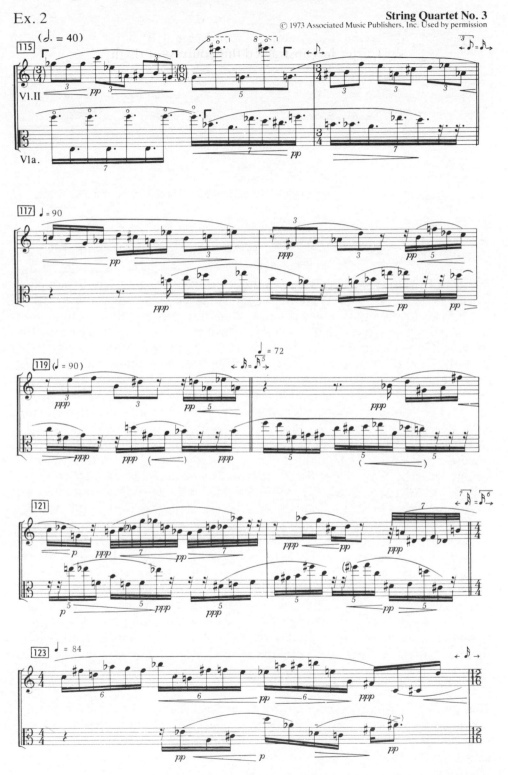

At bar 116 violin and viola play in a ratio of 9:7. The violin's pulse speed is MM 360; the viola's is MM 280.[5] At bar 117 the violin's pulse is renotated: it remains the same but is now written as semiquaver notes rather than quaver triplets. The viola takes up this speed (360) while the violin states cross speeds of MM 270 (ratio of 3:4) and MM 450 (5:4). Neither of these new speeds, though they are in simple proportions to the continuous pulse of 360, could have been notated without the previous tempo modulation. At bar 120 the MM 360 pulse is again renotated—now as quintuplet semiquavers in the viola. The violin introduces cross-pulses of MM 288 (ratio of 4:5) and MM 504 (7:5). At bar 123 the MM 504 pulse is renotated as sextuplet semiquavers. The viola enters with a pulse of MM 336 in a ratio of 4:6 (but note the accentuation in groups of five which prevents the formation of a simple polyrhythm). The process continues with new pulses introduced at speeds of MM 448, MM 588, MM 420, MM 525, MM 540. At bar 146 a maximum speed of MM 630 appears—the goal of the previous modulations.

This passage, like almost all of Carter's music, is notated conventionally, with simple metres and fairly regular barlines. The barlines are merely aids to performance, however, for the notated metre must never be heard. Similarly the cross-pulses must not be played as polyrhythms: the listener should not hear regularly coinciding patterns of, say 5:4. This would stress a single, unified pulse (the pulse of the coinciding beats) as in Chopin's polyrhythmic études, an effect contrary to the spirit of this music. The players certainly must *count* a unified pulse, but it must not be heard in the music. Instead, the listener must hear the complex interplay of distantly related pulse speeds.

Rhythmic Characters

The contrast of metronomic pulses is only one aspect of Carter's rhythmic language. Very often he superimposes rhythms that differ in character as well as speed—as at the opening of the Cello Sonata discussed above. Carter has said that the source of this technique was jazz, which contrasts the regular pulse of the rhythm section with the very free playing of the soloists — the strung-out cello line at the opening of the Sonata sounds like Lester Young. Carter has abstracted this contrast of rhythmic styles found in much popular music in order to articulate widely different temporal shapes simultaneously. There are four basic rhythmic characters in his music:

(1) *Metronomic pulses.* These are often indicated by the marking *sempre giusto* or even *meccanico.* Pulses must be played with a non-metric, irregularly accented articulation as the music carefully indicates. Regardless of where they appear in a notated tempo they must be played as even down-beats, not as syncopations. Carter often shows their simple pulse pattern with an alternative notation. For instance at bar 171 of the Second Quartet, the 2nd violin plays even pulses at MM 140 although the tempo of the passage is crotchet MM 175 (Ex. 3):

Ex. 3

(2) *Rubato.* The player must stretch the implied pulse expressively. This character is indicated by the markings *espressivo* or *quasi rubato,* 'quasi' because Carter tries to notate the expressive shape as precisely as possible. Nevertheless these passages must sound freer and warmer in expression than the pulse patterns. The viola line from bars 147 to 154 of the Second Quartet illustrates this style. It should sound like an evaded pulse, a series of upbeats (Ex. 4):

Ex. 4

(3) *Accelerating and ritarding pulses.* These create the illusion of a mechanical pulse projected on a curved temporal screen. They are not expressive characters, but dream-like time-structures, whirling out of control or perpetually running down. To notate either effect, Carter has had to depart from conventional notation. If a single instrument plays such a rhythm while the overall tempo remains fixed, he often uses a dotted arrow to indicate a constant acceleration or ritard. The exact rhythmic value of notes under the arrow is approximate; more important is the illusion of a constantly modulated pulse. Again such passages must be articulated as a series of downbeats and not as syncopations. The cello line from bars 248 to 260 of the Second Quartet illustrates a brief acceleration followed by a ritard and a longer acceleration; this complex shape is superimposed on two pulse speeds in the violins and a few rubato sighs in the viola (Ex. 5). Sometimes in Carter's music the overall tempo

Ex. 5

accelerates or ritards. Then the music is marked *accelerando* or *ritardando sempre,* and logarithmically derived metronome marks are given for every measure. This cyclonic effect can appear treacherous to performers. Carter usually notates it in terms of regular groups of measures which double or triple in speed, so that the music gradually goes from 'in three' to 'in one', a change players find familiar—even if the result is novel. Bars 563 to 587 of the Second Quartet illustrate a group acceleration. Through precise notation Carter is able to achieve effects of great subtelty here: the regular pulses in the 2nd violin at 569, which resist the accelerating tide; or the contrasted rates of acceleration between the cello and 1st violin from 583 on, where the cello accelerates at a constant rate while the violin accelerates at an accelerating rate (Ex. 6):

Ex. 6

* Violin II: in measures 568 and 569, the five accented C-sharps should be played as regular beats (*non accel.*).

(4) *Free rhythm.* The marking *fantastico* often calls for an improvisatory style, moving in and out of a pulsed feeling with flamboyant abandon. Although the rhythm is notated exactly, the player must articulate the music as if it were being thought up spontaneously, rather than counted. A passage from the violin cadenza of the Second Quartet (bars 385-419) illustrates this rhythmic character, with its extreme range of speeds and its silence-punctured continuity (Ex. 7):

Ex. 7

String Quartet No. 2
© 1961 Associated Music Publishers, Inc. Used by permission

Counterpoint of rhythmic characters

By superimposing different rhythmic characters Carter arrives at a multi-dimensional rhythmic counterpoint. Although notated in terms of a single metre, the overall texture is neither regularly metric nor rigidly unified. There

Ex. 8

String Quartet No. 2
© 1961 Associated Music Publishers, Inc. Used by permission

is no fixed relation of foreground and background. Each rhythmic character fades in and out of focus, changing the listener's perspective from moment to moment.

A counterpoint of all four rhythmic types can be seen at the end of the first movement of the Second Quartet (Ex. 8, bars 123-134). The 1st violin plays in a free style. The 2nd violin plays a steady pulse rhythm at MM 70—it sounds every seventh semiquaver. (The tempo is 163.3 to the dotted quaver so that the rate of semiquavers is MM 490). The viola plays in a rubato style. Its phrases usually mix values of quavers and dotted semiquavers (as at bar 125). These should not be articulated as distinct, fractional divisions of a steady beat; rather each phrase should be given an elastic articulation, as a small acceleration or ritard. The cello, beginning at 123, plays a long accelerating phrase, increasing its speed by a factor of 8. Brackets in the score indicate foreground material that passes quickly from instrument to instrument. The turning point of this passage occurs at bar 129 when the 2nd violin's accented pulse abruptly cuts off the long phrases of the other instruments, reducing them to fragments.

Large scale rhythmic organization; the Time Screen

The rich resources of Carter's rhythmic vocabulary could easily become incoherent. The mathematical possibilities of tempo modulation alone might produce a meaningless chaos of speeds. Carter takes great care to insure the coherence of his materials. Every work is based on an ordered articulation of its 'time screen', which is the sum of its rhythmic activity. The boundaries of this screen are the fastest and slowest tempi to be used in a piece; these are determined by the nature of the instruments and ensembles deployed. Once the range of tempi is defined a framework of relations is plotted within it. These will of course vary from work to work; but the Second Quartet shows a characteristic strategy. In this work the 2nd violin is the keeper of the pulse. Throughout, it sounds a near-heartbeat tempo of MM 70 (or its double MM 140—high blood pressure). The 2nd violin thus embodies a mechanical time-sense against which the other instruments project more fanciful chronometrics. The constant rate of pulse imposes limitations on the available tempi of the piece because they all must contain the values to express the MM 70 pulse rate. By renotating this pulse the tempi of the piece can be derived:

2nd violin pulse	Tempo	Ratio
♩.=70	♩=105	2:3
𝅗𝅥=70	♩=140	1:2
♩ ♪ 𝄼 =70	♩=112	5:8

♩=70	♪.=112	5:8
	♪=186.7	3:8
♩..=70	♪.=163.3	3:7
♩♪♪♪=70	♩=93.3	3:4
♩♪=70	♩=175	2:5
♩♪♪=70	♩=84	5:6
♩♪♪♪♪♪=70	♩.=60	7:6

Within this range of notational possibilities the formal development of rhythm is dynamic. Carter does not build works only out of pre-determined fixed values. He sets out values that will interact and transform one another. In the Second Quartet for instance, the four rhythmic characters gradually merge so that rhythmic types which begin as individual gestures become group events. The group acceleration at bar 563 has already been mentioned—it is an extension of the cello's rhythmic gestures throughout the piece. Preceding this passage is one that combines the styles of both violins. Beginning at 533 all four instruments articulate pulse rhythms that are interspersed with the *appassionato* flourishes of the 1st violin. The two patterns nearly coincide at bar 560 (an exact coincidence would have been more mathematically elegant—and musically static) just before the cello launches the accelerando (Ex.9 bars 558-63). The dramatic power of these passages depends on the clear exposition of opposites in the early part of the piece, and on Carter's skill at transforming the oppositions in order to create new and unforeseen configurations.

Ex. 9   **String Quartet No. 2**

Carter's rhythmic resources have grown with every work. He has told me that the rhythmic inventions of which he is most proud are the spiralling ritardandi and accelerandi of the Double Concerto and the vast polyrhythmic collision in the second movement of the Piano Concerto. These multilayered structures make the ocean of time palpable. Their complex field of forces, accents, and shapes can be terrifyingly unfamiliar—but the connections between these designs and the experiences one has in dreams or in everyday life become clear after several hearings. Similarly the rhythms may appear arcane at first but they do not remain so. Their emancipation from familiar principles allows us to hear a new universe of temporal experiences. As Charles Rosen has written:

> We realised that the absence of one dominant pulse did not mean a loss of control, but that it made possible a new and powerful expressive set of relations between the apparently independent voices. In fact Carter's rhythmic innovations—which are now famous—can be seen as affecting all the other elements of music, and even as radically altering our conception of the nature of music itself.[6]

Form

> I usually have at first a very specific plan of evolution for the whole work, with many of the details of the local events only very generally in mind. That is, I usually start with an idea of the sound, the musical character and the dramatic development of these, similar to the plot—or subject outline of a novel or play or the scenario of a movie. (FW 104)

The formal process of a work is often the prime source of Carter's inspiration. He sees himself as a shaper of time; and the form of a piece, the way it articulates time, is its compositional essence. Form, for Carter, does not mean the historical 'forms'; sonata allegro, rondo, passacaglia and so on. He abandoned these around 1948, when he began to seek a new kind of continuity and formal logic in his music.

The main principle of logic in European music since Haydn has been that of theme and development. The musical material in classical works is divided into perfect and imperfect manifestations; a theme is presented at the beginning of a piece, is broken up and then put together again. Thematic logic parallels the harmonic design of tonal music with its motion away from and back to the tonic. As music began to be heard in more evolutionary terms the treatment of themes became increasingly teleological. Works like the Franck Symphony move from mysterious fragments to a climactic statement of perfected material, an arrival that coincides with a long-delayed moment of harmonic definition.

In his search for formal principles more closely related to the new materials of twentieth-century music, Carter turned to the late works of Debussy,[7] such as *Jeux*, the three Sonatas and the Études, to such works of Stravinsky as the *Symphonies of Wind Instruments* and the Symphony in Three Movements, and to the works of Schoenberg's free atonal period, especially *Erwartung*. He also sought ways of applying the formal discoveries of Joyce, Cocteau, Eisenstein and Balanchine to an abstract musical discourse. From all these, rather than from the classical-romantic tradition, Carter derived means of creating works 'whose central interest is constituted by the way that everything that happens in them happens as and when it does in relationship to everything else'. (FW 92)

Epiphanic Development

Debussy's late works and some of Schoenberg's free atonal compositions show a new treatment of thematic material, so different in fact that the music has sometimes been termed athematic. 'Athematic' is not a very descriptive term; it implies that the music is built out of thin air. Robert Craft has correctly attacked the 'absurdity of the labels "atonal", "aharmonic" and so forth' and described *Erwartung* as 'almost purely thematic'.[8] Certainly *Erwartung* and *Jeux* have a tight and coherent motivic structure. What makes them seem themeless is the way these motifs appear in the music. They are rarely given the extended melodic treatment in high relief that one finds in a Brahms or Bruckner symphony. In *Erwartung* the motivic figures are brief, fragmentary and volatile, scattered around a constantly changing texture. In *Jeux*, which is much simpler in texture and continuity, the thematic material as first presented is purposely lacking in melodic contour or rhythmic shape; most of the themes are extremely simple scale or arpeggio figures, neutral in character. The result of Schoenberg's fragmentation and Debussy's neutralization of motifs is that the old distinction between theme and development is lost. There is never a privileged statement of thematic material in an ideal shape. Every motif is at once theme and development, a fleeting manifestation of one aspect of the basic sound-matter of the piece. The basic material—chords, scales, colours—generates a series of events in time, all of them related, none of them logically prior to the others. The continuity of the music is thus liberated from the older hierarchy of formed and deformed statements. Yet the music is not a random series of events. It is a purposive succession of deeply related forms which define moments in time and create a dense web of connections across time.

Rather than 'athematic', a more useful word to describe this new treatment of thematic development would be 'epiphanic'. James Joyce in his early works redefined the term 'epiphany' to mean a sudden, seemingly accidental outburst of enlightenment and understanding. As Carter has pointed out, Joyce's epiphanies are not isolated moments; rather they 'always occur as a result of a situation in which the person who is experiencing the events finally recognizes, in a "moment of truth" what they all mean'. A visual analogy for epiphanic forms can be found in the ballets of George Balanchine in which striking tableaux emerge from continuous movement. Carter has written, about works such as *Apollo, Four Temperaments* or *Agon*, that 'every individual momentary tableau . . . is something that the viewer has seen interestingly evolve, yet is also only a stage of a process that is going on to another point; and while every moment is a fascinating and beautiful thing in itself still what's much more fascinating is the continuity, the way each moment is being led up to and away from. . . .' (FW 99) Balanchine's practice of deriving the motifs and large shapes of a ballet from the conventional patterns of classical dance corresponds to Debussy's use of shapeless, atomic generating cells and Joyce's symbolic transformation of everyday objects. Abstract material is given meaning in time through an interplay of steps and tableaux, processes and moments.

Almost all of Carter's music is epiphanic rather than thematic in its formal logic. As early as the Symphony No. 1, continuous transformation of material replaced the theme-and-development polarity basic to the older symphonic style. Later on Carter greatly expanded the dramatic possibilities of epiphanic development by dividing up the basic material of a work into character-groups—associated constellations of intervals, chords, speeds and 'behaviour patterns'. In the Second String Quartet, each instrument has a repertory of intervals and rhythmic patterns which generates every event:

Instrument	Intervals	Rhythmic type	Expressive character
Violin I	m3, p5, M9, M10	free	bravura
Violin II	M3, M6, M7	pulse	laconic
Viola	aug4, m7, m9	rubato	espressivo
Cello	p4, m6, m10	accel.-ritard.	impetuous

Out of this genetic matter each instrument evolves patterns of behaviour. The 1st violin, the most outgoing, is revealed first. Looking at its part from bars 35 to 47 we can see how each phrase is a variation on the possible components of the assigned character (Ex. 10). The motto which opens the passage and appears in inversion at bar 46 is not a theme: it is a flamboyant gesture typical of the 1st violin's 'behaviour'. This passage gives the impression of free-association. The dramatic importance of the violin's part will only emerge as it begins to interact with the contrasting behaviour patterns of the other instruments. This interaction is heard most forcefully in the violin's cadenza beginning at bar 374 (Ex. 11).

Ex. 10

Ex. 11

Here the violin interweaves its own material with literal quotations of the other instruments: the viola is cited at 381, the cello at 384. The 1st violin seems to be inviting the other instruments to join in. Their silence, which interrupts the violin for six seconds at bar 405, might be termed an epiphany, a 'moment of truth'. The revelation of this moment is not an end in itself (as it would be in Ibsen) but a particular point along the work's dramatic curve, one revelation among many others (as in *Ulysses*). For the listener this palpable silence reveals the possible breakdown in ensemble that has been implied by the extreme dissociation of intrumental characters. The silence is also a momentary exposure of the music's anti-world, the negation of sound out of which the music springs. As anyone who has heard this moment in a live performance knows, it is Carter and not Cage who teaches us to listen to silence. (See Ex. 7, p. 32.)

Collage

Discontinuous, fragmented musical continuity can be called collage or cross-cutting by analogy with either cubist painting or movies, where they are familiar techniques of composition. The infrequent use of collage in earlier times has led to a certain misunderstanding of its emergence in recent music. Collage has been termed 'moment form', with the implication that time is now perceived only as a series of unrelated events. Although such thinking is a cliché of avant-garde thought, collage in fact enriches continuity. The absence of transition in much twentieth-century art allows many relationships to be established quickly and without explanation—an aspect of collage keenly understood by Eisenstein. The time-sense of a collage-form work, such as the *Sacre*, is therefore more directional than that of earlier music. While the movements of a baroque suite could easily change places, such rearrangement destroys the *Sacre*—as anyone who has seen Disney's *Fantasia* knows.

The fragmented continuity of Stravinsky's music has long fascinated Carter. In 1962 he had an opportunity to ask Stravinsky about it:

Through these recent years, when I saw him now and then, certain things that I wanted to make clearer, at least to myself, have nagged at me, but I was never able to formulate them into questions that would bring the answer I wanted. The possibility of such questions came to me first during a time when Robert Craft was conducting my Double Concerto in Los Angeles, and Mr and Mrs Stravinsky invited me to their house on North Wetherly Drive. A little discouraged and shy in the midst of such august figures as Spender, Isherwood, and Huxley, who were also there, I went off into a corner soon to be joined by Stravinsky himself, and we began musicians' talk until I got up the courage to ask him how he composed. At which he took me to his workroom, and showed me a large book of blank pages into which short fragments of musical sketches, roughly torn out of larger sketch-pages had been pasted. Since the original sketch pages had been papers of different qualities and colors and the musical fragments (sometimes only two or three notes) had been written on staves that were hand-drawn, often in quite fanciful curves, the scrapbook itself gave a very arresting visual appearance. This was the workbook for *The Flood*, which I don't think had yet been performed. He proceeded to explain how he chose fragments from his sketches, tore them out, reshuffled them in different orders until he found one that satisfied him, and then pasted them down. I was genuinely surprised to learn of such an unexpected way of composing, of which, if I had not known whose music it was, I might have had doubts as to the results. . . . Some time later I began to realise that what I saw corresponded to glimpses I had had of this technique in his music elsewhere. The description and quotation of Stravinsky telling how he cut up the final fugue in *Orpheus*, given in Nicholas Nabokov's *Old Friends and New Music*, as well as in a brilliant lecture by Edward Cone on the *Symphonies of Wind Instruments*, recalled to me how pervasive cross-cutting was in the music. I had not expected to see it so graphically demonstrated. (WEC 302-3)

(Stravinsky's method certainly sheds autobiographical light on the card shuffling scenes in *L'Histoire, Jeu de Cartes,* and *The Rake's Progress*.)

Carter had a further insight into Stravinsky's method in 1967 when he took the part of the soldier in a performance of *L'Histoire du Soldat*, with Aaron Copland narrating, Lukas Foss conducting and John Cage playing the devil. For the first time Carter realised that the scenario was made up of 'at least three almost disconnected stories presented one after another as if they were continuous'. The music was similarly produced by repeating little fragments in new forms, as the soldier's violin music turns into tango, waltz and foxtrot. The combination of continuous material and fragmented presentation produced music that 'holds together in a very new and telling way'. (WEC 304)[9]

A simple and striking collage form, typical of the works of the '50s, can be seen in Variation 7 of the Variations for Orchestra. The orchestra is divided into three groups: strings, brass and woodwinds. The strings propound a passionate recitative, doubled in sonorous octaves. The brass sound slow, tranquil chords which gradually swell in dynamics and dissonance. The woodwinds begin with a simple, melodic interval in the flute, which expands outwards to four voices, then back, without changing its dolce character. These three strata are cross-cut so that they never overlap. After three sequences of simple alternation, the strings and woodwinds cut each other into brief fragments, followed by climactic statements first in the strings then in the brass. The three layers do not interact; they proceed as if they were three independent pieces, each with its own contour, broken into fragments and shuffled together. Yet there are many implied relationships. As in movies, cross-cutting here functions as a metaphor for simultaneity; the alternating fragments form a temporal counterpoint. (Carter actually superimposes the three strata in Variation 9.) There are also tonal links between the groups. The pitch A in particular serves as a central focus for all three. It is heard in the opening brass chords, twice climactically in the strings, and cadentially in the woodwinds. G$\sharp$ and B$\flat$ serve as important 'directional

Ex. 12

41

pitches' which polarize the A (Ex. 12). The presence of strong tonal control in a fragmented texture ensures the effect of non-linear exposition rather than random exposure.[10]

In the '70s Carter expanded the technique of cross-cutting. A sequence of cross-cut events such as that heard in Variation 7 would now be superimposed contrapuntally on one or more other collaged sequences. In the Third Quartet, for instance, one duo plays six different kinds of material. Each of these 'movements' is divided in two, and the fragments are arranged in the order 1, 2, 3, 4, 3, 2, 1, 5, 6, 5, 4, 6. The other duo plays four movements, each broken into three fragments in the order: 1, 2, 3, 4, 2, 1, 4, 3, 2, 4, 1, 3. (Both sequences were chosen so that no succession of two movements appears twice). Each cross-cut stratum is also interrupted by silence so that all ten movements are heard in isolation somewhere in the piece. But the beginnings and endings of movements in one duo are always covered by a continuing movement in the other duo. Thus while the continuity of each strand is fragmented, the overall musical continuity is unbroken. Bars 286 to 291 illustrate this process of contrapuntal collage. The lower duo plays its Leggerissimo movement throughout. The upper duo ends its Largo tranquillo movement on the last beat of 289 and suddenly begins a new section, Appassionato, sharply different in gestures and harmony from the Largo (Ex. 13).

Ex. 13

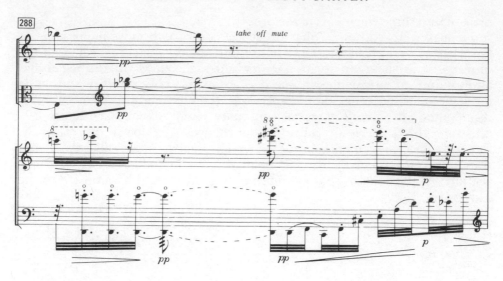

Compound Forms

Epiphanic thematic development combined with collaged fragmentation of material could easily produce intractable overall shapes. In exploring these techniques, Carter's challenge has been to find large shapes that would simplify the design of the music without oversimplifying it. Compound or portmanteau design has helped achieve formal clarity within a complex framework.

The use of contrasted large formal designs *simultaneously* finds some analogies in Berg's music.[11] In the *Kammerkonzert*, for example, the opening movement is at once a set of variations, and a sonata allegro. Such extensions of sonata form have precedents in Beethoven and Brahms, however, and the two designs reinforce each other. The boundaries between variations are clearly marked and correspond to the divisions of sonata form. The third movement of the *Kammerkonzert* is a rather more complex affair, superimposing all the materials of the first two movements. Because the themes exchange rhythmic and melodic contours, however, and because of the dominance of the typically Bergian *Hauptrhythmus*, the final impression is of a very complex but single-level design, not a superimposition of forms. Berg's operas perhaps come closer to a multilayered structure, because of their use of both Wagnerian leitmotif principles, and tightly organized short scenes each with a specific form. *Lulu* quite intriguingly links form with character by associating Alwa with a Rondo, Schoen with a Sonata, and Lulu with a set of Variations. These large character-forms are fragmented and spread across each act of the opera, somewhat in the way the movements in Carter's Third Quartet are cross-cut, but the large forms themselves do not interact. Perhaps the basic difference between the two composers is that for Berg form was still largely a matter of academic 'forms' whereas Carter seeks to derive unique designs from his material: 'The form I seek is Coleridge's "form as proceeding", and I try to avoid "shape as superinduced".' For the latter, he says, 'is either the death or the imprisonment of the thing; the former is its self-witnessing and self-effected sphere of agency'. (FW 101) (The characters in Berg's operas are all expressionistic stereotypes, which gives a dramatic dimension to his stereotyped formal structures.)

It might be said that Carter's compound forms stem from the conflict of epiphanic free-association and collage. The first technique emphasizes spontaneous continuity and the unbounded stream of consciousness. The second calls attention to the arbitrary control of the material by the artist. Epiphanic continuity contributes to the subjective time-world of the music; collage emphasizes the necessary links between the music and real time.

It is precisely the contrast of open processes and bounded structures which gave rise to the large-scale polyrhythmic form of the First Quartet. Carter has described it as follows:

> Note that while there are really four movements in this piece, only three are marked in the score as separate movements, and these three do not correspond to the four 'real' movements. The four 'real' movements are Fantasia, Allegro Scorrevole, Adagio and Variations. But the movements are all played *attacca,* with the pauses coming in the middle of the Allegro Scorrevole and near the beginning of the Variations. Thus there are only two pauses, dividing the piece into three sections. The reason for this unusual division of movements is that the tempo and character change, which occurs between what are usually called movements, is the goal, the climax of the techniques of metrical modulation which have been used. It would destroy the effect to break off the logical plan of the movement just at its high-point. Thus pauses can only come between sections using the same basic material. This is most obvious in the case of the pause before the movement marked Variations. In reality, at that point the Variations have already been going on for some time. (WEC 246)

As this description implies, the First Quartet can be listened to in (at least) two different ways. It can be heard as a succession of four movements, whose characters (though not their internal design) suggest classical practice: Fantasia, Allegro Scorrevole, Adagio and Variations. This mode of listening is reinforced by its familiarity, and by other gestures as well. The Allegro Scorrevole, for example, seems at first to be a Scherzo and Trio because of its sharp contrast of episodes. The four-movement pattern is undermined, however, by the two unexpected interruptions that occur in the middle of movements. Furthermore the Variations do not seem to have a clear theme; it is hard to say where this 'movement' begins. The listener is thus forced to seek alternative formal patterns. The three-fold division of the music suggests a contrasting design, one based not on fixed characters but on their transformation. The first part of the quartet expresses a process of fusion: unrelated contrapuntal lines of the opening converge (at bar 355) and are suddenly transformed into closely related fragments arranged in a sound-mosaic. The second movement evolves from the mosaic filigree to a new, simplified opposition of two elements, whose convergence releases the first unison rhythmic motion in the work (at bar 155). This singular moment of consolidation soon vanishes; the third movement attempts to reconstruct it through a process of continual acceleration. The acceleration process, however, whirls the music beyond its sought-after destination, curving it backwards in time so that it connects circularly with the beginning of the Quartet. Where the four-movement structure of the Quartet is classical, its three-part design is distinctly modern. One design is based on recurrence and boundaries, the other on transformations and ambiguities. The listener is invited to hear the music in both ways at once.

Large-scale formal patterns: circle, inverted arch, sine wave

Each of Carter's works is a 'large, unified musical action'. Free-associative continuity, collage, and super-imposed formal strategies are assimilated into an all-encompassing design. The various elements of the design 'interact with each other to produce a 'total' continuity and character effect, which, as the dialectical synthesis of the contributing sub-continuities and characters is irreducible to any one of these or to any "sum" of their qualities'. (FW 100)

That the overall form of a piece may be expressed in a simple gesture is not a new idea of Carter's. Schenkerian analysis sees almost all music as expressing a simple descending *Urlinie* moving towards resolution. Appreciating the power of such simple designs to clarify musical expression, Carter has sought large formal patterns *not* based on resolution. Three such patterns recur in his music: the circle, the inverted arch, and the sine wave.

Circular form

The endings of many of Carter's pieces flow into their beginnings in a manner recalling *Finnegans Wake*. Links between beginnings and endings of a work are familiar; Brahms and Bruckner were both fond of such gestures. In Carter's music, however, circular connections serve a different function. Where Brahms rounds out the motion of the Clarinet Quintet by alluding to the opening movement in the last variation of the finale, Carter's similar gesture in the Cello Sonata serves not to stop the work's motion but to extend it. The formal circle implies unbounded motion. It is an appropriate shape for music in which motion has replaced resolution as an aesthetic norm, and where transformation has replaced recurrence as a structural principle.

In the Cello Sonata a continuous circular design is achieved by eliding the separate movements. The third movement begins with material from the end of the second; the fourth, with material from the end of the third; and the first, with material from the end of the fourth. These connections are two-sided. They both reiterate and transform previously heard material. At the opening of the third movement, for instance, the cello repeats note for note a figure played by the piano in bars 202-3 of the second movement (Ex. 14). The pitches and absolute speeds (MM 560) are identical. In the second movement this speed is notated as quintuplet quavers; in the third it is written

Ex. 14

Cello Sonata
© 1953 Associated Music Publishers, Inc. Used by permission

as hemidemisemiquavers (♪). A fast pulse, heard in the context of a quick tempo (MM 112), is now projected on a very slow speed (MM 35). The repeated phrase is thus both an echo and a new beginning. The rhythmic proportions that permit this linkage, moreover, determine the tempo and character of the new movement. The Adagio therefore becomes not simply a contrast to the preceding Vivace, but a transmuted continuation of it. This process continues both between and within the other movements of the Sonata. By the end of the work it is established so strongly that the return of the materials of the first movement near the end appears as an anticipation rather than a re-capitulation. The opening of the first movement presents the same rhythmic texture as the close of the last, but with the instrumental roles reversed. By implication the cycle of transformation begins again.

Circular form is an illusion, a projection of subjective time, yet it is no less familiar for being illusory; and Carter is as clever with temporal sleights-of-hand as was Vladimir Nabokov. The Cello Sonata, for instance, is not an unbroken circle. It has a beginning and ending, but these do no correspond to their locations in real time. The break between the first and second movements is absolute. The music comes to a full stop, then launches a new motion. The first movement is in effect a summation of the others, and its close is the true conclusion of the Sonata. By beginning and ending in the middle of the work's formal processes and by placing its structural opening and close near the temporal centre, Carter indicates that motion itself is the music's reason for being, that its continuous journey is more important than its temporal destination.

Inverted arch form

Carter's music often reverses the arching formal curve heard in both Wagnerian and Bartokian music. Instead of building to a climax and then receding, his music will begin at a moment of great intensity, as if it were 'tuning in' on musical activity that had already begun. The music will gradually slow to a central stillpoint, and then revive, gaining in energy until it reaches or surpasses the opening moment. Such a parabolic form obviously reverses the cumulative construction found in most other music.

Cumulative forms are rational, additive, architectural. By contrast, Carter's inverted-arch designs might be termed experiential. The music bursts upon the listener. It is all pure, chaotic energy, too fast and dense to be understood. Gradually its outlines become clearer. But the more familiar the listener becomes with the sounds and patterns, the more those patterns lose their characteristic energy—the ear sometimes murders to dissect. A point of calm is reached, but serene repose only reveals that in slowing the music down in order to seize it we have lost its essence. So the mind begins to imagine new possibilities. Out of imaginative synthesis the musical energy is revived. The music spins faster and faster, beyond the mind's limited comprehension. Very often the music closes with the reflective quiet of a vanished encounter, a held breath, a fading vibration.

The inverted-arch appears in different shapes and sizes, from the grand design of the Variations for Orchestra to the brief span of 'Anaphora', whose text perfectly reflects Carter's formal psychology. The sectional format of the Variations provides a useful illustration of this design. The work begins with an introduction. Fragmented ideas are sounded simultaneously at a rapid-fire pace. Next comes the theme; but instead of the expected, simple exposition, some of the introduction's material seems to continue, superimposed on a theme-like melody, and also on new gigue-like material. The chaos of the opening is thus slightly reduced, as its amorphic motion is now focused in three strata. The superimposition of slow and fast material in the theme is separated out in the first two variations. Variation 1 clearly continues the gigue in light, bouncy music punctuated by flashes of more threatening substance. Variation 2 inverts this situation; it is *molto pesante*, densely contrapuntal with fleeting moments of clarity. With the fast and slow elements of the theme exposed, Variation 3 can now recombine them; but the effect is of subtraction rather than addition—the two characters won't mix and simply cancel each other out. Variation 4 literalizes the destructive pattern; the orchestra is reduced, contrast withers away and the tempo slows to stillness.

Variation 5 is the eye of the storm, nearly motionless. The orchestra becomes mysteriously undifferentiated; the only clear sound is a slap-stick. There are no conflicts, but also no shapes. Variation 6, a continuous accelerando, renews the work's motion. With Variation 7, the three opposed strata re-emerge. Variations 8 and 9 are additive, combining the simple elements of Variation 7 in contrapuntal schemes of increasing density. In the Finale all aspects of the piece are synthesized in a whirling fantasy, rapidly changing in sound and character and climaxing in an epiphany-like convergence of the three strata. This moment of revelation itself passes, however, and the musical ideas are swept away like leaves in the autumn wind.

Sine-wave design

Carter's forms, it should now be clear, do not aspire to architecture. His music is not built out of inert stone, but out of pulsing energies. The formal shapes described by the music are Carterian equations, graphs of endless curves. Many of his works trace a sine-wave-like pattern of activity. The music accelerates, reaches a climax of rapid motion, then plunges downward to a slowed motion, and then the music begins to accelerate again. The sine-wave motion complements the circular design Carter often seeks. Its shape also brings into relation the extremes of speed in a continuous pattern; it dramatically outlines the range of pulses in a work, placing the fastest and slowest speeds in sharp, central juxtaposition.

The First Quartet displays the sine pattern clearly. The opening Fantasia with its many different tempi creates the overall impression of gradually increasing motion. At what seems to be the limit of speed, a new and faster musical pace appears in the Scorrevole section—the sensation of 'going over the top' is very characteristic of this form. Controlled acceleration seems to be followed by free fall. The fast motion then gives way to a nearly stationary Adagio. After a lengthy exploration of stillness there is a sudden burst of motion—like a flash flood in the desert, but this burst fades to renewed stillness, an epicycle on the larger curve. The entire last section of the work is a continuous acceleration.

Because Carter's forms depend on patterns of motion rather than the repetition of fixed events, the listener who seeks milestones should look for turning points rather than recapitulations—but every work is different. The Carterian geometries of circle, arch and sine-wave are often combined in new configurations: spirals and ellipses. And the strict mathematical elegance of one work (say, the Third Quartet) is often followed by manneristic distortion in the next (the Duo). For Carter is finally far more interested in exploring the complex flow of events than in imposing reductive schemes on it.

Notes to Part 2

1. Allen Edwards: *Flawed Words and Stubborn Sounds*, a conversation with Elliott Carter (New York: Norton, 1971). All further references to this book will be indicated by FW.
2. See Grosvenor Cooper and Leonard Meyer: *The Rhythmic Structure of Music* (Chicago: University of Chicago Press, 1960), and Maury Yeston: *The Stratification of Musical Rhythm* (New Haven: Yale, 1976)
3. Carter's sense that tempo itself could be a structural factor was strongly reinforced by Rudolf Kolisch's article 'Tempo and Character in Beethoven's Music' in *Musical Quarterly*, vol. XXIX, 2 (April 1943) pp. 169–87
4. 'Metrical modulation' was a term first used by Richard Franko Goldman in *Musical Quarterly*, vol. XXXVII, 1 (January 1951) p. 87. Many of the tempo changes in that work *were* accompanied by changes in metre (see bars 15–20), but such 'metrical modulation' rarely occurs in the later music because simple metre is less prominent.
5. Unless otherwise indicated the metronome mark given indicates the absolute speed of the notes and not the tempo of beats. For example, the tempo at bar 116 in Ex. 2 is $\downarrow = 120$. The dotted septuplets in the viola part therefore have a speed of $7/3 \times 120 = 280$. Obviously these fast pulse-rates are not found on most metronomes, but they can easily be approximated by subdividing slower tempi.
6. Charles Rosen: 'One Easy Piece', in *New York Review of Books*, 20 no. 2 (22 Feb. 1973) pp. 25–9
7. Carter lectured on the Debussy sonatas at Princeton in 1947. Both the Cello Sonata and the Sonata for Flute, Oboe, Cello and Harpsichord owe much to late Debussy, and the

gigue-like theme in the last movement of the First Quartet almost quotes Debussy's Violin Sonata. Debussy had planned six sonatas; the last was to be written for a chamber ensemble combining the instruments used in all the previous sonatas. The orchestra of the Double Concerto comes very close to this ensemble, substituting percussion for Debussy's harp.

8. Robert Craft, notes to: *The Music of Arnold Schoenberg*, vol. I, Columbia (USA) M2S 679

9. The increasingly fragmented continuity of Carter's music after the Double Concerto reflects his growing interest in the collage-like continuity found in so much of Stravinsky's music. In the Third Quartet, for example, Carter contrasts sudden, Stravinskian shifts in continuity with his more habitual, Debussyan musical flow.

10. See Edward Cone: 'Stravinsky: The Progress of a Method', reprinted in *Perspectives on Schoenberg and Stravinsky*, ed. Boretz and Cone (Princeton: Princeton University Press, 1968) pp. 156–64

11. In *The Music of Alban Berg* (Berkeley: University of California, 1979) Douglas Jarman speculates briefly on Berg's possible influence on Carter; Stravinsky had earlier pointed out 'unknowing' resemblances. Carter denies such an influence and says that he really knew very little of Berg's music until well after his musical idiom had matured. He came upon the accelerando and ritardando in *Lulu*, Act I, after he had written the Variations, for instance. Both composers certainly share a dramatic conception of musical form and a preoccupation with purely rhythmic design. They both see time as the primary medium of music, both on the small and large scale, and thus treat musical time in a more structured way than an 'intuitive' composer like Schoenberg, yet in a more dynamic way than formalist composers like Bartok or Webern. Berg's gestural vocabulary, on the other hand, is very distant from Carter's music.

3

Musical Space: Texture and Harmony

The 'time screen' is a spatial metaphor for the horizontal motion of music through time. 'Musical space' is a metaphor for the vertical aspect of music, the entire range of available sounds. The frequent use of this term in recent discussions of music indicates that the range of sound can no longer be taken for granted as it has been since the advent of the standard four-voice texture in the late works of Dufay.[1] Soprano, alto, tenor, bass is yet another hierarchical arrangement associated with the reign of tonality. In the liberated discourse of recent music such a hierarchy no longer exists. To paraphrase Arshile Gorky, every time a composer begins to write he defines a new musical space. Liberated space perhaps appeared most clearly in Varèse's music with its reiteration of vertical sonorities spanning nearly the complete range of audible sounds, and also with its characteristic integration of non-pitched and sliding-pitched elements into the overall space. Even a linear piece by Varèse, like *Density 21.5*, is not 'melodic' but is an exploration of a specific space (the entire range of the flute, for example) projected on the time screen.

One of the clearest statements of liberated musical space in Carter's music is the first etude from *Eight Etudes and a Fantasy* (Ex. 15). The first two notes

Ex. 15   **Eight Etudes and a Fantasy**

53

of the piece, which span four octaves, define the possible range of the instruments. Immediately the situation becomes more complex than it ever does in Varèse, however. Each instrument begins to explore its own space. The parts constantly cross so that the overall tone colour varies with every note. The complex texture clears as the instruments partition the space in three: the flute defines the top, the bassoon, the bottom, and oboe and clarinet in octaves, the middle. This clarity is itself one variable aspect of the space—soon the lines converge and cross. In the closing phrase the instruments, moving first in pairs, then independently, swing through the extremes of their ranges, extending the opening space to five octaves in expanding intervals: unisons, thirds, tenths, and seventeenths. The intervals are not so much harmonies as bodies in musical space, each with its own specific gravity. Where the space of Varèse's music is thought of as a crystalline structure outside of time, in Carter the space of the work itself evolves. Musical space and musical time interact.

In traditional theory musical space is broken down into two aspects, counterpoint and harmony, whose chicken-and-egg relationship is the source of much theoretical debate. Stefan Wolpe[2] in his teaching suggested ways in which these two terms could be redefined to describe unbounded, emancipated musical space. Counterpoint, the relative motion of musical lines, activates space by differentiating it into clearly separate components. Harmony, the relationship between such lines, unifies musical space, making it clear that apparently separate sounds are part of an overall configuration. Much twentieth-century music, while extremely adventurous in its harmonies has been regressive and crude in its use of counterpoint; the discrepancy between the two has led to an impoverishment of musical space. In Carter's music a unique concept of musical space generates the polyphony and harmony of each piece, much as an overall pattern of motion in musical time generates rhythmic and formal events.

Texture

> . . . at a certain point I decided that the traditional categories, like 'theme and accompaniment' or 'subject and countersubject' really didn't deal with what began to seem to me the vast spectrum of kinds of relationship that the contributory vertical elements in the musical continuity can have with each other in respect of the past and future of a piece. . . . (FW 100)

The abandonment of the stereotyped contrapuntal textures of older music—canon, fugue, passacaglia, and so on—was a fundamental change that ushered in Carter's mature style. His mastery of these forms, which he pursued rigorously for three years with Nadia Boulanger, is evidenced on every page of his early works, from the ingenious *Canonic Suite* to the expansive and inventive choral prelude texture of *The Harmony of Morning* and the fugue of the Piano Sonata. Academic contrapuntal textures, however, express a conventional ordering of musical space. The space is divided up into voices, each with its own domain, and each related through common material. A leader-and-follower relationship in stating motifs

54

establishes the relative prominence of voices, so that even though lines are heard simultaneously there is always a clear hierarchy of relative importance. The foreground-background polarity becomes even more absolute in traditional non-imitative texture, such as the homophony of much nineteenth-century music, with its clear division of the musical space into melody and accompaniment.

In the mid 1940s Carter began to realise that the emancipated harmonic language of recent music required an emancipated texture. Within the European tradition there were several models of freer textures. The conversational polyphony of the classical string quartet with its free imitation and dramatic interaction of voices was one precedent. Operatic ensemble in which the moods and personalities of different characters are brought together and yet kept distinct was another—in particular Carter has stressed the ensembles in *Don Giovanni* and *Falstaff* as an influence on his work. The music of Charles Ives was perhaps most suggestive for textural innovation. Ives was fascinated with the polyphony of unrelated kinds of music. Hymn tunes, bells, rag-times, marches, the sounds of nature or the sound of the railroad are superimposed in his music to express a democracy of sounds rather than the usual hierarchy. Textures reminiscent of Ives's music can be heard throughout Carter's mature works, in abstract form, but they are subjected to transformational processes not found in Ives.

Carter's new approach to musical texture first appears in the Cello Sonata and First Quartet:

> These works . . . depend on a special dimension of time, that of 'multiple perspective', in which various contrasting characters are presented simultaneously—as was occasionally done in opera, for example, in the ballroom scene in *Don Giovanni*, or in the finale of *Aida*. Double and sometimes manifold character simultaneities, of course, present as our human experience often does, certain emotionally charged events as seen in the context of others, producing often a kind of irony which I am particularly interested in. In doing this so frequently, and by leading into and away from such moments in what seemed to me telling ways, I have, I think, been trying to make moments of music as rich in reference as I could and to do something that can be done only in music and yet that has rarely been achieved except in opera. (WEC 355-6)

'Multiple perspective' was achieved by many new techniques. Most important are the stratification of texture into superimposed but highly differentiated layers, mosaic elaboration of patterns out of simple material, and neutralization, the temporary submergence of contrapuntal strata in a unified sonority.

Stratification

In a canon or fugue, imitation is the basis of counterpoint. All the lines have similar material within a highly unified framework; double or triple counterpoint and the use of countersubjects serve to extend the musical unity, not to deny it. In stratified counterpoint, by contrast, the musical lines do not

Ex. 16

String Quartet No. 1
© 1956 Associated Music Publishers, Inc. Used by permission

imitate each other; they differ sharply in character. (The final scene in *Aida* provides a graphic illustration.) A clear instance of four-part stratified counterpoint in Carter's music appears near the opening of the First Quartet (bars 22-32) (Ex. 16). Each instrument plays at a different metronomic speed, with highly contrasted colours, intervals and expressive gestures. Unlike a Bach fugue, where the harmonic resultant of the lines is not only clear, but is the controlling structure, here the differentiation of character is the clearest structural guide, and the overall harmony seems unimportant, especially because the different speeds of each line prevent the sounding of simultaneous chords. Bach's counterpoint merges separate voices into a unified chorale. Carter's counterpoint lets voices move individually, like people on a city street.

Stratified counterpoint can be based on many-voiced textures as well as on single lines. From bar 85 to 126 of the second movement of the First Quartet, two textures, each previously heard separately, are superimposed. The violins play slow, continuous, tranquil music (related to the 1st violin's material in Ex. 16). Viola and cello play aggressive, heavy material that appears in violent bursts. The division is absolute; the instrumental pairs never trade characters. Their obstinate disregard for each other is the source of dramatic tension. The two pairs do interact in musical space, however. The violins make a continuous descent, while viola and cello mount ever higher (bar 122). In the course of the passage they exchange places in musical space, an 'unconscious' gesture of identity.

Traditional counterpoint is activated by dissonance, which disrupts the musical unity and pushes the music forward. Stratified counterpoint is activated by the transformation of each stratum and by interaction and intersection. The establishment of connections between strata is crucial for Carter, because it shows 'that the extreme dissociation between [strata] is neither a matter of random nor of indifference, but one to be heard as having an intense, almost fateful character'. (WEC 271)

The interaction of strata takes many forms in Carter's music; more than anything else such interplay is what the music is about. In the Adagio of the First Quartet, for example, the tense passage just described is followed by an attempted intersection. Viola and cello, still playing above the violins, now imitate their mood, and the 1st violin appears to echo (albeit tranquilly) the rugged lines of the viola. Confrontation seems to give way to co-operation; but the effort is short-lived and the polarized couples part company, withdrawing to their original widely-spaced positions as the 2nd violin climbs three octaves and the viola and cello plunge downwards.

The connections between strata are often less obviously dramatic and more structural. A tonal centre or a recurrent harmony can often relate elements that seem disparate. In the Adagio a four-note chord appears again and again both within and between the two duos. This chord (0,2,3,6) is based on the most important pitches of each duo: C#-E in viola and cello and E♭-G in the violins. In the first part of the Adagio, when each duo is heard separately, the lower duo is tonally centred on E, while the upper focuses on E♭. As the two duos are superimposed and begin to cross paths they also exchange tonal centres (see bars 120 and 121).

Carter often projects the stratification of musical space in real space. The players in the Second Quartet are asked to sit farther apart than usual, and the orchestras for the Double Concerto, Concerto for Orchestra and *Symphony of Three Orchestras* are given special seating arrangements which help to delineate the counterpoint of the music in space—the Concerto for Orchestra was even planned for performance in the round with its four groups encircling the audience. While such spatial separation is used mainly to make the texture of the music more clear, the motion of sound in space often becomes the most dramatic feature of the music, and an important means of connecting strata. The accelerandi and ritardandi heard at the centre of the Double Concerto circle around the orchestra clockwise, then counter-clockwise, unifying space and time in precisely plotted curves. Similarly the *Symphony of Three Orchestras* is planned so that the music sweeps across the audience in waves of sound.

Mosaic texture

A mosaic is a design built out of tiny fragments. Where the elements of stratified texture are clearly defined and contrasted, mosaic texture combines atoms of sound that are similar and simple in a tight pattern. Unlike traditional stretto, however, the close interplay of voices is free and fanciful, not canonically rigid.

Etude IV of the *Eight Etudes and a Fantasy* is Carter's most elegant mosaic. The musical material is limited to a rising minor second in the rhythm of two quavers always followed by a rest. That is all. No counter subjects, pedals or contrasting material of any kind. This minimal material, however, is articulated by all four instruments in changing juxtapositions and combinations. A surprisingly varied series of large patterns emerges: note the

Ex. 17

Eight Etudes and a Fantasy
© 1959 Associated Music Publishers, Inc. Used by permission

chromatic scale in *Klangfarbenmelodie* at bars 37-40 (Ex. 17), and the cross-accented ostinati at 78-83 (Ex. 18). Carter once pointed out to an audience that the structure of Etude IV was 'very similar to that of the parquet floor on which we are standing. You see it is made of small blocks of wood—all of the same dimension'. (WEC 245)

Ex. 18

Eight Etudes and a Fantasy
© 1959 Associated Music Publishers, Inc. Used by permission

Carter's polyphony, always dramatically conceived, expresses relationships between players. Stratified textures portray opposition or indifference. Mosaic textures tend towards greater unity. All players share the same material, but assert their individual freedom through minute differences in nuance. The music has the playfulness of children improvising a street game within strange and arbitrary rules.

Neutralization

The opposite of stratified musical space is neutralized space. Contrasts disappear; conflict gives way to co-operation. The individual timbres of instruments blend mysteriously. In Etudes III and VII Carter achieved neutralization radically by eliminating all contrasts of rhythm and pitch. Etude III is a D major triad sounded by four instruments in changing colours. Etude VII is a single pitch, G. The two studies are quite different in effect. The first is relaxed, peaceful. Change is slow and the dynamic range is very limited. The instruments 'sneak' their entrances so that we hear nearly imperceptible graduations of change in colour and intensity. Etude VII, by contrast, is dramatic. The instruments sustain the continuous note with overlapping crescendos, sforzandos and diminuendos. The tone colour is unstable, giving an impression of stasis and rapid motion at the same time.

Neutralization shifts the musical emphasis from pitch and rhythm to timbre and dynamics. Obviously Carter is indebted to the *Klanfarbenmelodie* of Schoenberg's *Chord-Colours*; but he places this effect in a dramatic continuum. In music as highly contrasted as Carter's, the abolition of contrast becomes a very special occurrence. Neutralization often articulates the low-point of a piece, its point of minimum energy and minimum differentiation— Variation 5 of the Variations for Orchestra exemplifies this usage. Where non-cooperation between instruments is the norm, the sharing of a pitch or the articulation of a common chord can become extremely poignant. In the beautiful Adagio near the end of the Brass Quintet, for instance, the instruments quietly celebrate the pure pleasure of playing together and in creating a music that is greater than the sum of its individual voices.

Harmony: Tonal or Atonal?

Harmony has been the most discussed aspect of twentieth-century music. Yet, perhaps due to the rapid evolution of idiom, there are few generally agreed-upon principles for analysing works even as distant in time as the Debussy Préludes. The Viennese composers' interest in unifying harmonic and thematic material, furthermore, has led many theorists to assume that such an identity always exists. The study of early atonal music in terms of set theory has grown out of this assumption, and it has provided many useful insights. Many of these studies, however, assume that 'atonal' music cannot be understood in terms of tonal centres, or 'pitch-priority'.[3] But when is a piece 'atonal'? And when does the structural role of 'pitch class sets' absolutely supersede that of tonic or polar design?

Carter, agreeing with Schoenberg and Stravinsky, dislikes the term 'atonality'. Schoenberg himself preferred 'the emancipation of dissonance'.[4] This expression has a precise, technical meaning. For nearly a thousand years musical intervals had been divided into two categories, consonant and dissonant. Since around 1450 the consonant intervals have been the unison, third, fifth, sixth and octave; the dissonances were the second, fourth, seventh and all augmented and diminished intervals. Dissonances were not necessarily unpleasant, but they were invariably unstable: they demanded resolution into the consonant intervals. This two-sided intervallic system served as the basic organization of musical space. It was the equivalent of the system of perspective in painting. Just as all points on a canvas were related to a single perspective grid which controlled their significance within the pictorial space, all pitches in a piece were related as dissonances or consonances, elements of motion or elements of rest.

The nineteenth century saw the gradual acceptance of almost all the dissonances as consonances. Schoenberg's proclamation of the emancipation of the dissonance merely recognized the fulfilment of this tendency; by 1908 none of the intervals seemed to demand resolution. A harmonic idiom could now make free use of all intervals. Schoenberg's music was not isolated in this discovery; Debussy's use of seconds, Ravel's use of sevenths and Scriabin's use of fourths and ninths point to a very similar harmonic usage. And the violent discords that Schoenberg soon began to employ for their expressive potential also appeared in the music of Mahler, Strauss and Stravinsky.

Music freely using all intervals may be called pan-intervallic. The presence or absence of tonality in such music is an open question. Ostinati and pedal points in many works of Debussy and Stravinsky often give one pitch a tonic function, even though this function is clearly not related to the familiar chords of major-minor tonality. The theorists of twelve-note music have tended to see such traces of tonality as vestigial. But the continued presence of polar functions even in the work of the Viennese masters perhaps indicates that the theorists have chosen to ignore some of the larger issues of tonal organization in emancipated harmony.

All this is by way of an introduction to Carter's harmonic practice, which extends the principle of emancipation to include all possible combinations of tones, but which has also developed non-serial means of achieving tonal coherence throughout a work. Although Carter has never made use of serial methods, his exploration of the chromatic universe owes much to the music of Webern and Schoenberg and to the theoretical insights of Milton Babbitt;[5] in this sense his music can be termed post-serial. However, rather than organize his music by the essentially linear means of the series, Carter has sought a more explicity harmonic approach based on the use of all possible intervals and chords, on recurrent harmonic units, and on 'primal sonorities', basic chords that assume tonic function throughout a work.

Intervallic music

Much twentieth-century music has isolated the sound of a single interval. Debussy's études in thirds, fourths, sixths and octaves, many works of Bartok, and some of Scriabin's late piano pieces treat one interval as the basic structural unit for both melody and harmony. Similar practice appears in such works of Webern as the Concerto and the String Quartet, whose series contain very few different intervals. In these works the absolute colour of a chosen interval replaces its relation to the dissonance-consonance polarity as the basis of musical coherence. Just as in older music the harmonic motion could be predicted in terms of the resolution of dissonance, in these works harmonic motion could be forecast in terms of the consistent use of certain intervals. In Webern's Quartet Op. 28, for example, we expect to hear minor seconds and major sevenths; in the Concerto Op. 24 we can predict thirds and sixths. The freeing of intervals from their dissonant or consonant functions and their new-found structural importance, finds its exact analogy in painting. In Matisse, for example, colour sheds its purely representational role and takes on an independent structural life.

In much music from Debussy's to Carter's the eleven intervals[6] of the chromatic scale serve as primary colours. Each one has unique acoustic qualities and expressive characteristics. Although Carter does not like over-literal accounts of inherent intervallic expression, he certainly recognizes and exploits the contrasting characters of the intervals in his music. He cautions, however, that sometimes he may find it interesting to use a secondary character of an interval instead of a more expected approach, rather 'like trying to paint a very restful picture using only reds'. His sense of intervallic character may be seen if we compare three works in which intervals are associated with specific expressive indications:

Interval	Third Quartet	Brass Quintet	Symphony of 3
m2	scorrevole	angry	angry
M2		flowing	flowing
m3	giocoso	humorous	accelerando*
M3	tranquillo	extravagant	floating*
P4	leggerissimo	vigorous	leggero
A4, D5	meccanico	menacing	espressivo, cantabile
P5	maestoso	majestic	bell-like
m6	espressivo	lightly	sostenuto*
M6	appassionato	lyric	espressivo
m7	grazioso	dramatic	grazioso
M7	furioso	furious	giocoso

*Descriptive words are the author's

Carter's harmonies begin with the interval. Coming after the harmonic researches of Bartok and Webern, however, Carter was able to expand their techniques. He sought an idiom that would exploit all eleven intervals, not just a limited number. Each of Carter's mature works places all the intervals in rigorously defined relations. In the Second Quartet, for example, they are divided between the four instruments:

Violin I: minor third, perfect fifth, major ninth, major tenth
Violin II: major third, major sixth, major seventh
Viola: augmented fourth, minor seventh, minor ninth
Cello: perfect fourth, minor sixth, minor tenth

(Minor and major seconds are not partitioned in this work; all the instruments use them.)

Because of the partitioning of intervals, each instrument has a limited harmonic colour analogous to the intervallically-restricted works of Webern. The constant nature of each part assures the strong and predictable harmonic structure found in Webern. Unlike Webern's practice, however, the four intervallically limited lines are combined so that all eleven intervals are present, creating a richer, more varied harmony, but without sacrificing any definition in harmonic character.

Chordal Music: the Harmony Book

Pan-intervallism, the co-ordinated use of all intervals, is a fundamental principle in Carter's music. He began to expand this practice in the Piano Concerto, written in 1963-4, whose harmony is based on the twelve three-note chords[7] numbered by Carter as follows:
3-1 (0,4,8)   3-2 (0,3,6)   3-3 (0,2,4)   3-4 (0,1,2)   3-5 (0,5,10)   (These five

contain one interval twice; they are unchanged when turned upside down.)

3-6 (0,3,7)   3-7 (0,1,6)   3-8 (0,2,6)   3-9 (0,1,5)   3-10 (0,2,5)   3-11 (0,1,4)
3-12 (0,1,3)   (These change when inverted.)

Like the intervals, the three-note chords have distinctive colours and properties. The first five are non-invertible. All the chords except 3-2, the diminished triad, can combine with transpositions or inversions of themselves to complete the chromatic scale.

In the Piano Concerto Carter achieves a coherent grammar for all these chords by means of partitioning. The orchestra plays chords 2,3,6,8,9 and 11; the piano and its concertino play chords 1,4,5,7,10 and 12. To isolate each chord further and give it a clear role in the musical discourse, each of them is associated with a metronomic speed; the mating of chord and speed results in easily identifiable musical characters. Chord 10, for instance, is always heard in light, scherzando passages, while chord 12 is sonorous, stately and expressive. The strong structural function of the chords is further achieved by identifying each of them with a predominant interval, and by limiting the positions of each chord to those which contain that interval. (If all positions were used, the intervallic content of the chords would overlap and make them difficult to distinguish, a problem that becomes even greater when larger chords are involved.)

Since the Piano Concerto, Carter has expanded his chordal harmony to include the twenty-nine four-note chords and the thirty-eight five-note chords (see Appendix B). In order to explore the properties of these chords he has gradually compiled a Harmony Book for his own use. This book at present numbers and analyses all chords up to and including those of eight notes. Carter analyses the chords for their intervallic content in all positions, for their content of smaller chords, and for their combinational resultants: for instance, what five-note chords result when one interval and one three-note chord are combined. The goal of these Rameauesque researches is a coherent use of all chordal combinations to produce harmonies at once rich and lucid.

All-interval tetrachords: the all-triad hexachord

Pan-intervallic harmony can become unfocused and obscure. Partitioning harmonic elements can clarify the harmonic structure of individual strands of music; but the overall harmony needs a source of coherence, a referential sound that will relate the partitioned harmonies to each other. Many twentieth-century works use a recurrent chord as a harmonic focus: Strauss's *Salome* and *Elektra*, Stravinsky's *Petrushka* and *Sacre*, Scriabin's late sonatas and orchestral works and several of the scenes in Berg's *Wozzeck* provide examples. The function of such chords is two-fold. They can provide a recurring sonority that becomes a recognizable norm in the course of the work, thus taking over the role of the major or minor triads in older music. They may also be repeated at the same pitch level to create a tonal centre. It should be noted that the repetition of chords does not necessarily lead to harmonic stasis. The establishment of a distinctive harmonic ambience through repetition allows for motion away from and back towards the tonic sonority; the directional tendency of the semitone becomes an important tool in defining such motion.

Recurring 'source-chords' appeared in Carter's music as early as the Symphony of 1942. In the piano and cello sonatas their use became increasingly rigorous; Carter was searching for chords that would contain the entire harmonic vocabulary of a work. In the First Quartet an all-interval tetrachord $(0,1,4,6)$ filled this purpose. This chord not only contains all six interval classes, but also pairs them uniquely (Chart 1):

Chart 1   The all-interval tetrachord $(0, 1, 4, 6)$

Its strong structural possibilities can be seen in the cello solo which opens the First Quartet; the chord is stated five times in different inversions and shapes (Ex. 19):

Ex. 19   **String Quartet No. 1**

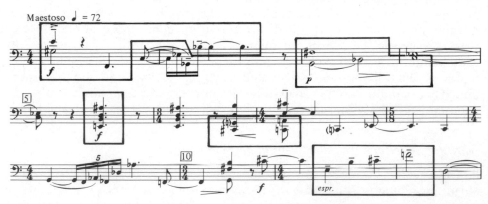

Note that in this passage and throughout the Quartet Carter uses chords closely related to $(0,1,4,6)$—$(0,2,5,8)$ in bar 2, $(0,1,3,7)$ in bar 6, $(0,3,4,7)$ in bar 7 differ from the source chord by only one pitch. The opening emphasis on the pitch E and its relation to F and E$^\flat$ is also a basic consideration in this passage: the harmony of F G$^\sharp$ and E first heard is repeated at bar 12 and bar 22, at the points where the other instruments join the cello. Such a stressed tonal emphasis has its consequences throughout the entire length of the work.[8]

The only other all-interval tetrachord is $(0,1,3,7)$—which Carter avoided at first because of its strongly tonal feeling; but it came into play in the Second Quartet and Double Concerto. In the Concerto, Carter partitioned the two chords: the harpsichord's orchestra plays (0,1,3,7) and the piano's plays (0,1,4,6). The intervals were also partitioned in order to differentiate the harmonies of the two orchestras as much as possible. Carter also explored eight-note harmony by combining each chord with itself and the chords with each other (see Chart 2). The complexity of this scheme and the real danger

Chart 2   Two all-interval tetrachords, with characteristic intervals used in the Double Concerto

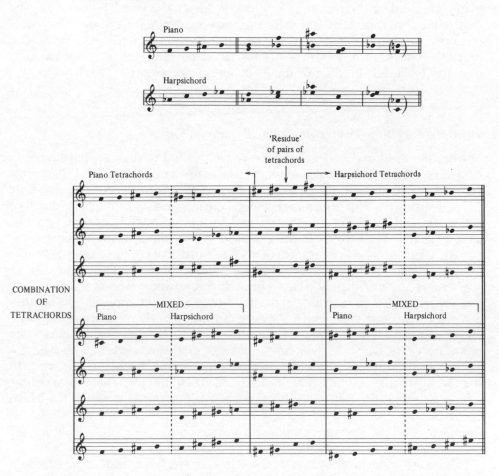

of a confusing redundancy between the two chords probably led Carter to explore chordal rather than intervallic harmonies in subsequent works.

In recent compositions based on all the three-note chords he has made use of the unique all-triad hexachord (0,1,2,4,7,8) as a source sonority. This chord contains all twelve triads in 10 pairs (Chart 3):

Chart 3   The all-triad hexachord (0, 1, 2, 4, 7, 8)

Like the all-interval tetrachords, this hexachord is universal; it can combine every element of the harmony into one recurrent sound. The most elegant deployment of this chord in Carter's music appears in 'Anaphora', where it is omnipresent but in constantly changing transpositions, positions, and triadic pairing. The harmony is thus always the same and yet always changing, maximally varied yet also maximally coherent (see Chart 31, 284).

Primal Sonorities: Twelve-note and all-interval 'tonics'

While the all-interval tetrachords were well suited to defining harmonies in quartets, larger ensembles demanded larger and more rigid harmonic structures. In the Double Concerto Carter first introduced a twelve-note primal sonority. This chord is repeated, untransposed, throughout much of the work. It thereby becomes the central harmonic structure of the Concerto, as well as the focus of its harmonic motion—in short, a twelve-note tonic chord. Untransposed reiteration of such a chord also creates a unique 'tonic-position' both for the pitches of the chord and for its constituent intervals.

The structure of the chord used in each composition reflects the harmonic vocabulary in use to such an extent that listeners are generally able to identify a work of Carter's with which they are familiar merely by hearing its primal chord. In the Double Concerto, the tonic chord emphasizes the intervallic elements of the work. In the Piano Concerto, piano and orchestra each have a prime chord built out of their respective three-note chords. In the Concerto for Orchestra the primal twelve-note chord articulates four three-note chords which generate the harmonies of the work's four movements. In the Third Quartet and *Symphony of Three Orchestras* all-interval twelve-note chords function as tonics, and thus emphasize a tonic position for all eleven intervals (Chart 4a, b, c).

The appearance of these tonic chords in each work is crucial to the structure and shape of the music. Their polar function, however, does not mean that they are used as chronological points of arrival and return as in classical tonal music. Carter is not interested in restoring a traditional sense of harmonic order. On the contrary, the existence of strongly ordered elements permits a more lucid articulation of disorder. In the Piano Concerto, for instance, the clear harmonic structure of the first movement is gradually abolished in the second. In the first movement a contrapuntal dialectic between all the three-note chords is controlled by two twelve-note tonics. In the second movement, however, the nature of the dialectic is redefined. Instead of a conflict between recognizable harmonic units, there is now a conflict between harmonic

Chart 4a   Interval scheme of Introduction   **Double Concerto**

RATIO		BETWEEN			SPEEDS		METRONOMIC SPEEDS	PIANO	HARPSICHORD
2					1/5	10	35	 [musical notation]	
	81					9	31½	 [musical notation]	
		25			1/6		29⅙		 [musical notation]
			32			8	28		 [musical notation]
				50	1/7		25	 [musical notation]	
				49		7	24½		 [musical notation]
			25		1/8		21⅞	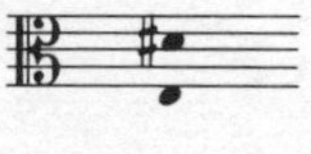 [musical notation]	
		18				6	21	 [musical notation]	
	50				1/9		19⁸⁄₉		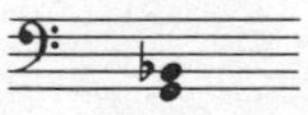 [musical notation]
1					1/10	5	17½		 [musical notation]

Chart 4b   Harmonic scheme

Piano Concerto

PIANO AND CONCERTINO { Intervals, Triads and Metronomic Speeds

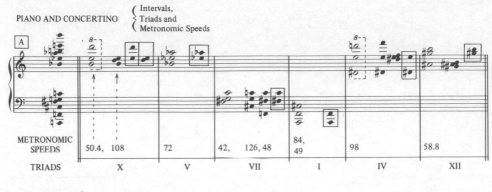

METRONOMIC SPEEDS	50.4, 108	72	42, 126, 48	84, 49	98	58.8
TRIADS	X	V	VII	I	IV	XII

ORCHESTRA { Intervals, Triads and Metronomic Speeds

METRONOMIC SPEEDS	110.25, 105	94.5, 88.2	63, 90	56, 54	73.5	60
TRIADS	II	VIII	IX	VI	XI	III

Chart 4c   Twelve-note chords in the:
a) Concerto for Orchestra
b) Third Quartet
c) *A Symphony of Three Orchestras*

(a)   (b)   (c)

definition and harmonic confusion. The orchestra plays dense clouds of sound whose harmonic nature become increasingly obscure. The piano's insistence on clarity is narrowed to a single pitch reiterated against the orchestra's saturated cluster. The extreme contrast of this moment would not make its stunning dramatic effect without the more orderly exposition of the first movement.

I hope that the foregoing discussion of Carter's idiom has provided a framework that can serve both theorists and more casual listeners in dealing with the apparent complexity of much of the music. Like most modernist art, Carter's music attempts to express complex experiences and feelings and rejects familiar and stereotyped forms of expression. But complexity is quite different from incoherence; indeed music that consists only of randomness and disorder soon seems stupefyingly simple. By contrast, the complexity of Carter's music grows from a lucid analysis of musical phenomena, and from a technique that is at once virtuosic and elegant. Contrapuntal music like Carter's is of course demanding on listeners, some of whom will always prefer Puccini to Bach. And his music is further demanding even to listeners devoted to earlier counterpoint because its polyphony does not derive from the forms of the past. The innovative techniques that Carter has devised, however, should be of secondary interest, even to musical theorists. To see the music only as an illustration of tempo modulation, for example, would be as misguided as to see *Tristan* only as an example of chromatic tonality, or the B Minor Mass only as a thesaurus of invertible counterpoint. For the essence of Carter's music is its energy and intensity, its drama and its beauty.

Notes to Part 3

1. See the discussion of musical space in Robert Cogan and Pozzi Escot: *Sonic Design* (Englewood Cliffs, N.J.: Prentice-Hall, 1976) pp. 15–85
2. I was fortunate to be able to discuss Wolpe's ideas with Irma Wolpe and two composers who studied with him, Ursula Mamlok and Howard Rovics
3. See Arthur Berger: 'Problems of Pitch Organization in Stravinsky', reprinted in *Perspectives in Schoenberg and Stravinsky*, op. cit. pp. 123–55
4. Charles Rosen: *Arnold Schoenberg*, op.cit. p. 16
5. Carter's copies of Webern's works are filled with detailed analytical observations, particularly of their harmonic designs. He feels, however, that his own harmonic practice is closer to the unordered-hexachordal works of Schoenberg, such as the String Trio. Carter published Babbitt's *Composition for Four Instruments* in *New Music* when he served as editor in the late '40s. He also chose works by Sessions, Nancarrow and Seeger for publication, all of which both reflected and refracted his musical thinking on the eve of the Cello Sonata and First Quartet.
6. The number of intervals should be explained. There are six interval-classes. Inversionally related intervals such as the minor third A–C and the major sixth C–A are considered members of the same interval-class. In most serial music this theoretical equivalence is also considered a musical one. Compositionally, however, a composer may choose to treat the inversionally-related intervals either as being interchangeable (as Webern) or distinct (as Carter usually does.) Indeed a composer could treat more than eleven intervals as distinct compositional elements, since ninths or twelfths, for example, are clearly different from seconds or fifths. Carter always takes great care to differentiate harmonic materials in his work, so that a large variety of harmonic elements can maintain their identity in complex, contrapuntal textures. Hence large chords are usually identified with smaller chords and intervals, and appear in spacings and inversions that make these family resemblances clear. The ambiguous nature of inversional relationships, equating sounds which are in fact rather different, would confuse such textures.

7. Carter uses the term 'chord' synonymously with Allen Forte's term 'pitch-class set'; that is to say, a chord is a collection of pitches defined by the number of pitches and by their intervallic relation
8. See Cogan and Escot: op. cit. pp. 204–5

4

Student Efforts, 1927–1936

Born in 1908, the year of Schoenberg's Second Quartet, Carter belongs to the first generation of composers who began their musical studies after radical changes in harmony, rhythm and texture had revealed a new, 'modern' music. Chronology is not a cause, however. Many composers younger than Carter are conservative aesthetically, and even today students inspired by the standard fare of concert halls and radio stations often begin composing in the styles of Mozart or Rachmaninov. Carter chose to be modern: as already said, the older music he heard—Beethoven, Bach, Wagner—bored him completely. The 'intensity and power' of the new music, by contrast, immediately attracted him:

> I can't give a date, but certainly the *Rite of Spring* was a very important and meaningful work, as were several of the works of Varèse like *Intégrales* and *Octandre,* and certainly the later works of Scriabin, particularly the *Poème de l'extase, Prométhée,* and the last preludes and sonatas, as well as Charles Ives's *Concord Sonata* and some of his songs. They were all very exciting and beautiful to me, and it was as a result of hearing and thinking about them that I decided to try composing. (FW 45)

Since almost none of the early attempts at composition remains, it is difficult now to judge the impact made by the works listed above. In the late '30s Carter destroyed nearly all his student efforts. Many of them were documented, however, in Claire Reis's *Composers in America,* published in 1938 (see p. 72). Of an entire page of listed works, only the short *Tarantella* and *To Music* (from the Madrigal Book) survived to later publication. Most of the rest were destroyed. (NB: The Symphony listed is not the 1942 Symphony No.1; the sequel-less number on the later score was perhaps used to distinguish it from the discarded 'zero' Symphony). Similarly the 1936 *Pocahontas* no longer exists and, according to the composer, was quite different from the published 1939 version, and shorter. Of the madrigals, *To Music* has been published; *Harvest Home,* performed and intriguingly described by Paul Rosenfeld as a leftist anthem, remains in manuscript. *The Ball Room Guide,* a long suite of dances written for Lincoln Kirstein, survives in manuscript in the form of the Prelude, Fanfare and Polka for Radio Orchestra (a work rather in the post-Satie style of Stravinsky's *Easy Pieces*

71

ELLIOTT COOK CARTER, JR.

Born in New York City in 1908, he studied music with Piston, Holst, and Hill for two years, after graduating from Harvard University in 1930. In 1933 he worked with Boulanger in Paris for a year. He has made his home in New York in recent years. Besides composing he writes criticism for *Modern Music*.

Performances of his compositions have been given by the Boston Symphony, Harvard Glee Club, and Harvard Classical Club. "Tarantella" was broadcast from Boston over WIXAL. "Pocahontas" has been performed by the Ballet Caravan.

COMPOSITIONS

ORCHESTRAL WORKS

	DURATION	PUBLISHER	DATE	
SYMPHONY	20 minutes	Manuscript	1937	*Destroyed*
CONCERTO FOR ENGLISH HORN AND ORCHESTRA		Manuscript	1937	*Never completed – destroyed*

CHORAL WORKS

	DURATION	PUBLISHER	DATE	
TARANTELLA *men's chorus, orchestra; arranged for piano. 4 hands*	6 minutes	Manuscript	1936	*Published*
MADRIGAL BOOK, 12 MADRIGALS FOR MIXED VOICES, 3, 4, 5, 6, 8 PARTS		Manuscript	1937	*Mostly destroyed*
ORATORIO—setting of Hart Crane's "The Bridge"		Manuscript	1937	*Project*

CHAMBER MUSIC

	DURATION	PUBLISHER	DATE	
FLUTE SONATA *flute, piano*	14 minutes	Manuscript	1934	*Destroyed*
FIRST STRING QUARTET	25 ,,	Manuscript	1935	,,
SECOND STRING QUARTET	16 ,,	Manuscript	1937	,,

STAGE WORKS AND FILM MUSIC

	DURATION	PUBLISHER	DATE	
INCIDENTAL MUSIC AND CHORUSES FOR SOPHOCLES' "PHILOCTETES" *men's chorus, oboe, percussion*	30 minutes	Manuscript	1933	*In manuscript*
INCIDENTAL MUSIC AND CHORUSES FOR PLAUTUS' "MOSTELLARIA" *men's chorus, bass solo, 10 piece chamber orchestra*	20 ,,	Manuscript	1936	,,
INCIDENTAL MUSIC AND CHORUSES FOR SHAKESPEARE'S "MUCH ADO ABOUT NOTHING" *women's chorus, 2 violi, 2 celli*	20 ,,	Manuscript	1937	*Project?*
TOM AND LILY—comic opera in one act *4 solo voices, small mixed chorus, chamber orchestra*	30 ,,	Manuscript	1934	*Destroyed*
POCAHONTAS—ballet in one act	18 ,,	Manuscript	1936	*See note*
THE BALL ROOM GUIDE—ballet	40 ,,	Manuscript	1937	*Mostly destroyed*
ONE ACT OPERA		Manuscript	1937	*Project ?*

that Carter told me he *should* have destroyed). The two quartets have no relationship to the later quartets; Carter says they sounded like Prokofiev. The incidental music for *Philoctetes* and *Mostellaria* exists in manuscript and will be discussed below.

In addition to these works, most of them begun during or directly after his study with Nadia Boulanger, Carter has spoken of a 'very advanced and complicated piano sonata, as well as some simpler settings of Joyce's Chamber Music', which he wrote in the 1920s and showed to Charles Ives. His letters to Ives reveal the one-time existence of yet another early string quartet, number 'minus three'. One of the Joyce songs accidentally survived because it was sent to Henry Cowell in 1928 with hopes of publication in *New Music*. Cowell never published it, but also did not return it until a few months before his death in 1965. Several other works, songs, piano pieces, and a ballet with scenario by James Agee entitled 'Bombs in the Icebox', are mentioned in the contributors' column in various issues of *Modern Music* during the late '30s, but, if they ever existed, were apparently destroyed.

Only two musical manuscripts survive from the pre-Boulanger years. These relics of Carter's pre-history show how his radical intentions were held back by a limited technique. Surprisingly, they betray almost no Ivesian influence. Carter has said that once he went to college he wanted to learn music step by step. Instead of the Ivesian extravagance that may have marked that very early piano sonata, both the Joyce song and the music for *Philoctetes* are reductively simple. Their stark textures reflect Carter's decision to write only music that was 'within my grasp to imagine and formulate clear ideas about'. Ives's music, despite the profound impact it made on Carter's imagination, remained beyond such precise comprehension. These remnants also reveal an interest in folk traditions that seems surprising in the light of Carter's later development. Again, however, it expressed his desire to start out at a very simple level of musical rhetoric. Because Carter refused to begin within a traditional European framework, imitating Mozart or Brahms, he went back to the most primitive musical situations he could imagine.

'My love is in a light attire', the long-lost fragment of a group of Joyce songs, is dated 1928 and dedicated to Laura Williams, at whose house in Tunisia Carter transcribed Arabic music during the summer of 1927. Although certain trappings of the score suggest advanced French music of the time, melodically and rhythmically it has a strong Arabic feeling. As in works of the same period by Milhaud and Ravel, bitonality is advertised by differing key signatures: the right hand of the piano has four sharps: the left hand and voice have none, but suggest G minor, and the song ends on a rather unconvincing final cadence in G major. The harmonically foreign notes of the right hand repeat an ostinato figure, evoking the sound of an *ud*. Although the $\frac{5}{8}$ metre must have seemed rather daringly angular for a love poem, it is interesting that Carter later returned to it for similarly light moods in the *Pastorale* and *Rose Family*. As is often the case in early efforts, the contrasting phrases of the piece—where the composer is not trying so hard to be modern—are more conventional, rather Debussyan, in fact.

Also surviving in manuscript, though in this case by intention, is the

73

incidental music Carter wrote in 1931 for a performance of *Philoctetes*, given in the original Greek by the Harvard Classical Club after Carter had left Harvard for Paris. This production, in which Harry Levin played Odysseus and Robert Fitzgerald Philoctetes, was directed by Milman Parry, who attempted to recreate a sense of irrational and ritualistic drama. Parry, searching for the folk roots of Greek culture, subsequently went to Yugoslavia to record the tribal bards who have continued Homeric narrative traditions to this day; these were the recordings Bartok transcribed at Columbia University in the '40s.

Carter did not know Parry's theories about the bardic basis of Homer; however, he anticipated this rediscovery of the folk basis of classical civilization. On the assumption that all primitive Mediterranean cultures must have been related, he wrote music which might be termed neo-Arab. In its scoring for offstage oboe, onstage drum (a dharbhouka is specified) and unison chorus, the music suggests the sonorities and textures of the traditional music Carter had transcribed in Tunisia, although there is no attempt to imitate the microtonal decorations of the Arabic style. The melodic line itself is based on classical Greek modes, occasionally quoting the surviving fragments of ancient Greek music, as Carter was later to do in *The Minotaur* in a very different sort of 'Greek' style. Carter researched the principles of Greek prosody; the sung rhythms follow the stress of the poetry and also make considerable use of hemiola; even such an early and simple piece exploits cross accent and polyrhythm. The music is not sophisticatedly pseudo-primitive like Milhaud's *Choéphores* or *l'Homme et Son Désir*. It is artless, modest, perhaps naive, but sensitive to the demands and style of the Classic Society's production.

When Carter returned to Cambridge, Massachusetts in 1936 in hopes of finding a job at Harvard he was commissioned, once again by the Harvard Classics Club, to write music for a performance of Plautus's *Mostellaria*. A march and two large arias written for this production remain in manuscript, and they show the immediate results of Carter's Parisian training. The music recalls certain pieces of Hindemith in its clear texture and brash, sometimes jazzy, mood. This style could be characterized as 'dissonant counterpoint', but Carter's keen literary wit and musical craft give the music a very distinct character. The *Canticum Philolachus* cleverly combines a chaconne, a mock-heroic recitative, and a frantic allegro based on a diminution of the chaconne theme. Ostinato bass structures were one of the clichés of the '30s, but here the structure perfectly mirrors the text. Philolaches pompously struggles to construct a philosophical analogy between a man and a house, comparing his own decay at the hands of love to the dilapidation of a fine house taken over by a careless new owner. The chaconne, a musical form which piles up developments on a repeated bass foundation, parallels the comic pedantry of Philolaches's build-up. The diminution of the bass motif instantly reveals his mock-pathetic decline and fall. Carter uses the chaconne form as an ironic device; the gesture is not neo-classical, but anti-classical, turning scholarly erudition back on itself.

The *Canticum Simonis* displays a similarly structural grasp of a dramatic situation. Simo first brags that his wife has cooked a fine lunch in order to get him into bed, then he admits that instead of going to bed he is walking to town, because his wife's desires would kill him. The first part of the aria is a boisterous march that would not be out of place in *Mahagonny*, but as Simo's power fades the march gives way to a pastorale that in turn fades out in a whimper—followed by a bang. The panache of both of these arias, the vivid way they present ironic and devious situations, makes one wish Carter had written more for musical theatre.

As a finale to the *Mostellaria,* Carter composed a *Tarantella* for chorus and orchestra to a text from Ovid's *Fasti.* The chorus was an immediate success and was often performed by the Harvard Glee Club; it is now Carter's earliest work to be published in its original form. With it we pass from Carter's pre-history to the beginnings of his surviving oeuvre, and to his now visible struggle to evolve a personal idiom.

5

Voyages, 1936–1948

Between 1936 and 1948, Carter produced a wide range of music: songs, choruses, ballets, large and small instrumental pieces and various symphonic works. Most of these compositions were published, though not all—Carter continued to discard or shelve pieces that did not satisfy him. From the perspective of the music he wrote after 1948, all the surviving works of this period are in the nature of creative etudes. Each reveals some aspect of Carter's later idiom, but even the greatest accomplishments of these years— the Piano Sonata and *The Minotaur*, which announce the later Carter's characteristic scope, density and tone—employ a rhythmic and harmonic language that he was later to abandon completely. These works are by-and-large not distinguishable from the later masterpieces in quality of technique, which quite early was supple and refined. Neither can they neutrally be termed a 'first practice', later to be superseded by a new idiom as with Monteverdi, or a stylistic 'period' in the manner of Stravinsky. Carter's early idiom was too unsettled to be termed a style.

Most of the works of 1936 to 1948 display basic conflicts: between experimental innovation and technical discipline, between a politically inspired desire for simplicity and a deep-seated need for complexity of expression. They contain these conflicting directions without fully resolving them—resolution would ultimately come not by deciding between the different claims of these tendencies, but by fundamentally redefining the basic elements of music.

The works of this period have too often been mislabeled 'neo-classical'. Despite certain outward trappings of neo-classicism—pandiatonic harmonies, clear rhythms, lucid textures—Carter's music of this time is too volatile to be classical. From the *Tarantella* of 1936 to the Woodwind Quintet of 1948 Carter in effect turned the neo-classical idiom against itself, sometimes, as in *The Harmony of Morning*, through subtle 'misreading', other times, as in the *Holiday Overture*, through disruptive mannerist distortions. The works of this period were exercises in sabotage—eventually Carter's energies had to burst the bounds of an alien practice.

The music he wrote from 1936 to 1948 was scorned at first by conservatives who could not grasp its complexity, and then neglected by a new generation of modernists embarrassed by its apparent simplicity. In both cases the musical public was the loser, deprived of a considerable and varied achievement. Carter's own attitude towards this period has changed with the years. After the stylistic and technical leap of the Cello Sonata in 1948, he even contemplated another reign of waste-basket terror for his early works. He banned performances of the Symphony No. 1 which had begun to be popular in England—it must have seemed to him like the unquiet ghost of a former existence. Now, Carter says, he is happy that he checked his self-critical drive. Increasingly these works have come into their own.

Because the music Carter wrote between 1936 and 1948 varies so widely in scale, from short songs and madrigals to large symphonic works and ballet scores, it will be best to discuss them according to genre.

Choral Works

The majority of Carter's compositions before 1948 are choral works, written for a variety of vocal ensembles. This emphasis may now appear surprising, for after *Emblems* of 1947, Carter never returned to the choral medium. However, because he had sung in and led many chorales and madrigal choirs at Harvard and in Paris, choral composing was a natural direction for him to take after he returned home from France. In Paris, he had organized choirs for the performance of older music; on his return to the States he transcribed a large number of medieval and renaissance works from manuscripts and old editions in the New York Public Library. Among these transcriptions are works by Pérotin, Machaut, Dufay, Obrecht, Ockeghem, Monte, Gabrieli and Gesualdo.

The *Tarantella*, originally the finale to *Mostellaria*, was first performed by the Harvard Glee Club in April 1937. It exists in two versions: with orchestral or four-hand piano accompaniment. The latter version was published by the Harvard Music Department in 1972, and later by Associated Music Publishers.

The text of the *Tarantella* is from Ovid's *Fasti*, book V, lines 183-99 and 331-77. It describes the Bacchic celebrations of May which were the occasion for performances of Plautus's comedies. Carter's earliest published piece is thus a rite of spring.

He took much of the melodic material from a book of Neapolitan tarantellas—the chorus of virile, urbane Roman youths therefore sings tunes associated with Calabrian peasant women. The sanctimoniousness of Latin is undermined by the plebeian cast of familiar everyday melodies. This transformation is precisely Dionysian, and the music portrays a Bacchic mood, without classical stylistic allusion or any suggestion of primitivism.

The texture of *Tarantella* is unacademically contrapuntal, constantly changing in density. As a medium, a male chorus is severely limited in range and colour. Carter overcame this weakness through contrapuntal invention—the choral colour may be grey but we hear the entire spectrum of grey, from one to four parts, from the widest possible spacing to a climactic cluster. As in the first of the Canonic studies, Carter here employed close canon at the octave and unison to create a sonorous web of echoed phrases. The extreme range of the accompaniment brilliantly sets off the palette of choral sonority.

Harmonically, the *Tarantella* is consistently polychordal—root harmonies are sounded with appoggiatura chords, usually a semitone away. The result is not bitonality, since the harmonic roots are clear, but rather a high level of harmonic tension stemming from the clash of six-note chords with the essentially diatonic vocal lines. These chords may suggest the influence of Milhaud, but Carter avoids the primitivism of *Les Choéphores*. The polychords in *Tarantella* are, moreover, part of a dynamically conceived harmonic design. The whole piece might be described as a labyrinthine search for the final cadence on D, a search that begins from tonal ambiguity, and is constantly coloured by the semitone relationships inherent in the polychords. The final cadence on D is thus prepared by a penultimate cadence on D♭, followed by a superimposition of E♭ on the D major harmonies in the chorus. Throughout the piece, D is approached by these contrary semitone motions, which are so uncharacteristic of traditional tonality, but are to become the basis of Carter's personal treatment of pandiatonic tonality.

The *Tarantella* is one continuous movement employing the development logic of sonata form but without the emphatic harmonic structure of the classical sonata. Carter represses the recapitulation of the opening material—which was deliberately unthematic to begin with—and postpones harmonic resolution until the very end. The *Tarantella* is thus formally the first of Carter's studies in sustained motion. The dynamic structure of this early work, which on the surface of things nowhere suggests the later Carter, shows how even in 1936 his basically dynamic concept of music placed him in oblique opposition to the restrained neo-classical style. Carter took from Stravinskian neo-classicism its purity of musical means, its preference for construction over colour and for clarity over sensationalism, but he rejected its formal stereotypes and stylistic allusions.

Unlike much of Carter's music from this period, *Tarantella* had a marked success. Goddard Lieberson (later of Columbia Records) wrote:

> Carter succeeded in writing something that even the Harvard boys couldn't be tight-lipped about! I wish I could convey with words the lift this music gave.[1]

After hearing the work, Carter's Harvard friend Lincoln Kirstein asked him to become musical director of his new touring company, Ballet Caravan, a position that soon led to the writing of the ballet, *Pocahontas*.

In a similar style to the *Tarantella,* but slighter, is *Let's Be Gay,* for women's chorus and two pianos, which was commissioned by Nicholas Nabokov for a production of John Gay's *The Beggar's Opera* at Wells College in upstate New York. The work continues the melding of popular-style melodic material and tangy polychordal harmonies, once again to express *carpe diem* revelry. Although he has saved the manuscript, Carter feels that this chorus is too inconsequential to merit publication.

In 1937 Carter organized a madrigal chorus in New York, and made the transcriptions of early music previously described. To complement these older works he embarked on composing a *Madrigal Book*. All that remains of this project is *To Music*, which was one of two settings of Robert Herrick for *a cappella* chorus. The other Herrick piece, *Harvest Home*, was performed in 1937 and reviewed by Paul Rosenfeld who thought that the line 'to the rough sickle, and crook'd scythe' indicated that the song was a leftist anthem—in the '30s apparently anything could be politicized. Whatever its political purpose (Carter doesn't recall any such intention), *Harvest Home* survives only in manuscript. It is a rather straightforward work, resembling the *Tarantella* but simpler in harmonic materials and design.

To Music sets Herrick's poem, 'To Music, To Becalm His Fever'. The poem praises music for its power to ease suffering—a potentially political argument in 1937 when the social function of art in a time of economic crisis was such an imposing issue. The poem's resolution, however, is unclear; the concluding flight to heaven is either a conventional trope for the music of the spheres, or an image of the poet's ultimate relief from worldly suffering—a macabre advertisement for music's powers. These disturbing textual elements were apparently not noticed at the time. The work won a WPA contest and was performed by Lehman Engel's Madrigal Singers in the spring of 1938, and subsequently by Varèse and his worker's chorus at the Greenwich House Music School. (Carter says Varèse made the music sound like Varèse.)

Along with the contemporaneous setting of 'Tell Me Where is Fancy Bred' and the Pavane from *Pocahontas*, *To Music* belongs to a brief neo-Jacobean phase in Carter's music. His Harvard room-mate, the musicologist Stephen Tuttle, had introduced him to the music of William Byrd, and to the *Fitzwilliam Virginal Book* and the English madrigal composers. In its modal melodic line, elegant melismas and flexible rhythmic accentuation *To Music* echoes the English madrigalists, as does its melancholy tone, which recalls Dowland and Wilbye. In harmony and texture, however, *To Music* was quite up-to-date. The texture fans out from four to seven parts and very dramatically, towards the end, a solo soprano soars above the choral mass in an evocation of the poet's heavenly flight.

Carter shapes the piece with a subtle and dynamic harmonic structure, but instead of the clashing semitones of the *Tarantella*, *To Music* exploits pandiatonicism, the harmonic technique that Stravinsky had developed in such works as the Serenade in A and *Apollo* and that was often called 'white-note' music at the time. This harmonic style was seen as a way of ordering and organizing the new harmonic vocabulary that had first appeared in chaotic form, a less radical Parisian parallel to Schoenberg's twelve-note method. The vertical combination of voices in *To Music* always lies within one scale, but is rarely simply triadic. Often two triads from a scale are superimposed, or non-triadic structures are derived from the scale, as in the seven-note pile-up of fourths (Ex. 20). Pandiatonicism here makes possible a much greater integration of the melodic harmonic materials than did the bitonal chord structures of the *Tarantella*.

Ex. 20

To Music

The overall harmonic design carefully supports the text. The work begins in F♯ aeolian, then moves to A aeolian and phrygian. The central stanza, which pictures the poet's feverish sufferings, sounds more chromatic, but actually lies within C♯ minor, exploiting the clash of raised and lowered leading notes that traditionally colours the minor mode. The tonality moves to C♯ major where the consuming fire dies down to a gentle licking flame—perhaps an over-traditional gesture. The music then returns to its opening F♯ tonality, but the ending—a cadence on B♭, a key that has not previously appeared—is completely unexpected. In traditional theory this tonality might be said to express the Picardy third in F♯ minor, but Carter explains it as a Doppler effect—the B♭ follows a preparation on B, and the sinking tonality suggests the poem's motion into the celestial distance. (Ives used a similar device at the close of *West London.*)

In his next choral work, *Heart Not So Heavy As Mine,* written in 1938, Carter greatly simplified his technique. The spare idiom and sharpened focus of this short work in effect constitute a critique of the Herrick chorus, which for all its melancholy beauty fails to convey the essential drama of its poem; the poet's agony and transformation are softened and obscured by the very richness of harmony and texture. By contrast, *Heart Not So Heavy As Mine* is a perfectly achieved musical drama in which harmony, counterpoint and form clarify and project the text. Whereas the Herrick chorus sounds at times uncomfortably like an updated madrigal, this setting of Emily Dickinson discovers fertile territory. It is the tiny seed of much later Carter, and also his first masterpiece.

Heart Not So Heavy As Mine is elegantly simple. The opening third of the work lies within the scale of B♭ aeolian (natural minor). Instead of harmonic motion, we hear the gradual saturation of a static tonality. The middle section similarly moves within G aeolian and phrygian, but with more ambiguity as to tonal centre, creating a growing harmonic tension which is released at the climactic recapitulation of the opening, a sudden return to B♭ aeolian, now strongly coloured by D♭. The final cadence in B♭ major is at once the relative and parallel major of the main tonal areas of the piece, and its shifting major-minor inflection echoes the climactic D♭ — all the tonal elements of the piece are brought to final resolution simply and clearly.

Carter's extreme restriction of harmonic motion allows him to create a very free and dramatically apt texture. The poem contrasts the isolation of the poet with the vitality of an unknown passer by, whistling a tune. Carter superimposes on a sustained tolling motif (suggestive of the *Dies Irae* or of Brahms Op. 118, No. 6) fragments of a livelier music. Both kinds of music migrate through the four voices, yielding a re-ordered collage of the poem's words which perfectly mirrors its drama. The very fact that both levels share the same pitches serves to heighten their rhythmic and expressive contrast. Echoing tones evoke a sense of spatial distance; the bell-like resonances of the sustained notes emphasize the silences that punctuate the whistler's tune, and the silence of these spaces is indeed frightening.

The form of the work also anticipates later developments in Carter's music. The climax occurs at the end of the phrase, 'without the knowing why', overlapping the return of the opening motif. The harmony suddenly moves from C minor to D♭ major, precisely at the melodic climax of the work, but is immediately pulled back to B♭ minor by the bass (Ex. 21). The climax is thus

Ex. 21   **Heart Not So Heavy As Mine**
                                        © 1939 Associated Music Publishers, Inc. Used by permission

at once a point of arrival and a point of departure; instead of stopping the musical motion it transforms and redirects it. This complex gesture is to appear again in the Symphony No. 1 and the Variations for Orchestra on a larger, more developed scale.

Musicians Wrestle Everywhere, written in 1945, confronts Emily Dickinson at her most dense and ambiguous. The poem is full of intimations of immortality, but its vision is at once vivid and uncertain, beyond metaphor and perhaps beyond belief. This is the one *a cappella* chorus (there is an optional string accompaniment) that Carter called a madrigal, but it is in no sense a pastiche. Carter here discovered a new kind of rhythmic counterpoint. The wrestling musicians appear in a riot of cross-accents; the regularly placed barlines serve only to co-ordinate traffic, for the accentuation of each voice is independent and constantly changing (Ex. 22). The way Carter

Ex. 22

Musicians Wrestle Everywhere
© 1948 Mercury Music Corp. Used by permission

springs the crossed-accents from the syllabic stress of the words (could non-English-speaking singers even attempt this piece?) suggests Renaissance practice, but no older madrigal goes this far in creating dizzying rhythmic cross-play.

Harmonically, *Musicians* extends the technique of controlled pandiatonic writing that *Heart Not So Heavy* had distilled to a pure state. The vertical combinations of notes are more dissonant, and the harmonic motion much faster and more unstable. After successive spins through all the sharp and flat keys—notice the enharmonic transformation at the madrigal's still centre—the music resolves on C major, the one tonality not previously stated. The double ending in simultaneous layers of loud and soft sound dramatically captures the central ambivalence of the poem, making the very purity of the final C major triad provocative and unsettling. Richard Franko Goldman, one of Carter's earliest and most perceptive champions, saw in this work the beginnings of Carter's later music; it certainly has a suggestive and original quality to its expression and structure that link it to the later works—it is philosophical music.[2]

Carter's three longer choral compositions, *The Defense of Corinth* (1941), *The Harmony of Morning* (1944) and *Emblems* (1947), are all major efforts. Both in scale and originality of form these little-known works were the main vehicles of Carter's development in the early 1940s. Each one is a unique conception, redefining the choral medium to express very different texts.

The Defense of Corinth, written in 1941 when Carter was teaching music, classics and mathematics at St John's College, Annapolis, is a comic work with serious overtones. Scored for men's chorus, piano duet and speaker, it combines narration, rhythmic recitation, choral speaking, whispering and hissing, with virtuosic sung polyphony. The source of such a novel exploitation of choral possibilities was probably not *Die Glückliche Hand* (which Carter knew) or *Moses and Aaron* (not published at the time)—which might come to mind first today—but rather Milhaud's *La Mort d'un Tyran* and *Les Choéphores* and Stravinsky's *Les Noces.* Carter's conception is new, however. He replaces Milhaud's primitive effects with a highly flexible and dramatic form: the chorus slowly emerges from the narrator's speech, its music gradually evolving from speech and isolated sung notes to a polyphony of speech and song; speech then drops out and the song mounts to a dense choral fugue, which then fades back into the narrator's words and a bare pianissimo cadence, two specks at the opposite ends of the piano. Carter constructs a curve which defines all the possibilities of his chosen medium in a single, inclusive continuum.

The complex form of the work serves an equally complex expressive goal. *The Defense of Corinth* is at once comic and cautionary. In choosing Rabelais's account of the tale of Diogenes and his tub (in a delightfully archaic seventeenth-century translation by Urquhart and Motteux) Carter had political motives, for in 1941, before the United States entered the war, this text could be read as two-sided allegory: a protest against American neutrality, and against the artist's own sense of uselessness at a time of national crisis.

The extraordinary sound-world of *The Defense of Corinth* equates Carter's music with Diogenes's tub. The music transforms noise into words and speech into song. The opening choral description of the Corinthians' preparation for the siege uses speech noises as musical sounds (Ex. 23). By contrast, the

Ex. 23

The Defense of Corinth
© 1950 Merion Music, Inc. Used by permission

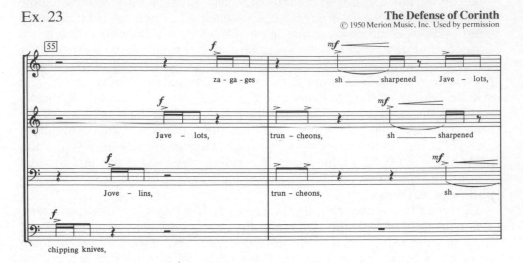

climactic double fugue celebrating Diogenes's downhill slide turns music back into noise, in a splattering of machine-gunned cross-accents (Ex. 24). Diogenes is the transforming agent, the composer, and like Diogenes Carter too wanted to show in the most dramatic way 'that not being engaged in any other office by the Republic, he thought it expedient to thunder and storm it so tempestuously upon the tub, that amongst a people so fervently busy and earnest at work, he alone might not seem a loitering slug and lazy fellow'.

Emblems, also written for the Harvard Glee Club, is *The Defense of Corinth*'s tragic counterpart. Like the *Defense, Emblems* is about the relationship of art and society. Although composed in 1947, it was not performed

Ex. 24

The Defense of Corinth
© 1950 Merion Music, Inc. Used by permission

until 1952 because of its difficulty—and has remained the ugly duckling of Carter's works. The text by Allen Tate, which has been subject to some surprising mis-readings—was suggested to Carter by his friend, the poet John Berryman.

To an even greater extent than *The Defense of Corinth, Emblems* has a distinctive structure and sound. The choral sonority is granitic, filling the total range of the male voice with up to eight-part harmony in spacious and dense

Ex. 25 **Emblems**

formations. The piano is not an accompaniment but an independent element; indeed the work might be termed a concerto for piano and chorus. The opening movement of the piece is entirely *a cappella*. The piano enters with a visionary bravura explosion at the beginning of the second movement (Ex. 25). This flourish is a stylized abstraction of a bass-drum roll traditional to a dirge; the movement is a funeral march. The piano's repeated bursts cover its entire range, slicing through the massive choral sonority (climactically at rehearsal number 160). The funeral march gradually fades away, continuing in the piano while the chorus begins the fast final section of the work. After briefly joining in the rapid, fugato motion, the piano evaporates, and the piece ends with a massive fortissimo slab of choral sonority, all the more intense for the absence of piano support.

Emblems is thus a symbolic musical drama with chorus and piano as opposed protagonists. This scenario stems from Carter's interpretation of the text. He has told me that he was particularly aware here of grammatical ambiguities and possible multiple readings of Tate's poem; the design of the music was constructed to project these internal conflicts of meaning. The poem deals with two subjects: the westward-moving settlement of America and the need to respond to death. (Carter feels that *Emblems* was so rarely performed because of this latter, 'un-American' subject—though it is precisely this pre-occupation that locates the work within the dominant tradition of American tragic art.) The poem symbolizes the forces of life and death through contrasting motion, the westward movement of the pioneers and their desire for burial by an eastward river. Instead of turning back, they carve out 'hollows of memory' by the river. In a society without traditions, art becomes the only way of understanding death, the only means of renewing the understanding of life in every generation; the poem concludes with a stunning image of comprehended primal nature:

> And the long sleep by the cool river
> They've slept full and long, till now the air
> Waits twilit for their echo, the burning shiver
> Of August strikes like a hawk the crouching hare.

Emblems was the first work Carter wrote after the Piano Sonata, and its vast scale and heroic tone are prepared by that crucial monument in Carter's career. The piano writing in *Emblems* recalls the Sonata though the harmonies are darker and less luminous, and the rhythms necessarily less free, because of the need to co-ordinate an ensemble. The harmonic structure is quite similar to the Sonata. It is based on a semitone opposition between B♭ and B♮, although the final resolution is sombrely downwards, contrasting with the Sonata's radiant upward cadences. The rhythmic retrenchment of the work, on the other hand, may explain its terminal role in Carter's choral output. To convey the density of the text, Carter simplified and slowed down his rhythms—the funeral march is perhaps the longest stretch of sustained slow music he ever wrote and, because it lacks the polyrhythmic tensions of the slow sections of his later music, it seems deficient in rhythmic force. Carter clearly felt that verbal and musical exposition called for very different speeds of presentation; words could never be articulated clearly at the rapid pulse or amid the contrapuntal density of the music he was beginning to write in the late 1940s. Coming between the Piano Sonata and the Cello Sonata, *Emblems* was written just when Carter was about to break through the sound-barrier of musical rhetoric. At this point, his new-found universe of high-speed musical complexity must have seemed incompatible with the demands of verbal clarity. Only after twenty-five years of experience with his mature idiom was he to return once again to the problem of setting poetry to music in *A Mirror on Which to Dwell.*

By contrast with the dense, heroic struggle of *Emblems, The Harmony of Morning,* written two years earlier, seems effortless. It is Carter's only composition for female chorus and orchestra, and his most expansive choral and instrumental conception, even though its text seems at first glance a slight affair. In *The Harmony of Morning,* he set 'Another Music' by Mark Van Doren, a poem neither dense nor modern, nor with any apparent social or political implications. Its subject however is central to Carter's work: the relation of music to both sound and thought. The poem traces a progression from the sounds of nature, to instrumental music, to the music of words: the diapason of musical experience.

To convey the poem's progression from sounds to ideas, Carter chose the form of cantus firmus variation, a form he uses with elegance and freedom. A single seven-note motif rings through the entire work, constantly recurring in varied guises. The accompaniment is an integral part of the drama: the poem's 'rage of the viols' gives rise to an energetic concertino for orchestra at the work's centre. The small instrumental ensemble, woodwind quintet, piano and strings, gives forth a luminous spray of colours—note the two perfect responses to 'sweet keys depressed', the bell-like sound achieved through pizzicato heterophony at letter T, the startling pianissimo chime of piano and plucked strings just before the conclusion. The choral sonority is similarly irridescent, particularly in the way it draws musical colours and accents from the sounds of the words; as in the marvellous fugato on 'but in the chambers of a brain/Are bells that clap an answer' (Ex. 26).

Ex. 26

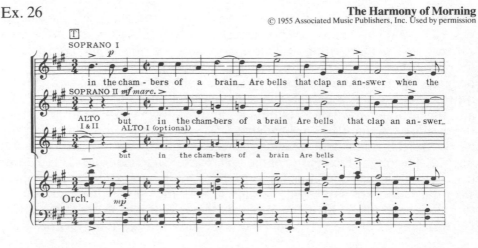

Harmonically, the work sums up the resources of the flexible, diatonic idiom that Carter first used in *Heart Not So Heavy As Mine,* and that he explored on an extensive scale in the Symphony No. 1. *The Harmony of Morning* is saturated with the sound of A major; at the same time it is constantly in harmonic motion. Typically subtle in harmonic function is the chordal frame of the central section of the piece. First stated as a juxtaposition of A major on D minor, it later returns a semitone lower: a section in A♭ prepares the return to the central A major tonality. This harmonic progression mirrors the high points in the work's vocal range—G♯ seems to be the highest sustained note, until the triumphant octave leap to high A on 'with truth'. The climactic statement of range dramatizes the most striking structural overlap of the work: the orchestra begins the coda with a sharp change in texture while the chorus continues its previous phrase, stretching it to a new climax against the sudden rhythmic burst in the orchestra (Ex. 27).

Songs

During the years of World War II Carter wrote many songs, but he discarded the bulk of his output. Five songs eventually were published, all written in

1942 and 1943. The evidence of other songs comes mainly from the contributors' column of *Modern Music,* which mentions a group of Whitman songs and several piano pieces at this time. Only one Whitman song survives, and no piano pieces, unless these were sketches for the Sonata. One additional song, *The Difference,* a duet written in 1944, remains in manuscript. All

Ex. 27

The Harmony of Morning
© 1955 Associated Music Publishers, Inc. Used by permission

but one of the existing songs set American poetry. During these war years Carter was interested in developing an American idiom—this intention certainly colours the contemporary Symphony No. 1 as well.

His earliest published song is pre-American, however, a setting of 'Tell Me Where is Fancy Bred', written at short notice in 1938, as incidental music for a recording of *The Merchant of Venice* by Orson Welles's famed Mercury Theatre. This was Carter's first piece to be recorded. The song, scored for low voice and guitar, was first published in 1972 with the guitar part edited by the guitarist-composer Stanley Silverman.

The style of the song echoes Campion and Dowland. The exquisite modal melody is drawn out in long sighing phrases, complemented by the simple, elegant counterpoint in the guitar—note the extraordinary intersection of the two parts on the word 'cradle'. This is the finest work of Carter's back-to-Byrd phase, and a wonderful, functional addition to the repertoire of Shakespeare songs.

Carter began his settings of American poetry with Robert Frost. Three of these songs are now published as a group, though this is misleading because *The Line Gang* calls for a heavier voice than either *The Dust of Snow* or *The Rose Family* require. Of all Carter's works, the Frost songs are written in the simplest idiom. They are the closest he comes to the light, charming vocal manner often found in Copland and Barber. *The Dust of Snow* and *The Rose Family* can be sung by a non-virtuoso (who can count) and would make nice encore numbers for a song recital. In a certain way, though, the 'charm' of these pieces is a little alien to Carter's compositional personality—he wants a larger canvas, a broader palette. The simple shifts in mood in these songs can seem a bit harmonically and emotionally pat—but they are attractive and not without subtleties. *The Dust of Snow* contrasts a long, slow-moving melodic line against a darting, staccato, syncopated accompaniment. The pentatonic vocal line captures Frost's matter-of-fact, New England intonation, while the piano's suggestion of sleigh bells sets off the poet's words in the blank spaces of a winter landscape.

The Rose Family is Frost's response to Gertrude Stein. Carter captures the poem's tongue-in-cheek delivery by setting it in a fast-moving $\frac{6}{8}$ metre, a little frantic, just a bit off-centre. (In harmony as well as metre the song echoes the slightly earlier *Pastoral*.) The major subtlety here is harmonic. Carter begins with fifth-dominated pentatonic material that gradually modulates away from its starting tonality and then back to it, travelling all round the circle of fifths in less than a minute. At its half-way point the song has moved from A♭ to A major (notated in the voice as B♭♭). The implications of this harmonic technique, at once extremely simple and yet capable of full chromatic saturation, were to be most fully realized in the first movement of the Piano Sonata. In fact the piano parts of all five of Carter's songs are preparations and sketches for that work.

The Line Gang portrays a noisy construction crew breaking through a forest to put up phone and telegraph lines. It was not published until 1975 and seems to fall between the light songs of 1942 and the epic vocal canvases of the following year. The musical punch-line, here an imitation of a telegraphic key-punch, though cleverly set up early in the song, also suggests a comic attitude not apparent in the text. Finally one feels that Frost's reticence was an alien and constraining vehicle for Carter's naturally expansive imagination.

In the two songs written in 1943 Carter turned in a very different direction, with significant results. In contrast to the tight-lipped aphorisms of Frost, Carter now set a vast, unruly catalogue poem of Whitman—*Warble for Lilac*

Time. The poem is a chaotic catch-all of spring-time reminiscences, in the course of which Whitman eventually transforms himself from outside observer to the voice of nature itself, indistinguishable from the warbling song of the birds. The singer, preferably a dramatic, even Wagnerian, soprano, must sustain vast, arched phrases over her entire range against the fast-flowing stream of the accompaniment. Although there exists an orchestral version of the song, Carter prefers the piano version (as revised in 1954) because a real virtuoso pianist can articulate the perpetually moving figuration without regular metric accents, creating an unbroken current of energy. When played in this way the song immediately suggests the *scorrevole* rhythmic texture of the Piano Sonata, and indeed of much later Carter, including the *Presto Volando* of the Concerto for Orchestra. The piano part of *Warble for Lilac Time* also firmly established the sonorous use of the entire keyboard with which Carter abolished the spinet style of neo-classical piano writing.

Harmonically, the song uses the pandiatonic idiom in a fluid way similar to *The Harmony of Morning*. From a simple diatonic opening the music gradually accelerates in harmonic motion; these speeding changes culminate in polychordal clashes. As in other works of this time, a semitone conflict, here between E and E♭, controls the harmony. The harmonic tension climaxes and resolves in the soaring melismatic setting of the words 'to sing', the climax of the song (Ex. 28). Despite the difficulties in performance that arise from the song's intense, expressive concept, *Warble* deserves to be heard more often; its torrent of sweeping melodic lines evokes Whitman at his most visionary.

Ex. 28

Carter's last and greatest song of this period, *Voyage*, sets Hart Crane's 'Infinite Consanguinity', one of a group of poems entitled 'Voyages' published in *White Buildings*. Carter discovered Crane's poetry in the 1920s when *White Buildings* and *The Bridge* first appeared, and he has obviously felt deep affinities with Crane—though on the surface it would be hard to imagine two more different people, beyond the fact that both were rebellious sons of wealthy families. Perhaps Carter saw in the flamboyant, self-destructive poet a *Doppelgänger*, a completing counterpart. Crane played out the role of *poète maudit,* abolishing the boundaries between his art and his life, pursuing chaos all the way to suicide—a suicide Carter portrays both in this song and in *A Symphony of Three Orchestras*. The mythical dimensions of Crane's struggle released the most intense qualities of Carter's personality into his music: *Voyage* seems to be the first work in which we hear his heroic-tragic voice, and his galactic sense of space. The song takes us into a very different world from the wit and wistfulness of much of his early music. Carter made the special nature of his relationship to Crane's poetry explicit in the unusual introductory essay he wrote for the song's first edition, and which is reprinted in the Appendix in its entirety to show Carter's care and sophistication in dealing with a text.

Voyage is a strikingly simple conception. The piano develops a single motif, which moves between slow, parallel outer voices. The motif is a Carter signature of this period; it engenders both the second movement of the Symphony No. 1, and the *Elegy* (in many ways a fraternal twin of *Voyage*). With this figure, Carter weaves a subtly evolving ostinato, constantly changing in rhythmic shape, so that a complex cross-accented texture results from the interplay of two strands in the accompaniment and the third element of the voice. As he did in *Warble,* Carter creates a polyphony of independent accents. The outer lines of the piano part gradually evolve into the dramatically tolling bells—echoing Crane's 'Broken Tower'—which dominate the central part of the song. The vocal line, preferably sung by a dramatic mezzo or heroic tenor, floats slowly and independently on the piano's tidal surface, joining it seemingly only at random moments of contact, an effect Carter was to extend in the Cello Sonata.

Harmonically the song reveals a new side of Carter's pandiatonic practice, which was greatly to influence the Piano Sonata. The song seems basically polytonal—the complete spectrum of tonalities appears to exist simultaneously, interwoven in ever-changing combinations. The slow parallel thirds of the piano's outer voices immediately give rise to polytonal cross currents that increase in tension until the climactic superimposition of G minor and E major at 'unto our body rocking' (Ex. 29). These pealing polytonal vibrations evoke a sense of vast, resonating space, most dramatically projected in the long, upward striding line under 'and where death if shed, Presumes no carnage, but this simple change'. The musical line is annihilated into a sudden pianissimo just as it reaches its goal. The final cadence is bitonal—E♭ major appears as an overtone of a B major bass. The harmonic conception is fundamentally contrapuntal. Each strand has its own tonal centre, and their combined motion produces six- and seven-note harmonies which replace

Ex. 29   **Voyage**
© 1973 Associated Music Publishers, Inc. Used by permission

tonal triads as the harmonic norm. This union of harmony and counterpoint is the basis of Carter's later harmonic technique.

An interesting addendum to the catalogue of Carter's songs is *The Difference,* written in 1944. It is a duet for soprano and baritone with piano accompaniment, to a poem by Mark Van Doren. When I asked Carter why he never published the song he said that he didn't think it was very good—I disagree with this judgement. The poem describes two people whose perception of reality is basically different—a very Carterian situation that he probably felt deserved a more dramatic and contrapuntal treatment than he gave it here. By his later standards the scale of the song is probably too small for the forces employed, and its working out too facile; but it is an attractive setting which surprisingly anticipates in texture and harmony parts of the Cello Sonata written four years later. The scale and shape Carter felt appropriate to two singers is not apparent in *The Difference*—it would emerge thirty-five years later in *Syringa.*

The Ballets

Carter's two ballets, *Pocahontas* and *The Minotaur,* frame his years of self-apprenticeship. *Pocahontas* includes music written as early as 1936, while *The Minotaur,* written in 1947, shares much material with the Cello Sonata of 1948 which can be considered the true beginning of Carter's mature phase. Perhaps the first thing to say about both ballets is that, like *Jeux* and *Daphnis et Chloé,* they failed in the theatre. *Pocahontas* was cast into obscurity by the brilliance of Copland's *Billy the Kid,* with which it shared a programme, and *The Minotaur* was similarly over-shadowed by the Stravinsky-Balanchine-Noguchi *Orpheus* which followed it by six months. The reasons for both theatrical failures were complex, having as much to do with choreography as with music, but the music itself was felt to be unduly 'thick', if not by music reviewers, certainly by the dance critics.

In neither of the two works did Carter follow the traditional closed forms of classical ballet. Instead, he created quite original symphonic forms—but this procedure always seems to be problematic for ballet choreographers and dancers who are accustomed to smaller, clearer formal units. Both *Jeux* and *Daphnis and Chloé,* so admirable in musical design, had great difficulty in supporting choreographic motion precisely because of their complex forms. Similarly, Stravinsky's most symphonic neo-classical ballet, *Jeu de Cartes,* was his one score that Balanchine was never able to choreograph successfully. Unlike Copland or Stravinsky, moreover, Carter is not essentially an illustrative composer—there would seem to be a basic conflict between the visual clarity needed in a theatrical work, and the contrapuntal bias of Carter's musical thinking. Both ballets thus represent side-tracks to Carter's development, but in differing ways. *Pocahontas* is a wildly uneven sampler of influences and inventions; *The Minotaur* is a deliberate invasion of enemy territory.

Pocahontas was commissioned by Carter's friend Lincoln Kirstein for a touring company called Ballet Caravan. This was the first of many attempts by Kirstein to bring ballet to America, attempts that culminated in the establishment of the New York City Ballet in 1948. Ballet Caravan was an odd, populist detour in Kirstein's career, very much in the spirit of the '30s. The company performed in small-town high schools and its repertoire clearly attempted to remake ballet in an American image. It included Paul Bowles's *Yankee Clipper,* Virgil Thomson's *Filling Station,* Copland's *Billy the Kid,* as well as *Pocahontas.* Balanchine played no part in this enterprise; in the 'American scene' mood of the '30s he was (for a time) resented as a foreigner.[3]

Kirstein wrote the scenario for *Pocahontas;* his original programme notes are reprinted in the published score:

When the English adventurers sailed into the bay by the outlet of the Virginia rivers they still thought of the strange new land not as a new continent but as a part of the East Indies Spice Isles. The people they found, subject to King Powhatan, were by no means the red nomads of the Western plains, but rather the gold-brown village-dwelling hunters and farmers—a race which has since disappeared completely.

Upon his arrival in the new land, the English explorer John Smith—now middle aged, a veteran of the Turkish wars and an experienced adventurer—accepted the cruelties of Powhatan's braves as the price of yet another adventure.

But the character of the young Indian princess Pocahontas was unexpected. Her capricious pity for him in rescuing Smith from the tortures of her kinsmen, her disgust with their savagery and her instinctive feeling for another civilization were something new.

And yet the white man's gifts were scarcely an improvement: firearms and firewater instead of tobacco and tomahawk. Guns and whiskey purchased the Indians and a handful of English seized America.

Symbolizing the naive trust and inherent tragedy of the original Americans, Pocahontas died in childbirth in England following her marriage to John Rolfe, Smith's protégé, and her presentation at the court of James I.

The idea and character of this ballet were suggested by 'Powhatan's Daughter', the second section of Hart Crane's poem *The Bridge*—particularly such lines as:

> There was a bed of leaves, and broken play;
> There was a veil upon you, Pocahontas, bride—
> O Princess whose brown lap was virgin May;
> And bridal flanks and eyes hid tawny pride.

Carter says that Kirstein was fascinated with Theodore de Bry's seventeenth-century engravings of idealized Indians costumed as Greek gods and goddesses among heavily caparisoned European conquerors. The scenic contrast between the well-padded Englishmen and Indians in classical ballet attire à la *Apollo* (well-realized by Karl Free) sparked Kirstein's plans—he even asked Carter for a concluding pavane that would be an early-American version of *Apollo's* apotheosis. The quotation from Hart Crane's *The Bridge* that appeared in the programme notes and is reprinted in the score was, Carter now says, an attempt to give the costume-inspired project some prestigious, poetic overtones—it was not, at any rate, a conscious influence on Carter's music for the ballet. The original version of *Pocahontas* was premièred on 17 August 1936 in Keene, New Hampshire, with choreography by Lew Christensen, and a cast including Lew Christensen, Ruthanna Boris, Charles Laskey, Harold Christensen and Erick Hawkins. This version had only piano accompaniment.

By 1939, when Ballet Caravan gave a New York season, *Pocahontas* was greatly revised and expanded. The biggest change in the music was the excision and replacement of material that later became the last movement of the Symphony No. 1—and which with its clean-cut, jaunty diatonicism must have sounded bizarrely out of place among the rugged features of the rest of the score. Unfortunately none of the earlier versions of the ballet still exists, so it is impossible to trace its musical development over the three years of gestation; nevertheless, the 1939 ballet, both in its complete form and in the Suite drawn from it, gives evidence of much stylistic and technical unevenness, the inevitable result of the extended process of revision at a time when Carter's musical personality was just beginning to evolve. The final version of the ballet was first performed on 24 May 1939 at the Martin Beck Theatre in New York, with Leda Anchutina, Erick Hawkins, Eugene Loring and Harold Christensen (doubling the role of John Smith with Todd Bolender). Also on the programme was *Billy the Kid,* an unfortunate juxtaposition.

The Suite from the ballet, which includes most of the full score, was published in two different versions. In 1941 the work won the Juilliard Publication Award and was printed in a deceptively attractive edition, studded with errors—Carter's errata list is twenty-five pages long! For a performance conducted in 1960 by Jacques-Louis Monod, he rather reluctantly engaged in a thorough-going revision of the score, urged on by Monod's scrupulous scanning of the work's details. Carter was working on the Double Concerto at this time and he must have felt light-years removed from the old ballet. The revised version was recorded by Monod and published in 1969.

Very little of *Pocahontas* sounds like later Carter—not in style, rhythm, harmony or orchestration. The shape of the Suite, however, *is* Carterian. The gradually subsiding motion from an opening explosion is a Carter fingerprint and is achieved there with memorable poignancy, as John Smith and John Rolf are gradually enveloped by the forest of the New World. The opening, explosive material, however, sounds rather like Milhaud (as Ernst Krenek once pointed out to Carter) and the calmer music starts out very much like Hindemith, before it begins to fade away. There are, however, also moments of great lyrical beauty in these opening sections that sound quite personal and original, from fig. 20 to the end of the second section, for example. Interestingly, these less derivative passages are also more characteristic of

Ex. 30

Carter in their counterpoint, which contrasts layers of different motion; at fig. 17 Carter superimposes a mysterious augmentation of Pocahontas's as-yet-unstated motif on top of the ⁶⁄₈ canter of the Smith-Rolfe material. At fig. 18 there is also an intriguing quotation in advance of a motif from the second movement of the Symphony No. 1, suggesting much interaction between the two scores in their formative stages. The motif, though prominently stated here, plays no important role elsewhere in the ballet.

The music for 'Princess Pocahontas and her Ladies' uses the rather exotic Pocahontas-motif as a frame for an un-Indian pop tune, whose cadenza-like extensions in the woodwinds perhaps suggest a jazz influence. At fig. 31, however, another section of beautifully restrained lyricism appears—one of the few passages in Carter that bring Mahler to mind, but very delicately: note the splendid interplay of violas and harp which supports the texture (Ex. 30). The clarinet cadenzas here foreshadow much more effective passages in the Symphony No. 1 and—in another universe—the Piano Concerto; but the orchestration of the last five bars of this section is inspired and well crafted.

The music for the 'Torture of John Smith' is the most uneven part of an uneven score. The basic shape is again distinctly personal, a tremendous build-up of violence released by a pianissimo echo—the barely audible resonance of harp and piano continues to ring after a sharp climactic chord for the whole orchestra. This effect is Carter's first use of a characteristically Ivesian gesture; indeed fig. 53 to 54 is Carter's only music of this period that *looks* like Ives on the page. Even at this stage, though, Carter was able to extend the gesture; the resonating piano and harp begin a new strand of music, taking the listener beyond the immediately shocking juxtaposition in volume. The musical materials of the torture scene, however, are less interesting than its shape. Smith's music sounds like a collection of neo-classical spare parts: there are passing echoes of Stravinsky, Hindemith, even Honegger. The more original Indian music, with its exotic percussion and dramatic silences, never quite seems to carry conviction—Copland did this kind of thing much better in the Gun Fight of *Billy the Kid*. The weakness of the music here stems from its surprising lack of counterpoint. It attempts to illustrate violence instead of creating it through structural polyphony, and the result is untypically square in rhythm and unfocused in sonority. When Carter needed a similarly riotous moment in *The Minotaur* he used a fugue texture, with much more precise effect and control of overall tension.

The Pavane that concludes *Pocahontas* is the double homage to Stravinsky's *Apollo* and the *Fitzwilliam Virginal Book* that Kirstein had requested. It beautifully achieves what it sets out to do though one feels that for Carter such an exercise in pastiche went against the grain. The more personal parts of the Finale are the delicate counterpoint at fig. 56 and the jaggedly punctuated fade-out at the conclusion, once again examples of Carter's inherent preference for polyphonic invention over simple illustration.

A decade after the first *Pocahontas*, Lincoln Kirstein again commissioned Carter to write a ballet, this time for Ballet Society, the immediate pre-decessor of the New York City Ballet. Ballet Society was as artistically élitist in character as Ballet Caravan had been populist—even the press had difficulty in getting into its exclusive performances held incongruously at the High School of Needle Trades in New York. Among its productions were Ravel's *L'Enfant et les sortilèges,* Balanchine's path-breaking choreography for Hindemith's *The Four Temperaments, The Seasons* (the first collaboration between John Cage and Merce Cunningham), and the Balanchine-Noguchi-Stravinsky landmark, *Orpheus.*

The Minotaur started out as a collaboration between Carter and Balanchine, who carefully worked out a scenario including the startling musical and scenic idea of transforming Pasiphae's heart beats into the hammer blows of workers building the labyrinth. The published score of the Suite contains the following synopsis:

Overture
Scene I—Pasiphae's apartments in the royal palace.
Pasiphae prepares secretly with her attendants for a tryst with the white bull.
Entrance of the bulls, summoned by the horn calls of Pasiphae's attendants. With a few companions, the white bull rushes in and a frantic
Bull's Dance with Pasiphae takes place. Blackout.
(Omitted in the Suite: Music during the change of scene suggesting the excited beat of Pasiphae's heart. When the curtain rises on the next scene, this beat turns into the pounding of hammers of stone cutters.)
Scene II—Before the Labyrinth. Some years later.

(Omitted in the Suite: The Minotaur is being imprisoned in a labyrinth as his mother, Pasiphae, tries to keep the workmen from building the walls. King Minos and Ariadne enter with Theseus leading a group of Greek captives who are to be sacrificed to the man-eating monster.)

Ariadne and Theseus are attracted to each other and dance a Pas de Deux. Despite Ariadne's pleading, her father commands that Theseus and his men be driven into

The Labyrinth.

Meanwhile Ariadne gives Theseus the end of a thread which is to lead him and his companions safely out of the maze.

Theseus's farewell on entering the labyrinth.

(Omitted in the Suite: Ariadne cautiously unwinds her thread from its spindle as Theseus enters the labyrinth pulling the thread after him.)

Theseus fights and kills the Minotaur, each gesture being transmitted to Ariadne through the thread.

Ariadne unwinds her thread to lead Theseus and his companions out of the maze. To her great dismay, the thread breaks.

Theseus and the Greeks emerge from the labyrinth and rejoice at their success. Then carrying oars and raising sails, but forgetting Ariadne,

Theseus and the Greeks prepare to leave Crete as the curtain falls.

Before Balanchine could choreograph the ballet, however, he left New York—and Ballet Society—for Paris, in an unsuccessful attempt to take over the Paris Ballet after the dismissal of Serge Lifar. Lifar was soon cleared of collaborationist charges and reinstated as director; Balanchine returned to New York in 1948, but meanwhile the choreography of *The Minotaur* had been assigned to Balanchine's young assistant John Taras. The magnificent sets and costumes were by Joan Junyer, and the cast included Elise Reiman, Francisco Moncion, Edward Bigelow and Tanaquil LeClerq as Ariadne. The première took place on 26 March 1947. The ballet received very mixed reviews: LeClerq made a great impression as did Junyer's sets, but the choreography was considered tentative and uneven. The dance critics found the music opaque—the auditorium at Needle Trades not being noted for its acoustics—but the music reviewers praised it: 'One could marvel at the extent of the work and complexity of thought that went into the process,' wrote Arthur Berger in the Herald Tribune. After two seasons *The Minotaur* was dropped and was never revived by the New York City Ballet. A new choreography by John Butler to the music from the Suite was staged in Boston in 1970. The Suite, which omits about one-third of the music, was recorded by Howard Hanson and the Eastman-Rochester Symphony Orchestra in 1956. (For several years this was the only orchestral work of Carter's available on disc.) The recording was very well received, but critics tended to label Carter a neo-classicist on the basis of the score—at the very time when his style had left neo-classicism far behind.

Perhaps more than any other work, *The Minotaur* presents problems for anyone attempting to trace Carter's development. Richard Franko Goldman, in a pioneering article on the first Quartet, went so far as to advise readers *not* to listen to *The Minotaur,* because of the misleading impression it would give of the composer's work.[5] Bayan Northcott similarly offered the cautionary explanation that in *The Minotaur*, Carter was deliberately tying up loose ends, bringing his first period to a close.[6]

The Minotaur problem can be stated simply: together with the Piano Sonata it is Carter's greatest achievement before 1948, a work of great lyrical beauty, compelling rhythmic force and distinctive emotional depth; but whereas the Sonata unmistakably points in the direction of Carter's later music, *The Minotaur* looks backwards, and in a peculiar, troubling manner. For if *Pocahontas* seemed to contain echoes of many other composers in a way natural to a young artist just beginning to seek his own style, *The Minotaur* seems, at first, perversely Stravinskian, deliberately contradicting many of the personal traits Carter's music had developed so strongly by 1947. Indeed passages such as figs. 73 to 75, or, even more, 107 to 109, seem like intentional allusions to Stravinsky's works—the spiccato strings and solo clarinet in an unmodulated *mezzoforte* are as characteristic of Stravinsky as they are unusual for Carter. The structural formations of the music, from the framing Maestoso whose horn duet so strikingly anticipates *Orpheus,* to the clearly juxtaposed sections of the Bull's Dance and Pas de Deux, also sound uncharacteristically close to the Russian master.

The derivative impression the score has made on some listeners, however, is superficial and deceptive. While the surface of the music suggests neo-classicism, its essential structure grows out of anti-classical procedures. The work embodies in its most extreme form the basic conflict running through almost all of Carter's music before 1948, the conflict between neo-classical restraint and a more dynamic and complex discourse. In *The Minotaur* this conflict emerges as a musical critique of Stravinskian practice whose destructive thrust cleared the way for the unforeseen, explosive *coup* of the Cello Sonata, and its radically new musical idiom.

Considering the almost paralysing influence of Stravinsky on Carter's generation, it is surprising how few echoes of his works there are in Carter's early output—Carter was wise enough to see just how personal Stravinsky's idiom was. How then can one account for the Stravinskian gestures of *The Minotaur*? The answer to this question probably lies in the original collaboration with Balanchine. The score is Balanchinian even more than it is Stravinskian—the angularity of motion, fast juxtapositions and tight rhythmic phrases seem tailored to Balanchine's choreographic style with its cubist distortions of Petipa.

Stravinsky and Balanchine shared the aesthetic values of modern classicism: a delight in using traditions, in irony, in elegant simplicity. Carter came to feel that he had to take this aesthetic a long step further. While he saw that Stravinsky's dynamic juxtaposition and cross-cuttings were among the few new formal premises of twentieth-century music, Carter began to smudge, overlap and superimpose Stravinsky's clearly demarcated events. Similarly, although Carter felt that Stravinsky's non-traditional use of traditions was an advance over, for example, Schoenberg's much more con-

Ex. 31

servative idea of musical history, he felt the need to go beyond the aesthetic ideals of neo-classicism. For Stravinsky, as for Balanchine, art grew out of a carefully created tension between traditions and violations of traditions. As Carter's art developed, however, it abolished stylistic and formal categories and set out to create in every work a complex, explosive interplay of unstable and constantly varied materials.

The Minotaur represents a deliberate collision between the anti-classical tendency of Carter's nearly-matured art and the high modernist mode of Stravinsky and Balanchine. It is Stravinsky taken to a second power— Stravinskian mannerisms form the normative background for Carter's distortions and inventions. Although this confrontation never emerged in the theatre—because of Balanchine's departure from the project—it can nevertheless be clearly heard in the music.

Before analysing the score it is necessary to show how the Suite differs from the complete ballet. While Carter feels that the Suite is preferable in the concert hall (suites are usually morning-after exercises in self-criticism) he insists that the entire score is necessary in the theatre; he viewed the new Boston choreography therefore as musically mistaken. The Suite omits two crucial structural events in the transformation of Pasiphae's heart beats into hammer blows, and the first statement of the music to which Ariadne unwinds her thread, music that is superimposed on a passacaglia bass when she rewinds the thread and it breaks. Although Carter may have felt that these events were too specifically theatrical to warrant inclusion in the Suite, they are absolutely necessary to the dramatic shape of the complete score. Two other omissions—a short, strange ostinato before the White Bull enters, and the long entrance march of Minos—are structurally less important, and musically less interesting than the rest of the music; they do contain bits of recapitulation which may have mirrored the dance, but seem redundant without it. It is a shame that there is no recording of the complete score, if for no other reason than to allow us to hear the hammer-blow music which was like nothing else Carter wrote at this time, but seems to anticipate the polyrhythmic explosions at the end of the Piano Concerto, and the thunderclaps in *A Symphony of Three Orchestras*. These hammer blows also make explicit the structural function of pulse throughout *The Minotaur*.

Two movements of the ballet are constructed on polyrhythmic principles. The propulsive Bull's Dance pits crotchets at MM 160 against dotted crotchets at 106.7 (Ex. 31). This is the familiar hemiola relationship of 3:2. What is new here is the absence of hierarchy between the two pulses: the music is essentially polyrhythmic, so that either pulse can be heard as background to the other. Carter for the first time is replacing the traditional rhythmic configuration of single pulse and fixed accent with a structure that grows from the conflicting accents of simultaneously stated pulses, pulses which furthermore are in a more tense relationship than the 2:1, 3:1 or 4:1 combinations of most European counterpoint. This passage almost crosses into the new rhythmic world of the First Quartet—but not quite.

The Pas de Deux, a section of mysterious beauty, is also based on two tempi, MM 120 and MM 80, that are related in a 3:2 ratio. The dance

Ex. 32

The Minotaur

alternates large sections built on each of these tempi, thereby creating a structure analogous to, but different from, the traditional and Stravinskian form of introduction, solo variations and concluding duet. In Carter's conclusion the two tempi fuse through cross-cutting. Alternating bars are built on the two different pulses. The interference pattern of the two tempi sounds at first like Stravinsky's shifting accentuation, but its structural source is the conflicting claims of the two pulses rather than the irregular accentuation of a single pulse unit (Ex. 32).

The pulse rate of the Pas de Deux reappears structurally in later parts of the ballet. The Passacaglia to which Ariadne rewinds her thread moves at crotchet=60, so that it can allude to the Pas de Deux, restating its quaver ostinato exactly by renotating in halved values. The pulse of MM 60 appears climactically at fig. 105 when a cross-accented grouping of five quavers sounds the pulse at the centre of a transformation in tempo from ♩.=152 to ♩=76; the semiquavers at fig. 107 are at the same speed as the dotted quavers at fig. 101.

The underground rhythmic organization of *The Minotaur* is part of its coherent and original sub-structure. The deceptively irregular accents and the major-minor dissonances of the music's surface are produced by coherent, hidden structural principles which never receive explicit thematic form; all the elements of the work are emanations from a hidden core. Most of the melodic shapes of *The Minotaur,* for example, were derived from the Seikilos Song—one of the few transcribed fragments of Greek music. But although Carter originally quoted (Ex. 33) this theme after fig. 104, he later cut the quotation out of the music, leaving variations without a stated theme and hiding the pervasive source of melodic unity.

Ex. 33   **Seikilos Song (The Minotaur)**

The harmonic structure of the work grows from a similar submerged principle, which, like the pulse system that unifies the work's rhythms, is to have great implications for Carter's subsequent development. The harmonies of *The Minotaur* sound far more chromatic and dissonant than even those of the Piano Sonata, because there are few of the pentatonic, pandiatonic, fifth-derived sounds of the Sonata. The tonal conflict is controlled by a set of four-note chords based on thirds and minor seconds, the ubiquitous semitones giving the work its distinctive colour. By combining pairs of thirds at the distance of a semitone, Carter derives the following seven source chords (Chart 5):

Chart 5   Chords in *The Minotaur*

These four-note groups control the harmonic and melodic idiom of *The Minotaur* with great consistency, though not with the relentless logic of similar practice in the Cello Sonata and later works. They are implicit, but not overtly stated in the opening Maestoso, and although they become increasingly explicit as the work continues, they always exist as subliminal cells rather than themes.

The formal structure of the ballet summarizes the strategies by which Carter undermines the deceptively Stravinskian surface. Most of Stravinsky's neo-classical ballets are suites of separate dances. There are few thematic connections between the dances, except for direct recapitulation as at the conclusions of *Apollo* and *Orpheus,* or the reiterated fanfares in *Agon.* By contrast, Carter's music always tends to eradicate formal boundaries, either through continuous evolution or by fragmentation and superimposition, so that, as in the Concerto for Orchestra or the Third Quartet, different 'movements' evolve simultaneously. In *The Minotaur* clearly demarcated sections turn out on closer inspection to overlap and interact. Because of the tightly controlled harmonic and rhythmic schemes, motivic cross-references abound—so much so that the listener hears a continuous, integrated permutation of materials rather than linear thematic development, or leitmotivic allusion. Behind many of these relationships is the Seikilos Song: the rising fifths that introduce the Bull's Dance (Ex. 34) state the opening motif of

Ex. 34 **The Minotaur**

© 1956 Associated Music Publishers, Inc. Used by permission

this melody most obviously, but other, veiled allusions abound, as in the cello line at fig. 10 (Ex. 35). Note how this passage in turn anticipates fig. 25, and how the oboe outline before fig. 27 returns as an accompaniment to the flute solo of the Pas de Deux. Similarly the Bull's pounding dotted crotchet motif returns in a lyrical guise in the ⅜ sections of the Pas de Deux. Balanchine's first idea, the heart beat/hammer blow transformation, may have been the source for this continuous process of thematic metamorphosis, much as, in the scenario, Ariadne and Theseus represent a mythical transformation of Pasiphae and the Bull.

In the closing sections of the ballet, contrasting material is gathered up by superimposition. A fugue announces the entrance of the Greek prisoners into the labyrinth; this is followed by a flute solo on a pedal point as Ariadne unwinds her thread. Fugue and pedal point are Stravinskian; but Carter then

Ex. 35 **The Minotaur**

© 1956 Associated Music Publishers, Inc. Used by permission

goes on to superimpose these two textures as Ariadne follows Theseus's movements as they are transmitted through the thread. When she rewinds the thread the flute solo is now placed over a ground bass, on top of which the fast, violent music of Theseus's struggle is later added. When the Greeks emerge from the labyrinth a new semitone motif appears—deceptively new, for it is the inversion of Pasiphae's music at the beginning of the score. The Greeks' rapid music is transmuted into a background for yet another flute solo at fig. 107. The Stravinsky-sounding strings here are in fact part of a Carterian textural and rhythmic modulation. The flute solo itself, though it sounds like Ariadne's earlier flute music, in fact states the horn theme of the Bull's Dance. To conclude the ballet the ground bass returns, bringing all the materials of the work to a climactic focus, which then fades away to a return of the opening Maestoso, the typical static frame of a Stravinskian collage, but equally the ending and starting point of a typically Carterian cycle.

Instrumental Works

Considering the central role played by chamber music in Carter's later phase, it is surprising that there are only four surviving chamber pieces from the years before 1948, and that they are all short and light. During this period of Carter's development it might be said that the vocal compositions functioned as the main exploratory vehicles, much as the quartets would later, while the chamber works were more in the nature of *pièces d'occasion*.

The *Canonic Suite* stems from the contrapuntal exercises Carter wrote for Mlle Boulanger. These pieces originally formed three of four 'Musical Studies' that were composed without any specific instrumentation or even any intention of performance. For a BMI competition in 1939, Carter arranged them for the unlikely but required combination of four alto saxophones, and in 1956 he rescored them, with slight revisions, for four clarinets (though they might work equally well if arranged for four violas or even four marimbas). The charm of these strict canons lies in their fresh insights into traditional and rigorous textures. The first is a four-part canon at the unison, and at the distance of a brisk crotchet. The constant stretto does not sound like canonic imitation in separate voices. The listener hears a complex changing texture that evolves mysteriously, adding and shedding tiny musical figures (Ex. 36). (This kind of process was to interest the 'minimalists' of the late '60s.) The second piece also grows out of an unusual canonic design. It simultaneously unfolds an original line, its diatonic inversion, retrograde and retrograde inversion. The technique (though not the style) recalls Berg's practice in the Chamber Concerto, but Carter's piece has a distinctive, melancholy feeling, and its complex palindromic form shapes this mood into an effortless arch. Harmonic motion, from modal diatonicism through enharmonic modulations and back again, matches the counterpoint in subtlety. The third piece, a tarantella, is a strict four-part canon, with each entrance a second higher than the one before. Its wealth of humour again masks the mechanics of its structure: the constantly rising imitative voices leap over each other with

Ex. 36

playfully mounting excitement. A fourth Study, a beautifully shaped Andante espressivo in the form of a double canon in inversion, exists only in manuscript. It contrasts a flowing line with rests and long isolated notes, creating a polyphony of contrasted motion in time, a texture that was to become the basis of Carter's later contrapuntal discoveries. Unfortunately its extended range prevented the same scoring as with the other pieces.

The *Pastoral* was written in 1940 for the oboist and cor anglais player Josef Marx. Although published—at Henry Cowell's insistence—as a viola piece with alternative parts for clarinet and cor anglais, Carter composed it for this last instrument and prefers that version. The *Pastoral,* together with the *Elegy,* the Frost songs and the Symphony No. 1 represents a brief bucolic phase in Carter's development. These works have a wistful mood that Carter soon intensified to his more characteristic emotional pitch. Unlike many of his later pieces, they are not difficult to play, and so make a good, if hardly typical, introduction to Carter for amateur performers.

Carter calls the *Pastoral* his Walter Piston piece. Its mild manner ('like a conversation in country surroundings') is more characteristic of his Harvard teacher than of himself. Piston's influence on Carter, however, should not be underestimated. Not only did Piston encourage him to go and study with Nadia Boulanger, but his music, which Carter began to know in the 1920s, forcefully illustrated the strengths of the new classicism. In 1978, for one of the concerts honouring his seventieth birthday, Carter asked that Piston's *Three Pieces* for flute, clarinet and bassoon of 1923 should be played, together with Leo Ornstein's Violin Sonata (1917). The wit, clarity and inventiveness of Piston's music still seemed like a gust of fresh air compared to Ornstein's post-Scriabin smog. The linear counterpoint of the *Pastoral* and its elegantly restrained use of jazz both derive from Piston. The work opens, however, with a Carter signature: the rising fifth motif from the Seikilos Song that he also uses in *Philoctetes, The Minotaur,* and 'Anaphora'.

The *Pastoral* is of particular interest because it is Carter's oldest surviving work for solo instrument and piano, and already indicates directions that he would follow in the Cello Sonata, and even in the Duo of 1974. Carter builds the piece out of contrasted sonorities, and employs a tensile rhythmic design. The formal plan by-passes classical procedures for an open form inspired by jazz improvisation. The work opens with a defining statement of the piano's sonority: a combination of sharp staccato attack and sustained decay sound which colours the piano part throughout (Ex. 37). The soloist enters with a

Ex. 37   **Pastoral**

pentatonic, lyrical theme, while the piano continues its material. The metre is ⅜ as in *The Rose Family*, which the *Pastoral* resembles in many ways, and this rhythmic pattern which is so often a strait-jacket is here treated with great flexibility. The ⅜ metric pattern is freely diminished and augmented with much cross-accentual play between the instruments. As the *Pastoral* develops, syncopated semiquaver motion gradually develops out of the opening material. By fig. 106 this new motion turns into a jazzy 'second theme' that has really been present for some time in incomplete form (Ex. 38). The two basic elements then alternate, leading to solo cadenzas and an accelerando conclusion.

Ex. 38

The *Pastoral*'s untraditional form and rhythmic complexity (for its day) point to later developments, as do—by contrast—its failings. The piece does not sustain the focus of its opening gestures. The sharp piano sonority with which it begins never evolves into a greater and more interesting design. Similarly the solo cadenzas seem to indicate climaxes that are not achieved. The music wants to go somewhere with all its rhythmic energy, but never finds a goal; instead, it doubles back on itself several times too many. Thematically the subtle evolution of one material out of the other becomes self-defeating, for it fails to provide real contrast. The final impression one has is of attractive material which lacks the tension to sustain the length of the piece.

In sharp contrast with the tentative procedures of the *Pastoral* is the beautifully achieved *Elegy,* which also exists in a variety of arrangements. It was written in 1943, originally for cello and piano. Carter was never pleased with the original scoring, and rearranged the work for a string quartet he met while on vacation in Maine in 1946, and again for string orchestra in 1952. In 1961 a final revision was made, now for viola and piano. Each of these arrangements shows an unmechanical attention to detail typical of the composer. The viola version in particular introduces a great deal of written-out rubato to separate the two instruments polyphonically, and also ends in tonal ambiguity, unlike the older, squarer, quartet and string orchestra versions.

If the *Pastoral* was an unsuccessful attempt to create a continuous instrumental arch, the *Elegy* poetically succeeds in attaining this Boulanger-inspired goal. It is a flowing, seamless meditation, its line carried forward by sensitive contrapuntal interplay and continuous harmonic motion. Thematically the piece is closely related to the slow movement of the Symphony No. 1 and the song *Voyage,* which it resembles in expressive mood and fluid continuity. Indeed the *Elegy* is closer to Carter's songs than to his later chamber works: it is pure sustained cantilena, not a study in dramatic contrast.

111

The Woodwind Quintet, written in 1948 and dedicated to Nadia Boulanger, presents the same problem for the annotator as does *The Minotaur,* though on a smaller scale. Technically it is a brilliant conception, with a Haydn-like inventiveness in instrumental counterpoint and a concise, original formal design. Expressively, however, it seems like a last backward glance—and a distant even ironic one—at the mild melancholy and witty good-cheer of the early '40s. Carter has said that he wrote the Quintet deliberately to be the kind of music Nadia Boulanger always wanted him to compose. Its untypical neutrality of tone seems like a pastiche of Boulanger's stylistic preferences—just as its extraordinary care of workmanship is a tribute to her teaching.

The work is in two movements, contrasting B minor and B♭ major in a way familiar from the Piano Sonata and *Emblems.* The opening texture is innovative. Each instrument plays individually characterized material: the flute, a lyrical theme; the oboe, a staccato, mechanical pulse; the clarinet, dramatically flamboyant runs; the horn, sustained notes; the bassoon, light, irregular staccato phrase groups (Ex. 39). In the course of the movement

Ex. 39

these personality traits are contrasted in various ways and migrate from instrument to instrument, so that at the recapitulation only the horn, the outsider of the ensemble, retains its original role. The contrast of instruments recalls places in Milhaud's six little symphonies, and anticipates as well the textures of Carter's Second Quartet and Brass Quintet; but it is not pursued here with far-reaching effect, for there is also much traditional thematic thinking at work and this tends to obscure the movement's instrumental contrasts.

The second movement is a brilliant, jazz-inspired rondo. The bouncy opening material returns in ever-intensified variations. Beginning with dramatically breathy fragments, the movement ignites in energy, sending up loudly syncopated bursts of sound like a miniature fireworks display. The intense rate of invention in this movement transforms its classical enclosure into a potent explosive—whether this gesture is comic or defiant or both is hard to say. The expressive contradictions of the work have not put off wind players, many of whom consider it the crown of the wind quintet repertory. Nevertheless, Carter's decision to write the Quintet à la Boulanger seems to prevent it from having his usual emotional scale. The *Eight Etudes and a Fantasy,* written a year later, show Carter more happily on his own turf; they are even more spectacular technically than the Woodwind Quintet, and more original in idiom and form.

Orchestral Music

During the '40s Carter wrote only two purely orchestral works. The Symphony No. 1, dedicated to his wife, Helen, was completed in December 1942 while the Carters were living in Santa Fe, New Mexico. It was premièred by Howard Hanson and The Eastman-Rochester Symphony Orchestra on 27 April 1944. Although it also received a reading by the New York Philharmonic under Mitropoulos (with Varèse present), it was never publicly performed by them or by any other major American orchestra, until Sarah Caldwell's performance with The Boston Symphony in 1976. (A pallid recording by the Louisville Orchestra in 1961 probably did not help matters.) The *Holiday Overture,* which celebrates the liberation of Paris, was written in the summer of 1944 in Saltaire, Fire Island, where the Carters were visited by Aaron Copland. Copland, who was composing *Appalachian Spring* at the time, helped the Overture to win the Independent Music Publishers' Contest in 1945. The prize was supposed to include a performance by Koussevitsky and the Boston Symphony, but Koussevitsky (who was on the jury that awarded the prize) never played the piece, and Carter had to steal the parts from the orchestra's library so that they could be duplicated for performance elsewhere. The première of this very American work therefore took place in 1946 in Frankfurt, Germany of all places; the Frankfurt Symphony had been re-established by the American Occupation Army and was anxious to establish de-nazified credentials by playing American music.

The unhappy tale with regard to performances of both these pieces stands in ironic contrast to the deliberately popular stamp of their musical idiom. Very much under the influence of Copland's works at that time, Carter was interested in using a musical language that would be accessible to a broad audience. Copland's music of the late '30s, beginning with *El Salon Mexico* and *Billy the Kid*, indicated to Carter the possibilities for a musical language that was modern without being élitist, and for an advanced music that would have a clear social function. Carter praised *El Salon Mexico* in a 1939 review in these political terms: 'He has discovered a kind of beautiful simplicity which bears a definite spiritual relationship to the simple, direct, and honest people of this continent' (WEC 46)—Carter was clearly in a WPA frame of mind in this untypical rhetoric, which nevertheless shows how pervasively the need for a broader-based serious music was felt.

Carter and Copland were personally very close at the time of these works. Copland suggested revisions in the Symphony, which Carter adopted, and tried, unsuccessfully, to persuade 'Koussie' to play the Overture—which much later became part of Copland's conducting repertoire. For Copland, the development of a popular idiom was at once a necessary political goal for a composer, an inherent aspect of the anti-romantic tendency that he strongly believed was the main force in the new music, and the perfect correlative of his music vision, which from the first was based on clear textures, song-like melody, dance-rhythms, and episodic structure. As early as 1925, he had produced a model populist work in *Music for the Theater*, but he then turned to a more abstract—though still contrapuntally simple—idiom in the Piano Variations and Short Symphony. Interestingly, his return to a wider audience was forecast in the article *he* wrote about Ives in 1933. Copland had given a concert at Yaddo in 1931—which Carter heard—including his Piano Variations and Seven Songs by Ives, among them *Charlie Rutledge,* Ives's parody of cowboy music, which quotes 'The Streets of Laredo', later used by Copland in *Billy the Kid*.

Carter's own attitude towards populism was mixed, even at this time. He admired the new-found directness of Copland's works, and sympathized with their political goal even to the extent of taking seriously the Hollywood Stalinism of the movie *North Star,* in which Copland Coplandized the *Internationale*. But he was suspicious of the vulnerability of populism to commercial taste at its most crass. As Carter's review of the music heard at the New York World's Fair of 1939 indicated, the serious artist's normal concern for audience appeal was being overwhelmed by a more traditional American variety of populism—commercial garbage, whether turned out by Kurt Weill and Vittorio Gianinni, who knew better, or by Robert Russell Bennett, who didn't need to. Happily forgotten works that passed for populism at the time such as George Kleinsinger's *I Hear America Singing* or Earl Robinson's *Ballad for Americans* (a leftist classic in my childhood) revealed to Carter that their composers seemed to go on 'the assumption...that the masses don't know anything about music and never will' (WEC 74). The term populism has indeed tended to be a misnomer. In American society, populist works have either been politically radical, like Blitzstein's *The Cradle Will Rock*—and

114

thus limited in appeal to a politically-conscious élite; or purely commercial, like Bernstein's Blitzstein-inspired *West Side Story,* which is indistinguishable in content and purpose from apparently less high-minded examples of commercial musical theatre: 'That's entertainment', as the song goes. Well-intentioned accessibility slides into money-making sentimentality, the picket line yields to the bottom line. Copland himself did not always avoid this all-too-American trap—though his political and professional idealism shielded him from the vulgarity of his imitators.

Carter's ambivalent reaction to populism was not simply an intellectual stance; more importantly it stemmed from the needs of his own musical personality. Where Copland is a poet of 'simple gifts' whose great talent is for the direct illustration of mood, Carter is a more complex artist, who expresses himself most personally through the creation of rich, labyrinthine musical structures. In both the Symphony No. 1 and the *Holiday Overture,* he subjected highly simplified, populist thematic material to a characteristically original and complex treatment. To many of his contemporaries the results seemed contradictory, confused and unsuccessful. ('Carter can write a tune' a reviewer wrote of the Symphony in *Modern Music,* 'but he can also surround it with a kind of esoteric tonal haze'.)[7] The works met with hostile resistance, not from audiences—who never heard them—but from conductors who decided that they were too difficult and modern to merit performance. The *Holiday Overture* was seen as 'another complicated Carter piece' and friends who saw the Piano Sonata that Carter was working on at this same time predicted that it would never be played because of its difficulties.

Ironically, considering its lack of acceptance when it first appeared, the Symphony No. 1 now seems in many ways to be a beautifully imagined embodiment of the populist ideal in its most humane and least polemical form. In this respect it resembles Copland's *Appalachian Spring* which it preceded by two years. The Symphony is a deliberately modest conception, scored for a small orchestra, and using the simplest of diatonic materials to make a serenely lyrical statement. It is a pastoral symphony, of a very original sort, completely free of the bombast and academicism all too characteristic of the symphonic form in the twentieth century—particularly when that form is used to express the sentiments of the 'People'.

Writing a symphony compels a composer to choose predecessors; the decision to employ a form so overloaded with historical associations demands a clear historical perspective. Carter in his Symphony No. 1 chose to work outside the main, German tradition of the symphony. There is none of the heroical rhetoric of the romantic symphonic style, no formal or stylistic allusion to the symphonic past. Carter instead turned primarily to recent American works as models: Sessions's Symphony No. 1 of 1927 which Carter copied out for his own analysis, Copland's Short Symphony (1933) and Roy Harris's Third Symphony (1938), the latter being the unavoidable Great American Symphony of the day. What he took—and what he rejected—from these models is very revealing. He borrowed Sessions's cross-accented rhythms and continuous development, but not his motoric, neo-baroque style. He borrowed Copland's clarity of statement and rhythmic emphasis,

Ex. 40

Symphony No. 1
© 1961 Associated Music Publishers, Inc. Used by permission

but not his bareness of texture. He borrowed Harris's openly evolving forms, but not his bombastic gestures.

The first movement of the Symphony No. 1 is the finest of the three, and the closest in structure to Carter's later music. Its form is quite original: exposition, development and recapitulation are replaced by a series of interlinked episodes, variations on two groups of musical material. These short events, each of them revealing a fresh aspect of the movement's primal matter, are not flat, static fragments but are transformational in character, structural crescendos or diminuendos moving towards a point of arrival which turns out to be a new point of departure. The ultimate goal of the work's motion comes at fig. 403, but the climax at that point dissolves precisely where the listener anticipates a structural downbeat and a new extension of the musical material begins (Ex. 40). (This is the climactic gesture that Carter first discovered in *Heart Not So Heavy As Mine.*)

The novel formal concept of this movement produces many moments of unusual poetic freshness, from the mysterious opening, with its instantaneous statement of the work's primary colours (interestingly—this opening was an afterthought; the work originally started at bar 3, without the rich string chords), to the evocative flute duet at 234, the salt-air background to the trumpet solo at 285, the cinematic dissolve at 320, or the subtle mixture of muted trumpets, plucked and sustained strings, and high woodwinds at 484. Considering the small forces deployed—double winds, timpani and strings—the movement's marvellously evocative orchestral colouring is all the more remarkable. Carter's anti-classicism again is the source of these discoveries. Although classically scaled, the orchestra is not dominated by the strings, with the other instruments used as secondary families, as is the case in classical and neo-classical scores; rather there is a continually changing interplay of all the available sonorities. This process of orchestral chemistry is reminiscent of Debussy who once wrote: 'The strings should form not a barrier, but a circle round the other instruments. The woodwinds should be dispersed: the bassoons with the cellos, the oboes and clarinets with the violins so that their entries should not produce a package effect.'[8] Without ever having heard Debussy's theory, Carter later followed this advice almost literally in the Concerto for Orchestra; in the Symphony No. 1 the conventionally-seated ensemble is blended in a similar way, producing a unique overall sonority. The kinship with *La Mer,* which one feels even without knowing that Carter was inspired by the sea- and land- scapes of Cape Cod in writing this movement, is spiritual rather than technical; Carter's Symphony emulates *La Mer*'s evocative powers without employing any of its illustrative devices. Perhaps the most singular trait of this movement is the way it transforms material as elemental and abstract as a major triad into an evocative and wistful mood. The distinctive colour of the work is constantly transformed and varied, and finally distilled down to the single line of a lightly floating clarinet solo.

The rhythmic design of the movement supports its formal innovations. Although the rhythms appear extremely simple—Carter says he is always amused when he sees 'all those quarter notes'—its structural premises are original. There are two basic pulses: a dotted minim value that establishes the gentle triple motion of the opening, and a minim pulse that appears at fig. 181. The cross accents inherent in this 3:2 relationship produce the rhythmic development of the score, either by superimposition of pulses or by rapid cross-cutting from one pulse system to the other. The metrical simplicity of the work is therefore deceptive. Instead of indicating a regular pattern of accentuation, the ¾ bars are themselves pulse units that are accented in irregular groupings, as arrows in the score point out. (Howard Hanson recommended to Carter a renotation in compound rhythms which might make this rhythmic design clearer, though it would have given the music a misleadingly slow appearance.) The tempo is extremely fluid, gradually accelerating from ♩.=MM 56 to 80. The minim pulse similarly accelerates from MM 84 to 120. The relationship of the tempi stays fixed—but the tempi themselves constantly change. The basic arch of speed is recapitulated in microcosm in the closing clarinet solo, whose rubato should give the sense of passing from a moderate speed to the fastest pulse of the movement and then slowing to stillness (Ex. 41).

As in many of Carter's works of this period, there is a basic harmonic opposition between B and B♭. These pitches are not fixed tonal centres but

Ex. 41

Symphony No. 1
© 1961 Associated Music Publishers, Inc. Used by permission

118

rather shifting centres of intervallic gravity whose enharmonic and directional implications are constantly reinterpreted. Tonally the work moves from B♭ minor to E major; but the true structural progression is from the bottom B♭ of the opening chord to the top B of the close (Chart 6). There is a similar

Chart 6   First movement: Harmonic scheme   **(Symphony No. 1)**

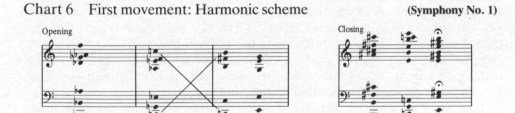

opposition between the sonorities of two basic chords, the first presented at the very beginning, and the second at fig. 27—a juxtaposition which again outlines a B♭/B polarity. The transformation of these two basic sonorities and the interplay of the two tonal poles colours all the episodes of the movement, which achieves its epiphanic form at the climactic harmonic change at fig. 401.

After the multi-level mosaic of the first movement, the second—slowly, gravely, flexible tempo—is a study in line, *la grande ligne* which for Nadia Boulanger was the essence of music. The movement sets forth a constantly developing, hymn-like melody of enormous breadth; the opening phrase is twenty-seven bars long. Unlike the first movement there is little contrasting material (a dotted-rhythm episode functions as a terrain that the main line must cross, not as independent matter.) The basic motif of the long melody, however, gradually breaks away to become a cantus firmus underpinning to the main melodic line, first as an ostinato under the long, lyrical trumpet solo, then as the foundation for freer polyphonic elaboration. These two elements—really facets of the same material—unite climactically at fig. 712, the apex of the movement's expressive arch.

The formal concept of the second movement is less original than that of the first. Brahms's Second Symphony and Mahler's Sixth provide classic precedents of slow movements built on endless melodic expansion. The movement, however, successfully sustains the pastoral tone and expressive evocation of the opening. The texture which frames the trumpet solo is typical in its lucidity: plucked and bowed violas sound an ostinato, while a fragmented counter-subject jumps from flutes to clarinets to cellos and bassoons and back, framing the central line. The counter-subject isolates the triplet motion which begins the trumpet line, playfully changing its rhythmic position with a simplicity and directness of wit reminiscent of Haydn (for example—Symphony No. 97, first movement bar 125 and following.) Unlike Brahms and Mahler, Carter does not set up a series of gradually mounting emotional waves leading to a climactic recapitulation. Instead, the music slowly rises in intensity to fig. 724, then gradually subsides, creating the impression of an uninterrupted curving motion. At the conclusion of the movement the superimposed cadences of the cantus firmus in the horn and the main melodic line in the violins—both lines drawn out in augmentation— bring the lyrical arch of the movement to a balanced rest.

The third movement—Vivaciously—was the first part of the Symphony to be composed. It stems from the original 1936 version of *Pocahontas,* and is not, surprisingly, simpler in materials and structure than the other two movements that were written five years later. (As noted in the discussion of *Pocahontas,* there are some intriguing clues in the ballet pointing to an earlier genesis for the slow movement as well.) The last movement originally contained a chorale-like recapitulation of the other movements. At Copland's suggestion Carter cut this passage (which occurred after fig. 1184), wisely freeing the light, comic mood of the piece from a Brucknerian (or Roy Harris-like) rhetorical device that it could not support.

The third movement pursues the conventions of American populism, replete with square-dance fiddles and a jazz-inflected solo on the $E^\flat$ clarinet. Carter explores this style with such disarming comic inventiveness, however, that even the Superior Person (as Tovey would say) can lower his moral guard and enjoy the musical pleasures as much as he would enjoy the events of a Haydn rondo. In a way, this comparison is Carter's goal: the third movement begins with a theme that suggests the last movement of Mozart's D minor Piano Concerto in melodic shape and rhythmic irregularity, but at the same time its major-minor harmony and arpeggiated accompaniment in the clarinets belong to the world of pop music (Ex. 42). Throughout the movement pop materials colour classical situations, as with the $\frac{5}{4}$ ostinato cross-rhythms at fig. 836, the solo trombone at 853 with its squeaky unison response in violins and oboes, the blues-tinted build-up to the return of the main theme at 927, the deliciously simple flute and clarinet duo over a sustained fifth in basses and cellos at 987. The cleverest collision of pop and classical styles comes in the central fugue with its heterophonic highlights in the trombone (so similar to Stravinsky's later Symphony in Three Movements) accenting the rough-hewn woodwind sonority. The final shrieking lick at the top of the clarinet register (at fig. 1238) not only caps the high spirits of the movement, smashing all traces of decorum, but also transforms the wistful clarinet cadenza of the first movement into jam-session frenzy.

Ex. 42   **Symphony No. 1**

The *Holiday Overture* seems at first to be a continuation of the festive mood of the Symphony's last movement, but it quickly evolves towards a contrapuntal complexity and instrumental virtuosity that undermine the light beginning. Indeed the work makes a more problematic impression than the Symphony as it passes from diatonic, minstrel-show Americana to striking dissonant explosions. The simple opening, reminiscent of Walton's *Portsmouth Point,* evolves into a dense contrapuntal design combining as many as five superimposed lines in prolation canon. If the opening suggests Walton, or Copland, the ending recalls Ives at his most violent: Carter constructed a musical continuity that gradually transforms the one into the other. The work is a carefully-built musical time-bomb.

The idiom of *Holiday Overture* is close to that of *Musicians Wrestle Everywhere.* Like that madrigal, the overture contains the germ of much of Carter's later explorations, even though its harmonic idiom is diatonic and its rhythms stem from simple syncopated units. The syncopation itself, however, is far from simple: from the beginning it immediately defies the regular bar-lines, giving rise to a freely cross-accented rhythmic polyphony. A second, slower element in the rhythmic texture appears in the muted trumpets at fig. 7, forming a background to the fast syncopation in the strings. At fig. 11 the strings superimpose a four-part sustained chorale (a continuation of the slow trumpet music) on rapid music in the woodwinds. The string chorale is highly irregular in rhythm. It does not create a static framework for the syncopated woodwinds, but functions as an independent stratum. The texture continues to snowball. At fig. 19 three levels of speed are superimposed—two of them internally contrapuntal. The brasses sound the chorale; the strings play an espressivo melody in canon that moves in the initial rhythmic units of syncopated crotchets and quavers; the woodwinds add a leggiero, freely imitative texture in quavers and semiquavers. After considerable fugal development, the tuba enters with the slowest material yet—a long augmentation of the chorale theme—underneath the continuing contrapuntal activity in the rest of the orchestra. The tuba line gradually moves upwards through the brasses in a vast forty-bar phrase. In the middle

Ex. 43

Holiday Overture
© 1946, 1962 Associated Music Publishers, Inc. Used by permission

The encircled notes in the brasses (and their doublings in other instruments) must be brought out so as to produce a descending arpeggio of increasing note-values.

of this phrase the rest of the orchestra begins a recapitulation of the opening material. The dramatic clash between the two formal and rhythmic layers indicates how far the music has evolved from its simple opening. This textural and structural collision in turn gives rise to dense, chordal detonations, coloured by flutter-tongued clusters in the horns. At fig. 30 the chorale theme is superimposed on itself in four different speeds, based on values of quavers, triplet crotchets, dotted crotchets and semibreves. At fig. 31 five speeds are superimposed in dense stretto, their cross-accents arranged to create a downward arpeggio of increasing note values sweeping from top to bottom of the orchestra and slowing the motion of the music to a tense halt (Ex. 43).

'In this our arduous time of sharp and shifting events, of despair and hope, of continual torment, of tension and, at last, cessation and relief, it may be that all those repercussions have left traces. . . .' So wrote Stravinsky, laconically, about his own Symphony in Three Movements composed in 1945. Though Carter's *Holiday Overture,* inspired by news of the liberation of Paris, does not mirror specific war episodes, as Stravinsky later said his Symphony did, its violence indicates a fundamental change in the structure of musical experience. The simultaneous statement of very fast and very slow motion, the elimination of a regularly-accented pulse, and the complex superimposition of contrapuntal textures force the listener into a purposely ambiguous and disturbing relationship with the musical events. The Overture turns into a violent collage—like the front page of a newspaper—which brings together contradictory, clashing forces in a dense time-experience at once sudden and slow, immediate and distant.

Piano Sonata

The Piano Sonata written in 1945 and 1946 is the greatest achievement of Carter's early years. Like most of the works of this phase, it looks in two directions: backwards to Copland, Debussy and Stravinsky, forwards to the First Quartet and beyond. But unlike most of the other early works it resolves its conflicting tendencies in a fully sustained musical vision whose scope and intensity match that of Carter's later music. The harmonic idiom of the Sonata is a summation of the possibilities of pandiatonic harmony. Its fugal second movement consolidates Carter's studies in traditional counterpoint. In its unique synthesis of instrumental treatment and temporal design, however, it leads directly to the concerns and discoveries of the works of Carter's maturity.

The basic premise of the Sonata is the interaction of a virtuoso soloist with the modern grand piano. The Sonata is specifically a *solo* work; free from the constraints of ensemble playing it pursues a rhythmic idiom at once complex in its metrical design and improvisatory in its manner of execution. The Sonata is also specifically pianistic. The piano is a seven-octave sound-source that is sustained not by scraping or blowing but by the decaying resonance of overtones. Chopin discovered this conception of the piano in his first étude; Carter's Sonata is a renewal of the grand piano sonority, but not in any way a return to nineteenth-century practice.

The style and technique of the Sonata seem at times to invoke Copland and Debussy. The opening phrases of both movements suggest Copland's Piano Sonata which predates Carter's by four years. Carter also cites, in passing, Copland's Piano Variations: these echoes I believe were intended as a homage (Ex. 44). Carter's Sonata is written in the tradition of Copland's piano music—it does not recall that of Stravinsky, Bartok, Schoenberg or Ives—but it transforms Copland's gestures into a recognizably new and personal idiom with a greater variety of moods and textures, and a greater contrapuntal density.

Ex. 44 (1)

Piano Sonata

(2)

Piano Variations *(Aaron Copland)*

Debussy's influence is less explicit, though the listener may hear echoes of *Les collines d'Anacapri* and *Jardins sous la pluie*. The textures and sonorities of the first movement particularly owe much to Debussy. But his larger impact on the piece lies in the realm of structure. As in Debussy's late works, the Piano Sonata avoids thematic development. Although there are many themes, these are generated by abstract material—intervals, chords, arpeggios. Out of this atomic matter, the music derives constantly new variations. The materials of the work combine, recombine, expand and contract, in a rich transformational pattern. The sonata is no longer a 'form', but a rushing stream echoing across a vast landscape.

The Piano Sonata is in two movements, both of them containing fast and slow music. The first movement has vestigial traces of sonata allegro design; the second is a portmanteau of slow movement and fugue. The two movements are united by an overall harmonic design and by a cross-network of anticipations and flashbacks. The cross-references seem free-associational rather than cyclical in design; they indicate an underlying deep structure made explicit only in the final coda.

The basic material of the Sonata expresses fundamental interconnections. The rhythm of the first movement relates the extreme fast and slow ranges of piano articulation in terms of a constant pulse unit, ♪ = MM 528. The music ranges in speed from the fastest possible keyboard figuration to the longest possible sounding-board resonance. The *scorrevole* sections of the first movement display the fast motion (Ex. 45) while the Maestoso passages

Ex. 45

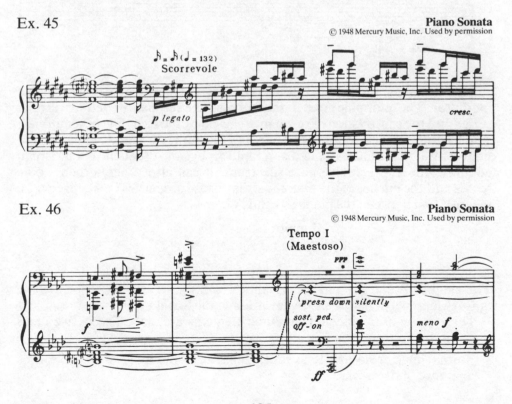

Ex. 46

present the sustained resonating material (Ex. 46). Mediating between these two extremes is a third tempo, espressivo, derived not from the nature of the instrument but from the expressive gestures of the performer (Ex. 47). The rhythmic structure of the music thus defines a continuum of man and instrument.

Ex. 47   **Piano Sonata**
© 1948 Mercury Music, Inc. Used by permission

The harmonic structure is similarly derived from two extremes and a mediator. The harmonic poles of the work are the resonances of the overtone series and the cancellation of resonance caused by the sounding of semitones. The bright overtone-series harmonies and the dark, chromatic semitones are linked by a cycle of fifths, stated as a rapid arpeggio. A sequence of fifths can generate the entire twelve-note spectrum. It can also generate pentatonic scales and the pitches of the diatonic scale. These properties are realized here in a relation between the pitches B and A♯:

B major
E B F♯ C♯ G♯ D♯ A♯ = B♭ F C G D A
B♭ major

The pitches B and A♯ and the tonalities of B major and B♭ major are the major elements of harmonic organization in the Sonata.

These basic harmonic and rhythmic elements are embodied in five ideas heard in the introduction (Ex. 48):

1. Initial jump from low B to much higher B—outlining of the sonorous expanse of the work.

126

2. Theme in thirds with downward leap of octave. This theme is later often played in 'harmonics' especially near the end of the whole work.
3. The rapid arpeggio figure which appears as an ornament to the above. This is confined to the first movement but fulfils a capacity of binding all the arpeggio material together.
4. Before the first rapid flight of arpeggios, a short motif A♯ A♯ G♯ in dotted rhythm appears with chordal harmonies. This is cyclical and appears in many places throughout the work.

Ex. 48   **Piano Sonata**

5. At the conclusion of the first flight of arpeggios a rising motif in octaves, marcato, in the bass, which occasionally occurs in the first movement and at the end of the first slow section before the beginning of the misterioso in the second movement.

[*from the composer's notes*]

As in the First Quartet the introduction contains the thematic material of the entire work; it is a microcosm of the Sonata's vast design.

The most striking feature of the first movement is its *scorrevole* writing. Rhythmically this 'scurrying' material appears in a rapid flow of semiquavers in constantly changing metrical groups. The metre is so irregular that Carter's editor, Kurt Stone, urged him to eliminate the metre marks altogether. The texture of the *scorrevole* is an innovative free counterpoint whose parts are related by the overtone series; an upper line is sustained by the sympathetic vibrations of the lower notes. Almost every accented note is heard as the second to sixth partial of a tone sounded below, a relationship made explicit by the use of 'harmonics' elsewhere in the piece. The formal design of the first movement pits the *scorrevole* material against two contrasted slower ideas, *Maestoso* and *espressivo,* which constantly attempt to interrupt the rapid music. As the movement progresses these slower elements are rejected in favour of the *scorrevole* material, which achieves epiphanic form in the meteor-shower-like coda with climactic repeated soundings of the highest B on the piano.

The second movement, Andante, begins with a bell-like motif whose new tonality of D minor still stresses the conflict between B and B♭. A lyrical melody gradually expands over an ostinato derived from the opening motif. After an intense development of the interplay of ostinato and cantilena, the bell motif returns interrupted by a rising third that alludes to the first movement and to the coming fugue subject. After a transition recalling the

128

first movement's introduction, there is a rapid, misterioso passage preparing for the statement of the fugue subject.

The design of the fugue is ingenious. The fugal exposition is followed by a series of episodes each based on a contraction of the fugue subject (Chart 7).

Chart 7 Shortenings of fugue subject (see Chart 8) **(Piano Sonata)**

Chart 8 Isorhythmic fugue episode **(Piano Sonata)**

129

The episodes are sometimes free, sometimes strict, with close three- and four-part canonic writing. A jazzy, white-note episode, sounding distant from the subject, is actually a strict isorhythmic variation, combining the rhythmic shape of the subject with a pentatonic melodic 'row' (Chart 8). In the next episode the complete subject gradually reappears. There now takes place an exposition in reverse, with fewer and fewer voices until the subject alone is stated in octaves. Harmonically the fugue moves upwards by semitones from B♭ to C♯. At the conclusion of the octave statement of the subject the opening material of the movement suddenly reappears—but in E♭ rather than the original D, preparing for one final harmonic resolution on B. The cantilena returns in an intensified form, leading to a climax which states the entire range and harmonic design of the Sonata, from the lowest B♭ to the highest B of the piano. This monumental sonority continues to ring as overtones to a held D♯–F♯, a minor third at the very centre of the keyboard— the core-sonority, it suddenly seems, of the entire work. In the coda the basic

Ex. 49

Piano Sonata

elements of both movements gradually fuse. The final chord is a glowing emanation of overtones from a primal three-octave B (the opening sound of the Sonata transposed by one octave) whose dying reverberations bring the work to a serene close (Ex. 49).

The Piano Sonata is at once original and achieved; there is not a tentative moment in its twenty-five-minute time span. What is most remarkable about the work when it is seen in the light of Carter's career, is that its idiom is wholly that of 'pre-Carter'. The harmonies derive from pandiatonicism, the rhythms rarely explore complex polyrhythmic relationships, and the formal procedures still adhere (however subversively) to classical categories. Carter now says, for example, that he *hates* fugues; a fugal texture would be as out of place in a work like the Double Concerto as would the Sonata's pentatonic melodic figures. Because the Piano Sonata does not sound like the later Carter, it presents an 'identity' problem to certain listeners. The usual response has been to regard it as a welcome anomaly among Carter's early works, a piece saved from its regressive idiom by formal and instrumental audacity. But this justification (for the unmistakable, abundant pleasures the work provides) will not do—the Sonata's idiom and formal structure are perfectly meshed and cannot be arbitrarily opposed. Indeed the great achievement of the Piano Sonata—and at the time it appeared it certainly ranked among the finest works ever written by an American composer—should instead form the basis of a general re-evaluation of Carter's early music. The composer whose idiom emerges in the Cello Sonata would not be possible without the struggles and achievements of *The Harmony of Morning, Voyage,* the Piano Sonata and *The Minotaur.* It might be said that the later Carter was the earlier Carter's greatest creation. But only a prodigiously prepared artist could have imagined, precisely plotted, and achieved the trajectory of that heroic leap into a new self.

Notes to Part 5

1. *Modern Music,* vol. XIV, 4 (May-June 1937)
2. *Musical Quarterly,* vol.XLIII, 2 (April 1957) p. 156
3. Kirstein at the same time created a more ambitious setting for Balanchine, The American Ballet, whose rather unsuccessful season at the Met included New York premières of *Jeu de Cartes* and *Le Baiser de la Fée.* Carter reviewed these enthusiastically (WEC 14–15).
4. 28 March 1947
5. Goldman: op. cit. p. 159
6. *Music and Musicians,* vol. 20 no. 12 (August 1972) pp. 28–39
7. Review by Bernard Rogers in *Modern Music,* vol. XXI, 4 (May-June 1944) p. 248
8. Stefan Jarocinski: *Debussy: Impressionism and Symbolism,* (London: Eulenburg, 1976) p. 139

6

Supreme Fictions, 1948–1955

In 1948, after completing the Woodwind Quintet and *The Minotaur,* Carter began work on a Vivace for cello and piano intended as the first movement of a Cello Sonata. As he sketched this movement, which compresses and extends the idiom of *The Minotaur,* he began to rethink the basic concept of an instrumental sonata, to imagine new ways of bringing these two very different instruments into a musical relationship. His ideas emerged more clearly in two further movements: an Adagio, which marks his first thoroughgoing use of tempo modulation, and an Allegro. By the time Carter had completed the outline of these movements his idiom had evolved so far beyond the Vivace that he felt compelled to preface the sonata with a new opening movement (Moderato) in order to tie the sonata together and state its novel rhythmic, harmonic and formal ideas at once. The opening of the Cello Sonata thus dramatically announces a new-found musical world.

Soon afterwards, Carter conceived a vast work built entirely on new premises. To prepare himself for this project he composed two sets of studies: the *Eight Etudes and a Fantasy* in 1949 and the *Six pieces for Timpani* in 1950. He then left New York for the Sonoran desert, near Tucson, Arizona, where in 1951 he completed the String Quartet No. 1. Two other large works soon consolidated and expanded the fully-realized idiom of the Quartet: the Sonata for Flute, Oboe, Cello and Harpsichord in 1952 and the Variations for Orchestra, composed in 1953 and 1954. There then followed a significant hiatus, as Carter prepared for a new creative leap—the String Quartet No. 2 of 1959. The works from the Cello Sonata to the Variations thus form a coherent group, a constellation centred around the First Quartet.

Carter's year in the Arizona desert is an emblem of creative transformation: he has called it his 'magic mountain'. The new idiom was discovered in isolation. The new works were intense inner voyages. They were written out of personal need with little thought given to their reception by players or audiences. The *Eight Etudes* and timpani pieces were conceived as compositional studies, not intended for performance, and the Quartet was written with the clear knowledge that such a demanding work might never be performed. The desert year liberated Carter from the tyranny of the audience.

Ironically, these works *were* performed, and they gave Carter, for the first time, an international reputation. After a performance of the Quartet in Rome in 1954, Dallapiccola and Petrassi greeted Carter as a new-found colleague. During the 1950s Carter's music was played at the festivals of contemporary music that had become such a conspicuous feature of post-war musical life in Europe.[1] Hans Rosbaud conducted the Variations and William Glock invited Carter to teach at the Dartington Summer School of Music where he met the very young generation of British composers (including Alexander Goehr, Peter Maxwell Davies and Harrison Birtwistle). As often happens with American artists, European success eventually led to acknowledgement of Carter's standing back home. But though Carter was awarded the Pulitzer Prize in 1960 for the Second Quartet, conductors in America remained hostile and orchestral performances scarce. The New York Philharmonic, for instance, did not play the Variations until 1972.

[II]

In the United States, the most notable phenomenon of the art of the '40s was the artist who was cut in two—individuals, such as Rothko, Guston, Gorky, who after years of working in one vein underwent a crisis out of which emerged a new artist with a new approach.[2]

Carter's breakthrough in the Cello Sonata was not an isolated phenomenon. In the late '40s New York gave birth to new developments in painting, jazz, dance, as well as in composed music. Like the painters DeKooning, Still, Pollock, Gorky, Rothko, Newman, Motherwell, Tomlin (and many others), the composers working in New York at this time shared a sense of radical discovery. Composers as different as Varèse, Wolpe, Cage, Feldman, Babbitt and Carter sought to create a new music, not the specifically American music the populists of the '30s worked for, but a new departure in the international movement of modernism, which had been centred in Paris before the war. New York now seemed the focus of the modernist movement, the New York of Frank O'Hara's *Second Avenue* and of Edwin Denby's 'Dancers, Buildings and People in the Street':

> . . . if you start looking at New York architecture, you will notice not only the sometimes extraordinary delicacy of the window framings, but also the standpipes, the grandiose plaques of granite and marble on the ground floors of office buildings, the windowless sidewalls, the careful though senseless marble ornaments. And then the masses, the way the office and the factory buildings pile up together in perspective. And under them the drive of the traffic, those brilliantly coloured trucks with their fanciful lettering, the violent paint on cars, signs, houses as well as lips. Sunsets turn the red-painted houses in the cross-streets to the flush of live rose-petals. And the summer sky of New York for that matter is as magnificent as the sky of Venice.[3]

Out of this energetic squalor, chaos, and beauty, a new art would be born.

133

Within a decade the achievement of the New York painters won them the central position in the modernist movement that they had set out to attain. Museums, galleries, and critics codified, canonized and championed the new painting. The composers were less fortunate. No institutions existed for the presentation of their work: no radio stations, no festivals, no orchestras with sufficient courage or rehearsal time to do new works justice, few critics able to understand the new music and educate an audience for it. As in the past, American composers had to turn to Europe for recognition, still cast in the role of young men from the provinces.

The politics of painting clearly shifted to New York in the '50s; in music, power remained in Europe. Because of the institutional strength of European music in the '50s, which led to the performance and publication of all sorts of radically difficult works, American music, largely unperformed and unpublished, was also largely excluded from musical history. Even in Copland's *The New Music,* the Darmstadt school appears as the centre of musical life; its concerns with serialism and chance appear as the defining aesthetic categories of the age.

In order to understand any of the New York music of the '50s the categories of the European avant-garde must be either radically redefined or thrown out all together. The best New York composers were interested in larger issues than 'serialism' or 'chance'. Like the painters, they were seeking to create what Wallace Stevens had termed a 'Supreme Fiction'.

The art critic Harold Rosenberg claimed that many of the painters were 'cut in two', undergoing a crisis out of which a new artist was born. This conversion often reflected a significant shift in subject matter. Advanced artists in the '30s and '40s sought to *illustrate* social struggles. But neither American society nor American culture really cared about the artists' political opinions; the painters looked back on their political art as 'poor art for poor people' as Arshile Gorky called it. According to Rosenberg the painters gradually began to see that instead of illustrating political conflict, their art could *enact* the inner conflicts they were experiencing: 'Action painting transferred into the artist's self the crisis of art and society.'[4] The new art was abstract. It did not illustrate or render reality—every painting would be a new reality. The new art was also expressionistic. Where previous abstract art had tended towards geometric design, New York painting derived from the psychological discoveries of both expressionism and surrealism. It was a metaphysical art in constant pursuit of the sublime.

The abstract expressionist style in music was most forcefully realized by Carter, Wolpe and Varèse. In the late '40s all three renewed their musical explorations in styles that broke sharply with the populism that had dominated American music. Because they sought a liberated musical discourse, none of them adopted the serialism of their European contemporaries, though they were very much aware of developments in Darmstadt and Paris. Perhaps because they were older than the leaders of the European avant-garde and had a longer familiarity with the works of the Viennese School, the New York composers took a more intuitive approach to musical innovation. Rather than pursue the statistical possibilities of the series, they set out directly to redefine musical time and space—Wolpe, for example, would bring his students to a window overlooking New York traffic and say 'Now compose *that*!' The music would be as dense and energetic as New York, as austere and vast as the desert.

Carter's works of this period fused the researches of New York's older avant-garde with those of European high modernism. Unlike earlier American experimental music, his works achieved a grandeur in scale and a complexity of expression unencumbered by the provincial quality of American concert life. They demanded and created a new audience. In contrast to the later works of Stravinsky, Schoenberg and Bartok, however, Carter's new compositions avoided the forms, textures and gestures of the European past. He thus combined the sophistication and complexity of the Europeans with the open-minded inventiveness of Americans such as Charles Ives and Conlon Nancarrow, both of whom he quoted in the First Quartet. To achieve this synthesis Carter developed many new formal, rhythmic and harmonic techniques. These were intuitive rather than systematic because they were means of discovery. Consequently the works of this period must first be approached in terms of their new poetic terrain.

[III]

The aesthetic values of Carter's new style and of much advanced New York art of the early 1950s are stated well in Wallace Stevens's 'Notes Towards A Supreme Fiction'.[5] The poem is in three parts:

(1) *It must be abstract*

> You must become an ignorant man again
> And see the sun again with an ignorant eye
> And see it clearly in the idea of it.

Abstraction means the rediscovery of the basic elements of the art, free of familiar associations. As Rothko said, when art rids itself of the familiar, 'transcendant experiences become possible'.[6] Abstract art transcends its materials in search of metaphysical qualities.

(2) *It must change*

> Two things of opposite natures seem to depend
> On one another, as a man depends
> On a woman, day on night, the imagined

> On the real. This is the origin of change.
> Winter and spring, cold copulars, embrace
> And forth the particulars of rapture come.

> Music falls on the silence like a sense,
> A passion that we feel, not understand.

Art must be in time, not outside it, in order to capture the 'metaphysical changes that occur/Merely in living as and where we live'.[7] Forms can no

135

longer simply contain developing materials, they must themselves evolve: 'I wanted to let the wind blow through the music,' as Carter has said of the First Quartet.

(3) *It must give pleasure*

> But the difficultest rigor is forthwith,
> On the image of what we see, to catch from that
> Irrational movement its unreasoning, . . .

Art stems from the pleasure-principle, and addresses itself to the primary processes of wonder and terror. Works of art should be larger than the rational mind: 'We reason about them with a later reason.' They should have the ambiguous, dense, unbounded—yet direct—reality of dreams.

Carter's mature works will be treated here in greater detail than the earlier ones. In order to avoid a note-by-note description of the music I have centred the discussion of each work on its larger concept, its basic materials, and its formal design. Because works like the Cello Sonata and the First Quartet show Carter's new compositional principles in their most straightforward terms they are discussed in rather more detail than the later works whose greater complexity arises from their more sophisticated use of these same principles. The circular design of the Cello Sonata, for example, reappears in a more refined way in the Third Quartet. The analysis of the later works therefore depends to some extent on the previous discussion.

Sonata for Violoncello and Piano

Occasion

The Cello Sonata was written for the cellist Bernard Greenhouse, who gave it its first performance with the pianist Anthony Makas at Town Hall, New York on 27 February 1950. The score is dated 'December 11, 1948. Dorset Vermont—New York'. The first edition was published by the Society for the Publication of American Music. A corrected edition, dated 1966, is published by AMP.

Materials

The idiom and form of the Cello Sonata grew out of an attempt to write a work that would exploit the differences between the two instruments rather than trying to disguise them. The implications of this strategy became increasingly apparent in the course of composition. Indeed the movement that is most severe in its articulation of instrumental contrast, the first movement, was composed last. The opening bars of the work, played by the piano alone, state the basic harmonic material for all four movements (see Ex. 1, p. 25 and Chart 9):

Chart 9 (Cello Sonata)

Six-note set   Four-note chords

The first bar contains a six-note set (0, 1, 2, 5, 7, 8) that is immediately repeated in transposed form; the set is not given consistent serial treatment, however. The opening chord, articulated as a minor third plus a perfect fifth, recurs throughout the work, as do other four-note chords combining these two intervals, or those of major sixths and perfect fourths. If the pitches of the original four-note chord are re-ordered they appear as two major thirds connected by a minor second. Three related four-note chords made of two major thirds and a minor second are heard melodically and harmonically throughout the work. An important motif first heard at bar 20 in the piano outlines the relationships of major thirds that are everywhere prominent (Ex. 50). The opening bar of the Sonata also emphasizes the pitches A♯ and B,

Ex. 50
Cello Sonata
© 1953 Associated Music Publishers, Inc. Used by permission

which assume an important polar function as they do in many of Carter's earlier works. However, the harmonic ambience of most of the Cello Sonata is significantly more chromatic than that of any of Carter's previous music, so that while the polar function of the pitch remains important it is no longer associated with diatonic scale patterns and chords. The semitone relationship between C and C♯ heard in bar 7 and between C♯ and D heard at the cello's entrance in bar 6 also plays a significant role in the work.

The harmonic materials presented at the beginning are neither thematic—the opening shape is not developed—nor serial in implication or treatment. The opening serves instead as a primal sonority whose characteristics define the nature of the musical exploration that follows. Many aspects of the initial sound—intervallic content, absolute pitch, spacing, rhythm, colour and character—take part in the evolving discourse of the piece. The opening thus presents the work's genetic matter; it is not its 'theme' any more than a man's chromosomes would be his vocation. In the Cello Sonata, for the first time in Carter's music, such genetic structure decisively replaces thematic exposition, and transformation now takes the place of development and recapitulation.

Form

As described earlier, the Cello Sonata is in four movements whose beginnings and endings are elided to suggest a circular design. Each movement begins with the transformation of material from the end of the previous movement. As the connection between the end of the fourth movement and the beginning of the first is much stronger than that between the first and second, the second movement functions as the beginning of the Sonata's trajectory while the first movement functions structurally as a summation rather than an exposition—it states material from all the other movements.

I. Moderato ♩=112   The contrast of instruments in sound and time appears immediately. The piano is a machine, ticking away at a regular pulse of MM 112. The cello sustains long notes over a grandly expansive melodic line whose rubato rhythmic shape never coincides with the piano's pulse. There are three huge phrases. The first, sixty-eight bars long, extends each instrument's distinctive character with mounting tension. The piano's pulse continues relentlessly, compounding its force with additional strata of pulsed contrapuntal lines (Ex. 51). The cello is equally unrelenting in its own

Ex. 51   **Cello Sonata**
© 1953 Associated Music Publishers, Inc. Used by permission

pursuits, but is more fanciful and discovers more varied material (the third movement is anticipated at bar 38; the second at 43). All that unites the two instruments is the shape of two rising major seconds heard in the cello bars 18–20 and then in the piano at 20–2. The piano, significantly, tends to give musical shapes definite, motivic form—there are several recurring mottos in its part including an important *Hauptrhythmus* pattern derived from the

Ex. 52

Cello Sonata
© 1953 Associated Music Publishers, Inc. Used by permission

opening bars (Ex. 52). The cello, by contrast, never articulates clear motifs; its character is far freer than the piano's. The piano marches, the cello swims.

The movement's second phrase (bars 68–103) contrasts sharply with the first. The cello begins alone with quiet flowing music that is gradually taken up by the piano. The instruments achieve a climactic intersection at bars 95–100. Although they both play at the same speed at this point, their directions diverge and their phrases do not correspond. The instruments therefore do not unite. They collide and then bounce away from each other.

The third phrase begins like the first; but it is a reversal not a recapitulation. Instead of building and intensifying, the music gradually fades away to the interval of the minor third. The instrumental characters are neutralized as their phrases break into fragments, and the music comes to a halt.

(NB: A more detailed analysis of this movement should trace its epiphanic design. The materials of the opening evolve into definitive form as the music progresses, so that every climax marks the arrival of a new event that has been prepared for but never previously stated. The fate of the C to C# opposition is particularly crucial in this respect because it receives the most climactic treatment (at bar 98). The emerging significance of the E–G minor third in the course of the movement also demands close attention. Yet another fruitful approach might be to compare the design of this movement with the first movement of Debussy's Cello Sonata.)

II. Vivace, molto leggero (♩=84)   Carter has pointed out that where the Moderato is an abstraction of jazz texture, the Vivace approaches jazz and pop music stylistically—but players who treat this energetic and driven music in too breezy a manner dilute its effect. In form and harmony the Vivace is close to the *Minotaur* Pas de Deux. Two sections alternate in an AB A B A design, whose proportions suggest a ternary form with coda. Unlike the usual ternary forms of scherzo movements, the middle section here is more intense in feeling than the opening. A and B are in a tempo ratio of 3:4 (♩=84 to ♩.=112 obtained by maintaining a constant value for the quaver). The pulse of B is thus identical with the tempo of the first movement, though this relationship is not made explicit by any thematic recall or allusion. Harmonically, the second movement—the last Carter was to write with a key signature—contrasts B major and B♭ minor, an opposition stated in the first two measures. Carter had extensively explored this polarity in the Piano Sonata and *Emblems;* here, however, the fluctuations between keys are far more rapid than before and moments of diatonic simplicity sound ironic rather than affirmative—Carter has described the more tonal parts of the movement as parodies of 'pop' music (see bars 37–40, for example). The contrasted tonalities of this movement tend increasingly to combine into chromatic figurations that emphasize the minor third, and in retrospect the listener may note that the apparent tonal opposition is in fact derived from the six-note cell heard at the beginning of the first movement. Minor thirds, often complemented by perfect fourths to form the 'key' four-note chord of the Sonata, dominate both the harmonic and thematic materials of the movement. The repeated downward thirds of the 'pop' tune phrases of A, are transformed in B into rapidly oscillating quintuplets and also into a *Dies Irae*-like motif that dominates the central section of the movement (Ex. 53). The

Ex. 53   **Cello Sonata**

composer does not recall his reasons for making this allusion—if he ever thought of it as such. The repeated emphasis on the cello's opening notes of the first movement, D and C♯, was perhaps more important as a structural consideration than as a liturgical echo, but the change in tone from the jazzy scherzando of the opening to the more impassioned, complex, and menacing expression of the B section seems crucial to the second movement's design, and its relation to the other movements. For as the Sonata continues, its character becomes increasingly provocative and unsettled.

III. Adagio ♩=35 ♪=70   The interaction of tempo and form tried out in the Vivace now yields a more complex pattern. The opening tempo is proportionally related to the tempo of the B sections of the Vivace. The cello's hemidemisemiquavers (♪) at the opening of the Adagio are at the same speed as the piano's quintuplet quavers of bars 198–203 of the Vivace ($8 \times 70 = 560$; $5 \times 112 = 560$). The cello makes this relation explicit by quoting the piano's oscillating minor thirds—the repetition is also a transformation, however; the piano's softly rocking motif becomes a ruggedly expressive ornament in a slow recitative. The change in character is further emphasized by the sharp contrast in speed, character and harmony between the cello's passionate lament and the calmly rising line in the piano. In terms of tempo

the movement might be described as having the form ABCACD. The tempo
of each section is:

$$A \; \eighthnote = 70$$
$$B \; \eighthnote = 60$$
$$C \; \eighthnote = 80$$
$$D \; \quarternote = 48$$

The A sections develop the wavering minor third motif of the opening. The B
section stresses the semitone relation of D and E♭. The C section is an
intensified variation of B. The D section is a coda. Unlike the second
movement, in the third the contrast between sections is obscured so that the
music seems to change tempo gradually. The piano's inability to compete
with the cello's melodic intensity contrasts the two instruments much more
distinctly than in the previous movement. By the end of the Adagio their
melodic shapes and gestures have become more dramatically opposed.

IV. Allegro (♩=120)   The piano begins by repeating part of the cello's
concluding phrase from the Adagio (Ex. 54). The speed of the cello's

Ex. 54

(1)   Third movement   (2)   Fourth movement

quintuplet demisemiquavers is now notated as semiquavers to give a new
tempo of MM 120, related to the B sections of the Adagio. Indeed the tempo
structure of the Allegro is a mutation of the Adagio. Again there are four
tempi: 120, 140, 160, 112. The form of the movement might suggest a very
developed rondo, but a more appropriate account of the music would note
that the rapid opening of the Allegro is deflected by the echoes of the second
and third movements, resisting their backward pull successfully until it is
suddenly transformed into the tempo of the first movement. The return of the
piano's MM 112 pulse at bar 147 (♩=140; ♩. thus equals 4/5 × 140=112) is the
climax of the entire Sonata and its first total realization of the poetic and
structural possibilities of Carter's new idiom (Ex. 55). Whereas earlier in the
Sonata proportional tempo changes had linked clearly distinct sections, here
the musical high point is achieved at the very moment of transformation
through a superimposition of tempos. The solid and imposing character that

marks so much of the Sonata here finally takes flight as the music seems to sweep over a great peak, and suddenly to discover an unforeseen terrain.

Ex. 55   **Cello Sonata**
© 1953 Associated Music Publishers, Inc. Used by permission

Like Schoenberg's Second Quartet and Stravinsky's *Agon,* Carter's Sonata for Cello and Piano evolved as it was composed. All three composers faced the problem of unifying works whose style had drastically changed. Schoenberg presented his evolution programmatically; each movement is more advanced than the one before. A linear motion from the musical past to the distant planets of the musical future appears in a progression suggested by the journey heavenwards of Mahler's Fourth Symphony. Stravinsky interrupts the linear evolution of style in *Agon* with a ritornello, creating a unified composition by the cross-cutting of evolving and static elements. Carter made *his* discovery of a new idiom the essence of the music. He neither explains nor disguises the music's motion from the familiar to the new; rather such transformation becomes the basis of the music's circular design, an emblem of constant renewal. For the Cello Sonata is the beginning of a journey in which each work will be a fresh departure.

Eight Etudes and a Fantasy
for Woodwind Quartet (flute, oboe, clarinet and bassoon) (1950)

Occasion

The *Eight Etudes* began as blackboard exercises. Carter taught a class in orchestration at Columbia University in 1949. The class had the services of a few excellent players trained by Richard Franko Goldman and the students were expected to compose works for that ensemble. Disappointed in his students' unimaginative efforts, Carter began to sketch small woodwind pieces on the blackboard, each one exploiting a different aspect of the ensemble. The Etudes became studies for Carter as well as his students. By isolating specific compositional problems he was able to explore new possibilities in construction and continuity and to discover many of the techniques that would become the basis of his mature style.[8]

Etude I   As described earlier, this Etude is a study of the musical space defined by the four woodwinds. Besides defining the limits of the available range, it contains a surprisingly large variety of textures—unisons, doublings, canonic imitation, free counterpoint of contrasting materials—all within twenty-four bars. Carter was particularly interested in the varied spacing and doubling of chords. The instruments constantly cross (as at bar 5) so that the sonority changes from chord to chord.

Etude II   A twenty-eight-note figure in flowing demisemiquavers is stated by each instrument at different transpositions. The statements are repeated exactly, but in changing temporal relation between instruments. While the melodic content of each line is fixed, the resulting harmony and texture are variable, as is the placement of entrances. Each instrument sustains the last note of the figure, which creates a changing harmonic pattern of its own, interrupting the fast motion. The four sustained pitches—F, F♯, A♭ and C♯—contain five of the six possible interval classes, so that the intervallic harmony between them also varies while the pitches stay fixed. For players, the challenge of this Etude lies in matching the articulation of the four instruments—the fast figure is easy for the flute, very tricky for the bassoon. As Samuel Baron has suggested, Etude II sounds like musicians warming up backstage before a concert. Carter says that it 'sounds like four birds that sing as birds do, sporadically, the same song over and over'.

Etude III   A D major triad is sustained throughout, its colour changing through the 'sneaked' entrances and smooth articulation of the instruments. Besides being a study in colour (like Schoenberg's famous Chord-Colours piece which is its model) the Etude, marked *Adagio possibile,* is also a study in breath control for the players, and its dynamic arch suggests one very long breath.

Etude IV (see p. 58)   The material is reduced to a rising semitone always heard in a rhythm of two adjacent quavers followed by a rest. The strict rules of the game produce a wide variety of configurations, as different doublings, spacings, and contrapuntal relations appear. The players must respond to their constantly changing role in the texture: sometimes they are contributing to a chromatic line, sometimes they link other instruments; elsewhere, as at the cross-rhythm ostinato at bar 78, each is an independent element (Ex. 56).

Ex. 56

Etude V   Like the first Etude, this is a study in space, but here the space is articulated in independent step-wise lines in order to explore the colours of different instrumental registers. The instruments are in a most unusual configuration, with oboe and bassoon in their high register and flute and clarinet in their low range. At bar 16 the space is turned upside down as a high A in the bassoon is taken over by the flute, which then moves down through its lowest register, pushing the other instruments deep into the bass. The cadence inverts the sonority heard at the close of Etude I.

Ex. 57

Etude VI   A study in colour-effects for individual instruments and ensemble. Double-, triple- and flutter-tonguing, as well as trills and harmonic fingering, are combined to create changing textures. The crossing of lines and echoing of pitches between instruments produces new varieties of the *Klangfarbenmelodie* effect heard in Etude III: the rapidly articulated four-note chord at bar 33 is particularly striking (Ex. 57). The extravagance of colour leads to extravagant formal gestures—the fast motion of the piece suddenly breaks into a slow flutter-tongued canon (reminiscent of *Pierrot Lunaire*) and a high trill in three instruments sets up a portentous (and comic) statement in the very low bassoon that will later reappear in the Fantasy.

Etude VII   A study on one note. The absence of any variation in pitch puts the emphasis on ensemble, colour and dynamic shapes. A three-part form is articulated by variations in attack and dynamics. Unlike the long, calm breath of Etude III, the dynamic envelope of this Etude is broad and unstable, suggesting fast motion, even though no entrances can be heard, and the tone is sustained without interruption. Note the two ensemble fortissimos at bars 19 and 21; the second is a dynamic retrograde of the first, and together they form a point of focus that gives the Etude a very strong shape despite the absence of pitch variation or clear rhythmic motifs (Ex. 58). This piece was played in Warsaw by the Dorian Quartet during the 1950s and Carter sometimes jokingly refers to himself as the father of modern Polish music.

Ex. 58

Eight Etudes and a Fantasy
© 1959 Associated Music Publishers, Inc. Used by permission

145

Certainly many versions of the one-note piece have followed it—none with its sure grasp of a particular mood, its precise articulation in imagined time.

Etude VIII   This double mosaic is perhaps the most difficult of all the Etudes to play, (and nearly thirty years after their composition they remain the most challenging pieces of woodwind ensemble to enter the repertory.) An uninterrupted stream of rapid semiquavers doubled in octaves passes from instrument to instrument in changing phrase-lengths and instrumental combinations. Against it, widely spaced single notes, mostly *sforzando* and short, but occasionally sustained, also pass across the instrumental space. The superimposed extremes in tempo and the constant traversal of the extreme ranges of the instruments suggest a synthesis of the techniques of all the Etudes that will be made explicit in the Fantasy.

Fantasy   Written after the Etudes, the Fantasy combines them all, giving the illusion that the Etudes are warming-up exercises for the episodes of an elaborate fugue. The Fantasy is both strict and innovative; it is Carter's virtuoso farewell to traditional contrapuntal procedures and at the same time a preparatory sketch for the Fantasia of the First Quartet with its novel textures and continuity. The fugal subject is eight bars long and derived from three of the Etudes (Ex. 59). The opening motif stems from the bassoon in bar

Ex. 59

Eight Etudes and a Fantasy
© 1959 Associated Music Publishers, Inc. Used by permission

52 of Etude VI. The septuplet semiquavers come from Etude VIII and move at the same speed as the semiquavers in that Etude. The cadential motif comes from bars 4–6 of the first Etude. The subject thus suggests two developmental paths both of which are pursued. There is traditional imitative development of the subject including stretti, double counterpoint and prolation canons, but this development is at the same time deflected and distorted by the appearance of the materials of the Etudes. Most importantly, the tempi of the Etudes transform the fugal development. The Fantasy begins at the tempo of Etude I. At bar 17 the tempo modulates to MM 126, the speed of Etude VII. At bar 35 the tempo of Etude II appears; at bar 48, the tempo of Etude VI; at bar 99 Etude IV rises to the surface. As the tempo modulates, reminiscences of the Etudes are heard as episodes in the fugue; the fugal subject continues on its way, undeterred by the interruptions but at new

speeds. The subject is heard at tempi of MM 84, 126 and 90; at bar 108 it appears at two tempi simultaneously, in the ratio of 4:7 (Ex. 60). The end of the Fantasy brings its two processes together. In a series of stretti, the subject accelerates, until it turns into a trill. Superimposed on the accelerating design is a statement of the subject in long-held notes, passing from instrument to instrument in *Klangfarbenmelodie* related to Etudes III and VII.

Ex. 60

Because of the length and difficulty of the *Eight Etudes* Carter has suggested several arrangements for performing excerpts from the work. Interestingly, he does not want Etudes III or VII to be played unless they are included in a group of at least five other Etudes—Carter is not interested in exploiting the sensational aspect of these studies, which some critics now see as 'minimalist', but insists that they should be placed in a context that shows how *Klangfarbenmelodie* can be related to other techniques. Similarly the Fantasy is not to be played unless preceded by at least Etudes I, IV, VII, VI, or VIII—its allusions to the Etudes make no sense unless they have already been heard. This last stipulation underscores the new formal concept of the Fantasy. If it were just a fugue it could stand on its own. The Fantasy, however, is not a fugue, but a situation *around* a fugue. By analogy with Carter's description of the Brass Quintet, the scenario of the Fantasy might be described as follows. Four players begin to play a fugue on a subject connected with the Etudes. As they hear other possible connections they pursue them, rather than the fugue, so that at several places reminiscences or extensions of the Etudes obliterate the fugal texture. The free-associative continuity of the piece accelerates as more connections between the Etudes are revealed, until the associative process itself whirls past the vanishing point, leaving only the fugue subject, which now appears as part of a much slower time-world.

Eight Pieces for Four Timpani

Occasion

In 1950 Carter wrote six studies for timpani. They were intended as compositional studies mainly in tempo modulation, but also in the manipulation of some of the four-note chords he was now using as a means of harmonic organization. He showed the pieces to many New York percussionists at the time—and was not pleased with the way they sounded. Only two, the Recitative and Improvisation, were published (in 1960) but the others circulated widely in photocopy and were often played. In the mid-'60s, Carter revised the pieces with the aid of the percussionist Jan Williams, in order to make them more effective in performance. He composed two additional pieces, Adagio and Canto, at this time, and dedicated them to Williams; these are the only two that require pedal timpani. The entire set of eight pieces was published in 1968, with the older ones dedicated to many of the percussionists who played them in the '50s. The eight pieces are an anthology, not a suite; and the composer, keenly aware of the limited colour of the timpani, specifies that not more than four of them should be played as a suite in public.

Whatever Carter's reservations about these pieces may have been, in their revised form they are equally compelling as formal designs and as instrumental vehicles. Whereas many percussion pieces degenerate into noise through lack of differentiation in timbre, Carter shapes the noises of percussion into music by stressing the many possible contrasts in timbre, range, dynamics and character. As with the *Eight Etudes,* the reduction of means was part of a deliberate search for basic new ways of putting music together. Each piece presents a specific rhythmic and timbral problem.

SAËTA (dedicated to Al Howard)   'An Andalusian song of improvisatory character sung during an outdoor religious procession, usually at Easter; said to be the descendant of a rain ceremony during which an arrow (saëta) was shot into the clouds to release the rain' (Composer's note). *Saëta* is both improvisatory and ritualistic in character. It is framed by a freely accelerating figure. The strictly notated rhythms within the frame gradually accelerate by means of tempo modulation, so that the process of the piece is the same as that of the frame, but in slow motion. The slowed motion also allows the polyphony of pulses to be articulated by contrasting dynamics and timbre, as in bars 20–4 (Ex. 61).

MOTO PERPETUO (to Paul Price)   An unbroken pulse of 480 is articulated in constantly changing accentual groups, but mostly in a very soft, light manner. Special cloth-covered rattan sticks are required to produce the desired light

Ex. 61 (♪ = 150)

Saëta (Eight Pieces for Four Timpani)
© 1969 Associated Music Publishers, Inc. Used by permission

tone quality. The tone colour changes with the accentuation as the drums are struck in different places. The overall effect is of a sustained sound rapidly flickering in colour. The four drums are tuned very close together to produce this unbroken effect. The four pitches—B♯, C♯, D♯, E—form the four-note chord which figures prominently in the *Eight Etudes*.

ADAGIO (to Jan Williams)   Written in 1966 and closely related to the timpani parts in the Piano Concerto, this study exploits pedal timpani to produce glissandi, vibratos, harmonics and sympathetic vibrations. Most of these effects are very quiet; they are heard as the decay of a few, dramatic, sharp attacks. The piece focuses attention on several aspects of timpani playing—change of pitch, resonances—usually regarded as peripheral 'noise'.

RECITATIVE (to Morris Lang)   Marked *Adagio drammatico,* this piece contrasts three ideas whose independent developments are cross-cut: a dramatic tremolo, a bolero rhythm, and an irregular heart-murmur pulse. The three converge and intersect in different ways. The heart beat comes out of the opening tremolo; the tremolo grows increasingly explosive and merges with the bolero figure. The heart pulse then takes over as the other figures fade away in fragments. The drums are tuned to G♯, A♯, C♯ and D, the all-interval chord used in the First Quartet. The complete range of intervals serves to define harmonic motion even with four unchanging pitches.

IMPROVISATION (to Paul Price)   A study in tempo modulation and free continuity. The tuning uses the same chord as the Moto Perpetuo but it is now widely spaced to allow greater contrasts in sound. The work is based on the cross-cutting of speeding and slowing materials. The illusion of improvised speed change is created through six co-ordinated tempi.

CANTO (to Jan Williams)   Written in 1966, this study for pedal timpani has a distinctive tone colour because of the combined effects of glissandi and snare drum sticks used to create an unbroken 'song'. Like the Adagio, then, the Canto brings to the fore the resonances and pitches that lie between the

149

normal sounds of the timpani. The use of snare drum sticks and rim shots moreover brings out the higher overtones of the drums, in their endless, otherworldly melody.

CANARIES (to Raymond Des Roches)   The title is a reference to a Renaissance dance imported from the 'wild men' of the Canary Islands—and not chirping birds, though the pun is probably intended. The music is a study in ⁶⁄₈ rhythms that anticipates the jig rhythms of the First Quartet and the Forlana of the Harpsichord Sonata. The dactyllic rhythm of the old dance serves as a contrast to the even pulses of many of Carter's rhythms and at the same time implies a polyrhythmic pattern that is exploited here in numerous ways. The different possible long-short patterns within the opening motif appear quickly, speeding up the pulse of the music so that within its first twenty bars the tempo has doubled. Later a constant pulse and an accelerating one are superimposed (Ex. 62), and towards the end the multiple speed layers of the piece are both combined polyrhythmically and cross-cut. The tuning once again uses the all-interval chord, now in a wide spacing.

Ex. 62

Canaries (Eight Pieces for Four Timpani)
© 1969 Associated Music Publishers, Inc. Used by permission

MARCH (to Saul Goodman)   The last piece is a very Ivesian jest, which some drummers also hear as a portrait of the New York Philharmonic's timpanist for fifty years—his conservative manner may be reflected in the one-five tuning of the piece. There are two marches, each at its own speed, one played with the heads of the sticks, the other with the butts (Ex. 63). The

Ex. 63

March (Eight Pieces for Four Timpani)
© 1969 Associated Music Publishers, Inc. Used by permission

contrapuntal play of the two turns the timpanist into a baton twirler, flipping the sticks from one end to the other. The shape of the piece suggests a hypothetical scenario which only those who have played in an American marching band could understand. Two drummers approach each other playing at different speeds. They meet and 'challenge' each other, imitating each other's figures and outdoing one another in virtuosity. Having established their equal credentials they then march away at different speeds. The compositional *leger de main* involved in constructing this little scene has to be matched by that of the player who takes both roles. The humour of this piece foreshadows 'A view of the Capitol from the Library of Congress'. (After a 'contemporary' concert in New York which ended with a selection of ragtimes and marches, Carter told me, 'what a good composer John Philip Sousa was!')

String Quartet No. 1 (1951)

Occasion

Carter has written the following about the origins of the First Quartet:

> The First Quartet was 'written largely for my own satisfaction and grew out of an effort to understand myself', as the late Joseph Wood Krutch (a neighbour during the 1950–51 year of this quartet) wrote of his book *The Modern Temper*. For there were so many emotional and expressive experiences that I kept having, and so many notions of processes and continuities, especially musical ones—fragments I could find no ways to use in my compositions—that I decided to leave my usual New York activities to seek the undisturbed quiet to work these out. The decision to stay in a place in the lower Sonora Desert near Tucson, Arizona, brought me by chance into contact with that superb naturalist Joe Krutch who was then writing *The Desert Year*. Our almost daily meetings led to fascinating talks about the ecology of the region—how birds, animals, insects, and

plants had adapted to the heat and the limited water supply, which consists of infrequent, spectacular, but brief cloudbursts that for an hour seem about to wash everything away, and then very long droughts. There were trips to remote places such as Carr Canyon, the wild-bird paradise, but mainly it was right around the house that exotica (for an Eastener) could be seen—comic road runners, giant suguaros, flowering octillos, all sharing this special dry world. It was indeed a kind of 'magic mountain' and its specialness (for me) certainly encouraged the specialness (for me at that time) of the Quartet as I worked on it during the fall and winter of '50 and the spring of '51. (WEC 275–6)

By going to the desert, Carter left his routine patterns of living in order to discover a new kind of time. Many of his friends refer to this time in the desert as a 'conversion', for a new composer emerged with the First Quartet, uncompromising and visionary:

I decided for once to write a work very interesting to myself, and so say to hell with the public and with the performers too. I wanted to write a work that carried out completely the various ideas I had at that time about the form of music, about texture and harmony—about everything. (FW 35)

The First Quartet was not commissioned but it was composed while Carter had a Guggenheim fellowship. Carter doubted if it would ever be performed. He submitted it, however, to the *Concours à Quatuor* of Liège, a competition he had found out about quite by accident. Although he felt that sending the score to Belgium (in the *nom de concours* of Chronometros) was like dropping a message-filled bottle off a boat in mid-ocean, he was later surprised to read that the Quartet had been awarded first prize. The Liège competition was supposed to give the première of its winning composition, but in fact the work was first played in New York before the prize was awarded, by the Walden Quartet on 26 February 1953 at McMillan Theater, Columbia University.[9] An important European performance was given by the Parrenin Quartet in Rome in April 1954 at a festival sponsored by the Congress for Cultural Freedom. This performance immediately established Carter's European reputation.[10]

Form

The form of the Quartet matches the heroic scale of Schoenberg's First Quartet, but owes little to the classical tradition. In its wealth of relationships it surpasses even Berg's *Lyric Suite*; where Berg's work is like a novel (as Boulez says), Carter's is cinematic. The First Quartet was probably the first musical composition of this century to rival the formal daring of Eliot, Joyce, Proust or Eisenstein.

The Quartet is divided contrapuntally into four movements and three parts. The movements—Fantasia, Allegro scorrevole, Adagio, Variations— flow into one another. The continuous stream of music is broken twice, thus dividing the music into three parts, but the breaks do not correspond to the divisions between movements and are heard as arbitrary interruptions of the musical flow, although both interruptions are part of the music's basic processes. Carter used this rather startling formal gesture because the essence of the piece is change, and the climactic moments are those which transform one movement into the next. To break between movements would have meant leaving out the crucial musical events of the work. The breaks during movements, in fact, serve to emphasize the essential continuity of the music, and particularly to dramatize the contrast between the special time world of the Quartet and the general, everyday time that surrounds it.

The fundamental harmonic matter of the First Quartet and some of its most important motifs are heard in the opening cello cadenza (Ex. 64). The

Ex. 64

all-interval four-note chord (0, 1, 4, 6) dominates this passage as it does the entire Quartet. Several chords closely related to it are also heard in the cadenza and are to play an important part in the work. Bars 3 and 4 forecast the upper duo of the Adagio, bars 5 and 6 the lower duo, while bars 7 and 8 anticipate one of the motifs from the Variations. What is not anticipated in the cadenza is the rhythmic structure of the work. The cadenza, inspired by Jean Cocteau's film *Le Sang d'un Poète,* frames the time-world of the Quartet, but lies outside it. The temporal frame represents measured time; the work itself explores a dream-like time-world.

Fantasia   The title implies a double meaning, bringing together Purcell and William James. The music is a contrapuntal study and also an evocation of the stream of consciousness. The counterpoint is not fugal. Instead of imitating each other, the instruments superimpose clearly different ideas. Five main themes (and many subsidiary ones) are presented in changing combinations—viewed academically the movement could be described as a study in double, triple and quadruple counterpoint, but it is far more than that. Some of the main themes are:

Chart 10 Fantasia: Main themes (String Quartet No. 1)

bars 12-16, 22-29, 91-103, 158-164, 178-180

bars 4-5, 22-32, 58-72, 106-138, 144-155

bars 25-35, 49-72, 131-138, 150-153, 296-300, 304-346

bars 27-36, 73-133, 282-352

bars 41-54, 300-303, 313-352

bars 50-59, 62-77, 103-109, 350-379

bars 22-26, 44-46, 67-68, 135-139, 144-147

bars 70-76, 112-138, 312-349

Each theme has a distinctive intervallic shape, gesture and absolute speed. Theme 4 begins with a quotation from the opening of Charles Ives's First Violin Sonata, a score Ives had given Carter. The tempo of the music changes very frequently as different speeds are superimposed, but there is rarely a sense of a simple tempo. The listener always hears cross-tempi which rapidly change in character as faster or slower strands come to prominence or fade into the background. The music is as strongly rhythmic as *Le Sacre,* but its constantly modulated speeds are to the ostinati of Stravinsky what the harmonies of *Tristan* are to those of Gluck.

Like the first movement of the Cello Sonata, the Fantasia is in three large sections. The opening (to bar 138) explores the combinational possibilities of the main themes. The middle section, launched after the viola's unexpected restatement of the opening cello cadenza, at bar 138, develops the rhythmic processes of the first section. The themes are distorted and transmuted under the influence of large polyrhythmic events such as the remarkable prolation at 198 where each line as it enters moves at a speed one and a half times faster than the previous line (Ex. 65). The third section begins at bar 282 in the viola but at 312 in the other instruments. (An overlap similar to that heard in the *Holiday Overture.*) At bar 312 the four main themes are superimposed. The Ives theme in the viola gradually accelerates until it approaches the speeds of

Ex. 65 **String Quartet No. 1**

Ex. 66

String Quartet No. 1
© 1956 Associated Music Publishers, Inc. Used by permission

(2)

the other themes. All four instruments move to the top of their ranges. At the climactic turning-point the four lines seem to fuse. The texture suddenly changes, and the Allegro scorrevole begins (Ex. 66).

Allegro scorrevole   The Fantasia's contrast of speeds gives way to a uniform motion of semiquavers at MM 540—a tempo heard in the Fantasia at bar 105 as the fastest pulse of the movement (the sound barrier is crossed once at 195 where MM 560 appears). Contrast of themes is similarly replaced by the mosaic development of a seven-note figure containing the four-note all-interval chords (Ex. 67). This figure is treated as a series. It is inverted, played backwards, transposed, fragmented, permuted. The rapid *scorrevole* motion alternates abruptly with sections of quiet sustained music (at bar 380). The earlier simultaneous occurrence of many speeds is replaced by the juxtaposition of extremes. The slow and fast music are related by the all-interval four-note chord. They thus appear as opposed aspects of a unified temporal experience. When the rapid motion is resumed at bar 442, fragments of the slow sections played in widely spaced short notes are now superimposed on the fast material on a texture like that of Etude VIII of the *Eight Etudes*. This double mosaic is interrupted by the breaks between

157

Ex. 67

sections I and II, and resumes after the break, seemingly (though not actually) where it left off. Once more the fast motion evaporates to expose slow music, but whereas when the slow material first appeared it gradually accelerated, here it continues to decelerate until it reaches the tempo of the Adagio.

Adagio   The Allegro scorrevole polarized musical time; the Adagio polarizes musical space. The quartet divides into two duos playing apparently unrelated music. Viola and cello sound a violently passionate recitative. The violins float tranquilly in distant vastness. The duos are heard separately, then are superimposed. The lower duo gradually ascends while the violins move slowly downwards, so that by bar 110 their opening vertical relationship is reversed; what was above is now below, what was below, above. At bar 130 the instruments attempt to reconcile their differences— but such a conventional synthesis is no longer possible and the two pairs restate their oppositions with climactic finality from bars 150 to 155. Once more the texture changes dramatically at a high point: all four instruments join in a rapid unbroken stream of semiquavers (Ex. 68). Against the flowing scales, angular motifs are projected in triple-stopped chords or in pizzicato. These motifs, beginning with the final viola and cello statement of the Adagio, are the themes of the Variation movement. They are subjected to the

Ex. 68

String Quartet No. 1

© 1956 Associated Music Publishers, Inc. Used by permission

159

Carter in Berlin, 1964, with page 54 of his Piano Concerto

plate I

plate II

top left   Carter and his wife Helen, Waccabuc, 1978

opposite   Igor Stravinsky and Carter, New York, 1962

above   Carter and Pierre Boulez, New York, 1977

plate III

above   Nadia Boulanger and Carter, Paris, 1954

top right   Carter and Aaron Copland, National Institute of Arts and Letters, 1974

opposite   Leonard Bernstein and Carter, New York recording session, 1970

plate IV

plate V

Carter in his workroom, New York, 1982

plate VI

left to right   Gustav Meier, Elliott Carter, Ralph Kirkpatrick and Charles Rosen,
Columbia Records Studio, 1961   *(Don Hunstein)*

plate VII

Helen Frost-Jones in 1938 (who became Carter's wife in 1939)

Elliott Carter in 1940

Elliott Carter in 1960

plate VIII

variation process as soon as they appear, spinning faster and faster until they vanish, leaving new slower motifs to the constant cyclonic process of the music. When the first group of themes have spun beyond the vanishing point the music suddenly breaks off.

Variations   Although Part III is entitled Variations, the variations have been in progress since bar 167 of Part II. The variations before the break, however, have an important structural role to play, as they will reappear at bar 334 to mark the completion of a variational cycle. The technique of the variations is based on acceleration; Carter has said: 'I wanted the wind to blow through the music.' Whereas the Fantasia gave the impression of stating all possible speeds at once, and the *scorrevole* and Adagio explored the extreme ranges of speed exposed by the Fantasia, the Variations recapitulate the entire range of speeds through constant acceleration.

There are seven main themes, here shown in their slowest form:

Chart 11   Variations: Main themes   **(String Quartet No. 1)**

Several of the themes are polyrhythmic; at the beginning of the Variations Carter quotes a passage from Conlon Nancarrow's Study No. 1 as a homage to his polyrhythmic explorations. As these themes accelerate, their component pulses are split between different instruments as at bars 209 and 294 (Ex. 69). Although accelerating variations can be found as far back as the

Ex. 69   **String Quartet No. 1**

Fitzwilliam Virginal Book, the form of this movement is basically different from older variations because so many themes are varied and their variants are both superimposed contrapuntally and juxtaposed formally, with new elements entering as others disappear.

As the themes accelerate, their character changes as well. The passacaglia-like minor thirds of the opening eventually turn into a tremolando, while the slow chorale-like chords gradually evolve back into the slashing polyrhythmic triple-stops first heard in the coda of II. Indeed, the recurrence of the coda of II at bar 334 of III serves as an important landmark. The listener now becomes aware that the themes have evolved into the motifs heard during the fade-out of II. The variational process does not stop here, however. The themes continue to accelerate into new forms, which begin to imply still larger cycles in time, connecting the Variations to the Fantasia. The slowest and last theme to appear (in the 1st violin at bar 281, Ex. 70) evolves very gradually

Ex. 70   **String Quartet No. 1**

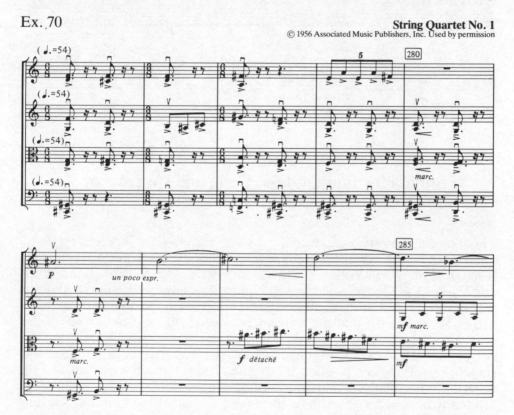

while the other material speeds off into the distance. Its intervals gradually expand as it accelerates, until it is finally transformed into the motif of the opening cello cadenza, now grandly expounded by the 1st violin (Ex. 71). With the most stunning gesture of all, the 1st violin completes the motion of the work in solitude, slowing the music to stillness on a celestial high E, a single star in the desert sky.

Ex. 71

Sonata for Flute, Oboe, Cello and Harpsichord

Occasion

The Sonata was commissioned by Sylvia Marlowe for her Harpsichord Quartet of New York in 1952, and first performed by that group at Carnegie Recital Hall, New York, 19 November 1953. The source of the commission—Miss Marlowe was not a champion of advanced music—and the fact that the First Quartet had yet to be performed at the time, led Carter to avoid, at least in the first two movements, the rhythmic complexities of the Quartet. The Sonata, however, is neither a compromise nor a step backwards. The First Quartet had demanded three years of experiment and sketching for its composition. Carter had spent much time calculating polyrhythmic relations and the harmonic possibilities of the all-interval tetrachord, in order to achieve the grand design of the Quartet. Having assimilated and mastered a new language, he was now able to use it in a quick, relaxed and improvisatory manner. The contrast between a hard-fought victory and a spontaneous celebration has many precedents in musical history: Beethoven's Third and Fourth Symphonies and Brahms's First and Second show a similar contrast. In Carter's oeuvre the alternation of experimental works that expand the language, and improvisatory ones that consolidate the new discoveries is a frequent pattern. In this respect the Brass

Quintet stands to the Third Quartet rather as this Sonata does to the First. But the Harpsichord Sonata also continues the researches of the Quartet. The third movement is as complex in its tempo modulations as the Fantasia of the Quartet, and the form of the Sonata is even more original than the Quartet's, for here process completely replaces motivic development as the basis of form. Carter has said that the rhythmic simplification of the first two movements was deliberate: he wanted to show that his new approach to musical form was broader in implication than the specific procedures used in the Quartet. He knew that he was thus once again setting his new technique and vision against hostile audiences and performers. The future successes of both the Quartet and the Sonata were to prove that 'strong, commanding works of art, no matter how strange they seem on their first appearance, sooner or later reach the public. Their intrinsic quality acts as a centripetal force that first educates the musical profession and finally the public to understand'. (WEC 190)

Materials

The idiom of the Sonata consolidates the achievements of Carter's works since the Cello Sonata. Its harmonies derive from the opening bars of the harpsichord (Chart 12). The rhythms, particularly in the first movement, are

Chart 12   Harmonic scheme   (Sonata for Flute, Oboe, Cello and Harpsichord)

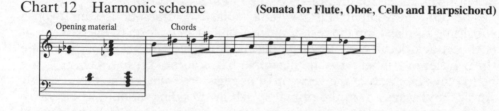

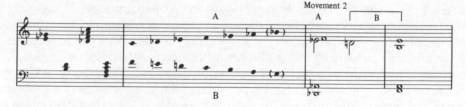

much simpler than those of the Quartet; and yet they sound even freer. Both the harmonic and rhythmic idioms sound so fresh because they serve a new sense of form. The temporal vision of the Sonata—a work sometimes mislabelled as a neo-classic divertimento—is as grand as that of the Quartet.

Form

The Sonata's form was determined by its instrumentation:

> My idea was to stress as much as possible the vast and wonderful array of tone-colors available on the modern harpsichord. . . . The three other instruments were used for the most part as a frame for the harpsichord.

This aim of using the wide variety of the harpsichord involved many tone-colors which can only be produced very softly and therefore conditioned very drastically the type and range of musical expression, all the details of shape, phrasing, rhythm, texture, as well as the large form. At that time (in 1952, before the harpsichord had made its way into pop) it seemed very important to have the harpsichord speak in a new voice, expressing characters unfamiliar to its extensive Baroque repertory. (WEC 272)

Carter was not interested in using the harpsichord as a vehicle for reviving elements of eighteenth-century style, as Falla had done in his Concerto, and Stravinsky in *The Rake's Progress*. He was first of all concerned to derive the musical substance from the particular sonorities of the instrument. The main characteristic of the harpsichord's sound is its sharp, percussive attack and rapid decay—the first movement is derived from this property. The modern harpsichord with its double manual, pedal stops, and—in the case of the Challis Carter wrote for—half-hitches for all stops, is also capable of many small but clear differentiations in tone colour. The second movement explores these possibilities. (The 'modern' harpsichord has gone out of fashion now as baroque specialists have come to prefer instruments closer to historical models. Appropriate as these may be for Cavalli operas or Scarlatti sonatas, however, historical instruments, especially those with hand stops, are not well suited for the Sonata or the Double Concerto.)

The first movement starts with a 'splashing dramatic gesture whose subsiding ripples form the rest of the movement'. The form of the movement is the attack-decay contour of the harpsichord shown in slow motion. The three other instruments sustain the upper harmonics of the harpsichord—the cello plays intensely at the very top of its register. There are no themes; only ripples and waves from the primal splash in subsiding motion. The style of playing at first is rubato: the initial energy stretches and propels the musical phrases. The harpsichord, however, gradually becomes clock-like in its gestures—true to its mechanistic form—as the other instruments continue to play freely (Ex. 72). At bar 30 the mechanical tendency of the harpsichord yields a steady pulse rhythm, its phrases reiterated in expanding cycles against fragments of rubato material in the other instruments. The steady ticking of the harpsichord, however, also serves to sustain its overtones—a function shared by flute, oboe and cello at the convergence of bars 45-50. Gradually the harpsichord moves outwards across its musical space, subduing the last fragments of the initial burst. The reinforcements and cancellations of the harpsichord's vibrating strings form nodal pulses which the regular rhythmic pulse makes explicit. When the entire range of the keyboard vibrates, the pulses cancel each other out and the music stops (Ex. 73). As in the Cello Sonata, the music appears to begin in the middle of an action, and the 'end' occurs at the very centre of the work. As in the First Quartet, the formal process of the music stems from a double time-scheme. The real time of attack-and-decay is projected into slow-motion illusionistic time.

The conceptual double time-scheme of the first movement continues in the second movement, but in a new form. The movement begins as a one-note

Ex. 72

Sonata for Flute, Oboe, Cello, and Harpsichord

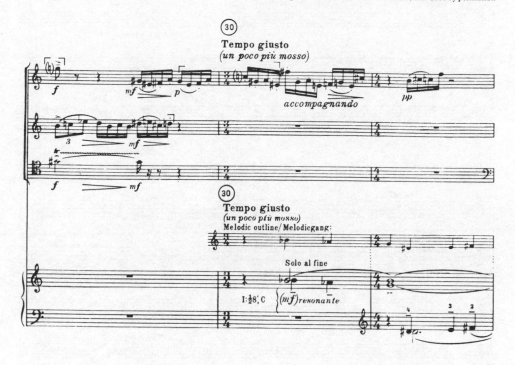

study, like the seventh Etude. The opening G, however, is the turning point of the Sonata, the low point of its formal curve. The instrumental trio and the harpsichord each begin to bring the music back to life with two streams of free association. These are fragmented and cross-cut without overlaps. Rapid cross-cutting exposes two contrasting developmental processes and allows all the changes in harpsichord registration to be heard. The form of the music again springs directly from the nature of the harpsichord—the movement is a study in alternating registration, with the other instruments stressing their unique ability to 'sneak' changes against the harpsichord's sudden shifts. The

168

Ex. 73

Sonata for Flute, Oboe, Cello, and Harpsichord
© 1962 Associated Music Publishers, Inc. Used by permission

harpsichord's continuity is abrupt and dramatic, while the others carry on a more sustained line of thought. As usually happens in Carter's music, the overall form is projected by changing degrees of similarity and contrast, as delicate moments of convergence alternate with dramatic or humorous non-cooperation as at bars 120–4. Almost every phrase contains a surprise twist, implying unforeseen developments. The very freedom of the Sonata's logic recalls Debussy's Sonata for Flute, Viola and Harp, a work classical in its wit rather than in its forms. As Charles Rosen writes at the close of *The Classical Style*:

> The true inheritors of the classical style were not those who maintained its traditions, but those, from Chopin to Debussy, who preserved its freedom as they gradually altered and finally destroyed the musical language which had made the creation of the style possible. (p. 460)

The Sonata celebrates the new freedom made possible by the language of the First Quartet.

The biggest surprise of the second movement comes at bar 155 with a sudden burst of fast music played together by all four instruments. This jazzy interlude implies multiple meanings. It sounds like a compression of all the music that has preceded it—note the rapid alternations in colour by all four instruments, particularly at bar 175 (Ex. 74). The entire passage may also be regarded as a new 'registration' of the ensemble, extending the juxtaposition of registers to a more complex formal level. The rapid motion of this passage can also be heard as an intersection with other time-planes of the piece; it echoes the opening of the first movement, though now with expanding rather than subsiding force. Perhaps this passage is the primal sound event of which the work's opening is just a reverberation. The interlude also prefigures the final movement—compare II bars 176–8 with III bars 283–6. Even after the harpsichord restores the original pattern of the second movement at bar 179,

Ex. 74   **Sonata for Flute, Oboe, Cello, and Harpsichord**

+Oboe { N=normal fingering/normaler Griff
{ S = in addition to normal fingering press low C♯ key (without D) to mute tone.
  Außer dem Normalgriff muß auch noch die iefe Cis=Klappe (ohne D) niedergedrückt
  werden, um den Ton zu dämpfen.

♦♦ sounds 8ᵛᵉ higher than written / klingt 8ᵛᵉ höher, als notiert.

both the cello and harpsichord continue with anticipations of the next movement. The final fortissimo G's, starting with a six-octave doubling in the harpsichord, then four in the instruments, then three in the instruments, then in unison, are only a barrier which the new stream of motion overcomes. Multiple layers of time in over-lapping motion are the essence of the Sonata's form.

The alternating time-strata of the second movement converge in the third, creating a riot of tempo modulations. The music begins in the rhythm of a forlana, a Venetian gondolier's dance, but bursts beyond the limits of

Ex. 75

Sonata for Flute, Oboe, Cello, and Harpsichord
© 1962 Associated Music Publishers, Inc. Used by permission

baroque style, as the harpsichord superimposes a faster tempo (bars 227–32, Ex. 75). The music now becomes a study in rapid motion and dazzling colours. If the first movement suggested the slowed-down motion of a single wave, the third is a speeded-up, multiple-exposed motion study, Carter's homage to one of his favourite works, the *Jeux de Vagues* from *La Mer*.

The rhythmic transformations of this movement all stem from the original forlana pattern, which is analysed polyrhythmically as the superimposition of a trochee on an even pulse. The trochee rhythm turns into a fast jig, while the pulse gives rise to many contrasted speeds of uniform motion, focused in two brilliant cadenza-like passages for the harpsichord. The continuity of the movement is 'cross-cut like a movie—at times it superimposes one dance on another'. (WEC 273) The collage technique of the second movement is thus combined with the overlapping design of the first, with faster and slower pulse strata added to the motion as it proceeds. The second cadenza sweeps upwards across the harpsichord's range, against fragments in the other

Ex. 76

Sonata for Flute, Oboe, Cello, and Harpsichord
© 1962 Associated Music Publishers, Inc. Used by permission

instruments that reach their fastest speed (675) after bar 445. The last flash of rapid music resonates as an echo in the beautiful closing bars that reveal the tranquil world lying beyond all motion (Ex. 76). This last gesture recalls the end of Ives's *The Housatonic at Stockbridge,* another water study. Carter's music, less representational than Ives's, is equally transcendental in its poetry. The Sonata is about time itself, and concludes with a rare glimpse of timelessness.

Variations for Orchestra

Occasion

The Variations were commissioned by the Louisville Orchestra. Aided by the Rockefeller Foundation, the Louisville has commissioned, performed and recorded hundreds of new works; the Rockefeller grant was an attempt to encourage new music and cultural decentralization at the same time. Carter's score was carefully tailored to conditions in Louisville, particularly the orchestra's small string sections. The opposition of strings, brass and woodwinds heard in much of the work were a means of balancing a full wind section against about half the normal body of strings; the solo string writing in several of the variations was a similar solution to this problem. The rhythmic language of the score at first appears as a concession, but in fact the ritarding and accelerating variations of the work were the most innovative rhythmic structures Carter had used so far and the most difficult in terms of ensemble.

The Variations were composed during the first of Carter's stays at the American Academy in Rome. He was a Fellow during 1953–54 and worked in the Casa Rustica where, he says, Liszt was supposed to have kept a mistress. The piece was completed in 1955 in Dorset, Vermont. The première was given by the Louisville Orchestra conducted by Robert Whitney in Columbia Auditorium, Louisville, Kentucky, on 21 April 1956. Despite the excellence of the Louisville recording, performances were few and far between. The New York Philharmonic did not play the Variations until 1972. The best interpreters of the work have been Hans Rosbaud, who conducted it in Donaueschingen in 1957 and Sir Georg Solti who has played it frequently with the Chicago Symphony Orchestra. The rather startling lack of interest in the Variations by American conductors served to deprive audiences of the most important orchestral work written in the United States during the '50s.

Concept

The last movement of the First Quartet had explored the possibilities of a new approach to variation form, a far more fluid and dynamic approach than the traditional conception. Instead of the usual division of theme and clearly differentiated variations, the elements of the piece were brought into constant interaction. In the Quartet, however, Carter had used only one means of variation, acceleration. In the Variations for Orchestra he wanted to use as many different kinds of variation as possible, both traditional and new; he studied Vincent D'Indy's chapter on variation in the *Course in Musical Composition,* which outlines all the traditional types in detail, and closely analysed his favourite example of the form, Bach's *Goldberg* Variations. He also studied Schoenberg's Variations, and lectured on them at the Dartington Summer School in 1957. Yet in fundamental ways his work is a reaction against Schoenberg's. Where the Viennese master had followed the formal conception of Brahms, Carter sought an entirely new formal approach:

> I have tried to give musical expression to experiences anyone living today must have when confronted with so many remarkable examples of unexpected types of changes and relationships of character, uncovered in the human sphere by psychologists and novelists, in the life cycle of insects and certain marine animals by biologists, indeed in every domain of art and science. (WEC 308–9)

Schoenberg's variations are a monument to new-found order, Carter's are a celebration of motion and change. Where traditional variations, including Schoenberg's, pursue a single motivic course and method, Carter's everywhere contrast materials and varitional processes.

Materials

There are three main elements: a theme and two ritornelli.

Chart 13   Structure of theme   **(Variations for Orchestra)**

Four-note cells (0, 2, 3, 6)

Three-note cells in Theme (0, 1, 3)

(0, 1, 4)

The theme is a seventy-four-note melody, which is treated as a series. The theme is unified by several recurring cells—a rising minor third, a cadential falling major third, the diminished seventh chord, and the four-note chord (0, 2, 3, 6). In the course of the work, segments of the theme are transposed, inverted, played backwards (see Chart 14). These familiar procedures, however, are treated quite freely. The Variations are not twelve-note music, though the theme contains two twelve-note sequences and Ritornello B is a twelve-note series; the contrapuntal techniques used by Carter derive more

Chart 14   Variants of theme   **(Variations for Orchestra)**

bar 102, inversion

bar 103

bar 130, interval expansion

from Renaissance and medieval practice than from the Second Viennese School. Other techniques, such as intervallic expnsion and contraction that are neither traditional nor serial, are also used as modes of transforming the theme—as will be seen below.

The ritornelli again are subject to variation, but of a more restricted kind. Ritornello A, heard descending in small intervals during the Theme, accelerates throughout the piece:

Chart 15　Ritornello A   （**Variations for Orchestra**）

Ritornello B, a twelve-note melody stated in two different guises during the introduction, is slower with every recurrence (Chart 16). The criss-crossed trajectories of the ritornelli outline the large formal shape of the work, which moves from extreme opposition to neutralization to renewed contrast.

INTRODUCTION   Three chords—one in the woodwinds, one in the strings (based on Ritornello B), the third in the brass (sounding the main four-note harmony of the theme)—immediately announce the three-layered scheme of the music. A cadential chord in the harp punctuates the opening gesture—the harp is to serve throughout as a connecting element. Immediately winds, brass and strings launch simultaneous elaborations of their material in contrasting speeds and textures. The three layers also pursue contrasted types of variation. The strings at bar 26 state Ritornello B; at bar 31 the ritornello is transformed, appearing in inversion and in a new rhythmic shape. The brass elaborate fragments of the theme in a developmental manner; in fact their material is the beginning of Variation I, and continues throughout the Introduction and Theme, gradually evolving into the jig rhythm of the first variation. The woodwinds meanwhile sound a continuous slow-moving line that is the preparation for Ritornello A. Statement, mutation, development and anticipation all appear simultaneously, immediately establishing a non-linear, multilayered conception of variation.

Chart 16   Ritornello B (twelve-note)   (Variations for Orchestra)

THEME   The woodwind line of the Introduction is taken up by two solo violins. Their tranquil music gradually descends through the Theme, changing colour as it moves downwards through the orchestra. This layer of music presents Ritornello A at its slowest speed. Against it, the theme proper unfolds in clearly articulated phrases. A third element, also moving through the orchestra's families, continues the brass music of the Introduction—the sextuplet semiquavers of the Theme move at the same speed as the semiquavers associated with this stratum in the Introduction. Again, three kinds

179

Ex. 77

Variations for Orchestra
© 1957 Associated Music Publishers, Inc. Used by permission

Ex. 78

Variations for Orchestra
© 1957 Associated Music Publishers, Inc. Used by permission

182

183

of variation are superimposed. The tranquil music of Ritornello A is gradually transformed in tessitura, while its speed and melodic shape remains constant. By contrast, the rapid sextuplet music changes by abrupt leaps in orchestration, texture and rhythmic shape; at bar 76 its rhythm is suddenly changed from a patter of rapid even notes to the trochaic pattern of the jig. Against these contrasted types of transmutation the unvaried theme is the one stable element, though it too varies in its phrase-shapes and orchestral colouring.

VARIATION 1   Vivace leggero ($\downarrow$. =168)   A developmental variation which continues the rapid material heard from the beginning of the work— the new semiquavers equal the old sextuplet semiquavers. The texture is light, the rhythm dancelike, and at first the variational technique seems to recall that of the *Goldberg* Variations, i.e. a constant rhythmic figuration elaborates the thematic skeleton. However, the *leggero* music is interrupted by aggressive statements of Ritornello B and by slow, quiet fragments of the theme in horn, strings and harp. These interruptions neutralize the jig material—it seems to evaporate in the course of the variation. Meanwhile at bar 106 Ritornello II appears, moving slowly upwards from the depths of the orchestra in plucked pulses. This sinister gesture belongs to Variation II, which thus begins in the middle of the first variation.

VARIATION 2 Pesante   All the values of the first variation are suddenly inverted. The music is heavy and slow, where it was light and fast. The texture is a parody of the traditional chorale variation. The theme is stated as a cantus firmus. Sounded against it are imitations at different speeds, which compress or expand the intervals of the theme. These mutations themselves give rise to dense imitative elaborations (Ex. 77). Twice the dark contrapuntal clouds part to reveal Ritornello A, which gradually increases in speed in the course of the variation, and fragments of Variation 1 in solo strings, lightly flowing at an ebbing pace.

VARIATION 3   The first two variations are here brought together. Dense espressivo music and light dance-like material alternate. The heavy texture of Variation 2 congeals into an eight-note chord—related to the opening string chord—whose doubling at a two-octave interval produces a luminous yet mysterious sonority. Against this chord the violins play an expressive mutation of Ritornello B—but after ten bars a sudden accelerando sweeps these massive gestures away, and developmental fragments of the theme appear in the woodwinds in a forlana variant of the first variation's jig rhythm. But the rapid music also fails to establish itself and fades back into a varied restatement of the opening chord. The two contrasted elements seem unable to proceed; instead they seem to cancel each other out. After a second acceleration the rhythm of the first variation fuses with the dynamics of the second in a loud dramatic stretto punctuated by Ritornello A.

VARIATION 4   A continuous ritardando; the speed is halved every four bars. The chamber orchestra scoring and slowing rhythm take up ideas heard at the end of Variation 2. The texture is a free double canon over an ostinato. A solo viola reiterates a four-bar phrase with small alterations, slowing to half its speed and then returning to its initial tempo every four bars. Against this more or less fixed pattern, solo violin and cello play a flowing line, imitated at first in inversion, which gradually slows in tempo across the entire variation; its rhythmic values are augmented from semiquavers at MM 800 to the entire duration of the four-bar units of the ritardando pattern (Ex. 78). A third element unfolds as a four-part canon in the woodwinds. The rhythmic values of this layer actually increase in speed; the woodwinds seem to attempt to accelerate but are pulled backwards by the slowing pulse. A fourth element appears in the background; the strings have plucked chords spaced further and further apart to form an irregular, spasmodic slowing pattern. (This material will continue through Variation 5.) All four elements are themselves variations of a basic type of rhythmic transformation—deceleration. As they slow down, however, their contrasts disappear. The winding down of rhythmic motion is the culmination of the neutralizing process that has marked each successive section since the beginning of the work.

VARIATION 5   The ritardando brings all the materials to a still point. The theme appears in purely harmonic form, without rhythmic shape, and moves mysteriously through the orchestra in changing colours. This variation combines both the calm and constrained aspects of stillness that Carter had explored in the *Klangfarben* studies in the *Eight Etudes*. Smoothly elided shifts of colour contrast with jagged outbreaks in the brass. At the centre of the variation is a harp cadenza that is cut off by the slapstick. Harp and percussion, which elsewhere serve to link stratified instrumental families, here come to the fore—creating a shadowy world of unformed echoes.

VARIATION 6   The music is notated as a constant acceleration; the tempo triples every six bars. As in Variation 4, the changing pulse is articulated by a canon. The subject, stated by the clarinet, is the retrograde inversion of the opening of the theme (Ex. 79). Successive entrances begin slower and become faster; the slowest statement begins in the cellos at bar 331. Although there is not the double canonic structure of Variation 4, a countersubject that first appears at bar 296 again seems to counteract the accelerating pattern, trying to introduce slower values that then get swept up by the quickening pace. Only the harp, which superimposes Ritornello A over the entire variation, seems to stand outside the accelerating tide.

Ex. 79   **Variations for Orchestra**

VARIATION 7   The return to life in the previous variation leads to a new differentiation of the materials. Three strands of music are cross-cut, never overlapping. The opposition of flutes, brass and strings may bring to mind Ives's *The Unanswered Question*. Each level presents a different kind of harmony. The strings play a rugged line in octave doublings; the woodwinds stress melodic and harmonic intervals; the brass intone rich chords. The contrasted densities of each part lead to different patterns of development. The strings gradually expand across musical space, first by way of Ritornello A at bar 388, later through agitated, accelerating motion. The woodwinds expand from single notes to five-note chords, then contract back to intervals, all within an unchanging dolce mood. The brass, slow and tranquil at first, gradually crescendo as their harmonies thicken, leading to a remarkable ten-note chord, telescoping the last notes of the theme, *ff* at bar 404 (Ex. 80).

186

Ex. 80

Variations for Orchestra

VARIATION 8   The dolce flute line of Variation 7 continues in slow motion, moving from flute to solo violin to clarinet. It is superimposed on jazzy giocoso music played very lightly by the rest of the orchestra, with much percussion colouring. Both ritornelli appear: Ritornello B at bar 422, now slowed to 90, Ritornello A at 435, speeded up to 180. As Ritornello A moves downwards, the scherzando music fades away, leaving the flute music, which grows denser and continues uninterrupted into the next variation.

VARIATION 9   The three strands of Variation 7 are here superimposed, making of Variation 8 a daydream-like interlude. The three strata move at different speeds: the strings mostly in semiquavers, the brass in dotted crotchets, the woodwinds in crotchet and minim triplets. The contrasting characters of the three groups are set in relief by a sharp staccato line in an unrelenting steady pulse that enters in the trumpet at bar 455. The trumpet line, though not intervallically based on the ritornelli, clearly relates to the statements of both ritornelli in the previous variation. Their light, jazzy pulses are here turned into the sound of Time itself, ticking away menacingly behind three levels of swirling clouds. All four elements build to a great climax which suddenly vanishes at the outset of the Finale.

FINALE   A rapid phantasmagoria, with fragments of all the previous variations, and new transformations swimming around in an unstable, bubbling musical soup. There are four contrasting sections plus an extended coda; all are played continuously and fade in and out of one another.

SECTION I Allegro molto   Thematic fragments moving at different speeds are projected on rapid triplet motion in the woodwinds. The fragments stem from the three strands in Variation 9 and the scherzando

Ex. 81

Variations for Orchestra
© 1957 Associated Music Publishers, Inc. Used by permission

material of Variation 8. Ritornello A cuts downwards through the orchestra at bar 500 against slowly rising chords in the strings.

SECTION II L'istesso tempo   The flute continues the dotted quaver pulse of the last section through two tempo modulations. Underneath, the flute, violas and celli begin an intense Andante espressivo, a free fugato derived from Ritornello B which appears at bar 534. At the climax of this phrase it is suddenly cut off by Ritornello A in plucked and tremolo strings, which are silenced in turn by a single chord on the harp, a gesture recalling the very beginning of the Introduction.

SECTION III Ancora più mosso   The woodwinds relaunch their triplet chatter, against expressive counterpoint of the strings, which continue the contrasting speeds of Section I, leading directly to:

SECTION IV Tempo I, which reinstates the opening speed and texture, now with growing density and excitement. The spiralling development is capped by a climactic statement of the theme's opening motif, which serves as transition to the coda. (Some listeners have compared this climax to that in Debussy's *Jeux,* although it is also foreshadowed in Carter's Symphony No. 1 and in *Heart Not So Heavy As Mine.*) A palpable effect of irresolution is produced by the sharp dissonance on the last note of the motto (Ex. 81) exactly where we expect a resolution—instead, new motion is begun.

CODA Meno mosso   The tripartite scheme is presented in its most heroic, rhetorical form. Trombones sound a noble variant of the theme's first half, while muted violins in unison state the second half of the theme in a long-lined tranquil melody. Below both lines the timpani expounds a cadenza, *con bravura, chiaro.* The texture is more complex than its first rousing impression may convey; when properly balanced, the contrast of simultaneous vast gestures so different in mood and sonority creates an effect that is both resolved and tense. At the climax of the brass phrase, the trombones dive down to a sustained pedal $B^\flat$, resonated in fluttertongued horn and trilled winds. As this sound tremor fades, Ritornello B is heard rising softly in basses and tuba, and then upwards to high string harmonics at its slowest rate of MM 32. Against it, at bar 633 Ritornello A rushes downwards from piccolo to the low 'D' on the harp at its fastest rate, 540. The pitches of Ritornello A are exactly those heard moving so slowly across the Theme. The criss-cross pattern of the two ritornelli in space, which dramatizes their cross-trajectories in time, sums up the grand design of the work, completing its 'large, unified musical action'.

Notes to Part 6

1. The Cello Sonata was played in Baden-Baden in 1955; the Variations in Donaueschingen in 1957: the *Eight Etudes* in Warsaw in 1958
2. Harold Rosenberg: *The De-definition of Art,* (New York: MacMillan, 1972) p. 194
3. Edwin Denby: *Dancers, Buildings and People in the Street,* (New York: Popular Library, 1965) pp. 178–9
4. Harold Rosenberg: *The Anxious Object,* (New York: Collier Books, 1964) p. 262

5. Wallace Stevens: *Selected Poems*, (London: Faber & Faber, 1953) pp. 99–131
6. Peter Selz: *Mark Rothko*, (New York: Museum of Modern Art, 1961) p. 9
7. See WEC p. 269
8. Etude II is echoed in Variation 2. Etude III is the model for Variation 5. The alternation of harmonic and normal fingerings in Etude VI reappears in the Sonata for Flute, Oboe, Cello and Harpsichord, as does the colour-play on G in Etude VII. Etude VIII anticipates the *scorrevole* passages of the First Quartet. The Fantasy was probably a sketch for the Fantasia of the Quartet—but their shapes are very different, as if Carter first tried out the more conventional contrapuntal devices that he chose *not* to use in the Quartet.
9. 'I remember that one of the professors got up at the end and said loudly, "The man who wrote that must be on the faculty or it would never have been played." ' (FW 35)
10. See William Glock's review in *Encounter* 2 no. 6, June 1954

7

Ideas of Disorder, 1959–1964

A four-year silence followed the Variations. From 1956 to 1960 Carter worked on two scores, the Second Quartet and the Double Concerto. Their long period of gestation indicates another leap in Carter's development. They are as far advanced beyond the Variations as the First Quartet had been beyond *The Minotaur*. The sharply innovative direction of these works may be explained in several ways. It was now clear to Carter that the perilous gamble of the First Quartet was entirely justified, for it had been successfully performed and well received. As a result, he felt free to pursue rhythmic and textural complexities to even more far-reaching conclusions. Furthermore, the radicalism of Carter's music was re-confirmed by developments in European music in the '50s. While American music still remained under the domination of conservative composers and performers, European music was revitalized largely through the influence of the Darmstadt school. Perhaps the most striking aspect of the European scene for an American was the performance of works whose difficulty or scale would have prohibited their appearance in America. Where American composers were (and still are) restricted by inescapable orchestral conditions—no exotic instruments, standard number of players, and a ten-hour maximum for rehearsal time—in Europe works as daunting as Stockhausen's *Gruppen,* Nono's *Canto Sospeso* or Boulez's *Marteau sans Maître* were given well-prepared performances, often broadcast throughout the continent. At the 1955 ISCM Festival in Baden-Baden where the Cello Sonata was performed, Carter was 'immediately impressed by what was, to me, extraordinary, for I witnessed what was said to be the fiftieth (or so) rehearsal of Boulez's *Marteau sans Maître,* at which the conductor, Hans Rosbaud, was still picking apart little details, patiently getting an instrument to play the part exactly as written with the right dynamics, and so on'. (WEC 266) The contrast with Carter's experiences at home, where the *Holiday Overture* was still considered 'unplayable', must have been startling. (Characteristically Carter's first response to the European situation was to encourage a first performance by the German radio of Ives's Fourth Symphony.) The virtuoso instrumental writing of the Second Quartet and Double Concerto reflect the liberating conditions of performance Carter discovered in Europe.

Many interests of the Darmstadt school intersected Carter's own develop-ment at this time. He welcomed their rejection of neo-classicism and admired their efforts to find a liberated musical discourse where 'tone color, register, attack, texture, perhaps dynamics, and time—the physical materials assume prime importance—are the subject matter of the composition, as space, the physical materials of painting and their types of application, have become the subject matter of the Abstract Expressionist painter'. (WEC 178) But Carter's considerable experience with advanced music since the '20s gave him a cautionary perspective on the European scene which the young generation of Europeans, who had grown up during the Hitler years, seemed to lack. Their new music was in effect 'neo-avante garde'—'to those familiar with musical history of the '20s very little that happens today seems really "advanced", although the present movement occasionally has more sophistication and interest than the foolish experiments of previous times'. (WEC 221) As in earlier experimental music (Carter must have been thinking in particular of Cowell's experiments and the theories of Schillinger, Hauer and Slonimsky) the preoccupation with physical sound was accompanied by an apparent indifference to 'the perception of these sounds, their possibilities of intel-lectual interrelation by the listener, and therefore, their possibilities of com-munication on a higher level. Most of the time the possibility of communica-tion is denied, or, if admitted, kept on the primitive level of any music that has only a sensuous effect'. (WEC 220) Without equivalent innovations in musical coherence and form 'even in the most stimulating sound combinations there is usually a stultifying intellectual poverty that no amount of arithmetic pat-terning will overcome; for either such a pattern can be heard by the listener, in which case it is usually far too simple to be of any interest, or it cannot, in which case an impression of pointless confusion results'. (WEC 221)

Carter's reviews of works by Boulez, Petrassi, Nilsson, Penderecki, Xenakis were astute and sympathetic. He understood that post-war European music was 'directed towards the disintegration of the routines and formulae that characterized the highly accomplished techniques of all previous, great Euro-pean composers'. Yet the prevalent naiveté of musical conception seemed insupportable, and the increasingly dadaistic attitude towards all culture seemed inapplicable to American society where musical tradition and culture in the European sense had only a superficial significance.

The two major techniques of the Darmstadt school were total serialization and aleatory composition, the first a rather deliberate misreading of Schoen-berg, the second a less deliberate but perhaps equal distortion of Cage. Despite their apparent opposition these techniques seemed to produce inter-changeable results. Carter found the processes of European serialism 'arbi-trary'. They lead to music that 'resembles the turning of a kaleidoscope and usually produces not much more—or less—interesting results. Indeed it can be fascinating to listen to the total repertory of pitches, note-values, timbres, registers, and dynamics being touched on in rapid succession and from a point of view we are unaccustomed to. But the cumulative effect of this is self-defeating since neither the attention nor memory is appealed to. For who can decipher, by ear, the complexities of total serialism in most works of the sort?'

(WEC 207) Carter's critique of the Darmstadt school was borne out by the subsequent development of composers as diverse as Boulez, Stockhausen, Ligeti as well as by that of younger composers. Peter Maxwell Davies, for instance, has recently deplored the systematic desensitization of musical elements that was the all-too-inevitable result of the serial kaleidoscope.[1]It was precisely this generalized use of all musical elements which related serial music to aleatory composition. As Carter pointed out in 1963:

> Aleatoric pieces with any degree of free choice are simply demonstrations of certain general methods of composition without ever becoming concrete individual works in which every detail, and aspect of order, contributes in some way to the total effect. In considering this kind of music, one cannot help thinking that for some composers it might very well have become a matter of indifference just what shapes the small details of a work would take, so long as a certain general effect is produced, and they came to think that it might be reasonable to let the performer choose how he wanted to make his effect—especially since so many listeners could not tell the difference anyway. (WEC 224)

Again Carter's critique anticipated the abandonment of chance by many composers originally involved with it.

[II]

When I asked Carter if the Second Quartet and Double Concerto might be seen on one level as a reaction to the Darmstadt school, he answered that he certainly did not think that this was the case at the time. He felt then that these works were a natural continuation of the First Quartet, though in retrospect he could see that they were in part a response to the European avant-garde. There is a pattern in Carter's development of selecting influences dialectically. He has often pursued musical developments that might have seemed alien, in order to expand his own techniques. As the painter Richard Hennessy pointed out to me, Carter's development recalls the words 'musicians wrestle everywhere'. Like Jacob, he wrestles with angels to become himself. As Carter's sense of his own individual style has become increasingly confident his confrontations with alien ideas and styles have grown more daring. With every such encounter, the expressive and technical domain of Carter's music has expanded.

If we compare the Second Quartet and Double Concerto with the First Quartet and the Variations we are immediately aware of a change in atmosphere. The confidence and expansiveness of the early pieces gives way to a mood of anxiety—not the *angst* of expressionism, but the ironic despair of black comedy. The music's disjointed surface expresses a fundamental conflict between order and disorder. In the European music of the '50s order, in the form of total serialism, and disorder, in the guise of aleatory procedures, were often indistinguishable. Carter seems to have recognized that the preoccupation with extreme, untraditional methods of ordering and disordering musical events exposed a basic expressive issue, closely tied to the forms of contemporary life. In societies where traditional forms of order no longer have an authentic standing, order and disorder take on ambivalent connotations. For the artist, order is associated with the meaning created in a work of art—it is the goal of creation. In contemporary society, however, order tends to take the inauthentic forms of authoritarianism and industrialism, the tyranny of politics and the regimentation of life by the machine. Very often older traditions, perhaps valid in their times, themselves become transformed into purely mechanical order, as Carter pointed out in contrasting the best of the new music with the continuing tradition of French organ 'improvisation' in which even given a twelve-note theme, the organist 'pulls out his stops and embarks on a half hour of variations, a passacaglia and fugue with many incidental canons; all quite audibly connected to the given theme, but all in the standard post-Franckian style with its romantic altered chords, its modulating sequences—and winding up, of course, with an apotheosis of the theme against a background of rapid arpeggiation. . . . The French organist . . . ticks away like a complicated clock, insensitive to the human meaning of its minutes and hours'. (WEC 188) Disorder has also taken on opposed resonances. Random chaos undermines meaning; and yet disorder may be a necessary rebellion against tyrannical order, an assertion of freedom in a world totally dedicated to making all experiences predictable.

In the Second Quartet, Double Concerto and Piano Concerto, Carter constructed new musical forms out of the manifold conflicts between order and disorder. The Second Quartet is an anti-quartet in which the very issue of playing together, usually taken for granted, becomes the formal crux of the work. The Double Concerto is a vast black-comic vision of a universe disintegrating into chaos. The Piano Concerto, in many ways a synthesis, sets the expressive freedom of the soloist against the relentless mechanical order—'insistent and brutal'—of the orchestral mass.

[III]

The expressive contrast of order and chaos was achieved through extensions of techniques Carter had developed in the early 1950s, but whereas the surface of the music became more fragmented, its underlying language became far more rigorous. The First Quartet and Variations still relied on thematic designs, even though handled in innovative ways. The works beginning with the Second Quartet replace themes with a comprehensive intervallic organization. Contrapuntally, the intervals are divided up among instruments or instrumental groups in order to create clearly contrasted linear patterns. Harmonically the intervals are consistently combined by the use of the two all-interval tetrachords, or twelve-note 'key' chords. Furthermore intervals are now associated rather strictly with metronomic speeds, with rhythmic shapes such as rubati and accelerandi, and with large 'behaviour patterns', gestural shapes of contrasting abruptness or sustained character. In terms of the American and European serialisms of the time Carter's extended technique could be termed 'partitioning' or 'group composition', in that large constellations of musical characteristics are formed out of the systematic exploration of a wide range of parameters. But if we contrast these works with, say, Milton Babbitt's Second Quartet of 1954 or Stockhausen's *Gruppen* of 1957, Carter's critique of serialism and his search for a less arbitrary order capable of creating coherent large shapes becomes clear. Babbitt's Quartet, whose intervallic treatment in some ways resembles Carter's Second Quartet, is a study in pre-planned elegance, devoid of drama. Stockhausen's work is certainly dramatic in its gestures, but its details seem random, and its continuity haphazard.[2] Carter, by contrast, sought a language that would be consistent enough to allow for a great deal of fragmentation, and flexible enough to sustain dramatic development:

> A work whose world is not clearly defined loses a great deal of possible power and interest; one whose world is too narrow and restricted runs the risk of being thin, although if the world is unusual enough this narrowness can produce a kind of hallucinatory quality—one that I do not concern myself with in my own works. (WEC 205)

Dramatic conflict between contrasting characters now became the essence of Carter's large formal designs:

> For I regard my scores as scenarios, auditory scenarios, for performers to act out with their instruments, dramatizing the players as individuals and participants in the ensemble. (WEC 208)

Less mechanically than his European contemporaries, who were introducing elements of chance in order to give the players a greater role in the music, Carter made each performer's musical interpretation and relation to the overall ensemble the core of the music's expression and form. Rather than demanding that the players 'improvise'—a task few classical musicians understand, and which rarely makes sense in a non-traditional context, Carter created *imagined* improvisations for distinct musical characters:

> You could say that a musical score is written to keep the performer from playing what he already knows and leads him to explore other new techniques and ideas. It is like a map leading a hiker through unknown country to new vistas and new terrain, revealing to him new possibilities of experience that he did not know he could have. (FW 79)

The dramatic forms of these works are all sustained by a systematic contrast of controlled and free elements, particularly in their rhythmic design. Pulse, which had dominated the surface rhythms of the First Quartet, now becomes even more significant in the overall structure. The Second Quartet is built around the pulse of 70 heard throughout in the 2nd Violin. In the Double Concerto and Piano Concerto speeds strictly associated with intervals or chords set up huge slow-moving polyrhythms extending across great expanses of the work, and contrasting with various kinds of rubato rhythms superimposed on them. These large, mysterious rhythmic patterns, so different in effect from the durational jumbles of serialized rhythms, appealed to Carter precisely because they were at once perceivable—regular pulse patterns are far clearer than designs based on many durational lengths—and unheard—no listener is aware that two pulses are in the precise ratio of 71:49. These large pulse designs that underlie the seemingly random and disjunct surfaces of the music thus embody the essential polivalent expression that Carter now pursued:

One of the things I like about this kind of effect at slow speeds is that at first these points of rhythm *don't* seem to have any graspable relation to each other and appear perplexing or perhaps chaotic, pointillist if you like. Then as these beats begin to converge toward a unison, you begin to become aware of their pattern, and to grasp the emerging rhythmic convergences. Conversely, the rhythm may at first appear clearly directional and structured and then seem to disintegrate into a floating, apparent incoherence. This sense of progression into extreme irregularity and back to perceptible order appears in many of my works. One of the things I hope to achieve is that it is audible from a number of different points of view, and, heard many times, with new and different things observed on each occasion. There is meant to be a sense of layers of meaning, resulting from a desire to achieve a richness of reference in unfamiliar ways. Hence these poly-rhythmic passages, which at times give the impression of almost hysterical disorganization are in the end part of a graspable order, and if they can be heard both ways, that's what I want. It's kind of terrifying in a way—you see, I always deal with things that have a very strong dramatic meaning to myself, and the conflict of chaos and order is particularly significant because it seems to be at the root of so many of the things important to us. (FW 114)

String Quartet No. 2

(Waccubuc, N.Y. 19 March 1959)

Commissioned by the Stanley String Quartet[3]
Awarded: The Pulitzer Prize 1960
      The New York Music Critics Circle Award, 1960
      The UNESCO First Prize, 1961
First performance: The Juilliard Quartet, N.Y.
      (Robert Mann, Isidore Cohen, Raphael Hillyer,
      Claus Adam)
      The Juilliard School, N.Y.
      25 March 1960

Hearing them (the First and Second Quartets) now, I get the impression of their living in different time worlds, the First in an expanded one, the Second in a condensed and concentrated one—although this was hardly a conscious opposition at the times of their composition. Each presents as different a version of the humanly experienced time as the two imagined by Thomas Mann in 'By the Ocean of Time', a chapter in *The Magic Mountain*, where he writes: 'It would not be hard to imagine the existence of creatures perhaps upon smaller planets than our own, practising a miniature time-economy . . . . And, contrariwise, one can conceive of a world so spacious that its time system too has a majestic stride . . . .

Although both quartets are concerned with motion, change, progression in which literal or mechanical repetition finds little place, yet the development of musical expression and thought during the eight years that separates them seems to me far-reaching. The difference, aside from that of time-scales, might be compared to the types of continuities found in Mann's own writings, where in the ealier ones, characters maintain their characterized identities with some revelatory changes throughout a work, while in the Joseph novels, each character is an exemplification of an archetype whose various other incarnations are constantly referred to (as Joyce does in another way in *Finnegans Wake*). Recurrence of ideas in the First Quartet is, then, more nearly literal than in the Second where recall brings back only certain traits of expression—'behavior patterns', speeds, and interval-sounds—that form the basis of an ever-changing series of incarnations but link these together as a group. The musical language of the Second Quartet emerged almost unconsciously through working during the '50s with ideas the First gave rise to. (WEC 274-5)

The Second Quartet, as its long list of prizes indicates, marked Carter's belated arrival in American musical life. Owing to its remarkable lucidity of technique it has probably been more analysed than any of his other works. Its stratified intervallic and rhythmic designs seemed close to the serialism emerging on American campuses in the late '50s, though the unbridgeable distance in temperament separating Carter from the academic serialists is obvious in the 'Shop Talk' interview given at Princeton in 1960, and in the unreprinted 'conversation' with Ben Boretz, published in Perspectives of New Music in 1971. Carter's own discussion of the Second Quartet makes it clear that the novel techniques of the piece stemmed from specific poetic considerations, which were themselves intensifications of the expressive researches of the First Quartet. Parts of the earlier Quartet sounded like four independent pieces being played simultaneously. This conceit—which subverts the social contract of ensemble playing—became the essence of the Second, which might have been entitled 'Four Players in Search of a Quartet'. Indeed Carter originally wanted the four instruments to sit as far apart as possible—'like characters in a Beckett play'—though this has proved impossible in live performance.

The technical clarity of the Second Quartet should be seen as a means to a dramatic end. Carter simplified the game-rules of his music in order to create a more complex, compact totality. As explained earlier, (see pp. 34 and 38) the musical elements are rigorously partitioned among the four instruments. Intervals, speeds, colours and gestures are divided up to create four 'character-continuities'. The 1st violin is 'fantastic, ornate, mercurial', the 2nd violin 'has a laconic, orderly character which is sometimes humorous'. The viola is 'expressive', the cello 'impetuous'. The resulting texture has little in common with that found in other quartets, though the contrast of characters may have been suggested by the second movement, 'Arguments', of Ives's Second Quartet—Ives's conservative, square, 2nd fiddle, Rollo, shares some traits with the 2nd violin here. Unlike the textures of a Haydn or Beethoven quartet, the four instruments do not share material—not until the fourth movement—nor do they play accompaniment, background figuration. Instead of sharing the burden of musical exposition, as in the obligato counterpoint of the classical quartet, here 'each instrument is like a character in an opera made up primarily of "quartets"'. (Carter had in mind particularly the quartets from *Aida* and *Otello*.) As in opera, the dramatic interest stems from the changing relations between characters. There are three kinds of relations in the Quartet: discipleship, companionship and confrontation. The instruments either imitate each other, co-operate to create overall effects, or oppose one another. The form of the work expresses these relations in terms of two interlaced processes. Within the frame of the introduction and coda, the four movements move towards greater co-operation, while the three cadenzas dramatize increasing opposition—the form is a double curve, played without interruption (Chart 17).

Chart 17   Formal plan

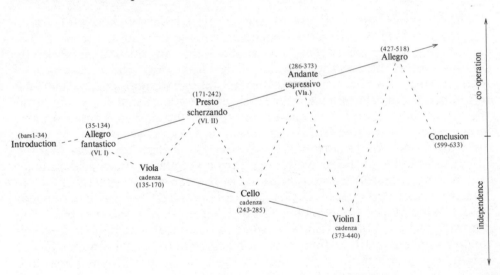

As Carter points out, the four characters are archetypes—not caricatures. They can be seen as archetypical musicians—the 1st violin is a virtuoso, interested mainly in showing off, the viola is a bit too-consistently doleful, the cello self-indulgently romantic; the 2nd violin, like a composer, tries to create order among its narcissistic neighbours. Psychologically the four could be termed manic, compulsive, depressive, expansive. But perhaps more relevantly to the specific forms the characters take on in the music, the four instruments exist in independent time-worlds—like the mysterious figures in Kafka's parables. The 1st violin plays in an extremely fragmented way, making sharp contrasts between fast and slow motion; it seems to exist in the moment, unaware of time. The 2nd violin recalls Carter's description of the

French organist's improvisations, 'ticking away like a complicated clock, insensitive to the human meaning of its minutes and hours'. The viola, playing with a constant expressive rubato, stretches and bends clock-time to match its moods, while the cello accelerates and ritards in great sweeping arcs, imposing its own subjective time-experience on the others, until it finally draws them all into a speeding whirlpool (bars 563–90).

The sharply opposed worlds of the four instruments as they are compressed and juxtaposed create a nervous, alienated mood, familiar from the experiences of urban life where many psychological types co-exist usually without cohering in a community. The music is fragile, punctured with silences and shadows. The characters could be drawn by Giacometti—they are always on the edge of a threatening emptiness. They express themselves in contrasting aphorisms of despair; even the opening cello phrase seems a contraction of the heroic cello cadenza that introduced the First Quartet—not a 'novel in a sigh', but a neurotic spasm.

Form

The Second Quartet synthesizes the formal patterns of the First Quartet and Variations for Orchestra. There are nine sections, played without a break:

Introduction, Allegro fantastico, Cadenza for Viola, Presto scherzando, Cadenza for Cello, Andante espressivo, Cadenza for Violin I, Allegro, Conclusion

These sections form an interwoven double-series, framed by the Introduction and Conclusion. The four 'movements' resemble, in their sequence of tempi, those of the First Quartet. The first three are dominated by one of the instruments: the Allegro fantastico by Violin I; the Presto scherzando by Violin II; the Andante espressivo by the Viola. In the four movements there is a progression from opposition to co-operation between the instruments. In the Allegro fantastico the florid character of the 1st violin contrasts with the fragmented statements by the other instruments, who gradually begin to assert themselves. In the Presto scherzando the 2nd violin maintains a steady pulse of MM 140 in pizzicato against the fragmented, filigree-like commentary of the other instruments, whose tempo is MM 175. With the Andante espressivo the instruments begin to imitate each other. The movement is a four-part distorted canon. Each phrase in the viola is imitated by the other instruments, in answers distorted by their own intervals and expressive habits (Ex. 82). In the final Allegro the instruments exchange characters and begin to build common structures. The connective function of the two all-interval tetrachords becomes increasingly clear, and a new rhythmic figure, containing all the polyrhythmic relations of the work, dominates the rhythm—see bars 458–69 and Chart 18. Beginning at bar 549 the pulse rhythm of the 2nd violin and the florid outbursts of the 1st are taken up by all the instruments in a large polyrhythmic design which leads to a group acceleration, an extension of a gesture previously used only by the cello. Precisely where all four instruments should fuse, however, at bar 588, there is a furious explosion of sound whose fragments float slowly away during the conclusion (Ex. 83).

Chart 18 'Fusion' motif **(String Quartet No. 2)**

Ex. 82

String Quartet No. 2
© 1961 Associated Music Publishers, Inc. Used by permission

200

Ex. 83

String Quartet No. 2
© 1961 Associated Music Publishers, Inc. Used by permission

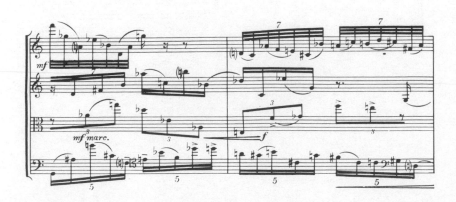

* Throughout the "Conclusion", all the notes of Violin II (usually pizzicato) end motives whose other note or notes are heard in another part.

The cadenzas form a contravening series, moving from co-operation to conflict. The viola's solo seems to be greeted by polite laughter, but the cello's large accelerating and retarding phrases are set against a relentless clockwork in the violins. Finally the 1st violin's cadenza is confronted by the indifference of the other instruments; a palpable silence interrupts the violin's music for four bars at bar 405.

The double series of movements thus creates a two-fold progression towards order and unity, and at the same time also towards disorder and non-cooperation. The double sequence also allows much of the material of the Quartet to be heard twice, in changed circumstances. The brash fioratura of the 1st violin in the opening movement becomes alienated and desperate in its cadenza. The viola's warmly expressive music sounds a bit preposterous during its cadenza, but returns to inspire the most emotionally intense music of the Quartet in the Andante espressivo. The cello does not dominate a movement; its cadenza however is the keystone of the work's arch, and its rhythmic contrast of free and mechanical shapes serves as the central image of the Quartet's polarities. Similarly the 2nd violin does not have a cadenza, because its relentless MM 70 pulse is the architectural basis of the Quartet's entire time-world. It alone seems to survive the concluding explosion; in the last pages of the Quartet the 2nd violin completes the fragmented phrases of the other instruments, and it ends the work with a soft statement of one of the all-interval chords plucked quietly at its heart-rate tempo (Ex. 84). Although some listeners have compared the 2nd violin's character to 'Rollo', the Philistine fiddler in Ives's Second Quartet, he may also represent an aspect of 'Chronometros' the time-measuring composer, E.C.

Ex. 84

String Quartet No. 2
© 1961 Associated Music Publishers, Inc. Used by permission

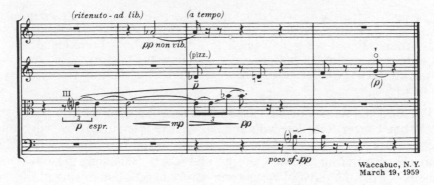

Waccabuc, N.Y.
March 19, 1959

Double Concerto for Harpsichord and Piano with Two Chamber Orchestras

Score dated Waccabuc, N.Y. August 1961 'To Paul Fromm'

This work was commissioned by the Fromm Music Foundation and first performed on 6 September 1961 at the concert of New American Music presented by the Fromm Music Foundation at the Grace Rainey Rogers Auditorium in New York for the Eighth Congress of the International Society for Musicology.

> Ralph Kirkpatrick, harpsichord
> Charles Rosen, piano
> Gustav Meier, conductor

Occasion

In 1956, Carter was asked by his friend Ralph Kirkpatrick to write a work for piano and harpsichord; the chances of performance for such a commission looked promising at the time, particularly in Germany. Later, this request was funded by a commission from the Fromm Music Foundation. Carter told Paul Fromm that the work would be exceedingly difficult, and Fromm promised that all necessary rehearsal time would be provided for the first performance—an extraordinarily generous arrangement. Fromm's impact on the musical situation in New York was to be crucial. At a time when the cause of new music in America was at one of its low points, Paul Fromm's active and involved philanthropy helped the performance and dissemination of new music to begin to approximate the fertile conditions in Europe. For the first time, Carter was free to write for a large ensemble without the intolerable restrictions imposed by American orchestras. The Double Concerto marked an unprecedented advance in ensemble virtuosity. The novelty and terror of the work as it was felt in the tense, hot late summer days of rehearsal has been well described by Charles Rosen:

> The mood of the first performance was one close to panic. In particular the last section of the piece, with one orchestra's part notated in ⅜, the other in

¾, caused special anxiety. 'I feel more like a traffic cop than a conductor', said Gustav Meier, trying to balance the sonority of one orchestra against another. Would we get through the piece without breaking down? We made it to the end. I had no clear idea how the performance went, but it turned out to be an enormous success with the public and, the next day, the critics.[4]

The unusual nature of the chosen instrumental combination posed problems that Carter wrestled with for five years, interrupted by work on the Second Quartet. Piano and harpsichord are distant cousins, sharing a keyboard, but differing in range, timbre and touch. Balancing these two mechanisms is only the most obvious compositional problem arising in the work. Most of the time the two instruments are kept out of each other's way, either through antiphonal treatment or by a clear contrast of registers. The piano plays mainly rapid filigree figures, rather than heavy, sonorous material that would have buried the more modest dynamic range of the harpsichord. In most performances, amplification has been used to boost the harpsichord, though Carter prefers unamplified sound when conditions in the hall are favourable. As Stravinsky pointed out, the contrast in volume is essential to the work's humour (as it is in the trombone/double bass duet in *Pulcinella*) and performances where the amplified harpsichord covers the entire ensemble are by no means faithful to the music. The purely acoustical problem of balance, however, was just part of the commission's larger challenge: to create a dramatic musical entity directly out of the contrasting sound characteristics of the two instruments, so that the music would not disguise their differences but would be *about* them on every level of composition.

Ensemble

The first solution to the troublesome solo pairing was the creation of a special ensemble:

> To join the piano and harpsichord into one world of music that could have many inner contrasts, I chose two small orchestras, each with two percussion players, and since this was to be an antiphonal piece, the two orchestras contained instruments that would underline the qualities of the soloists they were associated with and, in the case of the harpsichord, add dynamic volume to supplement its lack of dynamic range. (WEC 353)

Carter thus located his two soloists within two contrasting 'scales' of sound from unpitched percussive noises to sustained instrumental pitches, extending the percussive-pitched nature of both instruments outwards towards a vast, inclusive spectrum. The percussion itself is a highly differentiated sound-continuum with the drums, membranophones forming a 'continuous scale of clearly distinguishable pitch levels, as evenly spaced as possible, starting from the highest available bongo to the lowest available bass drum', and with metallophones and lignophones similarly arranged from soprano triangle down to low cow bell, from soprano cymbal to contrabass tamtam, and from slap-stick to temple blocks. The cymbal family was divided up between the four players to connect them in space, as at bar five where a cymbal roll moves around the orchestra counter-clockwise, prefiguring later interactions between sound and space. The percussion writing throughout is of an unprecedented refinement and sophistication, a quantum leap beyond Varèse's *Ionization,* and to this day the standard of virtuoso drumming; indeed the Double Concerto brought into existence a whole new generation of percussionists able to master its technical demands. Even greater than these, however, are the musical challenges the work poses for percussionists, for the Double Concerto was perhaps the first work to be written where the percussion is fully integrated into the ensemble, so that ideas constantly move across the sound spectrum from pitched instruments to unpitched percussion and back. Throughout the Double Concerto the percussion is the dominant sound, presenting the ideas of the work in their clearest form.

Carter assigned three of the four brass instruments to the harpsichord's ensemble, so that it could compete in volume with the piano's. The harpsichord's orchestra—flute, horn, trumpet, trombone, viola and double bass—has a 'baroque' sonority that is heightened by a 'dry' percussion section made up predominantly of metallophones (anvil, cowbells, gongs, tamtams) and lignophones (temple blocks, wood blocks and slap-sticks). The piano's orchestra—oboe, clarinet, bassoon, horn, violin and cello—is more expressive and 'classical', with its 'wet' percussion dominated by membranophones (bongos, snare drums, bass drums) capable of creating swelling dynamic shapes. Indeed dynamics are also treated as a wide continuum; in a note Carter has added to his score he requests that 'the dynamic range in performance should be very great:

as loud as possible: beginning of bar 5
middle of 310
end of 616
beginning of 619 (climax of piece)
for percussion, especially, middle of 654
as soft as possible: when accompanying the harpsichord particularly in its softer registrations as in 214–6.
Orchestra (not piano) from 465 to beginning of 475.

The structural function given to the entire spectrum of pitch and volume is complemented by a structural activation of space (Chart 19). The two groups of pitched instruments sit as far apart as possible, surrounded by the four evenly spaced percussionists to the rear of the stage and the soloists to the front. This plan is both antiphonal and circular; the music moves from left to right and back, and also clockwise and counter-clockwise in changing patterns.

The chosen ensemble, with its fundamental sound-spectrum ranging from seemingly undifferentiated 'noise' to articulated pitch, called forth a formal plan that would project this sonic continuum in time:

I . . . arrived at the idea of unpitched percussion groups, from which everything the two soloists did could be rhythmically derived. According to this notion, a 'primordial rhythm' expressed by the unpitched percussion would progressively take on pitches through the two resonating solo instruments, whose statements would then be elaborated and amplified by two

Chart 19   Approximate seating plan   **(Double Concerto)**

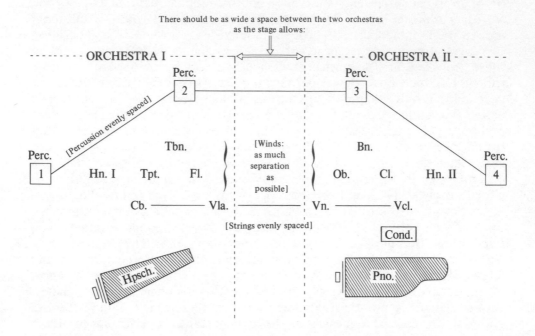

groups of sustaining pitched instruments. Finally at the beginning of a 'coda', there would be a gong crash, whose vibrating resonances would be 'orchestrated' as it died away, which would then be progressively re-absorbed by the unpitched percussion. (FW 104)

From the first, sound and structure were to be one; the work would 'get down to the physical origins of musical sound and . . . take off from there'. Rhythm would play an even more important role than it had in Carter's earlier music, and the shape of the piece would mirror its composition: a new world would be called into existence, then destroyed.

Concept

As Carter began working out his overall plan, two literary models suggested themselves: Lucretius's *De Rerum Natura,* and Pope's *Dunciad.* As in Lucretius's poem, the Double Concerto would bring a cosmos into existence by the seemingly random collision of falling atoms:

> All things keep on, in everlasting motion,
> Out of the infinite come the particles
> Speeding above, below, in endless dance . . .
> Surely the atoms never began by forming

A conscious pact, a treaty with each other,
Where they should stay apart, where come together
More likely, being so many, in many ways
Harassed and driven through the universe
From an infinity of time, by trying
All kinds of motion, every combination,
They came at last into such disposition
As now established the sum of things.

(I, Rolfe Humphries, trans.)[5]

Obviously, Lucretius expresses the relation of chaos and order in a strikingly modern way. As Carter has pointed out to me, there is something particularly hopeless about a genesis where accident gives way to rigidity devoid of a transcendental framework. Carter saw that the end of the work would undo this universe in the manner of Lucretius's 'Destruction of Athens' or the triumph of Chaos at the end of the *Dunciad*:

Nor public flame, nor private, dares to shine;
Nor human spark is left, nor glimpse divine!
Lo! thy dread empire, Chaos! is restored;
Light dies before thy uncreating word:
Thy hand, great Anarch! let the curtain fall;
And universal darkness buries all.

The texts of Lucretius and Pope helped Carter to define the work's dramatic form. He has often looked to non-musical works for strategies of design different from traditional musical procedures. The conclusion of the *Dunciad* is a kind of inside-out retrograde, 'uncreating' itself in ironic hyperbole. Lucretius and Pope, however, also seem relevant to the distinctive expressive colouring of the Double Concerto, its brittle sonority, rapid-fire, explosive continuity, and its avoidance of the lyricism so prevalent in Carter's other works. For the Concerto brilliantly evokes a mood of desperate comedy, as rationality totters on the brink of the irrational. Lucretius used science not as a form of knowledge but as an escape from the horrors of existence, like the plague that destroyed Athens:

On fire
They hurled their bodies, naked, into streams.
Many, with mouths wide-craving-open, plunged,
Headfirst into deep wells, from any height.

De Rerum Natura is an anatomy of disorder posing as science in a world always on the verge of dissolution:

There is never lack
Of outer space, available to take
The exploded rampart-rubble of the world.
The doors of death are always open wide:
For sky, for sun, for earth, for ocean's deeps
The vast and gaping emptiness lies in wait.

Pope's *Dunciad* is, similarly, an anatomy of cultural disorder, a *Narren-dämmerung,* as it is often termed, mock-heroically celebrating the powerlessness of enlightenment against the forces of stupidity, not only in politics and literature, but in music as well:

> Joy to great Chaos! let Division reign;
> Chromatic torture soon shall drive them hence,
> Break all their nerves, and fritter all their sense.

Listened to metaphorically, the Double Concerto, with its paired eighteenth-century protagonists surrounded by a shell of noise, may be heard to evoke the dark side of eighteenth-century rationalism; not the Encyclopedia and Dr Johnson's Dictionary, but The Battle of the Books, *Tristram Shandy, Le Neveu de Rameau,* Dr Johnson's madness. This is the side of the Enlightenment that the later twentieth century has discovered as its own mirror. Stravinsky's neo-classicism ended in Bedlam, but Bedlam itself, as Michel Foucault has pointed out, is a manifestation of rationality. The Double Concerto thus discovers an expressive terrain unusual in music—comic irony raised to a prophetic vision. Its polyrhythmic collisions, spiralling spatial trajectory, and vast fluctuations through the spectrum of sound are like an elaborate clockwork planetarium spinning out of control, a cosmic contraption. Where Carter had compressed his universe into the dense time-world of the Second Quartet, in the Double Concerto it explodes outwards in a vision of universal disorder, a cosmology of chaos that is also a triumph against the very disorder it so vibrantly evokes. Its mood is not far from much recent literature: Beckett's *Endgame* with its useless erudition, Nabokov's *Pale Fire* with its neo-Popean collision of real and imagined worlds, or the mad contrivances of Pynchon. At the same time, however, the Double Concerto of all Carter's works moves farthest from linguistic logic, towards an untranslatable, non-representational musical grammar.

Materials

The organizational techniques of the Double Concerto and the Second Quartet are closely related. All eleven intervals are partitioned between the two orchestras, and their harmonic combinations are largely defined by the two all-interval four-note chords—(0, 4, 6, 7) for the harpsichord and (0, 1, 4, 6) for the piano. These chords are then co-ordinated in ways suggested in Chart 2 (p. 65) 'in order to provide a somewhat ordered substructure (like the triadic harmony of the common practice period, but more freely used because it is not adhered to so strictly) as a source of many degrees of interrelation on several different levels at once'. (WEC 296) Because the intervals are divided into two groups rather than four as in the Second Quartet, the intervallic contrast of the two groups is less immediately apparent. The division of intervals, however, clearly opposes different harmonic colours. The harpsichord's intervals are 'dark'; the piano's 'bright'.

Harpsichord	Piano
Minor second (ninth)	Major second (ninth)
Minor third	Major third
Perfect fourth	Perfect fifth
Tritone	
Minor sixth	Major sixth
Minor seventh	Major seventh

In addition to the recurrent harmonic sonority of the two all-interval four-note chords, a sixteen-note chord shown in the interval chart appears quite frequently as an all-interval 'tonic'—see bars 39, 147–9, 158, 326–8 (piano) and 615, for literal restatements of this chord; many close mutations, usually related by the prominent major third on top, occur elsewhere.

As in the Second Quartet, the stratification of intervals is mirrored in the rhythmic organization. Where the Quartet associated intervals with contrasting rhythmic styles, here each interval (except the minor sixth) is given one or more speeds. These speeds divide up the ratio of 2:1 according to two mathematical series. Five speeds are in a ratio of whole numbers—10:9:8: 7:6:5—and five are in a ratio of reciprocals 1/10:1/9:1/8:1/7:1/6:1/5 (see Chart 4a, p. 67). The association of intervals and speeds thus gives each orchestra a rich repertoire of cross-rhythms and tempo modulations. Furthermore, each soloist 'specializes' in a polyrhythmic combination: 4:7 for the harpsichord and 3:5 in the piano. These are most clearly heard respectively in the Presto and Allegro scherzando, while the cadenzas for both instruments display the relationships between their contrasting intervallic speeds, most notably in the piano at bars 567–70 where five polyphonic strands, each made of one interval moving at its regular speed, are woven together (Ex. 85).

Ex. 85

Double Concerto

Form

Despite the similar intervallic and rhythmic rigour of the two works, the Double Concerto demands a different kind of listening from the Second Quartet. Where the Quartet was like 'an opera made up of quartets', the Concerto is more like a ballet in which two ensembles with distinctly different repertories of steps interact to form changing configurations:

> The form is that of confrontations of diversified action-patterns and a presentation of their mutual interreactions, conflicts, and resolutions, their growth and decay over various stretches of time.[6]

Motion is more important than gesture. The drama of the Concerto grows not out of contrasted musical characters, but from its imaginative 'choreography' of sound in time and space. (The closest balletic analogies might be such abstract works of Balanchine as *Movements for Piano and Orchestra* (1963) which Stravinsky termed a double concerto, or Symphony in Three Movements of 1972 with its independently deployed ensembles). Carter has himself pointed out this aspect of the Concerto in noting how the relation of soloists and ensembles evolves:

> In the central Adagio, the 'choreography' changes; the entire wind section, in centre stage (although still divided into groups) plays slow music, while in the background the two soloists, strings, and four percussionists surround the winds with accelerating and decelerating patterns that alternately move clockwise and counter-clockwise. (WEC 328)

In the Presto, moreover, the 'choreography' changes yet again, as all the sustaining instruments join the harpsichord, leaving the piano in isolation. The music throughout is as carefully composed in space as it is in time; Stravinsky, who was so fond of the work, particularly loved to 'visualize' it from the score.[7] Indeed many of the great effects of temporal and spatial choreography were sketched visually, without pitches: Carter's notebooks for the Concerto are filled with Carterian fantasies of colliding lines, curves and waves.

As in the Variations and the Second Quartet, the form of the Double Concerto is at once sectionalized and continuous. It falls into seven symmetrically arranged sections: Introduction, Cadenza for Harpsichord, Allegro scherzando, Adagio, Presto, two Cadenzas for Piano, Coda—the Adagio serves as keystone. Each movement is based on a distinctive integrative or disintegrative process. The Introduction and Coda are huge polyrhythmic patterns, bringing the atomic intervals of the work into alignment, and back into chaos. The Allegro scherzando is dominated by the piano and its ensemble, with interruptions by the harpsichord group. Re-enacting the introductory atomic collisions at a higher level of characterization, the two groups converge, then move apart. The Adagio contrasts a sustained chorale in the winds with unstable spirals for the soloists, strings and percussion, culminating in a great duet for piano and harpsichord in which the piano accelerates to its fastest speed and the harpsichord ritards to its slowest, 'like two opposed infinities that meet' as Charles Rosen has written. The Presto,

featuring the harpsichord, and so balancing the Allegro scherzando, is interrupted by the piano, playing Maestoso. Instead of the interaction of the
Allegro, however, here the two levels move farther apart, the disintegration
of texture being compounded by the percussion which re-enter after the
second piano cadenza, and drown the ensemble in a cadenza of their own.
Throughout the work there are constant cross-references, overlaps, echoes
and anticipations superimposed on the dialectical processes. As so often
happens in Carter's music, fantastic free-associational events are allowed to
violate a more logical, pre-determined design, in order to create multiple
perspectives. The symmetrical structure is articulated by a radically disjunct
continuity, starting and stopping unpredictably, a mosaic of unexpected
connections. Particularly remarkable in this respect are the many intersections with silence, for at no two places does the cessation of sound have the
same grammatical effect. The grand pause before the gong crash at bar 619,
where most other composers would have written a grand tutti crescendo, is
very typical of the work's surprising dramatic 'logic'.

Introduction

> . . . a strange kind of turbulence, a swarm
> of first beginnings, whose discordances
> Confused their intervals, connections, ways
> And weights and impacts, motions and collisions;
> And so the battles raged, because these forms
> Were so dissimilar, so various
> They could not rest in harmony, nor combine
> In any reciprocal movement. But at last
> Some parts began to learn their separate ways—
> Like elements joined with like, in some such way
> As to effect disclosure—a visible universe
> With parts arranged in order . . .
>
> (*De Rerum Natura* V, 434–45)

The music is set in motion with simultaneous accelerations and ritards in
the percussion, coming together in a climax at bar 5. As this intersection
subsides, two pulses emerge in a ratio of 49:50 (fifteen septuplet semiquavers
against twenty-one quintuplet semiquavers, at metronome speeds of 24.5 and
25 respectively.) These nearly indistinguishable pulses, introduced by rolled
cymbal and snare drums, begin to be orchestrated at bar 11, as the 24.5 pulse
is transformed into a tremolando minor second in the harpsichord's
orchestra, and the 25 pulse is heard in a tremolando major second in the
piano's orchestra; the intervals sound like overtones of the percussion.
Gradually the other intervals are placed in orbit, all emanating from
unpitched percussion at widening pulse speed ratios:

Bar				
	13–14	Perfect fourth (28)	Major seventh (21 7/8)	32:25
	16–17	Tritone (29 1/6)	Major sixth (21)	25:18
	20–23	Minor third (19 4/9)	Perfect fifth (31.5)	81:50
	35–36	Minor seventh (17.5)	Major third (35)	2:1

213

Amidst this pulsating primordial ocean, the soloists enter with tremulous vibrations, gradually building materials and gestures out of the intervallic atoms, but also flaring out suddenly with fully formulated character-patterns, forecasting later events. The piano anticipates its Allegro scherzando at bars 23, 29, 35, and 89; the harpsichord pre-figures its Presto at 33 and 50. Meanwhile the twin intervallic solar systems begin to approach two points of simultaneous accent. The two collisions are prepared by a huge crescendo, building from bar 41 to 46, and set off by synchronous strokes on tamtam and bass drum (each part of different pulse systems). The two ratio systems approach their rhythmic unisons in different ways. One system of pulses, related by ratios of whole numbers, approaches a unison attack on the downbeat of bar 45. The composite rhythm formed by these pulses produces a pattern of constant acceleration, heard clearly in the piano. The other system of pulses forms a pattern of accelerating acceleration, that is, the rate of acceleration is not constant but increases. These pulses collide at the downbeat of bar 46, and then continue to form a pattern of decelerating deceleration played by the harpsichord in bars 47 and 48 (Chart 20). The

Chart 20   Rhythmic scheme   (Double Concerto)

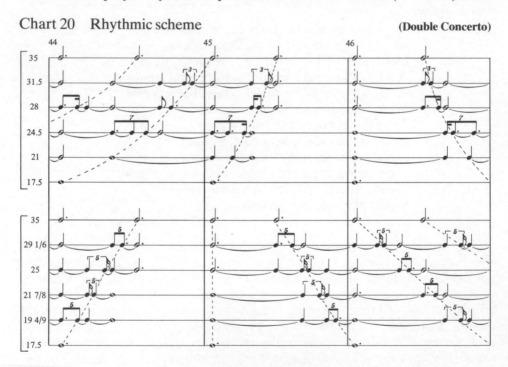

quiet, widely spaced notes in the piano from 46 on, heard against a fading burst of fast music in the harpsichord, are the continuation of its speed pattern, moving out of phase in regular pulses.

The second half of the Introduction continues the falling motion from the climax at bar 46, with each orchestra trying to launch its own fast material against the slowing solar wind. The music seems to come to a complete stop at bar 84, as a viola trill fades into a rolled cymbal. After a brief silence, the piano attempts to begin its Allegro movement, only to be overtaken by rhythmic accents in both orchestras, stressing a 4:3 speed ratio. Out of this new clash the harpsichord emerges with its cadenza.

Cadenza for Harpsichord

Many contrasting characters are heard in fleeting, aphoristic form. This improvisatory-sounding sequence is built on the harpsichord's intervals: minor second at MM 25.5 (bars 105–6), perfect fourth at MM 28 (bars 108–12), minor seventh at MM 17.5 (bars 113–5), tritone at MM 29 1/6 (bars 120–7), and minor third at 19 4/9 (bars 133–6). The cadenza also displays the full range of harpsichord stops and mutes. As in the Sonata for Harpsichord, Carter requires a very colourful modern instrument. The Challis he specifies in the score has two manuals:

Lower manual: 4', 8', 16' and coupler
Upper manual: 8'

All the stops have full and half positions, and both manuals have mutes. The work can only be properly realized on an instrument similarly capable of a large number of fast shifts in colour, giving the harpsichord a playful, quick-silver personality. (The virtuoso shifting of registers required in the work recalls an experience of Carter's from his Boulanger years: the Princess de Polignac, dressed in sneakers and an evening gown, played a Vivaldi organ concerto at her house on the Avenue Henri Martin. Mlle Boulanger gave Carter and another student specific directions for changing the stops with dizzying frequency while the elderly Singer sewing machine heiress played. Boulanger's students also sang choruses from Stravinsky's unperformed *Perséphone* on this occasion.)

The cadenza ends with a fanfare-like burst in the harpsichord's orchestra, which is swallowed up and dissolved rhythmically by the piano's orchestra, leaving the primal chord suspended in slow, quiet motion (bars 147–50). The pitched material once more fades into percussion, and then to a ten-second silence.

Allegro scherzando

> Then sun and moon were born, and went their rounds
> Between the earth and sky, with neither earth
> Nor sky appropriating either sphere.
> They were not heavy enough to sink and settle
> Into the earth, nor light enough to float
> Up to the ether, but their course was set
> Between the two; between the two they turn
> Like living bodies, their existence keeping
> A time, a place, as parts of the great world.

215

Their motion and their fixity resemble
Our own in this respect: that we can move
Some of our bodily members while the rest
Remain in quietude.

(*De Rerum Natura* V, 468–80)

Snare drums and bongos usher in fast, light music in the piano's orchestra. Rhythmically, this music develops the many possibilities of the relationships of 3:5 heard at the outset in the drums. This ratio appears not only as the polyrhythm of triplets against quintuplets, but also in a large number of related cross-accentual patterns (bars 223 and 224, for instance) and tempo modulations (bars 162–3.) Harmonically, the music emphasises the intervals of major third, perfect fifth, minor second, major sixth (in approximate descending order of importance.) The piano draws three of its intervals from the 'primal' chord in bar 158, then rearranges them in the spirit of fantastical improvisation that dominates the movement. Almost everywhere in the Allegro scherzando the piano plays in the upper half of its range and staccato, almost as an overtone of the snare drum and bongo figures which dominate the percussion.

The piano's playful music is cross-cut with slower music in the harpsichord's ensemble. Indeed the form of this movement may be compared with the second movement of the Sonata for Flute, Oboe, Cello and Harpsichord. Two independent strands are intertwined, each with its own intervals, chords, speeds and colours—like the sun and moon in alternating appearances. The rhythm of the montage is extremely unpredictable, ranging from the rapid jump cuts at bars 173, 178 and 258 to extensive, sustained statements by each side. In general, the harpsichord, playing mostly in its lower register, attempts to slow down the piano's motion, and opens up wide windows of slow time (as at the surprising silence, bar 197) on the contracted world of the piano. The piano 'retaliates' by unleashing its percussion, and itself turning into a percussion instrument, as with the accented clusters, bars 234–8, that are followed by a fast, blurred pedal effect, like a snare-drum roll (Ex. 86).

Unlike the Harpsichord Sonata, here there is considerable overlap between the two musical strands, beginning with the remarkable *Klangfarben* effect in bars 172–3, where a chord ricochets across the orchestra—note how it is transformed en route from one all-interval chord to the other, sustaining common notes through six rapid changes in colour (Ex. 87). From bars 234 to 251, large polyrhythmic patterns are heard between the two ensembles, all based on the ratio 7:5 that is also heard in fast motion between the soloists (bars 243–5). The twilight colour of rhythmic accents all in *piano* at bars 248–51 is particularly remarkable—a near-total eclipse as the two instrumental bodies move across each other's fields. In the course of the movement overlapping becomes the rule, as if the instruments no longer had the patience to wait for their entrances; note the beautiful brass 'penumbra' in the harpsichord's orchestra in bars 265–72, to the piano's increasingly brilliant figuration. After a sustained passage in the low harpsichord and flute, the piano unleashes its most violent explosion, followed by a climactic outbreak by all the percussion (bar 310). The harpsichord, however, in a Chaplinesque

Ex. 86

Double Concerto

© 1965 Associated Music Publishers, Inc. Used by permission

217

Ex. 87

*From the date of the Double Concerto (1961) onwards, Carter's scores—with the exception of the Brass Quintet and *A Symphony of Three Orchestras*—are nontransposed.

gesture, continues on its way and finally begins to impose a general ritard. This ushers in the Adagio as the harpsichord reaches its highest note—the four-foot F that brings in the crotales, the only pitched percussion instrument in the orchestra.

Adagio

> Now we turn
> to sing of stellar motion. The great flow
> Of heaven, as air turning, possibly may press
> Each polar axis of our atmosphere
> Holding it close both ways, with another stream
> Of air in flow above it, setting course
> In one direction only, with the stars
> Revolving, shining, swept along the flood.
> Or there may be another air below
> To make the arc revolve the other way
> As rivers turn the wheels of water-scoops.
> It's also possible that all the sky
> Is fixed in one position, while the stars
> Pursue their shining ways. The tides of ether
> May be shut in, over-compressed, revolve
> Seeking escape, and whirl the fiery stars
> To the Night-Thunderer's areas of the sky.
>   (*De Rerum Natura* V, 509–25)

Although the tempo, *Adagio,* is reached at bar 342, the new double configuration that defines this movement begins with the harpsichord ritardando at bar 321, which is countered by an accelerando beginning in the piano at 326. As noted before, the Adagio combines a slow chorale-like music in the winds with slowing and speeding figures which spin around the winds in space, through the percussion, strings and solo instruments. The Adagio can thus be heard as a symbolic configuration of order and chaos. The winds (whose notes are further sustained by the strings) sound the basic intervals of the work in tranquil, floating motion—the harmony of the spheres. The unstable spinning motion of the soloists and percussion imposes an Einsteinian astronomy on the platonic model of the wind-chorale. Compositionally it is interesting to see how Carter has re-interpreted his own rhythmic invention from the Variations, superimposing the elements of slowing, calm and acceleration that were distinct in the earlier work, in order to produce a more complex, dynamic shape: Ritard, Acceleration, Adagio, Ritard, Acceleration, Adagio, Acceleration. The rhythms projected on these warped time-screens are in fact simpler and more pulse-like in the Concerto, allowing the far more complicated overall shape to emerge clearly. For not only are the three motions interwoven, they are also choreographed in a spatial *Klangfarbenmelodie.* At bar 395 a constantly accelerating pulse moves counterclockwise around the orchestra, with just three or four notes played by each instrument (Ex. 88). A clockwise motion is similarly heard in

219

Ex. 88

Double Concerto

the percussion during the ritarding passages. Pitch, colour, time and space are brought together in a magical geometry.

The slow wind music evolves gradually from isolated intervals to a climactic superimposition of motifs at 404–6, which is beautifully sustained by the barely-audible strings moving at the slowest pulse-speed of the work, MM 9.3 in the viola and bass against MM 7.5 in violin and cello. As the music begins to build again, a new acceleration is launched with traumatic thuds on the bass drums. As pulses spin around the orchestra, a burst of wooden percussion sparks a long dazzling duet for the two soloists, accompanied by the last phrases of the chorale in the winds. The rhythmic plan of this duet surpasses everything that has come before in Carterian complexity. The harpsichord reaches a stable tempo at bar 433, while the piano continues to accelerate, playing nine increasingly fast beats against eight steady beats in the harpsichord. From bars 436 to 453 both instruments play continuous fast figuration at steady speeds of MM 560 for the harpsichord and MM 630 for the piano—in a ratio of 8:9. Through this clattering crossfire, bassoon and clarinet chant a slow line built on the piano's four-note chord, answered by the piccolo with the harpsichord's harmonic motif. At bar 453 the harpsichord and percussion begin to slow down, while the piano accelerates, unco-ordinated with the other instruments (Ex. 89). (As Charles Rosen has said, the only thing for the pianist to do is *not* to look at the conductor and just

Ex. 89

Double Concerto
© 1965 Associated Music Publishers, Inc. Used by permission

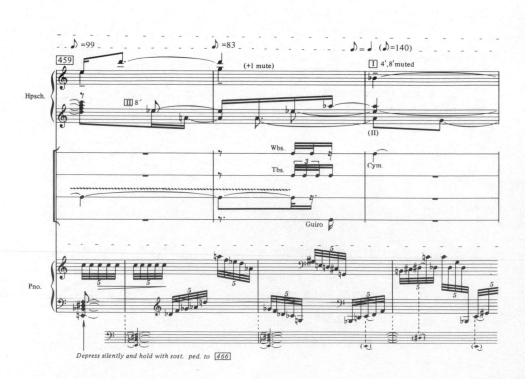

222

hope that everyone comes out together.) By bar 465 the harpsichord has slowed to silence, and the piano has sped past the vanishing point, a double infinitude of silence that is crowned by high chimes. The vast, mysterious space, evoked by the far-flung ringing of crotales, triangles and tamtam recalls the eerie calm of the First Quartet's 'desert places'. As in the Quartet, human expression tries to fill the empty space: the piano enters with a loud, questioning gesture. The question echoes in the metallic stillness and is repeated, remaining unanswered as the harpsichord begins its Presto.

Presto

> I have shown that all the reaches of the world
> Are mortal, that the heavens are born, and die.
> (*De Rerum Natura* VI, 37–8)

The Presto features the harpsichord, accompanied by all the winds and strings. The sprightly, angular material is based on the intervals of minor ninth, minor third, perfect fourth, minor sixth and minor seventh, which are heard from time to time in clarion bursts (555). The baroque-jazzy dotted rhythms derive from the seven against four polyrhythms, as can be seen at bars 509 to 512. The piano interrupts the Presto with Maestoso music, continuing the questioning mood heard at the end of the duet. For the first time in the piece, it plays predominantly in its bass register (while the harpsichord, winds and strings are in the treble) and stresses its most resonant intervals, major seventh and perfect fifth. The contrast of the two soloists is therefore very different in mood from that of the Allegro scherzando. There the piano and harpsichord seemed to move closer together; the light, staccato writing for the piano was an accommodation to the harpsichord, allowing it to compete as an equal. In the Presto the instruments stress their more natural traits—the harpsichord's speed against the piano's weight. There is no interaction between the parties; the oppositions grow stronger with each response. The harpsichord answers the piano's brooding prophecies with brilliant cascades of septuplets.

Cadenzas for Piano

Twice the piano expands its interjections into cadenzas. The first (bars 525–39) recalls the mood of the Allegro scherzando, and emphasises the intervals of major ninth and major third. The second cadenza, introduced by an exquisite soft filigree of sound as the two soloists intertwine, begins with the scherzando mood, grows more agitated, and reaches a climactic, oracular statement—five intervals moving at the five speeds associated with them in the Introduction. The prophecy gives ways to a brilliant display of power, as the piano rapidly resonates its entire musical space (see bar 577), setting off bursts in the percussion.

Presto (continued)

The percussion immerses the music in the destructive element of noise. Piano, harpsichord, winds and strings unite against the drums in futile assertive gestures fractured by percussive bursts. Note how the wind chorale from the Adagio is chopped up and compressed (bars 599–601), finally emerging as the Last Trump at 615—harmonically a restatement of the primal chord (Ex. 90). From bar 603 to 611 the percussion takes over the music in a mounting wave of cross-accents. After final convulsions by strings, soloists and winds, the drums re-assert their power—followed by a two-bar silence—a musical blackout.

Ex. 90

Double Concerto
© 1965 Associated Music Publishers, Inc. Used by permission

Coda

> In vain, in vain—the all-composing Hour
> Resistless falls: The Muse obeys the Power
> She comes! She comes! and sable Throne behold
> Of Night Primeval, and of Chaos old!
>
> (*Dunciad* IV, 626–30)

The coda begins with an enormous gong crash, orchestrated in a chord unlike any heard earlier in the work—a tower of tritones (Ex. 91). The gong crash projected in time becomes the form of the coda:

like a large gong, [it] dies away over many measures in wave-like patterns, with many diverse tone colours fading and returning—each time slightly different, and each time with less energy—until the work subsides to a quiet close. (WEC 328–9)

Ex. 91

Double Concerto

The texture of the Coda suggests a huge vibration with many smaller partials, all fading away in complex, periodic motion. Again, as in the Introduction, Carter planned his poetic effect geometrically. There are four simultaneous wave patterns (Chart 21). The main accents come every five bars in the

Chart 21   Wave patterns in Coda   (**Double Concerto**)

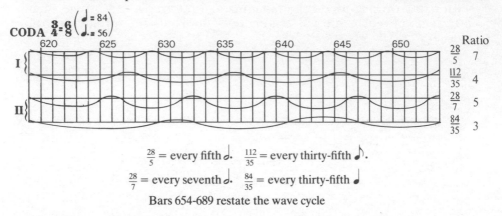

$\frac{28}{5}$ = every fifth $\musDottedHalf$. $\frac{112}{35}$ = every thirty-fifth $\musEighth$.

$\frac{28}{7}$ = every seventh $\musDottedHalf$. $\frac{84}{35}$ = every thirty-fifth $\musQuarter$

Bars 654-689 restate the wave cycle

harpsichord's orchestra (MM 5.6) and every seven bars in the piano's (MM 4) with secondary accents every 35 dotted quavers in the harpsichord's orchestra, and every 35 crotchets in the piano's. Since the Coda is seventy bars long, the overall 5:7 cycle is heard twice. Comparison bar-by-bar from 654 to the end with 619 to 653 reveals how the second half of the coda is a near-literal dying echo of the first half. The music no longer expands, it just resonates. Expression fades into physics. By bar 679 all that remains are the rolled cymbals and snare drum heard at the opening of the work. Reversing the sequence in the Introduction, these rolls swell into the last phrases of each soloist, then vanish in trills. The piano touches its highest note; the harpsichord sounds a cluster below the range of the piano. A last breath on the flute is cut off almost inaudibly by the claves, and the work ends.

> Thy hand, great Anarch! lets the curtain fall;
> And universal darkness buries All.
>
> (*Dunciad* IV, 655–6)

Here is what Stravinsky wrote about the Double Concerto:

I like the mood of Carter's Concerto, first of all. It is full of new-found good spirits, as his quartets were not. But the success of the piece is owing to the listener's eventual involvement and satisfaction in its form. That the Double Concerto should suggest Berg's towering example in general ways is not surprising, but I hear direct references to the Berg in it, too. (Carter is certainly not a naive composer, but I think these Berg bits are unknowing.) The passage from 432 (the piano entrance here is one of the finest things in the piece) to 460, and especially the flute at 436 and the bassoon at 441, remind me of the Berg, and the architectural plot of the solo instruments— their roles as alternate soloists, duo soloists, parts of ensemble groups— also is reminiscent of the Berg. The Concerto presents many interesting performance problems, not so much in instrumental technique—not in the wind and string parts anyway, though the percussion is a different matter— as in rhythm. The score introduces no metrical difficulties, and as the proportionalisms of tempos are easy to hear if the orchestras are reversed from the composer's seating plan so that the conductor stands next to the harpsichord, it is easy to conduct. Incidentally, the most effective example of an interlocking of tempos by a held-over beat pattern is precisely where it is most apparent (loudest): the percussion at measures 143–4. I do not think the chief rhythmic difficulty is in the notation—though I can imagine orchestra players complaining about that, and perhaps fidelity to the writing of the rhythmic series does make the instrumental parts momentarily more difficult to read: I mean, for example, four dotted sixteenths to the dotted quarter rather than 'four for three' without the dots, as I would now do it. The rhythmic problem of the Concerto is the old one common to most contemporary music. The player manages the notes, but cannot count the rests or feel irregular pulsations—or regular ones, but without simple patterns—when he is not playing.

I like not only the shape but also the sense of proportion in the Concerto, and I like the harpsichord and piano writing very much, too. And the intended high point, the coda, is the real climax of the piece. (This section is unclear, though, in the recording, where the rhythm is a blur and the dynamic plan is without profile. The question of dynamics in recording practice must be criticized more strongly than anyone has criticized it so far. The harpsichord is weak in volume by nature, or so the engineer assumes; but this weakness is overcompensated by about ninety percent in the recording.) I cannot comment upon or add to the composer's own analysis, but analysis as little explains a masterpiece or calls it into being as an ontological proof explains or causes the existence of God. There, the word is out. A masterpiece, by an American composer.[8]

Piano Concerto

The Concerto was commissioned by Jacob Lateiner through the Ford Foundation[9] and is dedicated 'To Igor Stravinsky on his 85th birthday with great admiration and friendship'. Carter began work on it in 1963 while he was composer in residence at the American Academy in Rome and continued in Berlin where he was invited by the Ford Foundation and the Berliner Senat to spend the year of 1964. Conditions in Berlin were so generous that Carter invited several of his students including Joel Chadabe, Alvin Curran and Frederic Rzewski to join him. He was later amused to realise that ever since Frederick the Great artists have been bribed to come to Berlin, which was always something of an eastern outpost of German culture. The Cold War tensions following the construction of the Berlin Wall certainly left their mark on the Concerto. Carter remembers the constant sound of machine-gun fire from a U.S. Army target range near his studio—a sound that echoes through the second movement. The isolation of Berlin and its hostile surrounding may have suggested the dramatic confrontation of piano and orchestra in the Concerto. It was completed in Waccabuc in 1965 and premiered by Jacob Lateiner and the Boston Symphony Orchestra conducted by Erich Leinsdorf on 6 January 1967.

Drama

Reviewing the first performance, Michael Steinberg wrote that 'Carter's Concerto established the most dramatic confrontation of solo and orchestra since Beethoven'.[10] Drama, as musical metaphor, is a slippery term; truisms such as 'Beethoven's music is too dramatic for opera' display a disturbing ambiguity, mainly because the word 'drama' is being used too narrowly. There are many kinds of musical drama: the rhetorical drama of baroque music, the formal drama of classical music, the lyrical melodrama of romantic music. All of these share a heightened sense of opposition, whether gestural or structural, and an assumed expressive mythology—the dramatic subject is defined by stylized gestures, moods and strategies.

Concerti are not always dramatic. As Charles Rosen points out, in the baroque concerto 'there is scarcely ever any effect of dramatic entrance'.[11] The same could be said of many late Romantic concerti, particularly those of Rachmaninov where the piano plays nearly continuously, and the dramatic element is reduced to the simple effect of intensification produced when a solo instrument plays a melody. Most twentieth-century concerti are either neo-baroque or neo-romantic. The first type, best exemplified by Stravinsky's Violin Concerto and *Capriccio,* avoid expressive drama. The soloist is first among peers, not a dramatic protagonist. The second type, exemplified not only by Rachmaninov and Sibelius but also by works as otherwise advanced as Schoenberg's Piano Concerto and Bartok's Violin Concerto, follows the dramatic conventions of the nineteenth century—the opposition of orchestral heroics and solo lyricism, or vice versa, leading to the inevitable climactic moment when the lyricism of a big tune is given full-blown Hollywood-heroic treatment. The neo-baroque concerto is aristocratic in its disdain of rhetoric, but runs the risk of losing all differentiation between solo and orchestra. In Stravinsky's *Capriccio,* for instance, the piano is more orchestral instrument than soloist. Most neo-romantic concerti, on the other hand, so safely follow expected procedures that they seem redundant—Brahms in plastic. The alternatives seem to have been no drama at all, or soap opera.

Breaking completely with past practice, Carter set out to discover a new dramatic meaning for the concerto form. As Michael Steinberg wrote, 'he has moved far from the Romantic concept of the soloist-hero cheered on by the crowd. Rather, the composer posits a conflict "between an individual of many changing moods and thoughts and an orchestra treated more or less monolithically—massed effects pitted against protean figures and expressions" (Carter's own words)'. The expressive world of the Concerto is thus typically modern. The soloist is not a hero but an anti-hero in an alien world. Perhaps more than any of Carter's other compositions the Piano Concerto exemplifies the values Harold Rosenberg found in action painting. The drama of the work focuses on the discovery of identity. The Concerto is not a *representation* of the search for identity, but a specific *enactment* of that search, in which the terms, issues and processes of self-discovery are themselves transformed. Formally, it is Carter's freest conception; expressively, it is his most intense.

Protagonists

The dramatic form of the Concerto arises from its particular ensemble. There are really two orchestras. The piano is surrounded by seven instruments: flute, cor anglais, bass clarinet, violin, viola, cello, bass. Where possible, this concertino should be spatially separated from the rest of the orchestra—Carter suggests three arrangements in the score. The concertino can be seen as a clever way of dealing with limited rehearsal time: the most demanding instrumental writing in the Concerto is entrusted to a group of soloists who—one assumes—will take more time learning their parts than that allocated by orchestral scheduling. This 'partitioning' of difficulty is expressive as well as practical, however. Not only does the concertino play more difficult music than the rest of the orchestra, its music is also more sensitive, lyrical and imaginative. The orchestra, by contrast, plays deliberately crude, massive music. Carter once described American orchestras as 'brontosaurs staggering with inertia and ossification'. In the Piano Concerto the orchestra is a musical brontosaur; unwittingly it portrays itself. The soloist and the concertino redefine virtuosity as freedom, vision and imagination, and so inevitably become locked in battle with the orchestral monster. The work thus transforms the architectonic group-opposition of the baroque concerto grosso and the metaphorical 'heroics' of the romantic concerto into a new conception. It can also be seen as a synthesis of the lyrical drama of the Second Quartet and the geometric choreography of the Double Concerto, with the concertino's lyricism and the orchestra's geometry placed on a collision course.

The two instrumental groups specialize in distinctly different sonorities. The piano and its consort are unendingly lyrical. The mechanical aspect of the piano, so prominent in the Double Concerto, is here suppressed. The solo part is almost always cantabile (even in the scherzando episodes of the first movement). Its long expressive lines, expanding and contracting in time, stretch cross the entire musical space of the piano in changing densities and harmonic colours. As Chopin demonstrated in his first étude of Op. 10, the piano is the spatial instrument par excellence, and the piano writing here explores voicings and intervallic distances with exquisite sensitivity: note, for instance, the beautiful contraction from wide-spread minor ninths to a cluster of minor seconds at bars 266-70, or the inventive figuration at 582–3, which, as Charles Rosen told me, reinterprets Chopin's first étude with ninths and sevenths substituting for octaves (Ex. 92). The solo instruments serve primarily to resonate the spatial explorations of the piano; the rich timbres of the solo winds, particularly the cor anglais and bass clarinet, bring out the mood of lyrical meditation. These auxiliary instruments do not appear in the orchestra and so give the concertino its distinctive colouring. Similarly the solo flute is often set against the metallic glare of piccolos in the orchestra to heighten the concertino's expressive timbre.

The sonority of the concertino is an idealization of chamber music: sensitive, singing, and with much interplay between instruments. By contrast, the orchestra is a machine, insistent and brutal. Individual instrumental colours

Ex. 92

Piano Concerto
© 1967 Associated Music Publishers, Inc. Used by permission

are repressed in favour of dark, mysterious, heterophonic mixtures; the swirling cluster at bar 78 is a typical early manifestation of the orchestral mass, which becomes increasingly molten as the first movement progresses—note the lava-flow of strings at bar 200, the divided violins at 245, and the climactic dust-storm at 312 with its seventy-note string cluster punctured by massed trills in the winds. The dissolution of this texture at bar 321 into harmonic wisps is perhaps an even more remarkable invention than the frontal storm itself. None of these dense textures is static; they evolve in time both internally and in relation to the concertino. The series of increasingly dense cloud formations in the first movement prepares for the great mesh of strings which covers the second—although that texture too is in constant atomic motion, changing in density, intervallic colour and real spatial configuration as the cloud moves across the divided strings. In the early '60s Carter was impressed by the 'textural' music of Xenakis, Penderecki, Ligeti and others, at least to the extent of writing that 'the isolation of single notes by pitch, dynamics and timbre . . . is a device that no longer seems to stimulate the writing of interesting music, while the thick, packed, dissonant textures and vivid juxtaposition of whole clusters or constellations of notes seems to lead, these days, to livelier results'. (WEC 225) Carter had in fact anticipated this European development: the Coda (and much else) of the Double Concerto is 'texture music'. But the inspiration for the string writing in the Concerto was Ives's *Fourth of July,* a score that has long intrigued Carter. While composing the second movement Carter left New York to go to Warsaw for a performance of the Double Concerto. His plane was grounded in London, however, and when he rang up some friends there he found out that at that very moment Frederik Prausnitz was rehearsing his Variations and the *Fourth of July*. Carter took a taxi and arrived just in time to hear the rehearsal of the dense string passages in the Ives, which convinced him that he was on the right track in the Piano Concerto.

The opposed instrumental groups are differentiated in their harmonic makeup. The basic harmonic unit is no longer the interval, as in Carter's earlier music, but the twelve possible three-note chords. Carter divides these triads between orchestra and concertino, identifying each three-note chord with a dominant interval and limiting the spacing and inversions of each chord in the interest of clear identification (see Chart 4b, p. 68). The stratification of intervals is similar to that of the Double Concerto, only here the piano is given the darker more expressive intervals, and both groups share the tritone (found in chords VII and VIII). The tritone functions throughout as a common element, linking the two instrumental groups; its pointed, plangent sound colours the entire work. The tritone's special function appears clearly at bar 18, where orchestra and concertino reiterate the same two pitches F and B—this important convergence also forecasts, far in advance, the dramatically repeated F's at bars 605–14. Four triads from each group are combined into two 'key' twelve-note chords that recur frequently and nearly literally throughout the first movement and at the beginning of the second. These two chords to a very great extent define the overall harmonic tone-colour of orchestra and concertino (as clearly contrasted at bars 344–8) and establish harmonic 'landmarks' for the free motion of the work.

Each triad is associated with from one to three metronome speeds, which are adhered to quite strictly in the first movement. These speeds fill in a spectrum between 126 and 42 (3:1) in whole number and reciprocal ratios similar to those used in the Double Concerto (see Chart 22). Twenty basic speeds in all are defined by this system, an extremely subtle gradation of the time-screen that is nevertheless all based on simple numerical ratios. Although the Concerto can be played (and probably, at present, *has* to be played) under the given tempo—Charles Rosen reduced the speeds to 5/6 of the given metronome markings—it is imperative that all tempo modulations should be strictly observed so that chordal speeds are maintained. Otherwise

Chart 22   Chord-tempi ratios   **(Piano Concerto)**

Chord	Piano	Orchestra	Ratios			
VII	126		21	1/7	18	1/6
II		110.25		1/8		
X	108		18			1/7
II		105			15	
IV	98			1/9	14	
VIII		94.5				1/8
IX		90	15			
VIII		88.2		1/10		
I	84		14		12	1/9
XI		73.5		1/12		
V	72		12			
IX		63		1/14	9	1/12
III		60	10			
XII	58.8			1/15		
VI		56			8	
VI		54	9			1/14
X	50.4					1/15
I	49			1/18	7	
VII	48		8			
VII	42		7	1/21	6	1/18

(header over Piano/Orchestra columns: Tempi – MM)

the distinctive character of each chord will not be heard in the constantly changing polyphonic collage. From bars 62 to 67, for instance, it is essential that chord X should continue straight across the tempo change at an unchanging pulse of MM 108—6/7 of the original tempo of MM 126 and 6/5 of the new tempo of 90 (Ex. 93). This uninterrupted pulse serves to link a scherzando episode combining speeds of 108 and 50.4, with a lighter and more delicate passage based on Chord V which moves at a speed of MM 72 in bars 68–74.

Ex. 93

Piano Concerto

Throughout the first movement, every triad is associated not only with a speed, but also with a distinctive mode of presentation. Each chord generates a characteristic kind of music, and these clear characters are combined contrapuntally in changing patterns between and within the concertino and orchestra. At bar 35, for example, the piano elaborates chord VII—its most important chord—while the orchestra combines the almost Mahlerian,

Ex. 94

Piano Concerto
© 1967 Associated Music Publishers, Inc. Used by permission

singing line generated by chord VIII, with the typical square rhythmic shapes of chord IX. By contrast, from bar 68 to 75 the piano contrapuntally combines the delicate character of chord V with the staccato articulation of chord X, while the orchestra sounds the cluster harmonies associated with chord III (Ex. 94). The piano's treatment of each chord tends to be imaginative and fanciful, always discovering new aspects of a chord's personality, and new combinations of chords and speeds. The orchestra's usage is more stereotyped; it tends to restate or intensify previously heard events. The solo instruments of the concertino occasionally act as messengers (as at bars 110–22 and 159–65) attempting to establish points of contact as the large behaviour patterns of piano and orchestra move farther and farther apart. This underlying divergent tendency, which achieves a climactic formulation at bars 312–23, controls the free-associational montage of short episodes in a subliminal way. The two groups seem to respond to each other, or to ignore each other, purely in passing—the larger pattern of interaction emerges only slowly. The listener's perception of the drama thus mirrors the piano soloist's evolving self-understanding.

233

Scenario

At the time of its première, Carter described the form of the Concerto with a biographical analogy:

> The piano is born, then the orchestra teaches it what to say. The piano learns. Then it learns the orchestra is wrong. They fight and the piano wins—not triumphantly, but with a few, weak, sad notes—sort of Charlie Chaplin, humorous. [12]

While such an explanation may have been a sop to the journalistic mind, a non-anecdotal biographical model for the work's form may be the most useful metaphorical guide. In this respect the Piano Concerto may be compared with Berg's clearly programmatic Violin Concerto. Like that work it is in two parts: the first might be termed childhood, adolescence or education; the second, maturity or self-discovery. Berg's Concerto is based on the specific story of Manon Gropius—birth, dancing, polio, death. Carter's Concerto is non-representational; not a biography, but a biographical meditation. In both works a mostly light, scherzando character in the first half gives way to intense, tragic opposition in the second, and the increase in tension stems from the expanded expressive freedom allotted to the soloist:

> I wanted the second movement to become a very free treatment of materials that in the first movement had been restricted to a more limited pattern of behaviour, and to open a broader, more expressive character. . . (FW 110)

The drama of the work increases as the piano slowly learns that 'the orchestra is wrong': the first movement can be thought of as the piano's *Éducation sentimentale*—in the second movement the piano asserts its identity in an increasingly alien world.

The two movements are really continuous, despite a twenty-second pause, which functions like the breaks in the First Quartet. They differ in their treatment of what Charles Rosen has seen as the major dramatic device of the concerto form:

> The most important fact about concerto form is that the audience waits for the soloist to enter, and when he stops playing they wait for him to begin again.

The first movement is a drama of entrances. The two instrumental groups are cross-cut, with varying degrees of overlap. Entrances are sometimes gradual, sometimes abrupt, continuing ideas from the other group, or interrupting the other's train of thought with sharply contrasting material. At many points the piano will establish a connection with the orchestra through a common note: at bars 79 and 80, the G♯ topping triad III in the clarinet is taken up in triad X by the piano (Ex. 95). In the early parts of the first movement the piano's exits are often balletic leaps into the wings, ushering in the orchestra with a virtuoso flourish—bars 22, 36, 74. Later, the dialogue becomes less polite. Contrasting moods interrupt each other with minimal interaction (bars 129–32 or, more intensely, 199–202) or become entangled in polyphonic struggle,

Ex. 95

as at 174–7. The increasingly deflected angles of contention between orchestra and concertino in the course of the first movement yield a drama of ironic non-cooperation—perhaps Carter's most distinctive expressive domain. A beautiful instance of this can be heard at bars 188–95. Here piano and orchestra cross each other's paths, each playing light, closely spaced three-note chords—chord III in the orchestra at MM 60; chord X in the piano at MM 48. At once distant and related, the two characters engage each other *en passant*; then the orchestra drops the game and the piano moves on (Ex. 96). Both the piano soloist and the conductor must be extremely sensitive to the nuances of these delicate, often humorous, moments of failed connection, out of which the larger, darker drama of the first movement grows.

In the second movement, superimposition replaces cross-cutting as the basic structural process. Here Carter constructs a drama of exits—who will

Ex. 96

stop playing first, piano or orchestra? The piano plays almost continuously, pausing only to let members of the concertino offer their ideas—notably in the three woodwind cadenzas: bass clarinet bars 438–63, cor anglais, 491–505, and flute, 529–43. Projected behind the concertino are two continuous processes in the orchestra: staccato pulses and dense, sustained chords in the strings—'a suffocating blanket of sound'. The apparent continuity of these processes is, interestingly, highly illusory. The string chord fades in and out, just as the many different pulse layers appear and disappear, seemingly moving in and out of consciousness.

In the second movement, the fundamental opposition between the soloist's freedom and the orchestra's tyranny—an opposition that was gradually revealed in the first movement—comes to the fore. After a transition (up to bar 375) during which the piano inverts the figures it was playing at the end of the first movement, as if trying to destroy the technique of that movement, the new, polarized texture emerges. The wall of strings is clearly an outgrowth of the clusters built from chord III earlier; now they evolve in harmonic colouring and density, until the musical space is saturated at bar

236

616. The staccato pulses that were associated in the first movement with chord XI become a giant polyrhythmic mechanism in the second, with many different staccato pulses at speeds from 105/13 to 105 ticking away until they appear to converge at bar 615. Against the orchestra's infernal time-machine the pianist plays with rhapsodic rhythmical freedom; the entire movement—which can be heard as an enormous expansion of the cello cadenza of the Second Quartet—is Carter's most extended vision of the clash between chronometric and chrono-ametric time-worlds. The pianist seems to be improvising a vast cadenza, freely using its intervals from the first movement, with the addition of perfect fifths and major sevenths 'stolen' from the orchestra's intervallic repertory. The rhythmic freedom of the piano part constantly threatens to violate notational decency—the hieroglyphic configurations force the player into an agogic, chrono-ametric rhythmic style—and crosses the traditional notational frontier at bar 522 where the concertino accelerates independently of the orchestra. The piano's rhapsodic meditation is interrupted three times by the woodwind cadenzas—Carter has called the bass clarinet, cor anglais and flute 'false comforters to the piano's Job'. These cadenzas extend the piano's lyricism to the concertino, but also set off the piano's unbounded expressive freedom from the more restricted lamentations of the 'comforters'.

As the staccato pulses come closer together and the string clusters become increasingly dense, the piano is gradually crowded out; its last foothold is a single F that fades away in accelerating repetition (Ex. 97). A rough blast in the brass, supported by strident tritones in the timpani, seems to seal the soloist's doom—but after a terrifying silence the concertino asserts itself with growing force, while sharp thunder claps in the orchestra unleash a cyclone of sound (see bars 656–60). The orchestra seems to be the voice answering Job out of the whirlwind, but the storm passes, and the piano concludes with a short, soft epilogue:

> The piano doesn't beat the orchestra down. It is victorious by being an individual—if there is a victory. Anyway, the orchestra stops before the piano does. Maybe that's a victory. I don't know. [13]

If the first movement of the Piano Concerto is Carter's most original formal invention, the second contains his most intense emotional drama. It is a music for the dark night of the soul, weaving together desperation and ravishing lyrical beauty—the bass clarinet solo in particular is a monument to pure melody. Like the Book of Job, the Concerto compresses vast, universal cataclysms into a compact frame, and is all the more intense for its restraint. The Concerto may be said to begin with an opposition of composer and orchestra, of the individual and the mass, but it ends as an epic confrontation of life against death. In order to transcend the disorder he had portrayed so strikingly in the Second Quartet and Double Concerto, Carter created a musical battle against chaos itself, and, in a 'Charlie Chaplin humorous' way, prevailed.

Stravinsky wrote Carter a letter (see p. 239), thanking him for the dedication.

Ex. 97

1218
~~1260~~ NORTH WETHERLY DRIVE

HOLLYWOOD ~~69~~ CALIFORNIA
90069

15 June 1968

Mr. Elliott Carter
Mead Street
Waccabuc, New York

Dear Elliott,

        My secretary finally found the blueprint
copy of the score and, at last, we listened to the
concerto yesterday. I am more delighted with it than
I can tell you. It is a masterpiece, and I like it
even more than the Double Concerto. I have not listened
to contemporary music lately; a batch of Xennakis a
few weeks ago and some other composers it would not be
very kind to mention. I have been steeped in late
Beethoven quartets, on the other hand, and have not tired
of them. So I came to your concerto with high demands
and quite fresh ears for an old man. I am very honored
to have my name on this score.

        We plan to fly to New York on the 26 of
June, and have reserved the usual rooms at the Pierre.
We expect to stay there until mid-August, then go to
Europe if the French revolution is over. There will be
an interesting concert in Cambridge, Mass. August 5,
playing some of the preliminary instrumental versions
of Les Noces, as well as my two new instrumentations of
Wolf's Geistliche Lieder and the Requiem Canticles. Perhaps you might go up, too.

        Please let me know if there is anything I
can do to help I Sang Yun. What an appalling story.

        If you see Natasha please tell her of our
plans. Many thanks, again, and with love from all of us
to you and Helen.

                    Igor Stravinsky

                    Igor Stravinsky

P.S.: I really can't judge the recorded performance, nor
can I honestly claim to have heard everything on page 54.

Notes to Part 7

1. In lectures at Dartington Summer School of Music, August 1978
2. Stockhausen told Paul Jacobs that he found the rhythmic innovations of the Cello Sonata and Variations very instructive. The tempo relationships in *Gruppen* and the ideas in 'How Time Passes' make an interesting contrast with Carter's methods and thinking.
3. The Stanley Quartet paid Carter 500 dollars for the Quartet. When they received it, however, they were overwhelmed by its difficulties, and never played it. In order to get the piece performed (by the Juilliard Quartet) Carter returned the commission money to them; their name has nevertheless remained on the published score.
4. Rosen: 'One Easy Piece', op. cit.
5. Lucretius: *The Way Things Are*, trans. Rolfe Humphries, (London: Indiana University Press, 1968)
6. Carter's notes to the now-deleted Epic recording
7. Lillian Libman: *And Music at the Close*, (New York: Norton, 1972) p. 238
8. Igor Stravinsky and Robert Craft: *Dialogues and a Diary*, (New York: Doubleday, 1963) pp. 47–9. Carter obviously differs with Stravinsky on 'unknowing' allusions to Berg, let alone the presence or absence of 'new-found good spirits'. Undoubtedly Stravinsky found the ironic emotional tone of the Double Concerto closer to his taste than the warmer lyricism of the quartets, and it may be precisely the lyrical element in Carter's music that linked it in Stravinsky's mind to Berg's. It might be noted here, since Stravinsky raises the notational issue, that Carter follows the notational conventions of Reneé Longy-Miquelle's *Principles of Music Theory*, which are particularly clear in notating polyrhythmic relationships. In his music, for example, the polyrhythm of 21:14 would be indicated by three groups of septulets against two of dotted septuplets; the internal 3:2 relationship is thus clearly shown. See Kurt Stone, 'Problems and Methods of Notation', and John MacIvor Perkins, 'Note Values', both reprinted in *Perspectives on Notation and Performance*, op. cit.
9. Bureaucratic methods of foundation funding were much in evidence. Carter was informed that Lateiner, whom he did not know, was commissioning a concerto through the Ford Foundation. When Carter told the Foundation that he would not write a piece unless he knew that the performer was sympathetic to his music he was informed that the press release had already gone out. Lateiner *did* know Carter's music well, so he accepted the commission, whereupon *someone* from the Foundation began to call every week or so to 'see how it was going'.
10. *Boston Globe*, 7 January 1967
11. Charles Rosen: *The Classical Style*, (New York: Norton, 1972) p. 196
12. *Time*, 13 January 1967, p. 44
13. *Newsweek*, 16 January 1967, p. 94

8

The Music of Our Climate, 1967–1974

> He had to choose. But it was not a choice
> Between excluding things. It was not a choice
> Between, but of. He chose to include the things
> That in each other are included, the whole,
> The complicate, the amassing harmony.
>   (Wallace Stevens, *Notes Toward a Supreme Fiction*)[1]

The Piano Concerto is a tragic vision whose prophetic darkness recalls the late paintings of Mark Rothko. Carter, however, was able to take his art beyond despair. He transcended the anxious battleground of the Piano Concerto through a leap of 'negative capability'. He identified with his opposite. The storm that threatened to obliterate the soloist in the Piano Concerto itself became the swirling, cyclonic texture of the Concerto for Orchestra. Carter now viewed destruction and innovation as inseparable, and perhaps realised that the confusion and even the banality around him were sources of imaginative creation. In *Vents* of St John Perse, which Carter used as a formal model for the Concerto for Orchestra, winds blowing over the American continent symbolize the interaction of destruction and innovation, a theme stated in a different form in 'The Poems of our Climate' by Wallace Stevens, from which Carter and Allen Edwards chose the title of their book of conversations:

> The imperfect is our paradise.
> Note that, in this bitterness, delight,
> Since the imperfect is so hot in us,
> Lies in flawed words and stubborn sounds.[2]

With the Concerto for Orchestra the mood of Carter's music becomes joyously celebratory, drawing delight from ever more complexly stubborn realms of sound.

Many listeners have found the works of this period more accessible than those they followed, even though their technical complexity seemed to increase exponentially. Their instrumental colour is immediately attractive; the Concerto for Orchestra glitters and shines like no earlier piece of Carter's. Yet both the surface brilliance of the music and its new formal richness derive

241

from a significant expansion in the technical resources of Carter's idiom. The harmony no longer stems from intervals, but rather from four-, five-, or six-note chords. Form now grows out of the contrapuntal interplay of movements, so that simultaneity becomes a formal as well as a polyphonic principle.

The jump from intervallic to chordal harmony had appeared in the first movement of the Piano Concerto. While composing that work, Carter began the Rameauesque speculations now compiled in his Harmony Book. The Concerto for Orchestra marks the first fruit of these researches. The impression the orchestral concerto gives of a greatly enlarged spectrum has as much to do with its harmonies as with its orchestral chemistry. For while intervallic harmony is limited to the eleven interval-classes, chordal harmony draws as well on the twelve three-note chords (and their nine-note complements), twenty-nine four-note (and eight-note) chords, thirty-eight five-note (and seven-note) chords and fifty six-note chords. Typically, Carter, having developed means for using all the intervals in each work, now found ways of ordering these greater harmonic resources, so that the music would gain in harmonic variety without becoming incoherent. The successful realization of the new harmonic idiom I believe marks the most important enrichment of harmony since Schoenberg. In these works the harmonies are not merely systematically consistent, they are imaginatively compelling. The listener is often surprised to find that, despite the cloud-like textures of the music, its pitch-sense and harmonic direction are forcefully palpable. Carter's specific means of reactivating pitch will be viewed more closely in the discussion of individual works.

The major formal innovation of this period is the contrapuntal treatment of movements. Carter's music has always broken down the boundaries between movements. In the Variations for Orchestra, for example, Variation 1 begins before the theme, and Variation 2 begins during Variation 1. With the Second Quartet, the partitioning of the musical texture in character-continuities further challenged the integrity of individual movements; the 2nd violin plays much the same music throughout the work, regardless of the movement in which it appears. In the Second Quartet and Double Concerto the movements might be likened to stage-sets on which the protagonists act. The different movements provided changing contexts for the ongoing drama. The Piano Concerto, however, pursued a new approach. Its first movement is a two-layered collage in which orchestra and concertino both draw on a repertory of musical characters. There is no longer a controlling context for the interaction; at every moment the superimposition of materials itself becomes the setting of musical action. Movements and character-continuities are merged. Form and content are brought together more closely, more explosively than before.

In the Concerto for Orchestra, formal polyphony is the music's essence. Four different movements, each with its own colour, character and mode of transformation, are fragmented and superimposed. The music springs from the confluence of four movements, much as the weather results from the interaction of vast atmospheric systems. Despite the sharply partitioned configuration of materials in all of these works, the music is what happens *between* the opposed strata as well as within them. The polyphony of movements makes these compositions at once more abstract and more colourful than their predecessors. We no longer sense the dramatic opposition of instrumental personalities, but of larger forces—clouds, glaciers, dust storms, tidal waves. The contrasted duos of the Third Quartet are not character-types like the instruments of the Second, they are basic ways of being: Apollo against Dionysus.

The glistening colours and energized textures of these works may reflect Carter's sense that an audience and performers now existed for his music. By the later '60s his achievement was widely appreciated. Pierre Boulez, formerly indifferent to Carter's music, now championed it; he conducted the Concerto for Orchestra twice at a special concert, discussing it publicly with the composer between performances and even going to the piano to illustrate its harmonies to the audience. He then directed the Concerto throughout Europe on the New York Philharmonic's tour, and, after he left the orchestra, gave Carter's works a prominent place in his concerts at IRCAM. The Double Concerto, which at the beginning of the decade had seemed so forbidding, was now played at least once a year in New York; the Cello Sonata had long since become a standard repertory piece. The enthusiastic support of ensembles such as Speculum Musicae, the Contemporary Chamber Ensemble, The American Brass Quintet, the Juilliard Quartet and the Composers Quartet (who give concerts of all three quartets) inspired Carter to expand still further the virtuosity of his instrumental writing. Carter premières had now become events. *Le tout New York,* painters, pocts, scholars, as well as musicians, filled Tully Hall for the first performance of the Third Quartet. The electric atmosphere of that performance—with the Juilliard Quartet's members tensely tapping their feet at different speeds, getting up in midstream to turn each other's ragged pages and playing nonetheless with furious concentration, will not soon be forgotten by anyone who was there.

Concerto for Orchestra

Occasion

Commissioned by the New York Philharmonic Symphony Society to celebrate its 125th anniversary, the Concerto was composed at the American Academy in Rome where, in order to get away from duties and obligations in New York, Carter once again became composer in residence. The Adagio movement was written at Villa Serbelloni, Bellagio, where Carter was invited for a month by the Rockefeller Foundation. He remembers his stay there for its violent thunderstorms which may have influenced the dramatic timpani writing of the Adagio. The Concerto was first performed at Philharmonic Hall on 5 February 1970. The dedication—omitted by printer's error from the published score—is to its first executants, the New York Philharmonic and its musical director Leonard Bernstein.

Concept

Although the orchestral concerto would seem to be a twentieth-century form, it stems from two older and opposed traditions. Hindemith's Concerto for Orchestra and Stravinsky's *Dumbarton Oaks* were revivals of the baroque concerto grosso. The orchestral concerti of Bartok and Lutoslawski by contrast extend the nineteenth century symphonic tradition; their combination of orchestral virtuosity and national sentiment looks back to Tchaikovsky's Fourth Symphony. Carter, while rejecting both these formal moulds, adapted certain aspects of them. His Concerto is a virtuoso symphonic work in which almost every player at some time becomes a soloist. Instead of the fixed concertino grouping of the concerto grosso, changing ensembles of soloists are drawn from the orchestral mass. Each string section, for instance, is given a group cadenza for seven soloists in the course of the work. Perhaps more in the tradition of Ives than of European music, the Concerto treats the orchestra as an idealized democratic society in which all the players are heard both as individuals and as part of a larger community.

Looking for a form that would dramatize his orchestral conception, Carter came upon *Vents* of St John Perse. This long Whitmanesque prose-poem describes winds blowing over the American plains destroying old, dried-up forms and sweeping in the new—a vision particularly relevant to the turbulent America of the late '60s. The poem's wide scope and rich imagery helped Carter to formulate his own design. Many of the poem's images—winds, the rustling of dry straw, clouds of flying insects—inspired the remarkably evocative sonic textures of the Concerto in which individual instruments combine in dazzling spray-like washes of sound. But the Concerto is not a tone poem. *Vents* suggested colours and gestures from which Carter abstracted a grand fresco of musical motion. The text of the poem remains as an aid to the audience, one possible interpretation of the music. With the text in mind, the listener may find in the Concerto something of an affirmative national work like the Bartok Concerto; it is perhaps Carter's most American vision, evoking an entire continent and a vast heterogeneous society in a state of turmoil. Indeed Carter hoped that the four orchestral groups might be seated around the audience so that the music could sweep across the concert hall like winds on the Great Plains. Less literal-minded listeners may prefer to hear the work as an impressionist wind study, Carter's aerial response to Debussy's *La Mer*. For those who prefer the more abstract pleasures of listening, the Concerto can be heard as a four-tiered kaleidoscopic collage of shimmering textures and pulsating rhythms all in a state of continuous flux. The many possible interpretations that the Concerto can sustain all stem from its structure; here Carter broke decisively from St John Perse's poem. Where *Vents* portrayed a sequential progression from death to rebirth, Carter chose to present the stages of this process simultaneously. Decay, destruction, despair and renewal are seamlessly interwoven.

Orchestra

Although scored for a normal orchestra with triple winds but with eight percussionists, the Concerto divides the ensemble into four groups, by tessitura:

A) violins, flutes, clarinets, metallic percussion. (Mov. II)
B) violas, oboes, trumpets, horns, snare drums. (Mov. IV)
C) cellos, bassoons, piano, marimba, harp, wooden percussion. (Mov. I)
D) basses, trombones, tuba, timpani. (Mov. III)

The division into groups is not absolute. Certain instruments, particularly oboes and horns, appear in more than one group, though usually in the background, and the strings occasionally cross boundaries to give a fuller sonority. The division by tessitura rather than by instrumental families is a Debussyan orchestral conception:

> The woodwinds should be dispersed: the bassoons with the cellos, the oboes and clarinets with the violins so that their entries should not produce a package effect. (See p. 131)

Like Debussy, Carter sought to achieve an orchestral sonority not based on the string choir. In the Concerto, as in the Double Concerto, the percussion forms the core of the orchesta's sound; it plays almost continuously throughout and the orchestral fabric constantly emerges from percussive sound, as at the very beginning of the work, where the string harmonics appear imperceptibly out of swelled rolls on triangle and suspended cymbals. Anyone listening to a percussion sectional rehearsal for the concerto would immediately hear how the entire sonority and shape of the music is present in the interplay of metal, skin and wooden percussive sounds.

The grouping of instruments by range rather than by colour allows for constant *Klangfarbenmelodie* and mosaic counterpoint within each of the four ensembles. Phrases and chords pass rapidly between instruments from strings to winds to percussion and back, producing a flickering surface. The imbrication of piano, harp, marimba and wooden percussion at bars 16–22 is a typical component of the orchestral tapestry. It might be noted here that the brilliant and fiendish piano writing in the Concerto was Carter's homage to the virtuosity of the Philharmonic's pianist, Paul Jacobs (much as the trumpet solo in *A Symphony of Three Orchestras* was for Gerard Schwarz). The rhythmic complexity of the piano part not only exploits Jacobs's particular mastery of polyrhythm, but also allows the conductor—who may be less comfortable with metrical intricacies—to follow the pianist through many of the work's more difficult tempo modulations, as at bars 40–1 (Ex. 98). (The verbal indications for tempo change were suggested to Carter by Bernstein and greatly facilitate the performance of the Concerto for conductors and players with an unsure grasp of tempo proportions.)

Materials

The music of each orchestral group is differentiated in harmony, rhythmic character and expression. Because Carter wanted to use the orchestra in a very full manner—as opposed, he has said, to the spare orchestration of late Stravinsky—he needed to devise a rich harmonic vocabulary for the work. The awkwardness in non-tonal music of octave doublings, the source of most

Ex. 98   **Concerto for Orchestra**
                                          © 1972 Associated Music Publishers, Inc. Used by permission

orchestral texture in the past, meant that the harmony would have to be based on many-voiced chords, capable of giving a full sonority without octave duplication. At the opening of the Concerto a twelve-note chord is heard in a swelling orchestral tutti; each instrumental group plays a three-note component of this chord which is the Concerto's primal sound. Starting from the contrasted intervals of these three-note chords, Carter divided all the three-, four-, and five-note chords among the four groups (Chart 23).

The harmonic resources of the Concerto—all intervals, three-, four-, and five-note chords and many seven-note chords—are vast; their strict partitioning on the basis of intervallic sound makes them coherent. The expanded possibilities for harmony opened up by the use of the thirty-eight five-note chords (and their seven-note complements) can be put into perspective if we recall that in tonal harmony only two such chords, the major and minor dominant ninths, are officially sanctioned. The listener wanting to explore Carter's harmonic vocabulary might begin with a passage like bar 146 (Ex. 99). Here five solo violins play in rhythmic unison at a rate of MM 630.

Ex. 99   **Concerto for Orchestra**
                                          © 1972 Associated Music Publishers, Inc. Used by permission

Each vertical sonority is a five-note chord associated with Group A; the harmony astonishingly changes with every septuplet demisemiquaver, giving the music a vibrant colour and a sense of motion that a slower, less inflected rate of harmonic change could not achieve (Chart 24).

Chart 24   Harmonic scheme   (Concerto for Orchestra)

Of course the music is not everywhere so dense or rapid in its harmonic motion (though frequently it is even more so); a more leisurely exposition of chordal harmonies can be heard in the clarinets at bars 342–4, where the three-note chords of group A drift by (Ex. 100). Throughout the work such

Ex. 100   **Concerto for Orchestra**
                                 © 1972 Associated Music Publishers, Inc. Used by permission

streams of chords, particularly in instrumental groups A and B, are the basis of the music's counterpoint and colour; they unite contrapuntally independent lines of solo instruments into clear harmonic vectors which are then set against the contrasted harmonies of the other orchestral units. At climactic moments all the harmonies merge back into the primal chord of the opening, as at bar 141 (Ex. 101). Occasionally the texture clears to reveal the basic intervals of each group as at bar 231, when a perfect fifth in the oboes suddenly appears in isolation and is then absorbed back into the orchestral cloud (Ex. 102). The constant fluctuation of the music from intervallic to chordal to saturated harmonies parallels and supports the rapid motion of instrumental colour between winds, strings and percussion.

249

Ex. 101

Concerto for Orchestra

Ex. 102

Concerto for Orchestra

Carter has related the character of each group's music to certain passages from *Vents*:[3]

C) 'For a whole century was rustling in the dry sound of its straw, amid strange desinences at the tips of husks of pods, at the tips of trembling things. . . .' (Mov. I)

The tenor-register ensemble, which dominates the first quarter of the work, plays moderately fast, expressive, rubato-style music in phrases that always slow down in speed, beginning faster and ending slower each time (Ex. 103). These fading rhetorical gestures perhaps also suggest 'the attrition and drought in the hearts of men'.

A) 'New lands, out there, in their very lofty perfume of humus and foliage. . . .
Those flights of insects going off in clouds to lose themselves at sea, like fragments of sacred texts. . . .' (Mov. II)

The soprano-register ensemble plays flowing, pulsed music first heard at a rapid speed, and dominates the second quarter of the piece, marked *Presto volando,* but gradually slows throughout the work (Ex. 104).

D) 'For man is in question, and his reintegration.
Will no one in the world raise his voice? Testimony for man.
Let the Poet speak, and let him guide the judgment!' (Mov. III)

The bass-register group, coming to the fore during the third quarter of the piece, plays slow, expressive music in phrases that accelerate, beginning slower and ending faster each time (Ex. 105).

B) 'And again man casts his shadow on the causeway of men.
And the smoke of man is on the roofs, the movement of men on the road,
And the season of man like a new theme on our lips. . . .' (Mov. IV)

The alto-register group plays swelling, pulsed music that gradually accelerates throughout the work and dominates the last quarter of the music (Ex. 106).

Carter's non-literal use of the poetic text can be seen in the instrumental assignments of materials. The cellos of group C are given 'romantic' gestures built out of major and minor sixths, but each such gesture is transformed by the dry, rattling sonorities of the piano, marimba and guiro—we can hear the meaning fade from these phrases as the cello cantilena rasps and crackles in the percussion. The prophetic utterances of Perse's Poet are assigned to groups of basses and the solo tuba, giving the heightened rhetoric a note of grotesque irony—Carter has said that he was not interested in the overblown, Whitmanesque gestures of some parts of the poem. A similar orchestral irony marks the relation of A and B. Whereas the violins and high woodwinds are given strikingly coloured *volando* material at first, in the course of the piece their fresh sonority fades away and the even more novel sounds of viola, brass

252

Ex. 103

Concerto for Orchestra
© 1972 Associated Music Publishers, Inc. Used by permission

and snare drums take their place; it is a rare orchestral work where the violas triumph over the violins.

If we set the poem aside and listen to the work more directly, it will be clear that the four orchestral groups are divided according to the basic characters of musical time often found in Carter's music. A and B are pulsed materials; C and D are rubato. A and C ritard; B and D accelerate. Furthermore, the rhythmic character of each group is also its mode of transformation. All four types of music are transfigured in the course of the music, so that their interaction is always changing. In the First Quartet, Carter had let the wind blow through the music of the Variations; in the Concerto for Orchestra four winds transform themselves and each other.

Form

The formal design of the Concerto is perhaps Carter's most complex structure; it combines several of his habitual shapes. The work can be heard as a continuous four-movement sine-wave sequence—Allegro, Presto volando, Maestoso, Allegro agitato, in which each movement features one of the orchestral groups, in the order C, A, D, B. However, all four groups are juxtaposed and superimposed throughout the music, so that the Concerto can also be heard as a cross-cut collage. Since the fragmented statements of each group's material are never literal repetitions, but are always transformations, the Concerto can be heard as a variational design. The intersecting tempo transformations of A and B, moreover, create an inverted arch pattern, so that there is a dramatic low point near the centre of the work (bars 350–3) where the differences in tempo between A and B are neutralized.

253

Ex. 104

Ex. 105

Concerto for Orchestra

These simultaneous designs stem from a large polyrhythmic formal conception, which is an expansion of the superimposed waves of the Double Concerto's coda. The main entrances of each instrumental group occur at regular intervals. The absolute tempi of these structural pulses are in the ratio 10:9:8:7 (Chart 25).

Chart 25   Structural polyrhythm   (Concerto for Orchestra)

The four groups thus fade in and out of the music each at a regular speed: Carter likes to derive the appearance of randomness from the certainty of natural laws. The structural pulses nearly coincide at the four climactic turning points (bars 141, 284, 488, 550) where the large movements begin. Each of these grand intersections recalls the twelve-note harmony and stormy texture of the opening, though they never repeat the opening literally. They appear like violent tornado gusts at once scattering the previously dominant material and launching new motion. The last such explosion (at bars 550–8) is closest in sound to the opening; the emergence of the solo piano out of the ratchet at bar 560 recalls bar 16 where C first bursts out of the primal chaos. The Coda following bar 560 reverses the pattern of the introduction, so that the work ends with a transformation of the opening's unpitched percussion into cadential chimes.

The large four-movement pattern and the criss-cross tempo design of A and B clarify and give direction to a highly fragmented variational structure. The Concerto is in fact a rapidly paced series of fragmented episodes, each one a variation of the material of the four groups. The contrapuntal combination of materials, the sequence of juxtaposition and the character of the materials themselves are all subject to change, so that while the vivid imagery of the music remains constant, its manifestations are always new. The four-movement design is really a method of placing one orchestral group in the foreground, to emphasize the most identifiable aspects of its character. The grand expressive gestures of C heard clearly at the opening become increasingly abstract and textural as the work progresses; the tidal waves of B, which eventually sweep the entire orchestra away in a *tutti accelerando,* only emerge slowly in the earlier parts of the Concerto. Although there is little exchange of material the nature of juxtaposition becomes more dramatic as the music unfolds. Where C and A seem to be casually interrupted during their movements, the prophetic rumblings of D give rise to a more antagonistic interaction of materials, while the fresh energies of B emerging out of the darkness at bar 419 seem to absorb all the other music in ever more rapid waves of sound; the music of the last quarter of the Concerto is perhaps the most exhilarating Carter has ever written.

257

Ex. 106

String Quartet No. 3

Occasion

The Third Quartet was commissioned by the Juilliard School for the Juilliard Quartet to whom it is dedicated. It was premièred by the Juilliard Quartet— Robert Mann, Earl Carlyss, Samuel Rhodes and Claus Adam—at Alice Tully Hall, Lincoln Center on 23 January 1973. The Quartet was awarded the Pulitzer Prize for Music in 1973, thirteen years after the Second Quartet was similarly honoured.

Concept

The Third Quartet is the most original of the three in its textures and form, and in its sheer sonority. It is also the most difficult to perform. Tempo modulations occur so frequently, and the relationships of cross-pulses are so complex that the Composers Quartet, the only ensemble yet to play all three quartets, has made use of a tape-recorded click-track giving each player his tempo. The Juilliard Quartet, it should be noted, has performed the Quartet without such assistance. The Quartet's rhythmic difficulties, however, are just the beginning. The work redefines instrumental virtuosity. Triple and quadruple stops abound and pizzicato passages demand a Segovian technique.

The sound, texture, and form of the Quartet are inextricable. The sonority is dense and mysterious—like a rain-forest. The musical materials are forcefully characterized, not in the psychological manner of the Second Quartet, but in terms of sonority. The listener feels the impact of each highly-coloured event: slashing chords, delicate filigree, clockwork pizzicato pulses, flamenco strumming, insect-like buzzing and scurrying, arching expressive lines, motionless wide-spaced intervals. Again unlike the spare, silence-punctured textures of the Second Quartet, the sounds of the Third are dense and overgrown. There is only one phrase in the entire work where the gesture of a single instrument emerges from the contrapuntal fabric (see the cello, bars 462–3.) Although the instruments are never called upon to produce untraditional sounds, the overall sonority is strikingly new.

The design of the Quartet grows from fundamental oppositions. Sensitive rubato and espressivo gestures are set against mechanical, strict, impersonal ones. The listener does not feel as in the Piano Concerto that these elements are warring, rather they all seem to be part of an expressive universe that is brought to life through their interaction. The opposition of gestures is reflected formally in the opposition of formal strategies. Carter was particularly interested here in developing a form that would be at once organic and fragmented. Events in the work are sometimes gratuitous acts, seemingly without motivation; yet the overall form is an unbroken circle. The music is at once a series of sharply contrasted moments and a continuous process.

The scheme of the work extrapolates that of the Adagio of the First Quartet: the four instruments are rigorously divided into two duos playing unrelated music. Where the divided ensemble was but one aspect of the First Quartet's variable contrapuntal texture, in the Third Quartet it is a constant. Violin II and the Viola form Duo II; Violin I and Cello, Duo I. The two duos pursue separate ways, never exchanging material. They are fundamentally opposed in rhythmic style: Duo II plays in strict tempo throughout; all of its material derives from complex cross-pulses. Duo I plays in a rubato style. The listener may invoke a number of analogies as suggested by this pairing of opposites—mechanism against living forms, the right hemisphere of the brain against the left, Apollo against Dionysus. But analogies fail; the Quartet is an intense confrontation of fundamental musical elements.

Materials

Duo II plays six different types of music—movements—each associated with an interval:
1) Maestoso—perfect fifth
2) Grazioso—minor seventh
3) Scorrevole—minor second
4) Pizzicato giusto, meccanico—diminished fifth
5) Large tranquillo—major third
6) Appassionato—major sixth

Duo I plays four movements:
1) Furioso—major seventh
2) Leggerissimo—perfect fourth
3) Andante espressivo—minor sixth
4) Pizzicato giocoso—minor third

Duo I uses the major second in all its movements, so that the eleven intervals are partitioned between the two duos. Although the material of each movement is clearly dominated by the sound of a single interval, the overall texture of the work is rarely intervallic. For this reason, Carter extends the harmonic partitioning to include all the three- and four-note chords. These are divided into three groups, one for each duo and a third for the harmony between duos. The overall harmony of the Quartet is controlled by a recurring all-interval twelve-note chord first heard in bar 15. The pitch location of each interval in this chord is stressed in each of the individual movements (Chart 26).

Texture

The Third Quartet is Carter's most rigorously contrapuntal work. Its technique may be traced to the renaissance counterpoint Carter mastered in Paris. The pulse rhythms of Duo II suggest cantus firmus; but the traditional species of academic counterpoint never extended to rhythmic proportions as complex as 63:64 and 20:21, both of which appear here. Similarly the flamboyant, free textures of Duo I can be seen as an extension of 'florid' counterpoint. As in renaissance polyphony the linear motion of each part and the harmonic relation between lines is governed by intervals; but rather than

NUMBERING OF CHORDS IS ACCORDING TO A PERSONAL ORDER

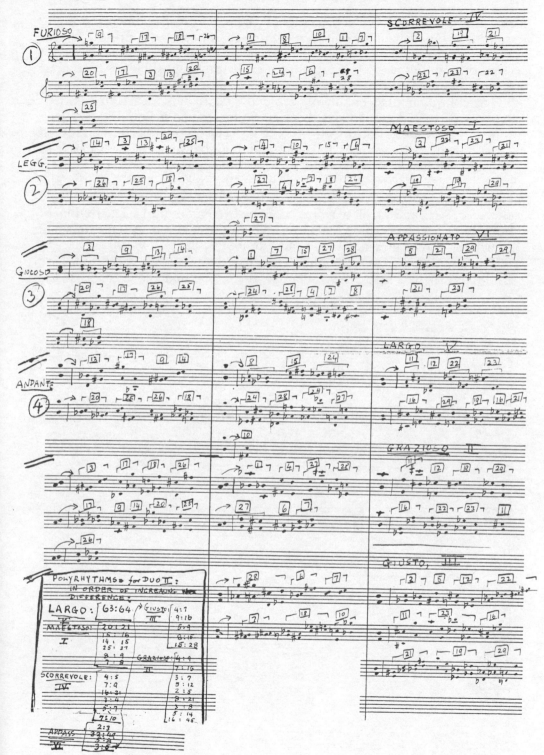

the traditional use of 'consonances', the controlling elements are the dominant intervals of each movement and the three- and four-note chords associated with them. Thus the polyphony has the rigour of older counterpoint but a much greater range of harmonic possibilities, and a far greater freedom of part-writing.

The contrapuntal technique of each duo is heard most clearly in isolation. At bars 67 to 72 Duo II plays its pizzicato meccanico material in changing ratios of cross-pulse (8:15; 9:10) (Ex. 107). The interval of the diminished fifth appears both linearly and contrapuntally between the two parts, as indicated by the dotted lines. At bars 96–105 the pizzicato giocoso of Duo I is heard alone. It stresses the interval of the minor third linearly and harmonically within each part; the overall harmony is governed by four-note chords 3, 9, 13 and 14, all of which combine two minor thirds. The rhythm of both lines is rubato; the changing subdivisions of the beat indicate small ritardandi and accelerandi within each phrase.

The counterpoint between duos—as when the two pizzicato episodes are combined at bars 90 to 96—although it may remind the listener of the

Ex. 107

String Quartet No. 3
© 1973 Associated Music Publishers, Inc. Used by permission

'textural' music of Ligeti or Xenakis, is perhaps closer to medieval music. Each duo is complete in itself, the superimposition of contrasted layers revealing a higher unity as intervals, chords and rhythmic styles interact. The play of intervals is particularly striking throughout. At bars 254–62 the major thirds of Duo II's *Largo tranquillo* are heard against the minor sixths of Duo I's *Andante espressivo*. The slow gliding motion of each duo contrasts the colours of two intervals that serial music often treats as equivalent (Ex. 108).

Unlike the textural music it superficially resembles, the Third Quartet is everywhere imbued with the spirit of polyphony. Every note in the densest intersection will be part of a strong linear design, so that there is an uninterrupted sense of motion. Every harmony is part of a rich but rigorous vocabulary of possibilities. Listeners returning to the Quartet are therefore often surprised by its sudden transformation before their ears from apparent chaos to clarity.

Ex. 108   **String Quartet No. 3**

Largo   tranquillo (stesso tempo)

Form

The movements of each duo are cross-cut in the following order:
Duo II 1, 2, 3, 4, 3, 2, 1, 5, 6, 5, 4, 6
Duo I   1, 2, 3, 4, 2, 1, 4, 3, 2, 4, 1, 3

These sequences are interspersed with silences so that all the movements of both duos are heard in isolation somewhere in the work. The ordering of movements ensures that no two of them in a duo are ever heard in the same succession. The superimposition of movements is planned so that every combination of movements between the two duos is heard. For the overall pattern see Chart 27.

Chart 27   Formal plan   **(String Quartet No. 3)**

Duo I (played continuously)   Duo II (played continuously)

```
 Furioso . . . . . . . . . . . . . . . . . . Maestoso ┐
 (pause) . . . . . . . . . . . . . . . . . . Maestoso │
┌Leggerissimo . . . . . . . . . . . . . . . Maestoso ┘
│Leggerissimo . . . . . . . . . . . . . . . . (pause)
└Leggerissimo . . . . . . . . . . . . . . . Grazioso ┐
┌Andante espressivo . . . . . . . . . . . . Grazioso ┘
└Andante espressivo . . . . . . Pizzicato giusto, meccanico ┐
 (pause) . . . . . . . . . . . Pizzicato giusto, meccanico │
┌Pizzicato giocoso . . . . . . Pizzicato giusto, meccanico ┘
│Pizzicato giocoso . . . . . . . . . . . . . . (pause)
└Pizzicato giocoso . . . . . . . . . . . . Scorrevole ┐
 (pause) . . . . . . . . . . . . . . . . . Scorrevole │
┌Leggerissimo . . . . . . . . . . . . . . . Scorrevole ┘
└Leggerissimo . . . . . . . . Pizzicato giusto, meccanico ┐
┌Furioso . . . . . . . . . . Pizzicato giusto, meccanico ┘
└Furioso . . . . . . . . . . . . . . . . . Grazioso ┐
 (pause) . . . . . . . . . . . . . . . . . Grazioso │
┌Pizzicato giocoso . . . . . . . . . . . . Grazioso ┘
└Pizzicato giocoso . . . . . . . . . . . . Maestoso ┐
┌Andante espressivo . . . . . . . . . . . . Maestoso ┘
│Andante espressivo . . . . . . . . . . . . . (pause)
└Andante espressivo . . . . . . . . . . Largo tranquillo ┐
 (pause) . . . . . . . . . . . . . . . Largo tranquillo │
┌Leggerissimo . . . . . . . . . . . . . Largo tranquillo ┘
└Leggerissimo . . . . . . . . . . . . . . Appassionato ┐
┌Pizzicato giocoso . . . . . . . . . . . . Appassionato ┘
└Pizzicato giocosso . . . . . . . . . . Largo tranquillo ┐
┌Furioso . . . . . . . . . . : . . . . Largo tranquillo ┘
│Furioso . . . . . . . . . . . . . . . . . . (pause)
└Furioso . . . . . . . . . . . . . . . . . Scorrevole ┐
┌Andante espressivo . . . . . . . . . . . Scorrevole ┘
└Andante espressivo . . . . . . . . . . . Appassionato ┐
 (short pause) . . . . . . . . . . . . . Appassionato │
 Furioso . . . . . . . . . . . . . . . . . Appassionato │
 Coda:Furioso; Andante;                                  │
    Leggerissimo; Pizzicato giocoso ┘ . . . . . Appassionato ┘
```

While Duo I has introduced all its material in the first third of the Quartet, Duo II does not reveal its Largo tranquillo and Appassionato material until the second half. Changes from movement to movement in each Duo are usually sudden, but are always covered by continuing music in the other Duo. The music is thus fragmented and continuous at the same time, combining the arbitrary, 'unmotivated' juxtapositions of collage with the 'motivated' continuity of organic development. Each movement, moreover, though broken up, has one climactic point, as well as more subdued passages, so that there is a continuous give-and-take between the duos in terms of relative importance.

Given the mathematical severity of its design, the Quartet is surprisingly clear and dramatic. Because the ten movements are cross-cut there is a great deal of non-literal recapitulation that serves to guide the listener through tangled rain-forests of sound. Moreover the sequence of movements emphasises the superimposition of similar materials: *Pizzicato giusto* with *Pizzicato giocoso* from 90–6; *Scorrevole* and *Leggerissimo* from 136–51; *Largo tranquillo* and *Andante espressivo* from 253–65; *Furioso* and *Appassionato,* 410–39. The sequence also brings the most extremely contrasted movements together near the end of the piece: *Furioso* against *Largo tranquillo* from 338–52 and *Scorrevole* against *Andante espressivo,* 381–95.

Critics who have found the Third Quartet too schematic have followed its plan instead of listening to the music. The Quartet is not a pre-ordained process, indeed its design is as poetic as it is rigorous. The Quartet's form is most reminiscent of literary works such as Faulkner's *As I Lay Dying* or Virginia Woolf's *The Waves* in which fractured episodes describe a continuous action from many different points of view. Every episode differs in its way of emerging, developing and fading out; each superimposed combination has its own poetry. Compare for example the frenzied collision of Leggerissimo and Scorrevole movements with the very different interplay of Leggerissimo and Andante espressivo. The movements are changed by their context, taking on new meaning with every recombination, so that the focus of the work gradually becomes the connections between the two Duos. Beginning at bar 396 these linkages are made explicit as the Appassionato of Duo II and the Furioso of Duo I are cross-cut at an increasingly rapid pace until they merge in the twelve-note tonic at 429. The harmonic arsenals of each duo are then unleashed in a cross-fire of held triple stops beginning at 443 (Ex. 109). This remarkable passage, the Quartet's climax, compresses the material of all the movements. Significantly the work does not end with this gesture. The solo cello at bar 462—with the one and only individual melodic statement of the Quartet—opens the texture: gradually fragments of all the movements build to a furious ending—which flows right into the Quartet's opening. The beginning and end of the work seem to express a single explosive instant; the body of the Quartet reveals smashed atoms, splitting and fusing in ever new forms.

Duo for Violin and Piano

Occasion

Commissioned by the McKim Fund in the Library of Congress and dedicated to the composer's wife, the Duo was completed on 27 April 1974 after a long gestation. It was first performed by Paul Zukofsky, violin and Gilbert Kalish, piano at a New York Philharmonic Prospective Encounter Concert at Cooper Union, New York, 21 March 1975. It was played twice on that occasion with violin and piano placed about thirty feet apart—not the composer's idea but a

THE MUSIC OF OUR CLIMATE, 1967-1974

Ex. 109

String Quartet No. 3
© 1973 Associated Music Publishers, Inc. Used by permission

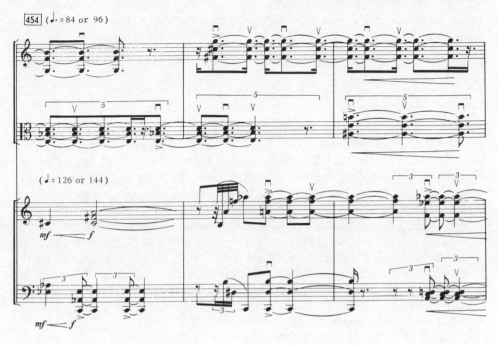

269

dramatic visual image of the musical design, in which the two ill-matched protagonists play equal but contrasting roles. The Duo was soon taken up by other violinists including Rolf Schulte, Robert Mann, Otto Armin, Regis Pasquier, Linda Quan and Ole Bøhn.

Concept

The twentieth century has been surprisingly rich in music for the problematical combination of violin and piano. The Sonata of Debussy, the two Sonatas of Bartok, Stravinsky's Duo Concertant and Schoenberg's Fantasy are all among the most personal and difficult of their composers' works. Carter's Duo though nowhere reminiscent of these compositions, is equally idiosyncratic; of the works of this period it is the one that gives listeners the most trouble. Yet Carter has said on several occasions that he considers it his finest composition, for it raises the achievement of the Third Quartet to a higher level and within a far more difficult medium. In the Quartet, Carter had reached an unprecedented complexity of form and texture by suppressing lyrical expression in favour of textural richness. In the Duo he synthesized the formal advances of the Quartet with the expressive explorations of the Piano Concerto. The result is a work of grand emotional range and density, that leads directly to the poetic concerns of *A Mirror on Which to Dwell* and *Syringa*.

Carter has written that the Duo 'draws its basic character primarily from the contrast between the sounds made by stroking the violin with a bow, that can be sensitively controlled during their duration and the sounds made by striking the piano that, once produced, die away and can only be controlled by being cut short' (WEC 329). The contrast in sound is extended to every element of composition. The instruments are stratified not only in their material—as in the Third Quartet—but also in their way of developing. The piano's music is textural. It is made of large-scale, highly contrasted episodes all built out of complex cross-pulse designs, whose polyphony grows from the contrast of lines, harmonic density and the variety of ways of striking the keyboard: legato, semi-staccato, staccato, martellato. The violin's music, by contrast, is expressive and sensitive. It contrasts many characters, not as 'movements', but in short phrases of a continuously developing line. Thus the two instruments articulate not just different material but contrasted formal processes. This opposition appears at the very opening of the work. Against an impassive, terrifyingly slow polyrhythmic exposition in the piano, whose texture is sustained without inflection for eighty-three bars, the violin plays a rough and passionate recitative, rapidly contrasting all of its expressive characters—appassionato, tenero, ruvido, espressivo—in mercurial, nervous phrases (Ex. 110). The dramatic scale of this passage, which Carter has compared to a man climbing a glacier, recalls the second movement of the Piano Concerto; but this is just the *opening* thrust of the Duo, and its emotional intensity ceaselessly spirals upwards.

Ex. 110

Duo for Violin and Piano
© 1976 Associated Music Publishers, Inc. Used by permission

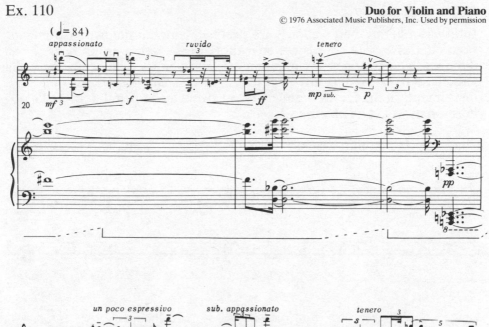

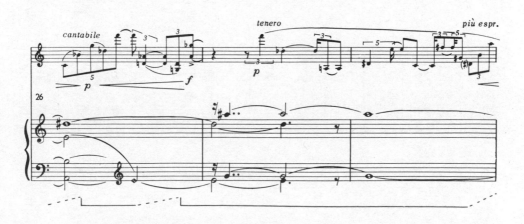

Materials and Form

Intervals and three-note chords are stratified between the two instruments. Four- and five-note chords are split three ways, with a group of the most dissonant and most consonant harmonies reserved for connecting the violin and piano (Chart 28). (Carter's objection to the spatial separation of the two instruments at the Duo's première sprang from a concern that these linking harmonies would be obscured.)

Chart 28   Harmonic scheme   (Duo for Violin and Piano)

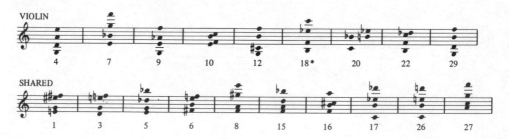

SHARED

As explained above, the form of the work is also stratified; the listener must perceive two formal processes at once. The piano has a series of contrasted movements: a slow polyrhythm of intervals and chords (bars 1–83, see Chart 29); a gradually accelerating scherzando built out of flowing cross-pulsed lines

Chart 29   Opening polyrhythm in piano ($\downarrow$=84)   **(Duo for Violin and Piano)**

minor 3rd = 72 ♪ = MM4.666

major 9th = 75 ♪ = 4.48

tritone or (0 46) = 73 ♪ = 4.603

minor 6th = 69 ♪ = 4.869

5-note chords = 56 ♪ = 6

in contrasted articulations (102–215, with significant interruptions); a pointillistic section based on a three-level polyrhythm of the bottom, middle and top of the piano's range (235–57); a delicate cantabile passage (266–89); a climactic loud, relentless, martellato polyrhythm, summing up all the piano's harmonic and pulse materials (290–309, Ex. 111); and a coda, combining previously heard material in a continuous fade-out, whose final, silence-fragmented tones dimly echo the work's opening. Against these highly contrasted episodes the violin's music gradually evolves out of the opening recitative. Despite many Paganiniesque flights of virtuosity—double-stopped harmonics, rapidly-changing chords—the violin's music is not colouristic but spatial in conception. The violin sweeps through its whole range in arching phrases (see 59–66, Ex. 112), emphasising its intensity of sound, against the piano's greater but less vibrant range. As the work continues, the violin's phrases grow longer, almost imperceptibly, so that it gradually takes over from the piano. From bar 315 onwards the violin builds to a climactic fusion of its materials, leading to an onset of fast music so rhapsodically irregular that it is only approximately co-ordinated with the piano (Ex. 113). In the course

273

Ex. 111

Duo for Violin and Piano
© 1976 Associated Music Publishers, Inc. Used by permission

of the violin's free flight the piano begins its fade-out, so that the last forty bars of the work are dominated by the violin with an unbroken phrase of heroic eloquence and poignant tenderness. As elsewhere in Carter's music, sensitivity triumphs; perhaps in no other work is its victory so heart-felt.

Carter has described the Duo as a series of ironic interactions. Throughout the work, violin and piano contrast sharply in mood. Yet the Duo introduces an irony beyond contrast. From time to time the protagonists seem to come together, as if by chance. Suddenly they find themselves occupying the same terrain (usually a fixed-pitch twelve-note chord); they listen to each other calmly, exchanging pitches while retaining their own harmonies. (See bars 84–94 and 218–31 for example.) In the polarized context of the Duo these magical interchanges seem as ironic as the most extreme contrasts. Like the surprising small revelations of everyday life, their appearance seems miraculous, for they arise from the natural and opposed continuities of each

Ex. 112

Duo for Violin and Piano
© 1976 Associated Music Publishers, Inc. Used by permission

instrument and seem to have no influence on the course of events, and yet they reveal the possibilities of communion. To me the Duo suggests two sleepers whose dreams move apart and converge; perhaps as Ursula Oppens has suggested, it's about love—as the dedication indicates.

Ex. 113

Duo for Violin and Piano

Brass Quintet

Occasion

Commissioned by and dedicated to the American Brass Quintet, the work was written between 15 May and 29 August 1974 and received its first performance in a Charles Ives Festival Broadcast of the BBC (see WÆC 322–5). Much of the Quintet was composed in Aspen where both Carter and the American Brass Quintet were in residence; Carter was able to try out many passages of the work as it was being composed.

Concept

Although the Brass Quintet was written very quickly, its form and textures seem nearly as complex as those of the Third Quartet—as if in composing the Quartet Carter had done enough contrapuntal research for another work which thus appeared effortlessly. The Quintet is in no way an occasional spin-off; it has its own extroverted grandeur.

A brass quintet is a tricky ensemble to balance and sustain. Trumpets and trombones, although related in timbre, do not overlap in range as the violin and cello do, and are very limited in tone-colours. The pairs of trumpets and trombones thus tend to pull apart in sonority. The horn, which should link the other instruments, is so different from them in sound that it only further splinters the ensemble. The solution many composers have tried of using a variety of mutes only compounds the problem; the mutes create the illusion of hearing not five unrelated instruments but ten or fifteen.

Carter's strategy for solving the Quintet's problem of disunity was typically structural. In order both to link all the members of the ensemble and yet also to produce great variety of tone colour, he built the work out of a series of duos and trios, using all the instrumental combinations possible. The Quintet is collaged out of these smaller ensembles (which always overlap) and also out of 'quodlibets' in which all five instruments display their individual characters, in the following sequence:

Q_1 3_1 2_1 Q_2 2_2 3_2 Q_3 3_3 2_3 Q_4 3_4 Horn Cadenza Q_5 2_4 3_5 Slow movement 2_5 Coda

Each trio and duo is based on a single interval, as is the horn cadenza:

trio 1—two trumpets and 1st trombone—minor sixth—'lightly'
duo 1— horn and 2nd trombone—perfect fourth—'vigorously'
duo 2—2nd trumpet and horn—minor third—'humorously'
trio 2—1st trumpet, horn, 2nd trombone—perfect fifth—'majestically'
trio 3—trumpets and horn—major second—'smoothly flowing'
duo 3—two trombones—major third—'extravagant'
trio 4—1st trumpet, trombones—major sixth—'lyrically'
horn cadenza—augmented fourth—'menacingly'
duo 4—trumpets—major seventh—'furious'
trio 5—horn and trombones—minor second—'angry'
duo 5—2nd trumpet, 1st trombone—minor seventh—'dramatic'

These different episodes and their intervals give each instrument a unique intervallic and gestural vocabulary which comes to the fore during the quodlibets:

trumpet 1		M2						p5	m6	M6			M7
trumpet 2		M2	m3						m6			m7	M7
horn	m2	M2	m3		p4	A4	p5						
trombone 1	m2			M3					m6	M6	m7		
trombone 2	m2			M3	p4			p5		M6			

The slow movement, first heard at the opening of the piece and anticipated during the quodlibets, brings all the harmonies of the work together.

As in the Second Quartet, there is a double structure, one emphasizing the total ensemble, the other its smaller components. The horn solo at the work's centre, with its menacing tritones and romantic echo effects (Triton's wreathèd horn?), represents the extreme in individualism, while the slow movement—given a climactic position unique in Carter's work—celebrates the pleasures of communal music-making. The expressive weight and surprising placement of the slow section may have been a reaction to the predominantly fast music of the Third Quartet, though all the works of the '70s use dramatic, assymetrical forms different from the more balanced designs of Carter's earlier music. The conflict in tendencies here is treated with much humour. Typical of Carter's playfulness is the ensemble's harmonic response to the horn. The horn's tritones—traditionally the most dissonant intervals—here sound romantically nostalgic. The other instruments counter them with cruel octaves—traditionally the most consonant intervals, but in the context of non-tonal music, shocking and disruptive. Consonance has become the devil in music.

The short episodes from which the Quintet is built are more sharply and variously characterized than those of the Third Quartet. In its remarkable range of moods the Quintet would be well suited to choreographic treatment. 'Pop' elements are heard in the jazzy music of duo 1 and in the concert-in-the-park 'cornet' solo of the 1st trumpet in trio 4 (201–32). The brilliant fanfare for two trumpets in duo 4 could almost stand on its own, as could the clownish acrobatics of the two trombones in duo 2 (bars 150–68), with their 'rips'. The superimposition of the trombones' glissandi on the cascading music of trio 2 is perhaps the most spectacular textural event of the work (Ex. 114), though the menacing eruption of the solo horn at the height of the 1st trumpet's soaring lyrical song is the most dramatic intersection of events.

Despite the brilliance of the duos and trios, however, the slow movement stands out as the climax of the work. Here finally the possibilities of the total ensemble are realized in a sustained harmonic meditation. Based on a fixed-pitch design, the music slowly changes in colour, density and harmony. In the course of the movement every interval, three-, four- and five-note chord is heard in an unbroken progression whose highpoint is the magical, radiant appearance of chord 7—the pentatonic scale at bar 383 (Chart 30). Just as the episodes of the Quintet demonstrated the expressive possibilities of each interval, so the slow movement reveals their luminous connections. It is an

277

encyclopaedic summation of the harmonic researches Carter began in the late
'60s, and its quietly confident tone, free of all anxiety, radiates a transcendent
joy not heard in Carter's music since *The Harmony of Morning*.

Ex. 114

Brass Quintet
© 1976 Associated Music Publishers, Inc. Used by permission

(A)

(B)

[Transposed score; Trumpets in B♭, Horn in F]

278

Chart 30   Harmonic scheme   **(Brass Quintet)**

bars 379-383 Harmony

5-23   5-11   4-3   5-24   5-9   4-11   5-15

4-17   5-16   4-27   5-23   4-14   5-7   4-4

Fixed pitches of the Adagio (358-384)

Notes to Part 8

1. Wallace Stevens: *Selected Poems,* op. cit. p. 124
2. Wallace Stevens: *Poems,* (New York: Vintage, 1959) p. 94
3. St John Perse: *Vents* ('Winds'), trans. Hugh Chisholm, (New York: Pantheon Books, Bollingen Series No. 34, 1953)

279

9

Music and Poetry, 1975–1979

In the '70s Carter completed as many works as in the two previous decades combined. The increased rate of composition—*A Symphony of Three Orchestras* was written in six months—has been matched by ever greater formal and poetic daring. Indeed the works from the Third Quartet onwards are so adventurous in conception that there is little in the way of traditional musical terminology that can be used to describe their forms, harmonies, or, in the case of *Syringa,* even their genre. While the continued exploration of abstract discourse in the Third Quartet, Duo and Brass Quintet was to be expected, Carter's preoccupation with the voice and with poetic subjects in the next three works seemed at first a surprising development.

Although the majority of his early works were vocal, Carter abandoned the voice after *Emblems.* The speed and contrapuntal density of his mature idiom must have seemed ill-suited to the needs of projecting a text clearly, and the rhythmic language developed from the Cello Sonata onwards was certainly beyond the technical range of most singers. And yet, as we have seen, in taking his music beyond the voice, Carter gave it the complexity of texture and continuity that have characterized modern poetry since the Symbolist movement—and that most modern music had failed to pursue. The intensely evocative colours of the Concerto for Orchestra, the collaged textures of the Third Quartet and Brass Quintet, and the ironically counterpointed continuities of the Duo can be seen as final preparations for Carter's return to the word. His idiom was now capable of clarity and complexity at the same time, so that it could project at once the surface and structure of the most challenging modern poetry.

Although the recent works are galactically distant in style from the earlier vocal compositions, there is a notable constancy in vocal and poetic treatment linking songs as different as *Warble for Lilac Time* and 'Sandpiper' (in *A Mirror on Which to Dwell*). The connections may be traced to the Boulanger years, when Carter sang through most of the Bach Cantatas. Conceptually, Carter's vocal treatment recalls Bach's. The voice is always one thread in a contrapuntal fabric. The vocal line thus seems 'instrumental' because it is set against instruments that never form a merely passive or decorative accompaniment. Very often a single instrument comes to the fore as an obbligato; Carter himself has compared the oboe part in 'Sandpiper' to the typical obbligati of Bach's arias. The double bass in the preceding song, 'Argument', has a similar function, though one that Bach would never have assigned to that instrument.

As with Bach, Carter's settings of texts are at once literal and structural. The musical design and materials of each setting stem from an almost palpable evocation of the words, yet there is no 'local colour'. Rather the oboe's chirps in 'Sandpiper', the guitar's Orphic strumming in *Syringa* and even the bits of *Stars and Stripes Forever* in 'A View of the Capitol from the Library of Congress' are all fundamental elements in compositional designs so powerful in their contrapuntal facture that they can integrate the most stunning literalism, the most spontaneous humour.

Hart Crane—whose poems inspired but are not sung in *A Symphony*—Elizabeth Bishop, and John Ashbery are poets of different generations, styles and moods. How can one composer interpret such varied sensibilities and styles? Carter sets a text to music in much the same way that Balanchine weds music to dance—both artists seek out material that will challenge and stimulate their own imaginations; they extend their own languages to encompass the creations of others. In Carter's settings there is no mannered, reductive rendering of the text; there are no interludes or parentheses indicating, in the tired romantic tradition, how the composer *feels* about the poems. Instead there is absolute artistic sympathy which clarifies the text for the listener. Carter is a dramatist of great range projecting his imagination onto personae far removed from his own personality. The Greek fragments he counterposed to John Ashbery's 'Syringa' are a good test case here. They do not represent the composer's point of view; rather they serve to dramatize the pathos of Ashbery's language, its sense of lost meaning, spent passion, 'hidden syllables'.

A Mirror on Which to Dwell
(Six poems of Elizabeth Bishop)

Occasion

A Mirror was commissioned by Speculum Musicae, New York's most prominent ensemble for contemporary music, in honour of the United States Bicentennial, with grants from the New York State Council on the Arts, the Mellon Foundation, Milton M. Scofield, Murray Socolof, Fred Sherry and Bernard E. Brandes. It is dedicated to the soprano Susan Davenny Wyner and Speculum Musicae who gave the first performance of *A Mirror,* conducted by Richard Fitz, at Hunter College Playhouse, New York City, 24 February 1976. The work is scored for nine players; each song has a different instrumentation.

Anaphora: Alto flute, oboe, clarinet B♭, vibraphone, piano, violin, viola, cello, bass

Argument: Alto flute, bass clarinet, four bongos, piano, cello, bass

Sandpiper: Oboe, piano, violin, viola, cello, bass

Insomnia: Piccolo, marimba, violin, viola

A View of the Capitol: Flute-piccolo, oboe, clarinet B♭ and E♭, one percussionist playing snare drum, bass drum, triangle, suspended cymbal, piano, violin, viola, cello, bass

O Breath: Alto flute, cor anglais, bass clarinet, suspended cymbal, bass drum, violin, viola, cello, bass

Concept

Because the songs were intended for a soprano, Carter sought out the works of female poets, so that the singer's dramatic relation to the text would be very direct. Robert Lowell recommended to Carter the poetry of Elizabeth Bishop, which had had a profound impact on his own development. At first glance her poems seem remote from the epic texts Carter has associated with his music—*De Rerum Natura* or *Vents*. Unlike these, Bishop's poems are specific, brief, unheroic. Yet the distinctive quality of her poems is their ability to move from the commonplace to the universal. The landscapes and domestic scenes have the intensity of anxiously precise observation and at the same time an epic spaciousness that extends the personal vision outwards:

> The world is a mist. And then the world is
> minute and vast and clear.
>
> *(Sandpiper)*[1]

Many of Bishop's poems deal with borders, coastlines, beaches—places where opposites meet but are never reconciled, like the lovers' bed in 'O Breath'. She views these complex oppositions with a calm and clear eye, which the composer of the Third Quartet obviously finds sympathetic.

The six songs of *A Mirror* are not connected; each has its own technique and colour. Carter chose and arranged them so as to reflect two aspects of Elizabeth Bishop's art: the geographical and the personal. Two groups of poems are interlaced. Three describe the relationship between the poet and the world: 'Anaphora', 'Sandpiper', 'A View of the Capitol from the Library of Congress'. The other three, appearing second, fourth and sixth, are about love. Both series move from the general to the specific. 'A View of the Capitol' is the most explicitly public and 'O Breath' the most intensely private, almost existing in a world beyond communication where both word and music are reduced to the common factor of breathing. 'Insomnia', containing the title of the cycle (also a reference to Speculum Musicae, music's mirror) is the emotional centre of the music.

Anaphora

> Each day with so much ceremony
> begins, with birds, with bells,
> with whistles from a factory;
> such white-gold skies our eyes
> first open on, such brilliant walls

that for a moment we wonder
'Where is the music coming from, the energy?
The day was meant for what ineffable creature
we must have missed?' Oh promptly he
appears and takes his earthly nature
    instantly, instantly falls
    victim of long intrigue,
    assuming memory and mortal
    mortal fatigue.

More slowly falling into sight
and showering into stippled faces,
darkening, condensing all his light;
in spite of all the dreaming
squandered upon him with that look,
suffers our uses and abuses,
sinks through the drift of bodies,
sinks through the drift of classes
to evening to the beggar in the park
who, weary, without lamp or book
    prepares stupendous studies:
    the fiery event
    of every day in endless
    endless assent.

The first poem is the most universal in subject, and receives the most abstract musical treatment. The title refers to a figure of speech in which a word is repeated in different clauses or lines, as with 'instantly' and 'mortal'. Its root meaning is 'carrying backwards', suggesting a recessional. The poem is a falling progression from the day's primal energy to man's mortal fatigue. The poet, 'the beggar in the park', reverses the fall through 'stupendous studies' and 'endless assent'. The pun implied in the last word perhaps suggests the poet's willed, even deceptive, inversion of reality. The poem is both cosmology and ontology; it creates a world and places the hapless poet in its midst to give it meaning.

The musical structure, one of the most remarkable designs in recent music, reflects the universal and fundamental theme of the poem. The pitches of the chromatic scale are each given a single octave position, forming a twelve-note chord whose pitches all lie within the range of the soprano (Chart 31). These are the only pitches used in the song. The entire twelve-note chord, however, rarely appears. A six-note chord, 6–35 (0, 1, 2, 4, 7, 8) is the recurrent harmonic unit. In changing transpositions, the chord is mapped on to the fixed twelve-note structure, assuming ever-changing intervallic shapes. This six-note chord has come to play a role in Carter's music as important as that of the all-interval tetrachords in earlier works. Like them it uniquely combines all possible elements of a lower order; it is the only six-note chord that contains all twelve three-note chords. In 'Anaphora' this property is made explicit: the hexachord is constantly articulated as the sum of two triads, in

Chart 31   Harmonic and rhythmic schemes   (Anaphora)

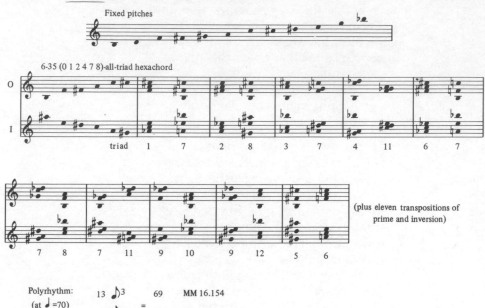

ever-changing combinations. (See the piano and vibraphone from bar 59 to the end, Ex. 115).

The resulting texture is both rigid and free. Despite the drastic limitations in pitch-content, the twenty-four possible transpositions of the hexachord in prime and inverted forms and their changing triadic presentation create a harmony of subtly shifting colours. The vocal line illuminates the myriad resources of the harmonic matrix by emphasizing one interval after another— perfect fifths, major and minor thirds, minor sevenths, and, climactically, major ninths. The rhythm of the song is as structurally conceived as its harmony. A rhythmic backbone is formed by a cross-pulse between piano and vibraphone (sometimes passing to the other instruments) in a tempo ratio of 65:69. The two instruments coincide only once, at bar 23, the poem's still

Ex. 115

Anaphora (A Mirror on Which to Dwell)
© 1977 Associated Music Publishers, Inc. Used by permission

centre. Against this constant polyrhythm the voice, beginning with a line of limitless energy and sweep, gradually slows and fades and then regains its initial force.

The music's harmonic and rhythmic structures serve to evoke and elucidate the text. The constant repetition of pitches in ever-new chordal transpositions and inversions is musical anaphora. The vocal trajectory mirrors the poem's theme of faded and recreated energies; the unique coincidence of the two crossed pulses occurs at the lowpoint of the ebbing initial burst, just before the poet's entrance. The shared pulse is thus a turning point, marking the birth of a new vision, the artist's reconstruction of life's primal force in 'stupendous studies'. The setting of 'stupendous' is climactic—and absolutely characteristic in its daring union of the literal and the structural. The voice leaps downwards nearly two octaves (Ex. 116). A stupendous jump, to be sure, but also the only melodic delineation of the song's harmonic extremes and the only time the voice articulates the two structural pulses.

Argument

> Days that cannot bring you near
> or will not,
> Distance trying to appear
> something more than obstinate,
> argue argue argue with me
> endlessly
> neither proving you less wanted nor less dear.

285

Ex. 116

Anaphora (A Mirror on Which to Dwell)
© 1977 Associated Music Publishers, Inc. Used by permission

Distance: Remember all that land
beneath the plane;
that coastline
of dim beaches deep in sand
stretching indistinguishably
all the way,
all the way to where my reasons end?

Days: And think
of all those cluttered instruments,
one to a fact,
canceling each other's experience; .
how they were
like some hideous calendar
'Compliments of Never & Forever, Inc. .'

The intimidating sound
of these voices
we must separately find
can and shall be vanquished:
Days and Distance disarrayed again
and gone
both for good and from the gentle battleground.

At once abstract and personal, 'Argument' portrays a lovers' dispute, as a
struggle between 'days' and 'distance', space and time—the basic categories
of human separation. The unified ensemble of 'Anaphora' is here split in two,
superimposing two arguments. The voice, supported by alto flute and bass
clarinet, is shadowed by the double bass, which plays an expressive,
grotesque anti-song aided by the cello. The vast space between soprano and

Chart 32 Harmonic scheme and materials (Argument)

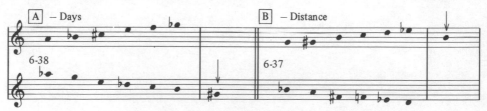

3 Disjunct elements:

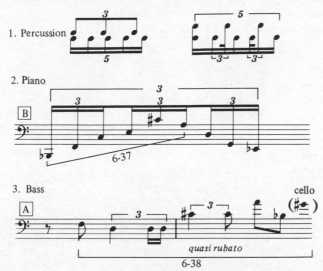

bass is filled in by a fast dialogue between piano and bongos. Each argument has its own harmonic and rhythmic design. The voice-bass viol dispute is associated with chord 6–38 (0, 1, 2, 5, 8, 9) and rubato rhythms. The piano-bongo skirmish uses chord 6–37 (0, 1, 3, 4, 7, 8) and fast pulse rhythms (Chart 32). The piano plays in nonuplets at the speed of MM 756 while the bongo superimposes triplet and quintuplet divisions of the MM 84 beat. The dual structure of the song is emphasized in the voice by two recurring pitches: G♯ heard with 'days' and B with 'distance'. The climactic montage of all these elements comes at bars 27–32 (Ex. 117).

The music here does not simply illustrate the words; rather the words seem themselves to be an image of Carter's music, built out of arguments. Yet both poem and music suggest a reconciliation. The 'gentle battleground' of the conclusion reminds us that the poem is about a lovers' quarrel. The music takes on a more intimate colouring as the piano—which has gradually ascended throughout the song—tinkles away at the top of the keyboard, echoed by fleeting fragments on the bongos.

Sandpiper

> The roaring alongside he takes for granted,
> and that every so often the world is bound to shake.
> He runs, he runs to the south, finical, awkward,
> in a state of controlled panic, a student of Blake.
>
> The beach hisses like fat. On his left, a sheet
> of interrupting water comes and goes
> and glazes over his dark and brittle feet.
> He runs, he runs straight through it, watching his toes.

—Watching, rather, the spaces of sand between them,
where (no detail too small) the Atlantic drains
rapidly backwards and downwards. As he runs,
he stares at the dragging grains.

The world is a mist. And then the world is
minute and vast and clear. The tide
is higher or lower. He couldn't tell you which.
His beak is focussed; he is preoccupied,

looking for something, something, something.
Poor bird, he is obsessed!
The millions of grains are black, white, tan, and gray,
mixed with quartz grains, rose and amethyst.

Ex. 117

Argument (A Mirror on Which to Dwell)
© 1977 Associated Music Publishers, Inc. Used by permission

The Sandpiper is 'a student of Blake', a poet obsessively seeking the world in a grain of sand. In the music the sandpiper appears as a frantic oboe pecking away at staccato semitones interspersed with multiphonic screeches. If the poem's bird is a self-parody of the poet, the oboe parodistically represents the composer fanatically choosing and placing notes, trying to impose order on a chaotic world (Carter played the oboe at Harvard).

The music meshes two elements. The oboe plays at the same speed throughout, MM 525, using the intervals of semitone, minor third and perfect fifth. The strings and piano, beautifully evoking hissing sands and breaking surf, play spacious harmonies derived from minor sixths, major sevenths and major ninths. The string rhythm is fluid, with frequent changes of tempo, all co-ordinated with the constant motion of the oboe (Chart 33).

Chart 33   Two elements   **(Sandpiper)**

A   Oboe: same note-lengths throughout ♪=M 525

semitones, minor thirds, perfect fifths

B   Strings and Piano: rubato – many changes in tempo
    Harmonies

The voice mediates between both elements, sometimes calm and spacious—'the world is a mist'—elsewhere as jumpy as the oboe, as in their Bach-like duet at bars 49–54.

Insomnia

> The moon in the bureau mirror
> looks out a million miles
> (and perhaps with pride, at herself,
> but she never, never smiles)
> far and away beyond sleep, or
> perhaps she's a daytime sleeper.
>
> By the Universe deserted,
> *she*'d tell it to go to hell,
> and she'd find a body of water,
> or a mirror, on which to dwell.
> So wrap up care in a cobweb
> and drop it down the well
>
> into that world inverted
> where left is always right,
> where the shadows are really the body,
> where we stay awake all night,
> where the heavens are shallow as the sea
> is now deep, and you love me.

291

Many listeners have noted the striking clarity of all the songs in *A Mirror*. 'Insomnia' is the simplest of them all; I can think of no other work of Carter's that achieves so much with such spare strokes; the inverted thirds at:

> where left is always right

are exquisitely mimetic. Yet even the sparse texture of the song, scored for just four instruments, suggests several layers of feelings. The high slow-moving lines of piccolo and violin contrast with the nervous repeated rattle of the marimba and viola, reflecting the poem's contrast of an insomniac with the reflected moon. Piccolo and violin outline a cross-pulse of 84:85 (every fourteenth quintuplet against every seventeenth sextuplet of the slow MM 54 pulse). Marimba and viola play at steady speeds of MM 648, 432 and 324, until bar 23 where they join the flute and violin as the singer describes the 'inverted' world dwelling on the mirror. All the harmonic material of the song is derived from the first four pitches of the voice and their inversion which immediately follows (Chart 34).

Chart 34   Three elements   (Insomnia)

A   Marimba + Viola

B   Piccolo + Violin: polyrhythm of 85: 84

$$17 \quad \flat^6 \quad : \quad 14 \quad \flat^5$$

C   Voice-palindromes to suggest Mirror

Motif of C :

Chords

292

The ease with which the song evokes the thoughts of an active mind in the still hours of the night may be explained, in part, by noting that the composer has occasional bouts of insomnia himself, which he usually tries to fight off by conjugating irregular Italian, German or Greek verbs.

A View of the Capitol from the Library of Congress

Moving from left to left, the light
is heavy on the Dome, and coarse.
One small lunette turns it aside
and blankly stares off to the side
like a big white old wall-eyed horse.

On the east steps the Air Force Band
in uniforms of Air Force blue
is playing hard and loud, but—queer—
the music doesn't quite come through.

It comes in snatches, dim then keen,
then mute, and yet there is no breeze.
The giant trees stand in between.
I think the trees must intervene,

catching the music in their leaves
like gold-dust, till each big leaf sags.
Unceasingly the little flags
feed their limp stripes into the air,
and the band's efforts vanish there.

Great shades, edge over,
give the music room.
The gathered brasses want to go
boom—boom.

A Mirror was a Bicentennial commission and 'A View' responds to the occasion, portraying the relation of artist and government comically (how else?). The poet's playful, perverse images of the Capitol set off a jumbled, Ivesian texture. Again there are two elements (Chart 35). The Maestoso opening describes not the Capitol dome but the giant trees which block the view and muffle the sound of the Air Force band. The band's Sousa-like small-intervalled fragments are projected on majestic major ninths. The rhythmic structure also inverts the expected confrontation. The opening tempo remains constant in the voice and the viola, which plays an important obbligato. The band music by contrast is unsteady and out of phase. The song's tone is just slightly menacing, for all its comedy. At the close, 'the gathered brasses want to go boom-boom' drops an ominous Cold War hint that Carter underscores by having the 'booms' intensely whispered. The texture of the song may suggest Charles Ives, but instead of Ives's idealized vision of a harmonious democracy, 'A View' gives a more realistic picture of the tense relation between the artist and American society.

293

Chart 35   Two elements   (A View of The Capitol)

Background

'Alla marcia'

O Breath

> Beneath that loved   and celebrated breast,
> silent, bored really   blindly veined,
> grieves, maybe   lives and lets
> live, passes   bets,
> something moving   but invisibly,
> and with what clamour   why restrained
> I cannot fathom   even a ripple.
> (See the thin flying   of nine black hairs
> four around one five the other nipple,   ·
> flying almost intolerably   on your own breath.)
> Equivocal, but what we have in common's   bound to be there,
> whatever we must own   equivalents for,
> something that maybe I   could bargain with
> and make a separate peace   beneath
> within   if never with.

The poet looks at her sleeping lover and finds that all that unites them is breathing. Each of the poems in *A Mirror* is about the attempt to cross a boundary. 'O Breath' is the ultimate statement of this theme in its most intimate human form. The music counterposes two kinds of breathing. The soprano sings gasping melismatic fragments, as if out of breath. Her florid line is punctured with rests which mirror the split lines of the poem. The vocal line uses every interval except perfect fifth and minor seventh. These two intervals dominate the slow, swelling chords heard in the orchestra. The instrumental texture suggests the rise and fall of a deep sleeper's breath; it is based on a three-part polyrhythm of every forty-third sixth of a beat, every thirty-seventh fifth of a beat and every sixty-fifth ninth of a beat. Of course this pattern is not meant to be recognized; the complex cross-play of very slow pulses (MM 8.372, 8.108 and 8.308) gives the impression of a regular pulse surrounded by slightly irregular swelling and fading. By contrast the soprano's rhythm is extremely free.

Once again the conception of the song is starkly simple. Yet without any Bergian demands for empathy it devastatingly evokes an unnamed emotion somewhere between acceptance and despair. The modesty and humanity of all the songs in *A Mirror on Which to Dwell* are a tribute to Elizabeth Bishop's pursuit of the innermost feelings of everyday existence.

A Symphony of Three Orchestras

Occasion

Begun in June 1976 and completed on 31 December of that year, *A Symphony* was commissioned by the New York Philharmonic under a grant to six orchestras (Boston, Chicago, Cleveland, Los Angeles, New York and Philadelphia) from the National Endowment for the Arts in honour of the United States Bicentennial. The NEA plan was that each orchestra would commission one work but perform all six commissioned works; the more conservative orchestras have not yet kept their part of the agreement. The score is dedicated to Pierre Boulez and the New York Philharmonic, who gave *A Symphony* its première at Avery Fisher Hall, 17 February 1977.

Concept

Ever since discovering Hart Crane's poem *The Bridge* while he was at Harvard, Carter had planned to set it as a large choral cantata. Although Crane entered his music in *Pocahontas,* whose scenario was derived from *The Bridge,* and in *Voyage,* the projected cantata languished, chiefly because of the absence of large professional choruses in America who could perform Carter's music. Finally Carter decided to transform the choral setting into a symphonic work whose sounds, textures and forms would evoke Crane's life and work in purely abstract terms. Neither a traditional symphony nor a tone poem, *A Symphony of Three Orchestras* might best be termed a 'portrait of Hart Crane' to be set beside *Pli selon pli,* Boulez's 'portrait' of Mallarmé; the two works, whose composers greatly admire each other's music, are at least as different as the two poets they portray.

Hart Crane flamboyantly lived out the conflicting values of the modernism of the American '20s; he leapt to his death in the Gulf of Mexico in 1932. Like Eliot and Pound, he wrote of a world which (as Carter has said) 'for all its fascinating modernism, would eventually prove a paralyzing wasteland, depriving him of his poetic gift, even destroying him completely'. Unlike Eliot or Pound, Crane was unable to escape to Europe. His fate was more distinctly and tragically American—as perhaps was his poetry which is at once nihilistic and monumental, jazzy and Miltonic. Though occasionally pretentious, awkward or intoxicatedly reckless in syntax, his poems often achieve the epic vision of modern America Crane self-consciously strove for. While he certainly does not rank with the greatest modern poets, Crane's visionary strengths and tragic failings are emblematic of the New York avant-garde of the 1920s, the milieu in which Carter first decided to become a composer. Crane, moreover, as a *poète maudit* symbolizes in extreme form the perilous position of the American artist. For those unfamiliar with Crane's story, Robert Lowell's 'Words for Hart Crane'[2] can well illustrate what his life and work mean to Carter:

> When the Pulitzers showered on some dope
> or screw who flushed our dry mouths out with soap

few people would consider why I took
to stalking sailors, and scattered Uncle Sam's
phoney gold-plated laurels to the birds.
Because I knew my Whitman like a book
Stranger in America, tell my country: I,
Catullus redivivus, once the rage
of the Village and Paris, used to play my role
of homosexual, wolfing the stray lambs
who hungered by the Place de la Concorde.
My profit was a pocket with a hole.
Who asks for me, the Shelley of my age,
must lay his heart out for my bed and board.

Crane's poetry compresses past, present and future in a fragmented cinematic montage:

I think of cinemas, panoramic sleights
With multitudes bent toward some flashing scene.[3]

The Brooklyn Bridge in Crane's poem is at once mythical and real, spanning a river and a continent, linking the Indian past with the mechanical future. To suggest the dense, flickering imagery of Crane's poems Carter conceived a work for three orchestras of contrasting sonorities whose music would unfold simultaneously. As in the Concerto for Orchestra, much of the music's sound-imagery was suggested by the text. The opening, which John Russell has called the definitive portrait of New York in sound, evokes:

How many dawns, chill from his rippling rest
The seagull's wings shall dip and pivot him,
Shedding white rings of tumult, building high
Over the chained bay waters Liberty—

Then, with inviolate curve, forsake our eyes
As apparitional as sails that cross
Some page of figures to be filed away;
—Till elevators drop us from our day. . . .[4]

The transition from natural to mechanical motion in these lines is a general theme of *The Bridge,* and inspired the form of *A Symphony.* The music, like the poem, describes a continuous descent:

Lead-perforated fuselage, escutcheoned wings
Lift agonized quittance, tilting from the invisible brink
Now eagle bright, now
                        quarry-hid, twist-
                                    -ing, sink with
Enormous repercussive list-
                        -ings down
Giddily spiraled
                    gauntlets, upturned, unlooping

in guerrilla sleights, trapped in combustion gyr-
Ing, dance the curdled depth
                              down whizzing
Zodiacs, dashed
            (now nearing fast the Cape!)
                          down gravitation's
                              vortex into crashed
. . . dispersion . . . into mashed and shapeless débris . . . .[5]

A related theme is that of fallen men, like Rip Van Winkle, whom Carter says may be heard in the Scherzando movement of Orchestra III:

> *And Rip forgot the office hours,*
> *and he forgot the pay:*
> *Van Winkle sweeps a tenement*
> *way down on Avenue A,*[6]

Crane's Rip Van Winkle is not comic; he is human debris, like the hoboes who appear later in the poem:

> Behind
> My father's cannery works I used to see
> Rail-squatters ranged in nomad raillery,
> The ancient men—wifeless or runaway
> Hobo-trekkers that forever search
> An empire wilderness of freight and rails.[7]

The world's fall from natural beauty to mechanical terror and the fall of men are themes that appear more autobiographically in Crane's other poems. Carter has said that the bell-like movement in Orchestra II was inspired by 'The Broken Tower':

> The bell-rope that gathers God at dawn
> Dispatches me as though I dropped down the knell
> Of a spent day. . . .
> The bells, I say the bells break down their tower;
> And swing I know not where. Their tongues engrave
> Membrane through marrow, my long-scattered score
> Of broken intervals. . . . And I, their sexton slave! . . .[8]

The connections between the falling bells, symbolising the disappearance of faith, and Crane's own death are even more explicit in 'The Return':

> The sea raised up a campanile . . . The wind I heard
> Of brine partaking, whirling spout in shower
> Of column kiss—that breakers spouted, sheared
> Back into bosom—me—her, into natal power . . .[9]

For Crane made his poems inseparable from his life and death; *A Symphony* evokes at once the poems and the man in a continuous descent whose inviolate curve, like the poet's life, is suddenly broken:

297

> The forked crash of split thunder parts
> Our hearing momentwise . . .

The music evokes life and death, lyrical motion and paralysis in a continuous span built from fragments of shattered images, 'one arc synoptic of all tides below'.

Materials

A standard symphony orchestra (triple winds, five horns, five percussionists) is divided into three contrasting groups:

Orchestra I: brass, timpani, strings

Orchestra II: three clarinets, vibraphone, chimes, xylophone, marimba, long drum, low tom-tom, piano, four violins, six cellos, two basses

Orchestra III: woodwinds (without clarinets), horns, metal percussion, strings (no cellos)

Orchestra II seated at the centre is a concertante group, each of whose movements is dominated by solo instruments. The outer orchestras play more textural music.

Chart 36   Twelve movements   (A Symphony of Three Orchestras)

Orchestra I: Brass, timpani, strings.

Movement	Bars	Interval	Chord	Speed	Character-colour
1	38-46 237-259	m6	 *(musical notation)*	MM 12	sostenuto
2	55-89 207-226	A4	 *(musical notation)*	60	molto espr.
3	105-121 157-192	M2	 *(musical notation)*	420	flowing
4	127-142 273-309	m2 m9	 *(musical notation)*	120 140~	angry

Orchestra II: 3 Clarinets, Vibraphone, chimes, xylophone, marimba, Piano, 4 violins, 6 celli, 2 basses.

Movement	Bars	Interval	Chord	Speed	Character-colour
1	50-67 131-164	P5	 *(musical notation)*	45	bell-like
2	82-112 250-264	m7	 *(musical notation)*	240	grazioso (clarinets)
3	178-199 298-318	A4	 *(musical notation)*	80	cantabile, espr. (celli)
4	215-242 268-285	m3	 *(musical notation)*	accel. to 540	accelerating (piano)

Orchestra III: Flutes, oboes, bassoons, horns, violins, violas, basses, non-pitched percussion.

1	40-61 291-314	M7		360	giocoso
2	75-100 185-221	M3		24	sostenuto
3	108-136 233-245	P4		180	flutter-tongue tremolandi
4	150-171 254-280	M6		105	espr. cantabile

Introduction bars 1-39; Coda, bars 318-394

Each orchestra has four movements—the work's only trace of traditional symphonic form—which are split and cross-cut. The twelve movements are distinct in harmony, timbre, expressive character and tempo (Chart 36).

The harmonic motion of the work is controlled by the interplay of the dominant intervals and triad of each movement with a recurrent forty-five-note 'tonic' chord, made up of four versions of an all-interval twelve-note chord three of whose notes are the same (Chart 37).

Chart 37   Four versions of all-interval chord (5, 10, 4, 2, 7, 9, 1, 6, 3, 11, 8) = 45-note 'tonic chord'

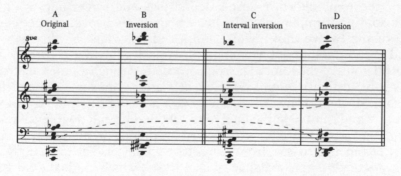

Each interval of the twelve movements has four fixed positions in the forty-five-note chord, which focus harmonic motion within them (Chart 38).

Form

The word 'Symphony' here denotes not form but process, the bringing together of sounds. Stravinsky implied this meaning in his Symphonies of Wind Instruments. There, disparate materials gradually merge in a nearly static chorale. Carter's materials are more fluid than Stravinsky's; their convergence yields fission, not fusion.

Chart 38   Location of each interval of the twelve movements in the four fixed
            all-interval chords

A,B,C,D designate the four all-interval chords.

Roman numerals indicate each of the three orchestras.

Arabic numeral indicates movement number.

The work falls into three distinct parts: an Introduction in which the highest notes of the tonic chord in suspended strings and screeching woodwinds frame a soaring trumpet solo; the main body of the work, a three-levelled collage of the twelve movements; and a coda in which all the material is reduced to chordal sounds beginning with explosive thunder-chords sounding the central notes of the tonic. The coda proceeds through a series of terrifying factory-noise ostinati, unprecedented in Carter's music, to a concluding piano solo, diving downwards to the lowest notes of the tonic chord which reverberate and rumble in the final notes of the tuba and double basses. The introduction and coda are the extremes of the double dramatic trajectories of the work, from high to low, from lyrical to mechanical. The main body of the music is a kaleidoscopic mélange of characters, which gradually transforms the opening trumpet flight into the piano's clattering descent.

A Symphony of Three Orchestras is Carter's most complex exploration of collage. Not only are there more movements and strata than in the Third Quartet; the motion of the music is also much faster. Listeners do not have time to analyse the constituent elements of the texture, but must let the rapid currents of the music carry them along. The seemingly chaotic whirlpool of sonic textures follows a regular and elegant pattern, however. The music sweeps across the orchestra in swelling waves, beginning with one orchestra alone, mounting to two, cresting to three, then subsiding. Each 'trough' is a unique isolated occurrence of one of the twelve movements. The following chart outlines the form of the middle section of the work, from bar 40 to 318, identifying the movements by the number of their dominant triad:

Orchestra I	Orchestra II	Orchestra III
1-augmented triads	5-bells	11-scherzando
8-espressivo	10-clarinets (grazioso)	6-major & minor triads
3-flowing	7-cellos	9-leggero
4-angry	2-piano (accel.)	12-cantabile

```
I    1          8 8 8 8 8          3 3 3      4 4 4            3 3 3
II           5 5 5         10 10 10 10 10            5 5 5 5 5
III 11 11 11 11      6 6 6        9 9 9 9 9              12 12 12


I    3 3          8 8 8        1 1 1 1 1            4 4 4 4 4
II   7 7 7         2 2 2 2 2          10 10 10      2 2 2        7 7 7
III      6 6 6 6 6          9 9 9          12 12 12 12 12        11 11 11
```

Each vertical unit in the chart lasts about fifteen seconds. Obviously it would have been impossible to use every combination of movements as the Third Quartet had done. The montage of movements was selected for variety; the most active materials of each orchestra are reserved for the final intersection, bars 300–9. Because of the great speed of textural change, the interest of the music lies not so much in the interplay of materials as in the constant transformation of the entire tapestry as movements are added and subtracted. Each exposure of a single movement appears as the end of one transmutational progression and the beginning of the next. Repeated hearings reveal ever-receding echoes of the trumpet's opening flight—in the flowing movement of Orchestra I (see bars 169–76), in the grazioso music for the clarinets beginning at 82, and in the shimmering leggero movement of Orchestra III, as well as in the constantly encroaching intimations of mortality.

The thunder-chords which blot out the last traces of expressive music in Orchestra II are the climactic 'sounding-together' of the symphony. As the last wisps of solo violins disappear the silence between thunder claps becomes awesome, terrifying. (As a young boy Carter was once nearly struck by lightning.) The coda that follows is a transformed world. A few fragments of the earlier music, 'mashed and shapeless debris', remain: the violas of Orchestra III, the cellos of Orchestra II, and the trumpets of Orchestra I give intense but fading restatements of their lyrical material. But these are dispersed by frighteningly extended, mechanical ostinati, built of scattered intervals, each repeated at a different frequency (bars 348–52). With a grotesque halo of xylophone and marimba, echoing the screeching gulls of the opening bars, the piano, the transformed persona of the opening trumpet, leaps downward, *con bravura*.

Syringa

Occasion

Dedicated to Sir William and Lady Glock, *Syringa* was made possible by a Composer-Librettist Grant from the National Endowment for the Arts. It was first performed at Alice Tully Hall, Lincoln Center on 10 December 1978, the eve of Carter's seventieth birthday, as the central focus of a year long retrospective festival of his music by New York's contemporary music ensembles. The first performers were Jan de Gaetani, mezzo-soprano, Thomas Paul, bass, and Speculum Musicae conducted by Harvey Sollberger. The prominent guitar part was played by Scott Kuney. *Syringa* is scored for mezzo-soprano, bass, guitar, alto flute, cor anglais, bass clarinet (doubling B♭ clarinet), trombone, percussion (marimba, vibraphone, bongos, tom-toms), violin, viola, cello, bass, and piano.

Concept

John Ashbery, born in 1927, is the most important poet of the present avant-garde New York school. Influenced both by the dreamlike collage of French surrealism and by the open-ended philosophical discourse of Wallace Stevens, his poetry revives the syntactical experiments of Hart Crane, but without any trace of romantic heroism. His tone goes beyond the controlled anxiety of Elizabeth Bishop to a distinct blend of dead-pan irony, camp humour and exquisite lyricism. For Ashbery, the very act of writing poetry often seems impossible and absurd, merely a matter of random inclusions and exclusions. Not surprisingly, then, he has been strongly influenced by John Cage; his long poem *Europe* reads like a transcription of a performance of Cage's piece for twelve radios. In his later works, however, Ashbery has seemed to stress the lyrical possibilities still present in a disordered world, and has cited the influence of Carter's music on *Three Poems* and *The Skaters*. Ashbery himself approached Carter with the idea of a collaboration; he may have been surprised by the non-musical aspect of Carter's contribution, his assembling of Greek fragments to superimpose on Ashbery's poem.

For Carter, Ashbery's poetry presented many challenges and difficulties; its jokiness and irony and its jolting shifts in diction from the lofty to the vernacular were qualities not found in Carter's earlier music. Ashbery reads his poetry in a flat, common-sensical way, as if his wildest flights of syntactical fancy were perfectly obvious in their meaning. What is not said in Ashbery's poems is often as important as the printed text. Their relentless irony is a strategy of understatement. The poems are rent by silences and cut-off phrases, implying realms of experience too painful to mention. It is poetry after Beckett.

After reading through all of Ashbery's published and unpublished poems, Carter decided to use two singers as in Cavalieri's *Rappresentazione di anima e di corpo* which he brought into a lesson one day saying 'I've found the solution!' The work-in-progress would not be a song cycle like *A Mirror* but a new genre: a polytextual motet, a cantata, a chamber opera, a vocal double

302

concerto—all in one. The text of Ashbery's poem would be superimposed on its implied subtext.

Carter worked quite hard at the Greek text, both in its selection and its scansion, starting with his classics textbooks from Harvard, and later doing research at the British Museum. He interrupted work to take a short vacation in Morocco where he visited the ruins of the Roman city of Volubilis. There he came upon the 'house of Orpheus' where there was a large circular mosaic of Orpheus playing his lyre surrounded by a small concert audience of birds and beasts. It suggested to him the idea of Orpheus singing and playing, attracting his audience one by one. *Syringa* starts with the bass singer and guitar alone and one by one each of the instruments, the conductor and the mezzo are drawn in by the spell of the music. Carter later learned that Ashbery had written 'Syringa' while listening to Monteverdi's *Orfeo*. He saw this as a further justification for a texture something like a Monteverdi madrigal for two voices and accompaniment with a formal looseness similar to Monteverdi's 'arioso'.

John Ashbery's 'Syringa' is a typically oblique and distanced treatment of the Orpheus story. In Carter's setting the mezzo-soprano sings Ashbery's words in a flat patter remarkably close to the poet's own inflection and also reminiscent of Carter's Robert Frost songs. The bass sings a text in classical Greek, made up of fragments chosen by Carter to suggest the contrasts implied by the poem 'in whose tales are hidden syllables/Of what happened so long before'. What Ashbery mainly leaves unsaid is Orpheus's passion. His Orpheus is a very modern poet, too aware of the futility of his art. Apollo, no less, tells him:

> 'Leave it all on earth
> Your lute, what point? Why pick at a dull pavan few care to
> Follow, except a few birds of dusty feather,
> Not vivid performances of the past.'[10]

The whole poem is a response to the god's rather academic despair, celebrating the fresh discoveries of the present moment against the claims of a lost past. The bass gives a vivid performance, intense and emotional, but in words whose meaning is lost. Carter assembled a collage of classical Greek texts mostly dealing with aspects of the Orphic cult which developed, Carter enjoys saying, when, after his dismemberment, Orpheus's head floated across the Aegean, still singing. In wide-arching phrases of extravagant lyricism the bass sings of a world of undistanced passion, set in motion by the demands of Eros.

If Orpheus in Ashbery's poem appears as a self-portrait of the poet, Carter's music seems like an idealized embodiment of all those expressive qualities most personal to the composer. He has often said that the true medium of musical composition is not sound but time. *Syringa* celebrates time; it is a ceaselessly flowing temporal stream. Where many artists have attempted to rescue their art from time, Ashbery and Carter honour the quality of temporal passage, and its inherent nexus of the destructive and the creative:

> ... music passes, emblematic
> Of life and how you cannot isolate a note of it
> And say it is good or bad. . . .
> For although memories of a season, for example,
> Melt into a single snapshot, one cannot guard, treasure
> That stalled moment, It too is flowing, fleeting,
> It is a picture of flowing scenery, though living, mortal,
> Over which an abstract action is laid out in blunt,
> Harsh strokes.

Or as Heraclitus says in the Greek text: 'What is is like the current of a river.'

The two texts contain the whole of time, from creation—'Time gave birth to the egg'—to a distant future, 'When all record of these people and their lives/Has disappeared into libraries, onto microfilm'. Each text evokes motion in time. In Ashbery's poem all experience seems to vanish like Eurydice into *les temps perdus*. The words are merely 'a record of pebbles along the way'. The Greek text portrays a world ravished by time: 'Eros has shaken my soul like the wind which comes from the mountains and fells trees.' Ashbery's irony and the Greeks' daemonic passion are superimposed by Carter as related aspects of temporal experience: the very sense of time lost stems from the violent intensity of each present moment.

Materials and form

Syringa synthesizes the formal complexity of the Duo with the evocative clarity of *A Mirror on Which to Dwell*. As in the Duo, the singers spin forth contrasted musical characters and continuities, whose intersections are ironic, surprising, revelatory. The main structural contrast between the voices is the size of their intervals. Carter built the work on six seven-note chords, all of which fulfil two conditions: they contain the all-triad hexachord, 6–35 (0, 1, 2, 4, 7, 8) and they contain two statements of a triad (Chart 39). Soprano and bass thus often sing notes based on the same three-note chord, with the soprano in close position and the bass in open, as at bars 24–5 (Ex. 118). One of the main chords used is 7–4 (0, 1, 2, 4, 6, 7, 8), containing not only 6–35 in two versions but also 6–7 (0, 1, 2, 6, 7, 8), which can be spaced in such a way as to make a triad built of fourths (0, 5, 10) superimposed on one

Chart 39   Harmonic basis   (Syringa)

6-35 (0 1 2 4 7 8)-all-triad hexachord

7-4 (0 1 2 4 6 7 8)

triads stated twice

3-4   3-5   3-7   3-9

Ex. 118

Syringa

built of fifths (0, 7, 14). This chord with its relation to the open strings of the guitar appears all through the work and is featured at the moment when the bass sings that Orpheus was only a musician (kitharodos), at bars 299–300 (Ex. 119).

The soprano sings throughout in simple pulse rhythms that contrast with the rhapsodic phrases of the bass. As in *A Symphony of Three Orchestras*, however, the music's basic processes go by too fast for the structural contrasts to be analysed by the listener. What is heard is a series of sharp sonic images that emerge and disappear into the musical flow, vanishing as the words

Ex. 119

Syringa

themselves disappear in time. At every point the music finds a striking correlative to the words, from the opening bars where creation is heard in the sound of sharply plucked guitar strings, casting the first musical atoms into motion, to Apollo's sudden appearance announced by cor anglais and vibraphone, to the beautiful melodic descent 'at the way music passes', and the ravishing guitar arabesque, set off against the vibraphone at 'a bluish cloud' (Ex. 120).

Ex. 120

Syringa

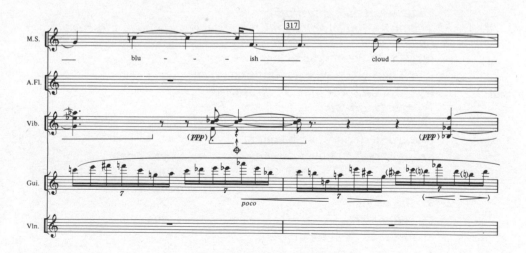

Because of the music's remarkable identification with the text—each seems to describe the other—the best approach to the form of the piece for the listener is the words. Here is a collage of both texts, roughly indicating their temporal relation as well as indications of the Greek sources, identified at the end:

bar
numbers

5   *Chronos (Time) gave birth to the world-egg*
    Fair flowing Ocean was the first to marry
    and he wedded his sister Tethys,[1]

21   Orpheus liked the glad personal quality
    Of the things beneath the sky. Of course, Eurydice was a part
    Of this.
    daughter of the same mother

28   *Then Eros fairest among the immortal gods, who unloosens the*
    body

37   *(exclamations of despair* [2]

25   Then one day, everything changed.

40   *For you, oh, only one, oh, dear wife*
    Woe, alas, oh fate!
            He rends
    Rocks into fissures with lament.

56   *drops of poison flow in exchange for my heart's grief.* [3]
              Gullies, hummocks

55   Can't withstand it. The sky shudders from one horizon
    To the other
    O, evil, alas
    almost ready to give up wholeness.

58   *For, doom, fathomless, approaches* [4]

308

61   Then Apollo quietly told him: 'Leave it all on earth.
Your lute, what point? Why pick at a dull pavan few care to
Follow, except a few birds of dusty feather,
Not vivid performances of the past.'

71   *But what life would there be, what joy without golden Aphrodite?*
                                        But why not?
All other things must change too.
The seasons are no longer what they once were,
But it is the nature of things to be seen only once,
As they happen along, bumping into other things, getting along
*May I die when I am no longer concerned with secret love
and gentle gifts* [5]
Somehow. That's where Orpheus made his mistake.

87   Of course Eurydice vanished into the shade;
She would have even if he hadn't turned around.

90   *There can be nothing unexpected, nothing impossible, nothing
marvellous since Zeus, Olympian father out of midday made night,
obscuring the light of the sun.* [6]

104   No use standing there like a gray stone toga as the whole wheel
Of recorded history flashes past, struck dumb, unable to utter an
      intelligent
Comment on the most thought-provoking element in its train.

110   *Dream in the black night, Eros, sweet god.* [7]

117   Only love stays on the brain, and something these people,
These other ones, call life.

129   *Eros has shaken my soul like the wind which comes from the
mountains and fells trees* [8]
Singing accurately

138   So that the notes mount straight up out of the well of
If I catch a brief glimpse of you

Dim noon and rival the tiny, sparkling yellow flowers
Growing around the brink of the quarry, encapsulizes
I can't say a word, my tongue is torn
The different weights of the things.
*and under my skin a subtle fire runs, my eyes don't see,
and my ears buzz.* [9] *Once again Eros, who unloosens my body*

162   But it isn't enough
To just go on singing. Orpheus realised this
And didn't mind so much about his reward being in heaven
torments me—bitter-sweet, invincible monster [10]
After the Bacchantes had torn him apart, driven
Half out of their minds by his music, what it was doing to them.

178   *Saving the seed of fire* [11]
Some say it was for his treatment of Eurydice.
But probably the music had more to do with it, and

187   The way music passes, emblematic
Of life and how you cannot isolate a note of it

190   *Cool waters from above sing as they flow through the*
          apple orchard
          And say it is good or bad. You must
          Wait till it's over. 'The end crowns all,'
          and from the trembling leaves sleep falls down. [12]
          Meaning also that the 'tableau'
          Is wrong. For although memories, of a season, for example,
          Melt into a single snapshot, one cannot guard, treasure
212   That stalled moment. It too is flowing, fleeting;
211   *In the spring quinces and pomegranates are watered by the river*
          It is a picture of flowing scenery, though living, mortal,
          Over which an abstract action is laid out in blunt,
221   Harsh strokes.
          in the undefiled maidens' garden
                                And to ask more than this
          Is to become the tossing reed of that slow,
          vines grow with shading vine-leaves.
          Powerful stream, the trailing grasses
          Playfully tugged at, but to participate in the action
          For me however Eros never sleeps
          No more than this.
          but by burning lightening and freezing wind a scorching frenzy
          sent by the Cyprian has captured my heart
          since childhood. [13]
                         Then in the lowering gentian sky
250   Electric twitches are faintly apparent first, then burst forth
          Into a shower of fixed, cream-coloured flares. The horses
259   Have each seen a share of the truth, though each thinks,
          'I'm a maverick. Nothing of this is happening to me,
          Though I can understand the language of birds, and
          The itinerary of the lights caught in the storm is fully
             apparent to me.
272   *Orpheus, unrewarded, they sent back from Hades,*
274   Their jousting ends in music much
          As trees move more easily in the wind after a summer storm
          And is happening in lacy shadows of shore-trees, now, day
             after day.'
          They showed him only a phantom of the wife for whom he came;
          her real self they would not bestow; for he was considered a coward
          since he was a musician, and would not have the heart
          to die of love. [14]
301   But how late to be regretting all this, even
          Bearing in mind that regrets are always late, too late!
          To which Orpheus, a bluish cloud with white contours,
          Replies that these are of course not regrets at all,
322   *All things change;*
          Merely a careful, scholarly setting down of
          You cannot step twice into the same river

Unquestioned facts, a record of pebbles along the way.
333 *What is is like the current of a river.*[15]
330 And no matter how all this disappeared,
Or got where it was going, it is no longer
Material for a poem. Its subject
340 Matters too much, and not enough, standing there helplessly
While the poem streaked by, its tail afire, a bad
346 *soon, clearly and sweetly he played on his lyre,*
Comet screaming hate and disaster, but so turned inward
*he lifted up his voice and sang, and lovely was the sound of
his voice that followed.*
That the meaning, good or other, can never
Become known. The singer thinks
He sang the story of the immortal gods
359 Constructively, builds up his chant in progressive stages
Like a skyscraper, but
*and of the dark earth, how the first was born
and how a task was allotted to each.*
                                    at the last minute turns away.
The song is engulfed in an instant in blackness
372 *First among the gods he honored Mnemosyne (Memory), mother of
the Muses in his song . . .*[16]
Which must in turn flood the whole continent
With blackness, for it cannot see. The singer
377 Must then pass out of sight, not even relieved
Of the evil burthen of the words.
389 *Apollo, Apollo, guardian, destroying me, you have crushed
me utterly.*[17]
406 *Begone, go away, save your present mind.*[18]
                                    Stellification
412 Is for the few, and comes about much later
Alas, woe![19]
When all record of these people and their lives
413 *The body is the sign (tomb) of the soul*[20]
Has disappeared into libraries, onto microfilm.
416 *saving the seed of fire*
A few are still interested in them. 'But what about
So-and-so?' is still asked on occasion. But they lie
420 *Of Ge (Earth) and Uranus (Sky) were born the children Oceanus
andTethys*
422 Frozen and out of touch until an arbitrary chorus
Speaks of a totally different incident with a similar name
In whose tale are hidden syllables
Of what happened so long before that
431 *body, sign (soma, sema)*[21]
In some small town, one indifferent summer.

311

Sources of Greek texts:
 1. Otto Kern, *Orphicorum fragmenta*, Berlin, 1922, No. 54
 2. Quoted by Plato (Socrates) in *Cratylus*, 402 C, as being part of an actual poem by Orpheus.
 3. Hesiod, *Theogony*, 120
 4. Exclamatory passages from Aeschylus, mostly from Cassandra's lines in *Agamemnon*; except for bar 40 and bar 58 which are from Euripides's *Alcestis*
 5. Mimnermus-Diehl, 1 (E. Diehl, *Anthologia Lyrica*, Leipzig, 1922)
 6. Archilochus-Diehl, 74
 7. Sappho-Diehl, 67
 8. Sappho-Diehl, 44
 9. Sappho-Diehl, 2 (excerpt)
 10. Sappho-Diehl, 137
 11. Homer, *Odyssey*, Book V, 490
 12. Sappho-Diehl, 5
 13. Ibycus-Diehl, 6
 14. Plato, *Symposium*
 15. Plato, *Cratylus*, 402 A (quoted from Heraclitus)
 16. Homeric Hymn, IV, *To Hermes*, 425–30
 17. Aeschylus, *Agamemnon*, 1091–2
 18. Aeschylus, *Prometheus Bound*, 392
 19. Aeschylus, *Agamemnon*, 1307, 1072
 20. Orphis saying—discussed by Plato, *Cratylus*, 400 C
 21. Plato, *Timaeus*, 40 E

Carter first used his college text book, *Greek Lyric Poets* by M. H. Morgan, revised by C. B. Gulick (Harvard University Press, 1929). Although he later found that classical scholarship has subsequently improved some of the texts chosen, he decided to use the version in the Harvard text.

The intersections of the two layers of text are everchanging, sometimes close in meaning, at other times distant. Often they are related by sound, not meaning. The Greek *Pheou,* an exclamation of despair, echoes 'Orpheus'; *Stellou,* 'be gone', sets off 'Stellification is for the few', Ashbery's conflation of Orpheus and Chaucer's Troilus. 'One indifferent summer', the final phrase in English, echoes the Orphic cult words, *soma, sema* that conclude the Greek. The orchestra surrounds these linguistic confrontations in a glowing double-aegis of sound. It is not divided into two rigidly opposed ensembles; rather its configuration is protean in colour, volume and density, ranging from the exquisite interplay of guitar and vibraphone to violent outbursts in the drums, piano and trombone.

Carter describes the form of *Syringa* as a series of short vocal pieces by the bass with commentary by the mezzo. Thus, as in the Duo, one part, here the bass, is sectional while the other, the mezzo, is free-associational in development. The sections of the bass part are:

1 (bars 1–35)   Creation myth. The bass breaks down on the word 'athanatoisi', immortal.

2 (36–59)   Lament for Eurydice. This is interrupted by Apollo as music critic.

3 (71–113)   Songs about Eros.

4 (116–265)   Songs of the power of love, its pleasures and torments.

5 (272–309)   Orpheus's story as seen by Socrates (Plato).

6 (322–80)   Heraclitus on time and a description of Hermes, who made the lyre, demonstrating its use to Apollo.

7 (389–412)   Cassandra's curse, and Prometheus's warning—both criticisms of Apollo.

8 (413–end)   Recall of opening texts and Orphic sayings.

The poetic quality magically projected by *Syringa* is instantaneous:

> But it is the nature of things to be seen only once
> As they happen along, bumping into other things, getting along
> Somehow.

There are no musical recurrences. *Syringa* allows its listeners no formal guides or fixed landmarks. It demands that we plunge into the river of time. For the Daedalian schemes of Carter's recent works have not been ends in themselves; he has no interest in constructing stone labyrinths. Rather he seeks to lead us through the maze of temporal experience with unbroken, intertwined strands of sound.

Night Fantasies

Carter's first work for solo piano since the Piano Sonata of 1946 was composed in Waccabuc and at the American Academy in Rome between June 1979 and 12 April 1980. It was commissioned by, and dedicated to, four New York pianists: Paul Jacobs, Gilbert Kalish, Ursula Oppens, and Charles Rosen. The commission was made possible by the American Music Center in New York. Miss Oppens gave the world première of *Night Fantasies* at the Bath Festival on 2 June 1980.

All four pianists have a long association with Carter's music. Paul Jacobs has recorded the Cello Sonata, the Sonata for Flute, Oboe, Cello and Harpsichord, and the Double Concerto (playing the harpsichord). As pianist of the New York Philharmonic he has also recorded the virtuoso piano parts written especially for him in the Concerto for Orchestra and *A Symphony of Three Orchestras*. Gilbert Kalish has recorded the Double Concerto (at the piano) and the Duo, which he premièred with Paul Zukofsky. Charles Rosen was the first piano soloist of the Double Concerto. He has recorded that work twice and performed it many times over the last twenty years. The Piano Sonata has been in his active repertory for over a quarter of a century, and in recent years he has also played the Piano Concerto. Ursula Oppens holds the distinction of being the only person to perform both solo parts of the Double Concerto (not at the same time!). She also played the Piano Concerto with the New York Philharmonic at concerts honouring Carter's seventieth birthday, and has taken part in many of the chamber works with the ensemble Speculum Musicae which she helped found.

It must have been a great pleasure for the composer to be able to write a piece expressly for performers with such a sure command of his style. The very existence of four such pianists is remarkable in itself, and it indicates the extraordinary relationship that Carter has formed over the years with a large group of musicians whose performances have greatly speeded the acceptance of his music. Carter is often known as a performer's composer, an epithet that may appear puzzling to those 'star' performers of today who never play today's music, or even the music of the last fifty years. Carter's commitment to performers is one of his most firmly held convictions, for he feels that only good performances can persuade an audience of the music's value. The performers in turn know that he always writes with them in mind; his music stretches their technique but does not violate it. The dense abundance of notational devices in his music, which some players at first find dizzying, is the result not of compulsiveness but of Carter's generosity in trying to give as much help as he can to lead the performers to a vivid interpretation of the music. Jacobs, Kalish, Rosen and Oppens have returned the favour, and welcomed the challenge of mastering a new repertory and of developing a new tradition of performance practice. All four pianists, moreover, possess the gift of connecting the new music to the older repertory, of which they are acknowledged masters. The four dedicatees of *Night Fantasies*, unlike too many perennial specialists in contemporary music, play new works because they want to, not because they have to. Carter's dedication honours both their virtuosity and their idealism.

As soon as the commission was announced, its unusual nature provoked speculation. Would Carter write a work for four pianos, or one with multiple formal pathways (as in Boulez's Third Sonata) so that each player could give the piece a unique form? Carter told the pianists that the new work would contain passages particularly suited to their musical personalities— prompting some critics to find in the piece a fantasy *à clef*. *Night Fantasies*, however, turned out to be both less sensational and more profound in its response to the commission than these lesser fantasies had anticipated. And in its use of the piano, too, the piece is at once conservative—no drumming, plucking, or singing along—and far-reaching in its innovations.

The title deliberately evokes Schumann; Carter has called the work a 'sort of contemporary *Kreisleriana*'. The relation to Schumann is not stylistic, however. The style of *Night Fantasies*, and particularly its use of the piano, stems from Carter's preceding works, especially the Duo. Carter has also denied any attempt to paint musical portraits as Schumann is said to have done. The link with *Kreisleriana* is purely conceptual. Carter set out to write a large-scale work whose form would be as different as possible from that of a sonata. Schumann had discovered just such a principle in *Papillons*, *Carnaval*, and his other sequences of short character pieces. These compositions are not sonatas, suites or anthologies. They are song cycles without words. They evoke and sustain a large dramatic argument through the juxtaposition of contrasting moods rather than through thematic development or recapitulation. Although each short piece could stand on its own (as a Chopin prelude or a Mendelssohn song-without-words can), in context they take on a dramatic resonance. Their contrasting characters interact to form a large design whose 'story' is mysteriously implied but nowhere stated. Links between pieces are achieved not by thematic recurrence or variation but by transformations that give a more ambiguous sense of causality than the more rigorous means of a sonata would. The G-minor movements in *Kreisleriana,* for instance, are all related, but how and why? Mystery is the essence of the form.

Like *Kreisleriana,* then, *Night Fantasies* is built out of many contrasting episodes. Carter, however, collages fragments of his episodes so that they appear, evolve and vanish, sometimes growing imperceptibly out of one another, elsewhere appearing suddenly, sharply interrupting the previous mood. The work is a twenty-minute-long movement, an unbroken span constructed out of many brief events whose beginnings and endings are often elided or blurred. Carter has compared the continuity of the music to the unpunctuated poems of Mallarmé or William Carlos Williams where phrases, thoughts and images are ambiguously dovetailed, so that multiple readings are not only possible but inevitable. He has also likened the music to the unclear thoughts of an insomniac on a wakeful night, a condition he found sharply etched in Robert Lowell's poem 'Myopia: A Night':[11]

> Bed, glasses off, and all's
> ramshackle, streaky, weird
> for the near-sighted, just
> a foot away.
> > > > > The light's
> still on an instant. Here
> are the blurred titles, here
> the books are blue hills, browns,
> greens, fields, or color.
> > > > > This
> is the departure strip,
> the dream road.

Schumann, Mallarmé, Lowell—Carter is suggesting helpful analogies, not dropping hints. There are no figures in this carpet. *Night Fantasies* springs from Carter's own world. It continues and extends the improvisational and spontaneous manner of the Duo and *Syringa*—a *Syringa* without words, or a Duo whose external instrumental conflict has been internalized, absorbed by a single instrument and a single performer. The piano here is not the percussive contraption it has become in much recent music, but a mirror of the mind (as it often is in Schumann), a mind in a state of semi-conscious but fertile meditation. The music is at once calm and nervous, sustained and unstable. The breathless rate of change and the deliberate ambiguity of gesture are the essential elements of the music's poetic world—and they are also Carter's creative response to his commission. For *Night Fantasies* in its succession of fugitive visions creates a musical ambience of such sensitivity that it will amplify the tiniest facet of each interpreter's musical personality. The music is not a portrait of the performers, but it is composed so that each interpretation will be a self-portrait.

Musical Space and Harmony

In writing for solo piano Carter denied himself the opposition of protagonists that has become habitual in his recent scores. These oppositions are here absorbed into the musical space of a single instrument. Instead of the lateral contrasts of singers and texts in *Syringa,* the conflicts within *Night Fantasies* are vertical. The surface of the music is an ambiguous reflection of its deep, latent content: true to its title the piece has the structure of a dream. Its deep foundation is rigorous and regular; its musical surface is improvisatory and changeable. This conflict, source of the work's spontaneity and inevitability, is further complicated for the listener because the deep structure is never given explicit presentation. The musical events we hear are all distorting prisms of the unrevealed framework. And—again as in dreams—because we are not aware of the rigorous basis of events, the relation of contrasting or similar episodes is always somewhat obscured or tentative. The rational structure of the music is hidden in shadow. Its surface is a magical sequence of flares and beacons, fireflies and fireworks in the dark.

As was already clear in the Piano Sonata, the piano for Carter is the spatial instrument *par excellence.* It has a huge range that is unified by a consistent mode of attack and by the resonance made possible by the pedals. In the Sonata, Carter emphasised the role of the overtone series in the piano's musical space, and used a few elemental contrasts of materials and textures: fast, slow and moderate materials in the first movement; arioso and fugue in the second. In *Night Fantasies*, he sought a much greater variety of sounds and textures. Quite early in the course of composing the work he told me that he had already written fifty different kinds of piano music, and was now looking for ways to bring them together. The variety of textures in the work is remarkable, especially considering the absence of imitative textures such as canons or fugatos. The performer is called upon to use a great range of dynamics and touch—from leggerissimo to marcatissimo, from staccato to cantabile. The music covers the spectrum of the keyboard in ever-changing configurations, so that the resultant tone colour continually varies.

It was in fact precisely through the organization of the space of the keyboard that Carter achieved the link between his many textures. For *Night Fantasies* he has discovered a new means of integrating harmony and musical space. In most music the harmonic structure is projected onto its instrumental space; chords are transposed, inverted and doubled within the field of available notes. Carter here based the music on eighty-eight all-interval twelve-note chords that function both as harmony and as a special composition of the piano's space. Instead of projecting harmonic objects on the instrumental field, he *composed* the field. The eighty-eight chords share a structural property: each interval is paired symmetrically with its inversional equivalent (minor second with major seventh, major second with minor seventh, minor third with major sixth, major third with minor sixth, perfect fourth with perfect fifth) around a central non-invertible tritone (Chart 40). The frequent pairing of inversionally-related intervals in the music stems from this chordal property as does the texture of the 'recitativo collerico' at

Chart 40   Principal one of 88 all-interval chords   **(Night Fantasies)**

(used in bars 3-14)

bar 235 with its centrally located tritones framed by a chordal accompaniment. The eighty-eight chords are further related because they all derive from just four hexachords (numbers 3–6) that contain every interval except the tritone.

The harmonic technique of *Night Fantasies* marks a culmination and breakthrough in Carter's exploration of all-interval chords. These chords have played an increasingly important role in his music not only because of their structure, but, even more, because of their sonority. As each interval occurs only once, the overall harmonic sound of the chord dominates its intervallic components—whereas in a chord made up of one or two intervals, these intervals will tend to dominate the sound of the chord. Of course, the sonority of the all-interval twelve-note chords is complex, but this very complexity is a source of their structural clarity—no other chords sound like them. Even in comparison to Carter's most recent works, *Night Fantasies* has an altogether new harmonic coloration.

Two aspects of the chordal structure will be most apparent to the listener. By using all possible chords of this type, Carter emphasises the opposition of large and small intervals. This opposition is at once the constant structure of the work's harmony and the source of its ever-changing sound. Throughout the work close and open spacings are contrasted, and as these spacings change position relative to the keyboard the sonority of the piano changes accordingly. Close chords in the bass paired with wide-spaced notes in the treble have a very different resonance from their inversion. Carter makes use of every possible gradation of spatial contrast (within the limits of the chordal structure) so that in the course of the work the total spectrum has been explored and elucidated. At first the listener will notice mainly the heightened contrasts of registers and spacings; later the many connections established between these contrasts will become apparent. As in his other music, Carter often uses the familiar linkage of common notes to connect his uncommon chords. A few pitches may be sustained, for instance, as a kind of pedal throughout a passage, and many different chords containing these pitches are sounded against them. This method appears most clearly in the last pages of the work where a four-note chord (pairing major seventh and minor ninth) is sounded repeatedly against fragments of all the twelve-note

317

chords that include it. This four-note chord tolls seventeen times, gradually fading and seeming to absorb all the fragments of the work until its final appearance silences them. (Perhaps—just perhaps—this final cadence is also an echo of the quiet G-minor conclusion of *Kreisleriana*.)

The second compositional property of the all-interval twelve-note chords is their ability to transform smaller intervallic structures. Carter explored this property in 'Anaphora' by projecting many transpositions of one six-note chord on a fixed twelve-note chord. In *Night Fantasies* the procedure is far more varied, for a large number of chords and intervals are projected on the vast array of all-interval chords. Sometimes a single class of intervals is emphasised: the fourths and fifths of the opening tranquillo music, or the minor thirds and major sixths from bar 15–26, or the ninths and sevenths near the end. Elsewhere three-note chords come to the fore: (0, 2, 5) at bars 70–9, or (0, 1, 5) in the capriccioso material beginning at 195. Still elsewhere four-note chords are stressed, notably Carter's old favourite (0, 1, 4, 6) at 123–8. By contrast with Carter's other music, however, these relatively discrete harmonies are not the main elements of the musical design. Instead, they serve to reveal different aspects of the all-interval chords that form the music's underlying spatial structure. Consequently, clear intervallic or chordal material often appears mixed with less clearly-defined harmonies. At bar 27, for example, the minor thirds of the previous passage suddenly become part of chord (0, 1, 4) which itself is used to introduce the region of a new all-interval chord in bars 32–6. The music next becomes dominated by the major third, the sum of the previously stressed intervals. Thirds and seconds are then combined into four-note chords in the important passage from 42 to 55 that returns in altered but recognizable form at 417 to 431. By frequently changing his focus from simple intervallic patterns to the all-interval patterns of the deep structure, Carter achieves the ambiguity of character that is the distinctive expressive domain of the work.

Form and Structure

The rhythmic structure of *Night Fantasies* displays an internal conflict parallel to that of its harmonic design. Carter began with a desire to write many contrasting types of music, and, as in the harmony, he sought a temporal design that would link these episodes in a coherent sequence. Unlike the Third Quartet and *A Symphony of Three Orchestras*, *Night Fantasies* does not obey a constructivist scheme of musical return. Some episodes come back in clearly recognizable form: the four-note chords at bars 42 and 417, for example, or the capriccioso music whose speed, harmony and tessitura remain constant throughout. Other material returns but in a transformed manner: the *recitativo collerico*, for instance, spawns a number of episodes clearly related to it in gesture and texture, and yet different in intervallic makeup and melodic contour. Some episodes return only briefly and in altered states: the mechanical nightingale of bars 157–67 is echoed in a quite different context at bars 215–16. Still other episodes are gradually replaced by their opposites: the spacious fifths of the opening correspond structurally to the clangorous ninths of the close. The various episodes of *Night Fantasies* might thus be said to possess contrasting half-lives. Some of them change slowly, some more quickly, others decay even as they are sounded. These juxtaposed rates of transformation again contribute to the ambiguous climate of the music, for as the materials change their contrasts and connections change as well. Like *Syringa, Night Fantasies* seems always to be discovering the unexpected present moment, provoking the listener's memory in order to surprise and confound it.

Although *Night Fantasies* avoids any large points of arrival along its path, the overall shape of the piece creates a context for the many small events that flash by. Carter describes the work as a fast movement interrupted (as in Schumann) by slow 'trios' that gradually turns into a slow movement interrupted by fast 'trios'. Fast and slow episodes thus gradually exchange roles of foreground and background—a difference the performer should make clear. The characters of both fast and slow music also evolve in the course of the work. Several distinct types of fast music (fantastico, marcato, cantabile, leggero, appassionato) are heard before the most sustained fast section (capriccioso leggerissimo) appears. These all return as 'trios' during the second half of the piece, with the marcato passages becoming increasingly prominent. Similarly the slow music changes in character from the barely audible tranquillo opening, floating chords, and brief, static ostinati, to increasingly intense lyrical utterances, most clearly heard in the extravagant beauty of the melodic line at bars 377–87. Typical of the work's reversals of focus is the way this passage returns at bar 417 with its melodic line 'erased' and its chordal accompaniment now the dominant event. Slow and fast materials finally merge at their points of greatest intensity with the harsh chords of bar 472 and following; from this climax of fusion the music gradually subsides.

In order to ensure the coherence of the music in time, Carter quite early in its composition constructed a system of pulses that runs from the beginning to the end. There are two pulse rates, MM 10.8 and 8.75; they coincide only at the down-beat of bar 3 and on the final notes of the piece. The polyrhythm formed is 216:175, and every pulse of both rates is played, though they rarely appear in isolation. Thus, just as Carter composed the musical space of the work, he also composed its 'real' time; this rhythmic design moreover corresponds to the chordal substructure in its poetic function. It is at once hidden and controlling. The relentless pulses might be compared to a clock in an insomniac's room, its ticking passing in and out of the listener's consciousness. Never before has Carter systematically composed real time into a piece of these dimensions with such absolute rigour, and never before has the contrast of clock time and psychological time been presented structurally rather than dramatically—though of course for the insomniac the clock can become the most terrifying of dramatic personae. Although the cross-pulse is mostly hidden in the faster motion of the musical surface, many of the events of the music owe their drama to the partially revealed deep structure of musical time: all that remains of the erased recitative at bar 419, for example, is the underlying pulse whose isolated notes now bear the

Chart 41   Field of tempi

(Night Fantasies)

Tempi	Pulses	Surface speed
MM 94.5 = ♩	5/54 = 8.75*	♪^{5} = 472.5
	4/35 = 10.8	♪ = 378
MM 47.25 = ♩	5/27 = 8.75	♪^{5} = 236.25
	8/35 = 10.8	♪ = 378
MM 42 = ♩.	5/24 = 8.75	♪.^{5} = 210
	9/35 = 10.8	♪^{3} = 378
MM 63 = ♩	5/36 = 8.75	♪^{5} = 315
	6/35 = 10.8	♪ = 378
MM 126 = ♩	5/72 = 8.75	♪ = 630
	3/35 = 10.8	♪^{3} = 378
MM 90 = ♩.	7/72 = 8.75	♪.^{7} = 630
	3/25 = 10.8	♪ = 270
MM 45 = ♩	7/36 = 8.75	♪^{7} = 315
	6/25 = 10.8	♪^{3} = 270
MM 30 = ♩.	7/24 = 8.75	♪.^{7} = 210
	9/25 = 10.8	♪^{3} = 270
MM 67.5 = ♩	7/54 = 8.75	♪^{7} = 472.5
	4/25 = 10.8	♪ = 270
MM 78.75 = ♩.	1/9 = 8.75	♩. = 78.75
	24/175 = 10.8	♪ = 1890

*The fraction means that the pulse rate is equal to fifty-four quintuplets

expressive burden of the vanished melody. The slower pulse becomes most audible towards the close when it is heard in the repeated four-note chord that gradually extinguishes the music.

The relation of surface events to the underlying polyrhythm is mostly hidden, and yet it is a fully controlling link. Having chosen the two pulse rates, Carter could use only those tempi that would allow every pulse to be precisely notated. The slow pulses thus determined an entire field of tempi and generated all the faster speeds and polyrhythms used in the piece (Chart 41). Needless to say, in performance the many gradations of speed must be rigorously observed to ensure both the steadiness of the underlying pulses and the temporal variety of the musical surface.

Night Fantasies commands interest for its virtuoso demands and its structural originality, and yet its most distinctive feature is its meditative character, rather different from the dramatic mode of most of Carter's music. America, whose composers so often feel isolated, has produced a uniquely private genre of piano music. Though often difficult to play, works in this genre are not extroverted show pieces. Rather they seem intense acts of self-communion. One thinks of Ives's 'Thoreau', of Ruggles's *Evocations,* of the closing pages of Copland's Piano Sonata, and of his Piano Fantasy and *Night Thoughts*. *Night Fantasies* reaffirms this meditative tradition, so expressive of peace and anguish, and extends it in Carter's most personal manner.

Notes to Part 9

1. Elizabeth Bishop: *Complete Poems*, (New York: Farrar, Straus and Giroux, 1969)
2. Robert Lowell: *Life Studies*, (New York: Farrar, Straus and Cudahy, 1959)
3. *The Complete Poems of Hart Crane*, (New York: Liveright, 1958) p. 3
4. Ibid.
5. Ibid. pp. 38–9
6. Ibid, p. 13
7. Ibid. p. 17
8. Ibid. p. 139
9. Ibid. p. 163
10. John Ashbery: *Houseboat Days*, (New York: Penguin, 1977) pp. 69–71
11. Robert Lowell: *Selected Poems*, (New York: Farrar, Straus and Giroux, 1977) p. 114

Appendix A

Three Occasional Pieces

Canon for 3
Igor Stravinsky In Memoriam (1971)

Written as a memorial to Stravinsky, *Canon for 3* first appeared in *Tempo* No. 98, one of two issues of tributes by composers. It is written for 'three equal instrumental voices'. Performances have been given with three trumpets, flugelhorn, cornet and trumpet, and oboe, clarinet and trumpet. Other combinations are certainly possible.

The short work combines canonic rigour with a typically Carterian textural transformation. It is a strict canon, with the second voice in inversion at the tritone; the third voice repeats the first exactly. After the third voice has restated the subject, the continuing canonic motion of all three parts produces first the inversion at the tritone and then the original subject as a *Klangfarbenmelodie* formed by the three lines. The voices thus merge, and independence gives way to unity. The Canon combines renaisssance and twentieth-century techniques, a feat that Stravinsky of all composers would have appreciated.

A Fantasy about Purcell's Fantasia upon One Note
for Brass Quintet (1974)

A Fantasy was written as a Christmas present for the American Brass Quintet who had just given the première of the Brass Quintet. Carter has long admired Purcell's music, and in particular the fantasias for viols which were an important inspiration for the First Quartet. The *Fantasia upon One Note* has a special appeal because of the contrapuntal ingenuity involved in building a work over a continuous pedal, and because of the rhythmic structure, based on doubling and then re-doubling the pulse-rate of the music against the constant durations of the drone. In arranging the piece Carter strove to make the drone always audible, which it rarely is when the Fantasia is performed on viols, and to articulate and phrase the music so that its contrapuntal structure would be clear. The extremely detailed notation of dynamics and attack indicates Carter's impatience with the unvaried and colourless renderings of older music which too often pass for authentic.

Carter's Fantasy, as distinct from Purcell's, is another one-note study, like Etude VII. He transforms Purcell's sustained drone into a tolling bell-like tone which passes from instrument to instrument, and thereby changes subtly in colour. Carter frames Purcell's music with an introductory two bars of *Klangfarbenmelodie* in which the constant B♭ is given two different scorings, and by a concluding three bars that sustain the B♭ beyond the last cadence in an echo-like sound. The frame makes clear the double structure of fantasy/ fantasia. The listener can hear Carter's Fantasy as a background to Purcell's original, or hear Purcell's contrapuntal web as a background for Carter's study in changing colours.

Birthday Fanfare for Sir William Glock's 70th, 3 May 1978
for 3 trumpets, vibraphone and chimes

The fanfare is a brief birthday greeting—almost a singing telegram—to Carter's friend and long-time champion. Three trumpets, one playing quintuplets, the second, semiquavers, the third triplets, are set against expressive mysterious music for the vibraphone with a final cadence appropriately given to the chimes. The material recalls *A Symphony of Three Orchestras,* but it is subtly derived from the song 'Happy Birthday to You'. The song appears in melodic fragments, inversions and retrogrades, and is also the pervasive source of the fanfare's harmony. Chord 3–9 (0, 1, 5) is the constant harmonic unit; in the form 0, 4, 5 it occurs melodically at the beginning and end of the song.

Although Carter invested much ingenuity in revealing and concealing the birthday tune, he feels that the fanfare is too slight to merit further performance after its intended occasion.

Appendix B

Carter's Listing of three- to six-note chords

Computations of all possible chords in the chromatic scale have been made by Haba, Slonimsky, Schillinger, and more recently by Allen Forte, who introduced the term 'pitch-class set' and the use of set theory into this field of speculation. Carter began to make his own list of chords around the time of the Piano Concerto. His method was intuitive and pragmatic, related to the compositional needs at hand. His ordering differs from Forte's, but they agree on basic definitions and on the number of chords. Although Carter's numbering is in no way superior to Forte's, his habitual use of his own numbering in discussing and sketching his music makes a knowledge of his system necessary for a detailed understanding of the music. In the list of chords given below the order number appears first, and the numbers inside the parentheses indicate semitones above the first note of the chord. The chords are given in their closest position. (Readers interested in a more detailed description of the premises of this list should see Allen Forte, *The Structure of Atonal Music* (New Haven, 1973) pp. 1–21.)

Three-note chords
1 (0 4 8)
2 (0 3 6)
3 (0 2 4)
4 (0 1 2)
5 (0 2 7)
6 (0 3 7)
7 (0 1 6)
8 (0 2 6)
9 (0 1 5)
10 (0 2 5)
11 (0 1 4)
12 (0 1 3)

Four-note chords
1 (0 1 2 3)
2 (0 1 6 7)
3 (0 2 3 5)
4 (0 2 5 7)
5 (0 3 6 9)
6 (0 1 2 7)
7 (0 1 3 6)
8 (0 1 4 5)
9 (0 1 3 4)
10 (0 1 5 6)
11 (0 2 4 6)
12 (0 2 6 8)
13 (0 3 4 7)
14 (0 3 5 8)
15 (0 1 5 8)
16 (0 2 4 8)
17 (0 1 2 4)
18 (0 1 4 6) all-interval
19 (0 1 5 7)
20 (0 1 2 5)
21 (0 1 4 7)
22 (0 1 2 6)
23 (0 1 3 7) all-interval
24 (0 3 4 8)
25 (0 2 3 7)
26 (0 1 3 5)
27 (0 2 4 7)
28 (0 2 3 6)
29 (0 2 5 8)

Five-note chords

1 (0 1 2 3 4)	11 (0 1 2 3 5)	21 (0 1 4 5 8)	31 (0 1 3 6 7)
2 (0 2 3 4 6)	12 (0 1 2 3 6)	22 (0 1 3 5 7)	32 (0 1 3 6 8)
3 (0 3 4 5 8)	13 (0 1 2 3 7)	23 (0 1 3 5 8)	33 (0 1 3 6 9)
4 (0 1 2 6 8)	14 (0 1 2 4 5)	24 (0 2 3 5 8)	34 (0 1 3 7 8)
5 (0 1 3 5 6)	15 (0 1 2 4 6)	25 (0 2 3 5 7)	35 (0 1 4 5 7)
6 (0 2 4 6 8)	16 (0 1 2 4 7)	26 (0 2 4 5 8)	36 (0 2 3 6 8)
7 (0 2 4 7 9)	17 (0 1 2 4 8)	27 (0 1 2 5 6)	37 (0 1 4 6 8)
8 (0 1 4 7 8)	18 (0 2 3 4 7)	28 (0 1 2 5 7)	38 (0 1 4 7 9)
9 (0 2 4 6 9)	19 (0 1 3 4 6)	29 (0 1 2 5 8)	
10 (0 1 3 4 8)	20 (0 1 3 4 7)	30 (0 1 2 6 7)	

Six-note chords

1 (0 2 4 6 8 10)	14 (0 2 3 5 6 9)	27 (0 2 3 5 6 8)	40 (0 1 2 4 6 9)
2 (0 1 4 5 8 9)	15 (0 1 3 6 7 9)	28 (0 2 3 4 6 9)	41 (0 2 3 4 5 8)
3 (0 1 3 4 5 8)	16 (0 1 2 3 6 7)	29 (0 1 3 4 6 7)	42 (0 1 3 4 5 7)
4 (0 1 2 3 4 5)	17 (0 1 2 5 7 8)	30 (0 1 2 3 6 9)	43 (0 1 3 5 6 8)
5 (0 2 3 4 5 7)	18 (0 2 3 5 7 9)	31 (0 1 4 6 7 9)	44 (0 1 2 4 7 9)
6 (0 2 4 5 7 9)	19 (0 1 2 3 4 6)	32 (0 1 3 6 8 9)	45 (0 1 2 3 6 8)
7 (0 1 2 6 7 8)	20 (0 1 2 3 5 7)	33 (0 1 2 5 6 7)	46 (0 1 2 4 6 7)
8 (0 1 4 5 7 9)	21 (0 1 3 5 6 9)	34 (0 1 2 3 7 8)	47 (0 1 2 4 5 7)
9 (0 1 3 5 7 9)	22 (0 1 3 4 7 9)	35 (0 1 2 4 7 8) all-triad	48 (0 1 2 3 5 8)
10 (0 1 2 4 6 8)	23 (0 1 2 3 4 8)	36 (0 1 2 5 6 8)	49 (0 1 2 3 5 6)
11 (0 1 4 5 6 8)	24 (0 1 2 4 5 6)	37 (0 1 3 4 7 8)	50 (0 1 2 3 4 7)
12 (0 2 3 4 6 8)	25 (0 1 2 5 7 9)	38 (0 1 2 5 6 9)	
13 (0 1 2 4 5 8)	26 (0 1 3 5 7 8)	39 (0 1 3 4 6 8)	

Appendix C

Carter's note on *Voyage*

A Commentary on the Poem by the Composer

To help the singer (and possibly the listener) in forming an interpretation of the text of this song (the third in a series of six 'Voyages' by Hart Crane), it would perhaps be pertinent to describe something of what it has meant to the composer.

As with most poetry, this poem can be read in several ways. I venture neither to deal with them exhaustively nor least of all to construct a definitive interpretation. In the music I have tried to reflect its poetic meaning and lyrical beauty. Without going into the psychological and emotional implications which every line challenges, I would like to give a short account of its meaning (for me) on the most matter-of-fact level.

There are three protagonists: the Sea which is the medium through which everything in the poem moves and changes and to which every idea is referred, Love (to whom the poem is addressed) and the Poet.

The argument (stripped of symbols and conditions) runs something like this: since Love is never far from his thoughts and represents the most desirable of conditions (first section, lines 1–8) the Poet entreats Love to allow him to go safely through an ordeal which will bring him under Love's power (second section, lines 1–8).

The Sea is thought of under several aspects. In the first section, the relation of sea to sky suggests the unifying, harmonizing power of love; while in the second, the sea forms an obstacle to be voyaged through to reach Love. At the end of each part, the transforming power of the sea (with the peril of loss of identity) looms up as a danger which, by implication, is like that of love. This transforming power is exemplified in the ordering of images and ideas in the poem itself, which uses many metaphors and moves rapidly from one level of meaning to another.

Love, in the same manner, is in one place an actual person and in another seems transformed into the principle or power under whose spell the Poet wishes to come. In the following line-by-line analysis, I assume (for purposes of simplicity) that the poem is addressed to the power, Love, although it can just as well be explained in terms of a particular person. In this respect the poem has a double meaning.

The Poet first envisions the Sea as bearing a relationship infinite in time, in space as well as in proximity to all things. It is like the mother of all; like a great blood stream uniting all in a common bond (line 1).

Considered from this point of view, which was suggested by the close relationship of sea and sky that the light of day reveals, the sea is comparable to love (lines 2–4).

Coming down to the particular scene or experience that may have suggested the poem, the Poet then describes his beloved and himself swimming in the sea. He follows no path far removed from his beloved, and, maintaining the level of meaning taken for the first four lines, this would naturally imply that his thoughts are constantly with Love (lines 5–7).

The section closes with a hint of the dangers lurking in the sea pictured as grasping at both swimmers with hand-like waves that could transform them into relics by disintegrating their bodies (lines 7–8). In another poem, Crane wrote: 'The dice of drowned men's bones', which suggests the meaning implied here.

In the second section (which is one long sentence: 'And so, . . . Permit me voyage, love, into your hands . . .'), the Poet turns to consider the ordeal he must undergo in order to come under the spell of Love. Using other elements of the swimming scene, the ordeal is represented metaphorically as a voyage into the depths, a rise to the surface and a swim over the waves to reach the floating body of his beloved. The different depths of the sea suggest a turbulent architectural façade before which he rises, with gates at the bottom, pillars and pediments above them, and on top a roof of waves reflecting glittering lights and stars (lines 9–14).

Then once again the Poet becomes aware of the danger involved in the voyage. Death at sea is not bloody but a disintegration into relics scattered over the bottom from one end of the world to the other. It is like the transformation of a poet's experience that suffers disintegration and reorganization into word-relics made into a poem by the subtle poetic art (lines 14–15).

In the final line the Poet asks permission of Love to be allowed to complete his ordeal or voyage safely and to come under its power, wishing to surrender himself wholly to it.

I have purposely avoided an attempt to explain the ordeal described metaphorically in the poem, for that would involve a much lengthier discussion than there is room for here. Certainly the tragic career of Hart Crane himself throws one kind of light on the matter. In fact, viewed autobiographically, this particular work can be considered as a prophecy of his own personal voyage through life, which met its end when he wilfully extinguished himself in the hands of the sea.

Elliott Carter
(1945)

Chronological Catalogue of Works

1928   *My love is in a light attire*
               for voice and piano
            Unpublished

1931   Incidental music for Sophocles's *Philoctetes*
               for baritone, tenor, men's chorus and chamber orchestra
            1st perf. Harvard Classical Club, 15 March 1933
            Unpublished

1936   Incidental music for Plautus's *Mostellaria*
               for baritone, tenor, men's chorus and chamber orchestra
            1st perf. Harvard Classical Club, 15 April 1936
            Unpublished

              Tarantella (finale to *Mostellaria*)
               for men's chorus (TTBB) and piano, 4-hands, or orchestra
            1st perf. Harvard Glee Club, G. Wallace Wordsworth, conductor, 29 April 1937
            Pub. AMP (piano version only)

1937   *Let's Be Gay*
               for women's chorus (SSAA) and 2 pianos
            1st perf. Wells College Glee Club, Nicholas Nabokov, conductor. Spring 1938
            Unpublished

              Harvest Home
               for chorus (SATB) a cappella
            1st perf. Lehman Engel Madrigal Singers. New York, Spring 1938
            Unpublished

To Music
   for mixed chorus (SSAATTBB) a cappella
1st perf. Lehman Engel Madrigal Singers. New York, Spring
   1938
Pub. Peer

1938   *Prelude, Fanfare and Polka*
           for small orchestra
        Unpublished

        Tell Me Where Is Fancy Bred
           for alto voice and guitar
        Recorded by Orson Welles and the Mercury Theater as inci-
           dental music for *The Merchant of Venice*
        Pub. AMP (1972), guitar part ed. Stanley Silverman

        Heart Not So Heavy As Mine
           for chorus (SATB) a cappella
        1st perf. Temple Emanu-El Choir, Lazare Saminsky, conductor.
           New York, 31 March 1939
        Pub. AMP (originally Arrow Music Press)

1939   *Pocahontas*
           Ballet Legend in one act for orchestra
        1st perf. Ballet Caravan, Fritz Kitzinger, conductor. New York,
        24 May 1939
        Pub. AMP

        Suite from *Pocahontas*
        Pub. Edwin Kalmus; revised version (1961) AMP

        Canonic Suite
           Musical Studies
        a) for Quartet of alto saxophones
        Pub. BMI, 1945
        b) revised for 4 clarinets
        Pub. AMP, 1956
        Andante Espressivo, a fourth study, unpublished

1940   *Pastoral*
           for viola or cor anglais or clarinet and piano
        1st perf. Ralph Hersh, viola; Elliott Carter, piano, New York,
        1942. Joseph Marx, cor anglais, 12 November 1944
        Pub. New Music 18 No. 3 (April 1945); Presser

1941   *The Defense of Corinth*
           for speaker, men's chorus and piano 4-hands
        1st perf. Harvard Glee Club, G. Wallace Woodworth,
        conductor, 12 March 1942
        Pub. Presser

1942   Symphony No. 1
                   for orchestra
                1st perf. Eastman-Rochester Symphony Orchestra, Howard
                   Hanson, conductor. Rochester, N.Y., 27 April 1944
                Pub. AMP (revised version 1954)

1942 (?)   *Elegy* (Adagio)
                a) for cello and piano
                Unpublished
                b) for string quartet (revised 1946)
                1st perf. Lanier Quartet, Eliot, Maine, 21 August 1946
                Pub. Peer
                c) for string orchestra (revised 1952)
                1st perf. David Broekman, conductor. New York, 1 March 1953
                Pub. Peer
                d) for viola and piano (revised 1961)
                1st perf. George Humphrey, viola; Alice Canady, piano.
                   Cambridge, Mass. 16 April 1963
                Pub. Peer

1942   *Three Poems by Robert Frost*
                   for voice and piano
                i. Dust of Snow ii. The Rose Family iii. The Line Gang
                Pub. AMP

1943   *Warble for Lilac Time*
                   for soprano or tenor and piano, or soprano and small
                   orchestra
                1st perf. Helen Boatwright and Yaddo Orchestra, Frederick
                   Fennell, conductor. Saratoga Springs, N.Y., 14 September
                   1946
                Pub. Peer

                Voyage
                   for medium voice and piano, orchestral version 1975 (rev.
                   1979)
                1st perf. Helen Boatwright, soprano; Helmut Baerwald, piano.
                   New York, 16 March 1947
                Pub. AMP (originally Valley Music Press)

1944   *The Difference*
                   for soprano, baritone and piano
                Unpublished

                Holiday Overture
                   for orchestra
                1st perf. Frankfurt Symphony Orchestra, Hans Blumer,
                   conductor, 1946
                Pub. Arrow Press revised version (1961) AMP

The Harmony of Morning
for women's chorus (SSAA) and chamber orchestra
1st perf. Temple Emanu-El Choir, Lazare Saminsky, conductor.
New York, 25 February 1945
Pub. AMP

1945   *Musicians Wrestle Everywhere*
for chorus (SSATB) with optional string accompaniment
1st perf. Randolph Singers, David Randolph, conductor. New
York, 12 February 1946
Pub. Presser (originally Mercury)

1946   Piano Sonata
1st perf. Webster Aitken. New York, 16 February 1947: (broadcast) James Sykes. New York, 5 March 1947
Pub. Presser (originally Mercury)

1947   *The Minotaur*
Ballet in one act and two scenes for orchestra
1st perf. Ballet Society, Leon Barzin, conductor. New York,
26 March 1947
Pub. AMP

Suite from *The Minotaur*
Pub. AMP c.1956

Emblems
for men's chorus (TTBB) and piano solo
1st perf. Harvard Glee Club, G. Wallace Woodworth, conductor
(Part II only). New York, 3 April 1951: Colgate College
Singers (first complete performance). European tour,
Summer 1952
Pub. Presser (orginally Mercury)

1948   Woodwind Quintet
1st perf. Martin Orenstein (flute), David Abosch (oboe), Louis
Paul (clarinet), Pinson Bobo (horn) and Mark Popkin
(bassoon). New York, 27 February 1949
Pub. AMP

Sonata for Violoncello and Piano
1st perf. Bernard Greenhouse, cello; Anthony Makas, piano.
New York, 27 February 1950
Pub. AMP (originally Society for the Publication of American
Music); revised edition 1966

1949   *Eight Etudes and a Fantasy*
for flute, oboe, clarinet and bassoon
1st perf. New York Woodwind Quintet—Murray Panitz (flute),
Jerome Roth (oboe), David Glazier (clarinet) and Bernard
Garfield (bassoon). New York, 28 October 1952
Pub. AMP

1950   Timpani Pieces
i. Recitative and Improvisation
Pub. AMP (1960)
ii. Saëta, Moto Perpetuo, Canaries, March
Pub. AMP with the above and Adagio and Canto of 1966 (q.v.)
as *Eight Pieces for Four Timpani*. All were revised in 1966 with
the aid of Jan Williams

1951   String Quartet No. 1
1st perf. Walden Quartet (Homer Schmitt, Bernard Goodman,
John Garvey and Robert Swenson). New York, 26 February
1953
Pub. AMP

1952   Sonata for Flute, Oboe, Cello and Harpsichord
1st perf. Harpsichord Quartet (Sylvia Marlowe, Claude
Monteux, Henry Shulman and Bernard Greenhouse).
New York, 19 November 1953
Pub. AMP

1953–55   Variations for Orchestra
1st perf. Louisville Orchestra, Robert Whitney, conductor.
Louisville, Ky. 21 April 1956
Pub. AMP

1959   String Quartet No. 2
1st perf. The Juilliard Quartet (Robert Mann, Isidore Cohen,
Raphael Hillyer and Claus Adam). New York, 25 March 1960
Pub. AMP

1961   Double Concerto for Harpsichord and Piano
with 2 chamber orchestras
1st perf. Ralph Kirkpatrick, harpsichord; Charles Rosen, piano;
Gustav Meier, conductor. New York, 6 September 1961
Pub. AMP

1965   Piano Concerto
1st perf. Jacob Lateiner, piano, Boston Symphony Orchestra,
Erich Leinsdorf, conductor. Boston, 6 January 1967
Pub. AMP

1966   Adagio and Canto for Timpani
Pub. in *Eight Pieces for Four Timpani,* AMP

1969   Concerto for Orchestra
1st perf. New York Philharmonic Orchestra, Leonard
Bernstein, conductor. New York, 5 February 1970
Pub. AMP

1971   String Quartet No. 3
1st perf. Juilliard Quartet (Robert Mann, Earl Carlyss, Samuel Rhodes and Claus Adam). New York, 23 January 1973
Pub. AMP

Canon for 3
In memoriam Igor Stravinsky, for equal instrumental voices
1st perf. Joel Timm (oboe), Alan Blustein (clarinet) and James Stubb (trumpet). New York, 23 January 1972
Pub. AMP (also in *Tempo,* No. 98)

1974   Duo for Violin and Piano
1st perf. Paul Zukofsky, violin; Gilbert Kalish, piano. New York, 5 March 1975
Pub. AMP

Brass Quintet
for 2 trumpets, horn, tenor and bass trombones
1st perf. American Brass Quintet (Robert Biddlecombe, Edward Birdwell, Louis Ranger, Raymond Mase and Herbert Rankin). BBC broadcast, 20 October 1974
Pub. AMP

A Fantasy on Purcell's 'Fantasia on One Note'
for brass quintet
1st perf. American Brass Quintet. New York, January 1975
Pub. AMP

1975   *A Mirror On Which To Dwell*
for soprano and chamber orchestra
1st perf. Susan Davenny Wyner, Speculum Musicae, Richard Fitz, conductor. New York, 24 February 1976
Pub. AMP

1976   *A Symphony of Three Orchestras*
1st perf. New York Philharmonic Orchestra, Pierre Boulez, conductor. New York, 17 February 1977
Pub. AMP

1978   *Birthday Fanfare*
for Sir William Glock's 70th, for 3 trumpets, vibraphone and glockenspiel
1st perf. London, 3 May 1978.
Unpublished

Syringa
for mezzo-soprano, baritone and chamber orchestra
1st perf. Jan DeGaetani, Thomas Paul, Speculum Musicae, Harvey Sollberger, conductor. New York, 10 December 1978
Pub. AMP

1980   *Night Fantasies*
         for solo piano
         1st perf. Ursula Oppens. Bath Festival, 2 June 1980

Key: AMP – Associated Music Publishers, New York
     Mercury – Music Press and Mercury Music Corp., New York
     Peer – Peer International, New York
     Presser – Theodore Presser, Bryn Mawr, Pennsylvania

A Selective Bibliography

compiled by
John Shepard

Writings by Elliott Carter

Citations for writings which have been reprinted in the collection *The Writings of Elliott Carter* (Bloomington: Indiana University Press, 1977) are followed by the abbreviation WEC and the page numbers from that collection.

'New York Season, 1937', *Modern Music* 14 no. 2 (Jan.–Feb. 1937), 90–1, WEC 3–5

'Late Winter, New York', *Modern Music* 14 no. 3 (Mar.–Apr. 1937), 147, WEC 5–10

'The Sleeping Beauty', *Modern Music* 14 no. 3 (Mar.–Apr. 1937), 173, WEC 10–11

'Season's End in New York', *Modern Music* 14 no. 4 (May–June 1937), 215–16, WEC 11–13

'With the Dancers', *Modern Music* 14 no. 4 (May–June 1937), 237–9, WEC 14–15

'Opening Notes, New York', *Modern Music* 15 no. 1 (Nov.–Dec. 1937), 36, WEC 16–17

'In the Theatre', *Modern Music* 15 no. 1 (Nov.–Dec. 1937), 51–3, WEC 17–19

'With the Dancers', *Modern Music* 15 no. 1 (Nov.–Dec. 1937), 55–6, WEC 19–20

'Homage to Ravel', *Modern Music* 15 no. 2 (Jan.–Feb. 1938), 96, WEC 21

'Vacation Novelties, New York', *Modern Music* 15 no. 2 (Jan.–Feb. 1938), 96, WEC 21–2

'With the Dancers', *Modern Music* 15 no. 2 (Jan.–Feb. 1938), 118–22, WEC 23–6

'Musical Reactions—Bold and Otherwise', *Modern Music* 15 no. 3 (Mar.–Apr. 1938), 199, WEC 27

'Orchestras and Audiences: Winter, 1938', *Modern Music* 15 no. 3 (Mar.–Apr. 1938), 167–71, WEC 28–31

'Recent Festival in Rochester', *Modern Music* 15 no. 4 (May–June 1938), 241–3, WEC 31–3

'Season's End, New York, 1938', *Modern Music* 15 no. 4 (May–June 1938), 228–32, WEC 34–8

'Coolidge Crusade, WPA, New York Season', *Modern Music* 16 no. 1 (Nov.–Dec. 1938), 33–7, WEC 39–43

'Once Again Swing; also "American Music"', *Modern Music* 16 no. 2 (Jan.–Feb. 1939), 99–103, WEC 43–7

'The Case of Mr Ives; Winter Notes', *Modern Music* 16 no. 3 (Mar.–Apr. 1939), 172–6, WEC 48–51

'O Fair World of Music', *Modern Music* 16 no. 4 (May–June 1939), 238–42, WEC 55–9

'Season of Hindemith and Americans', *Modern Music* 16 no. 4 (May–June 1939), 249–53, WEC 60–3

'New York Season Opens', *Modern Music* 17 no. 1 (Oct.–Nov. 1939), 34–7, WEC 64–8

'American Music on the New York Scene', *Modern Music* 17 no. 2 (Jan.–Feb. 1940), 93–7, WEC 68–74

'Stravinsky and Other Moderns in 1940', *Modern Music* 17 no. 3 (Mar.–Apr. 1940), 164–70, WEC 74–81

'The Changing Scene', *Modern Music* 17 no. 4 (May–June 1940), 237–40, WEC 81–5

Laboratory manuals on music, written while a teacher at St John's College, Annapolis, Md, 1941; mimeographed
    'Manual of Musical Notation', (1 Mar. 1941) p. 22
    'Musical Intervals and Scales', (First Year Laboratory, Exercise 15) 16 pp.
    'The Greek Diatonic Scale', (First Year Laboratory, Exercise 16) 14 pp.
    'The Just Scale and Its Uses', (First Year Laboratory, Exercise 17) 20 pp.

'Composers by the Alphabet', *Modern Music* 19 no. 1 (Nov.–Dec. 1941), 70

'Films and Theatre', *Modern Music* 20 no. 3 (Mar.–Apr. 1943), 205–6, WEC 86–7

'American Figure with Landscape', [Henry F. Gilbert] *Modern Music* 20 no. 4 (May–June 1943), 219–25, WEC 87–93

'Theatre and Films', *Modern Music* 20 no. 4 (May–June 1943), 282–3, WEC 93–5

'Theatre and Films', *Modern Music* 21 no. 1 (Nov.–Dec. 1943), 50–2, WEC 95–8; excerpt about *One Touch of Venus* reprinted in German (tr. Josef Heinzelmann), in *Über Kurt Weill,* ed. David Drew (Frankfurt: Suhrkamp Verlag, 1975), 137–8

'New Compositions', *Saturday Review* 27 no. 4 (22 Jan. 1944), 32–3

'Charles Ives, His Vision and Challenge', *Modern Music* 21 no. 4 (May–June 1944), 199–202, WEC 98–102

'Music as a Liberal Art', *Modern Music* 22 no. 1 (Nov.–Dec. 1944), 12–16, WEC 102–6

'What's New in Music', *Saturday Review* 28 no. 3 (20 Jan. 1945), 13–14, 34

'Vassar Choir Concert Features Belgian Music', *New York Herald Tribune* (15 Mar. 1945)

'Gabriel Fauré', *Listen* 6 no. 1 (May 1945), 8–9, 12, WEC 107–10

'A Commentary on the Poem [*Voyages* III by Hart Crane] by the Composer', Preface to the first edition of *Voyage* (South Hadley, Mass.: The Valley Music Press, 1945), 1 p.

'New Publications of Music', *Saturday Review* 29 no. 4 (26 Jan. 1946), 34, 36,38, WEC 111–16

'Scores for Graham: Festival at Columbia', *Modern Music* 23 no. 1 (Winter 1946), 53–5, WEC 116–18

'Fallacy of the Mechanistic Approach', [review of *The Schillinger System of Musical Composition*] *Modern Music* 23 no. 3 (Summer 1946), 228–30, WEC 118–21

'Walter Piston', *Musical Quarterly* 32 no. 3 (July 1946), 354–73, WEC 121–40; condensed version in *The Book of Modern Composers* 2nd ed., rev. & enl. (New York: Alfred A. Knopf, 1950), 498–508

'The Composer's Viewpoint', *National Music Council Bulletin* 7 no. 1 (Sept. 1946), 10, WEC 140–3

'An American Destiny', [Charles Ives] *Listen* 9 no. 1 (Nov. 1946), 4–7,WEC 143–50

'The Genial Sage', in *Paul Rosenfeld, Voyager in the Arts,* ed. Jerome Mellquist and Lucie Wiese (New York: Creative Age Press, 1948), 163–5

'The Function of the Composer in Teaching the General College Student', *Bulletin of the Society of Music in the Liberal Arts College* 3 no. 1 (1952), Supplement 3, WEC 150–8

'Wallingford Riegger', *American Composers Alliance Bulletin* 2 no. 1 (Feb. 1952), 3–5, WEC 158–9

'The Illinois Festival—Enormous and Active', *New York Herald Tribune* (5 Apr. 1953); reprinted in *Bulletin of the American Composers Alliance* 3 no. 2 (Summer 1953), 17

'Music of the Twentieth Century', *Encyclopaedia Britannica* (Chicago: Encyclopaedia Britannica, 1953), XVI 16–18

'La Musique aux Etats-Unis', *Synthèses,* (Brussels) 9 no. 96 (May 1954), 206–11

'The Rhythmic Basis of American Music', *Score* 12 (June 1955), 27–32, WEC 160–6

Autobiographical sketch written for *The 25th Anniversary Report of the Harvard Class of 1930* (Cambridge, Mass.: Harvard University Press, 1955), 165–9

'Current Chronicle: New York', [review of Roger Sessions's Violin Concerto] *Musical Quarterly* 45 no. 3 (July 1959), 375–81, WEC 166–73

'Current Chronicle: Italy', [review of ISCM festival in Rome] *Musical Quarterly* 45 no. 4 (Oct. 1959), 530–41, WEC 173–84

'Uno paso adelante', *Buenos Aires Musical* 14 special number (Dec. 1959), 63–7; reprinted in English ('A Further Step'), in *The American Composer Speaks 1770–1965,* ed. Gilbert Chase (Baton Rouge: Louisiana State University Press, 1966), 245–54, WEC 185–91

'The Composer's Choices', commissioned by the Fromm Foundation for a radio broadcast (196?), WEC 192–7

'Sixty Staves to Read: This Was One of the Problems Faced by ISCM Jury in Cologne', *New York Times* (24 Jan. 1960), WEC 197–9

'Shop Talk by an American Composer', *Musical Quarterly* 46 no. 2 (Apr. 1960), 189–201; reprinted in *Problems of Modern Music* ed. Paul Henry Lang (New York: W. W. Norton, 1960), 51–63, and in *Contemporary Composers on Contemporary Music,* ed. Elliott Schwartz and Barney Childs (New York: Holt, Rinehart and Winston, 1967), 261–73, WEC 199–211

'Current Chronicle: Germany', [reviews of Shostakovitch's *Lady Macbeth of Mzensk* and Nicolas Nabokov's *Rasputin's End*] *Musical Quarterly* 46 no. 3 (July 1960), 367–71, WEC 212–16

'Variationer for orkester', *Nutida Musik* 4 (1960/61)

'The Milieu of the American Composer', *Perspectives of New Music* 1 no. 1 (Fall 1962), 149–51; reprinted in *High Fidelity and Musical America* 27 no. 9 (Sept. 1977), 6, MA 27, WEC 216–18

'Letter from Europe', *Perspectives of New Music* 1 no. 2 (Spring 1963), 195–205, WEC 219–30

'Letter to the editor', [reply to Gardner Read's criticism of Carter's notation] *Journal of Music Theory* 7 no. 2 (Winter 1963), 270–3

'Expressionism and American Music', *Perspectives of New Music* 4 no. 1 (Fall-Winter 1965), 1–13; reprinted in *Perspectives on American Composers* ed. Benjamin Boretz and Edward T. Cone (New York: W. W. Norton, 1971), 217–29, WEC 230–43

'The Time Dimension in Music', *Music Journal* 23 no. 8 (Nov. 1965), 29–30, WEC 243–7

'Current Chronicle: New York', [Edward Steuermann] *Musical Quarterly* 52 no. 1 (Jan. 1966), WEC 248–55

'Elliott Carter Objects', [letter to the editor in response to an article by Harold Schonberg] *New York Times* (20 Oct. 1968)

Introduction to a poetry reading session by W. H. Auden, Hunter College Playhouse, January 1969, WEC 256–7

Sleeve notes for Nonesuch H-71234 (1969 recording of Sonata for Violoncello and Piano, and Sonata for Flute, Oboe, Cello and Harpsichord), WEC 269–73

'String Quartet No. 2 (1959)', *Alice Tully Hall Program* (15 Apr. 1970), WEC 273–4

'Conversation with Elliott Carter', by Benjamin Boretz, *Perspectives of New Music* 8 no. 2 (Spring-Summer 1970), 1–22

Sleeve notes for Nonesuch H-71249 (1970 recording of String Quartets Nos. 1 and 2), WEC 274–9

'The Composer Is a University Commodity', [reply to the questionnaire 'The Composer in Academia—Reflections on a Theme of Stravinsky'] *College Music Symposium* 10 (Fall 1970), 68–70, WEC 279–82

'Elliott Carter', in *The Orchestral Composer's Point of View* ed. Robert Stephen Hines (Norman, Okla.: University of Oklahoma Press, 1970), 39–61, WEC 282–300

'Igor Stravinsky, 1882–1971', *Perspectives of New Music* 9 no. 2 (1971), 1–6, WEC 301–6

Flawed Words and Stubborn Sounds, A Conversation with Elliott Carter by Allen Edwards, (New York: W. W. Norton, 1971)

'Variations for Orchestra', *Philharmonic Hall Program* (Apr. 1972), WEC 308–10

'Music Criticism', [read over the BBC August 1972 as part of the series *Composers and Criticism*, ed. Elaine Padmore], WEC 310–18

'In memoriam: Stefan Wolpe, 1902–1972', *Perspectives of New Music* 11 no. 1 (Fall-Winter 1972), 3–5, WEC 318–20

'Acceptance by Mr Carter of the Gold Medal for Music', *Proceedings of the American Academy of Arts and Letters and the National Institute of Arts and Letters* 2nd series no. 22 (1972), 34

'Igor Stravinsky, 1882–1971', *Proceedings of the American Academy of Arts and Letters and the National Institute of Arts and Letters* 2nd series no. 22 (1972), 84–6, WEC 306–8

'Stefan Wolpe (1902–1972), In Memoriam', *Tempo* 102 (1972), 17–18; revised version in *Proceedings of the American Academy of Arts and Letters and the National Institute of Arts and Letters* 2nd series no. 23 (1973), 115–17

Introductory talk for the BBC première of the Brass Quintet (20 Oct. 1974), WEC 322–5

Reminiscence written for *Charles Ives Remembered* by Vivian Perlis (New Haven: Yale University Press, 1974), 131–45, WEC 258–69

Sleeve note for Columbia (USA) M32738 (1974 recording of String Quartet No. 3), WEC 320–2

'Documents of a Friendship with Ives', *Parnassus* 3 no. 2 (Spring-Summer 1975), 300–15; reprinted in *Tempo* 117 (June 1976), 2–10, WEC 331–43

Sleeve note for Nonesuch H71314 (1975 recording of Double Concerto, and Duo for Violin and Piano), WEC 326–30

'To Think of Milton Babbitt', *Perspectives of New Music* 14 no. 2, 15 no. 1 (double issue 1976), 29–31

'Foreword', *Sonic Design* by Robert Cogan and Pozzi Escot (Englewood Cliffs, N.J.: Prentice-Hall, 1976), ix

'Music and the Time Screen', *Current Thought in Musicology*, ed. John W. Grubbs (Austin: University of Texas Press, 1976), 63–88, WEC 343–65

'Was ist amerikanische Musik?', *Oesterreichische Musikzeitschrift* 31 no. 10 (Oct. 1976), 468–70; translated ('What Is American Music?'), and published in *Oesterreichische Musikzeitschrift* special English language issue (Oct. 1976), 4–6

'France Amérique Ltd.', *Paris–New York* (Paris: Centre national d'art et de culture Georges Pompidou; Musée national d'art moderne, 1977), 6–11

'A Symphony of Three Orchestras', *Avery Fisher Hall Program* (17–22 Feb. 1977), WEC 366–7

The Writings of Elliott Carter: An American Composer Looks at Modern Music, ed. Else Stone and Kurt Stone (Bloomington: Indiana University Press, 1977)

'On Edgard Varèse', *The New Worlds of Edgard Varèse*, ed. Sherman van Solkema (New York: Institute for Studies in American Music, Brooklyn College, 1979), 1–7, [originally written in French and read over transatlantic telephone 29 Oct. 1975 for a programme broadcast by Radio-France (ORTF)]

'Insomnia', from *A Mirror on Which to Dwell*, MS reproduced in *World Literature Today* 51 no. 1 (Winter 1977), 20–2

'Elliott Carter', [interview by Marvin A. Wolfthal] (in Italian), *La Musica* (Milan) 3 no. 14 (Oct. 1979), 232–3

Interview with George Gelles *Amacadmy* (The Newsletter of the American Academy in Rome) (Jul. 1979)

'Foreword', *Selected Essays and Reviews 1948–1968* by Richard Franko Goldman, ed. Dorothy Klotzman (New York: Institute for Studies in American Music, Brooklyn College, 1980), vii-ix

Autobiographical sketch written for *Harvard Class of 1930 Fiftieth Anniversary Report* (Cambridge, Mass.: Harvard University Press, 1980), 836–8

Writings about Elliott Carter

Citations for articles by Richard Franko Goldman which have been reprinted in his *Selected Essays and Reviews, 1948–1968* (New York: Institute for Studies in American Music, Brooklyn College, 1980) are followed by the abbreviation RFG and the page numbers from that collection.

Austin, William W.: *Music in the 20th Century, from Debussy through Stravinsky* (New York: W. W. Norton, 1966), 442–4

Blyth, Alan: 'Elliott Carter on musical vocabulary', *The Times* (10 Jan. 1968), 7

Boulez, Pierre: *Elliott Carter: A Birthday Tribute,* (London: AMP/Schirmer, 1978), 8

Boykan, Martin: 'Elliott Carter and Postwar Composers', *Perspectives of New Music* 2 no. 2 (Spring-Summer 1964), 125–8

Bradshaw, Susan: 'Passage du XXᵉ siècle: au-delà des Viennois', *Passage du XXᵉ siècle,* 1re partie (Jan.–Jul. 1977), IRCAM—Centre Georges Pompidou, 58–9

Brandt, William E.: 'The Music of Elliott Carter: Simultaneity and Complexity', *Music Educators Journal* 60 no. 9 (May 1974), 24–32

'Carter, Elliott', *Current Biography* (Nov. 1960), 7–8

'Carter Vogue', *Time* 105 (10 Feb. 1975), 65

Chase, Gilbert: *America's Music, from the Pilgrims to the Present* rev. 2nd edn. (New York: McGraw-Hill, 1966), 567–9

Clements, Andrew: 'Elliott Carter Views American Music', *Music and Musicians* 26 no. 7 (Mar. 1978), 32–4

Collaer, Paul: *La Musique moderne, 1905–1955* (Brussels: Elsevier, 1955), 267

Composers Quartet: *Elliott Carter: A Birthday Tribute* (London: AMP/ Schirmer, 1978), 9

Copland, Aaron: 'America's Young Men of Music', *Music and Musicians* 9 no. 4 (Dec. 1960), 11

——— 'Presentation to Elliott C. Carter of the Gold Medal for Music', *Proceedings of the American Academy of Arts and Letters and the National Institute of Arts and Letters* 2nd series no. 22 (1972), 32–3

Daniel, Oliver: *Elliott Carter* (New York: Broadcast Music, Inc., 1962)

Davies, Peter Maxwell: *Elliott Carter: A Birthday Tribute* (London: AMP/ Schirmer, 1978), 9

Davis, Peter G.: 'Speculum Musicae Celebrates Elliott Carter at 70', *New York Times* (11 Dec. 1978), 18

DeRhen, Andrew: 'League-ISCM: Carter Works', *High Fidelity and Musical America* 29 no. 2 (Feb. 1979), MA22–MA24

Driver, Christopher: 'A Composer Deeply Respected', *The Guardian* (25 Aug. 1975), 6

Edmunds, John and Gordon Boelzner: *Some Twentieth-Century American Composers, A Selective Bibliography* (New York: The New York Public Library, 1959), 25–7

'Elite Composer', *Time* 67 no. 22 (28 May 1956), 48

'Elliott Carter', in 'Contributors to This Issue', *Score* 12 (June 1955), 94

Ellsworth, Ray E.: 'Classic Modern', *Down Beat* 24 no. 19 (19 Sept. 1957), 36

Ericson, Raymond: 'Carter on the Record', *New York Times* (1 Feb. 1970)

Ewen, David: *Composers since 1900, A Biographical and Critical Guide* (New York: H. W. Wilson, 1969), 116–19

Flanagan, William: 'Elliott Carter', *The International Cyclopedia of Music and Musicians* ed.-in-chief Oscar Thompson, ed. of 10th edn. Bruce Bohle (New York: Dodd, Mead, 1975), 366–8

Fromm, Paul: *Elliott Carter: A Birthday Tribute* (London: AMP/Schirmer, 1978), 10

Gauthier, André: 'Elliott Carter: "A la manière de Rameau"', *Les Nouvelles Littéraires* 55 no. 2569 (27 Jan.–3 Feb. 1977), 13

Glanville-Hicks, Peggy: 'Elliott Carter', *Grove's Dictionary of Music and Musicians* 5th edn., ed. Eric Blom (New York: St Martin's, 1955), II, 97–8

——— *Grove's* . . . supplement (New York: St Martin's, 1961), 63–4

Glock, William: 'A Note on Elliott Carter', *Score* 12 (June 1955), 47–52

——— *Elliott Carter: A Birthday Tribute* (London: AMP/Schirmer, 1978), 8

——— Laudatio auf Elliott Carter (Zug: Ernst-von-Siemens-Stiftung, 1981)

Goldman, Richard Franko: 'Current Chronicle: New York', *Musical Quarterly* 37 no. 1 (Jan. 1951), 83–9, RFG 69–74

——— 'The Music of Elliott Carter', *Musical Quarterly* 43 no. 2 (Apr. 1957), 151–70, RFG 33–47

——— 'Music In The United States', *New Oxford History of Music, Volume X: The Modern Age 1890–1960* ed. Martin Cooper (London: Oxford University Press, 1974), 630–4

Griffiths, Paul: *The Musical Times* 115 no. 1572 (Feb. 1974), 154

Hamilton, David: 'Amidst the Mountains: Contemporary Music', *High Fidelity and Musical America* 23 no. 12 (Dec. 1973), MA20-MA21

Hansen, Peter S.: *An Introduction to Twentieth-Century Music* 3rd edn. (Boston: Allyn and Bacon, 1971), 355–6, 405–7

Henahan, Donal: *New York Times* (1 Nov. 1974)

____ 'Elliott Carter Has a Birthday', *New York Times* (17 Feb. 1969)

Henderson, Robert: 'Elliott Carter', *Music and Musicians* 14 no. 5 (Jan. 1966), 20–3

Hitchcock, Hugh Wiley: *Music in the United States* 2nd edn. (Englewood Cliffs, N.J.: Prentice-Hall, 1974), 228–31

Hurwitz, Robert: 'Elliott Carter: The Communication of Time', [interview] *Changes in the Arts* 78 (Nov. 1972), 10–11

Jackson, Richard, ed.: *Elliott Carter: Sketches and Scores in Manuscript,* [NYPL exhibit catalogue; bibl; illus.] (New York: The New York Public Library, 1973)

Kastendieck, Miles: *BMI, The Many Worlds of Music* 3 (1973), 36–7

Keats, Sheila: 'Reference Articles on American Composers: An Index', *Juilliard Review* 1 no. 3 (Fall 1954), 24

Kerner, Leighton: 'Elliott Carter Wrestles at 70', *Village Voice* (25 Dec. 1978), 87–8

____ 'The Eloquence of Elliott Carter', *Village Voice* (11 Nov. 1974)

Koegler, Horst: 'Blick in die Welt', *Musica* 12 no. 6 (June 1958), 363

____ 'Europäer hören amerikanische Musik', *Der Monat* 10 no. 117 (June 1958), 68–73

____ 'Begegnungen mit Elliott Carter', *Melos* 26 (1959), 256–8

Kolodin, Irving: 'Carter in Retrospect', *Saturday Review* (8 May 1971)

Kostelanetz, Richard: 'The Astounding Success of Elliott Carter', *High Fidelity* 18 no. 5 (May 1968), 41–5

____ *Master Minds: Portraits of Contemporary American Artists and Intellectuals* (New York: Macmillan, 1969), 289–303

Kozinn, Allan: 'Elliott Carter at 70, Something to Whistle', *Soho Weekly News* (14 Dec. 1978), 30, 71

Machlis, Joseph: *Introduction to Contemporary Music* 2nd edn. (New York: W. W. Norton, 1979), 505–14

Martin, William R., and Julius Drossin: *Music of the Twentieth Century* (Englewood Cliffs, N.J.: Prentice-Hall, 1980), 238–47

Mayer, Martin: 'Elliott Carter: Out of the Desert and Into the Concert Hall', *New York Times* (10 Dec. 1978), 21, 36

Mellers, Wilfrid: *Music in a New Found Land* (New York: Alfred A. Knopf, 1965), 102–21

Northcott, Bayan: *The New Grove Dictionary of Music and Musicians,* ed. Stanley Sadie (London: Macmillan, 1980), III, 831–6

____ 'Carter in Perspective', *The Musical Times* 119 no. 1630 (Dec. 1978), 1039–41

____ 'Elliott Carter—Continuity and Coherence', *Music and Musicians* 20 no. 12 (Aug. 1972), 28–39

'People Are Talking About . . .', *Vogue* 165 (Apr. 1975), 152–3

Ponsonby, Robert: *Elliott Carter: A Birthday Tribute* (London: AMP/ Schirmer, 1978), 9

Reis, Claire: 'Elliott Cook Carter, Jr.', *Composers in America* (New York: Macmillan, 1947), 60–2

Rorem, Ned: 'Elliott Carter' *New Republic* 166 (26 Feb. 1972), 22

—— 'Messiaen and Carter at 70', *The Listener* 100 (14 Dec. 1978), 806–7

—— 'Messiaen and Carter On Their Birthdays', *Tempo* 127 (Dec. 1978), 22–4

Rosen, Charles: 'Carter, Elliott', *Dictionary of Contemporary Music,* ed. John Vinton (New York: E. P. Dutton & Co, 1974), 127–9

Rosenfeld, Paul: 'The Newest American Composers', *Modern Music* 15 no. 3 (Mar.–Apr. 1938), 157–8

Rossiter, Frank R.: *Charles Ives and His America* (New York: Liveright, 1975), 285–7, 293–4

Salzman, Eric: *Twentieth-Century Music: An Introduction* 2nd edn. (Englewood Cliffs, N.J: Prentice-Hall, 1974), 163–4

Saminsky, Lazare: *Living Music of the Americas* (New York: Howell, Soskin and Crown, 1949), 92–4

Schiff, David: 'Carter in the Seventies', *Tempo* 130 (Sept. 1979), 2–10

Shneerson, Grigorii: *Portrety Amerikanskikh Kompozitorov* (Moscow: Muzyka, 1977), 135–50

Skulsky, Abraham: 'Elliott Carter', *Bulletin of the American Composers Alliance* 3 no. 2 (Summer 1953), 2–16

—— 'The High Cost of Creativity', *HiFi Review* 2 no. 5 (May 1959), 31–6

Slonimsky, Nicolas: 'Elliott Cook Carter, Jr.', *Baker's Biographical Dictionary of Musicians* 5th edn. (New York: G. Schirmer, 1958), 257–8

—— *Baker's . . .*1971 supplement (New York: G. Schirmer, 1971), 41

—— *Baker's . . .*6th edn. (New York: Schirmer Books, 1978), 284

Smith, Patrick J.: 'Elliott Carter, Musician of the Month', *High Fidelity and Musical America* 23 no. 8 (Aug. 1973), MA4-MA5

Steinberg, Michael: 'Elliott Carter: an American Original at Seventy', *Keynote* 2 no. 10 (Dec. 1978), 8–14

—— 'Introduction', *Elliott Carter: Sketches and Scores in Manuscript* ed. Richard Jackson (New York: The New York Public Library, 1973), 7–9

Stone, Kurt: 'Problems and Methods of Notation', *Perspectives of New Music* 1 no. 2 (Spring 1963), 9–26

—— 'Current Chronicle: New York', *Musical Quarterly* 55 no. 4 (Oct. 1969), 559–72

Stravinsky, Igor, and Robert Craft: *Dialogues and a Diary* (London: Faber & Faber, 1968), 99–101

Sykes, James: 'The Music of Elliott Carter', *The Listener* (31 May 1962), 969

Thomson, Virgil: *American Music Since 1910* (New York: Holt, Rinehart and Winston, 1970), 84, 130

Vlad, Roman: 'Elliott Carter', *La Rassegna musicale* 24 no. 4 (Oct.–Dec. 1954), 369–71

Walsh, Stephen: 'Disagreeable Stimulus', *The Listener* 94 (4 Sept. 1975), 312–3

Weber, J. F.: 'An Elliott Carter Discography', *Association for Recorded Sound Collections Journal* 8 no. 1 (1976), 33–9
—— *Carter and Schuman* (Utica, N.Y.: J. F. Weber, 1978), 1–10
Whittall, Arnold: 'Elliott Carter', *First American Music Conference: Keele University . . . 18–21 April 1975* (Keele: University of Keele, Dept of Music [1977?]), 82–98
Zanetti, Emilia: *Enciclopedia dello Spettacolo* (Rome: Casa Editrice le Maschere, 1956), III, 126

Writings about Individual Works of Elliott Carter

Citations for articles by Richard Franko Goldman which have been reprinted in his Selected Essays and Reviews 1948–1968 (New York: Institute for Studies in American Music, Brooklyn College, 1980) are followed by the abbreviation RFG and the page numbers from that collection.

BRASS QUINTET

Griffiths, Paul: *The Musical Times* 115 no. 1582 (Dec. 1974), 1069
Hamilton, David: *The Nation* (11 Jan. 1975)
Kerner, Leighton: 'Solid Gold Chamber Music', *Village Voice* (13 Jan. 1975)
Kolodin, Irving: *Saturday Review/World* (25 Jan. 1975), 50–2
Porter, Andrew: *New Yorker* 50 no. 5 (30 Dec. 1974), 55
Rockwell, John: *New York Times* (17 Dec. 1974)
Saylor, Bruce: *High Fidelity and Musical America* 25 no. 4 (Apr. 1975), MA29—MA30
Villatico, Dino: 'Attenti alle asprezze servono tutte a nascondere Debussy', *La Repubblica* (Rome) (16 June 1978)
Weber, William: *Los Angeles Times* (14 Feb. 1975)

CONCERTO FOR ORCHESTRA

Cott, Jon: *Rolling Stone* 80 (15 Apr. 1971), 46
Griffiths, Paul: 'Proms', *The Musical Times* 116 no. 1592 (Oct. 1975), 894–5
Hamilton, David: *The Nation* 210 (2 Mar. 1970), 253–4
—— *High Fidelity* 20 no. 5 (May 1970), 22
—— *High Fidelity* 20 no. 3 (Mar. 1971), 82
Jacobson, Robert: *Saturday Review* 53 (21 Feb. 1970), 50
Kenyon, Nicholas: *Music and Musicians* 24 no. 2 (Oct. 1975), 50, 52, 54
Kerner, Leighton: *Village Voice* (26 Mar. 1970)
—— 'Whirlwinds to Whispers', *Village Voice* (21 Feb. 1974)
Sadie, Stanley: *The Times* (11 Aug. 1972)
Schonberg, Harold: *New York Times* (6 Feb. 1970)
Shawe-Taylor, Desmond: 'Flux and Turmoil', *New Yorker* 49 no. 52 (18 Feb. 1974), 104–6

Smith, Patrick J.: *High Fidelity and Musical America* 20 no. 5 (May 1970), section 2: 21, 24
Steinberg, Michael: *Boston Globe* (15 Feb. 1970)

THE DEFENSE OF CORINTH

Avshalomoff, Jacob: *Music Library Association Notes* 7 no. 3 (June 1950), 442–3
Berger, Arthur: *New York Herald Tribune* (19 Dec. 1951)
Goldman, Richard Franko: RFG 35–6
Perkins, Francis D.: *New York Herald Tribune* (6 Apr. 1942)
Williams, Alexander: *Boston Herald* (13 Mar. 1942)

DOUBLE CONCERTO

'American Concerto Given First U.K. Performance', *The Times* (27 Apr. 1962)
Archibald, Bruce: *Musical Quarterly* 63 no. 2 (Apr. 1977), 287–9
DeLone, Richard P.: 'Timbre and Texture in Twentieth-Century Music', *Aspects of Twentieth-Century Music* ed. Gary E. Wittlich (Englewood Cliffs N.J.: Prentice-Hall, 1975), 198–207
Fuller, David: *Music Library Association Notes* 22 no. 1 (Fall 1965), 819–20
Goldman, Richard Franko: RFG 135–6, 138–41
Hamilton, David: *The Nation* 218 no. 3 (19 Jan. 1974), 93–4
Harrison, Max: *The Times* (31 Jul. 1970)
Northcott, Bayan: 'Crosstalk', *New Statesman* 86 no. 2230 (14 Dec. 1973), 920–1
Porter, Andrew: 'Marvelous Performers', *New Yorker* 50 no. 38 (11 Nov. 1974), 199–200, 203
Rich, Alan: *New York Times* (22 Jul. 1962)
Rosen, Charles: 'One Easy Piece', *New York Review of Books* 20 no. 2 (1973), 25–9
Salzman, Eric: *New York Times* (7 Sept. 1961)
Stravinsky, Igor, and Robert Craft: *Dialogues and a Diary* (Faber & Faber, 1968), 99–101
Wilson, Carolyn: 'Time and Motion', *Records and Recording* 11 no. 5 (Feb. 1968), 21–3

DUO FOR VIOLIN AND PIANO

Archibald, Bruce: *Musical Quarterly* 63 no. 2 (Apr. 1977), 289
Condé, Gérard: 'Le "Duo", d'Elliott Carter', *Le Monde* (29 May 1976)
Crichton, Ronald: *Financial Times* (1 June 1976)
Ericson, Raymond: *New York Times* (23 Mar. 1975)
Northcott, Bayan: *Tempo* 116 (Mar. 1976), 29
Porter, Andrew: 'Duo', *New Yorker* 51 no. 7 (7 Apr. 1975), 129–30

EIGHT ETUDES AND A FANTASY FOR WOODWIND QUARTET

Eyer, Ronald: *Musical America* 72 no. 14 (15 Nov. 1952), 8
Frankenstein, Alfred: 'Recordings', *High Fidelity* 8 no. 5 (May 1958), 54
Goldman, Richard Franko: RFG 133
Harrison, Jay S.: *New York Herald Tribune* (29 Oct. 1952)
Winold, Allen: 'Rhythm in Twentieth-Century Music', *Aspects of Twentieth-Century Music* ed. Gary E. Wittlich (Englewood Cliffs N.J.: Prentice Hall, 1975), 230–1

EIGHT PIECES FOR FOUR TIMPANI

Larrick, Geary H.: *Percussionist* 12 no. 1 (Fall 1974), 12–15
McCormick, Robert M.: *Percussionist* 12 no. 1 (Fall 1974), 7–11

EMBLEMS

Goldman, Richard Franko: RFG 40–2

THE HARMONY OF MORNING

Goldman, Richard Franko: RFG 35–6
Thomson, Virgil: *New York Herald Tribune* (27 Feb. 1945)

HOLIDAY OVERTURE

Biancolli, Louis: *New York World-Telegram* (19 Apr. 1960)
Goldman, Richard Franko: RFG 37, 67–68
Jacobson, Bernard: *Chicago Daily News* (10 Apr. 1970)
Lang, Paul Henry: *New York Herald Tribune* (26 Apr. 1957)
Stadlen, Peter: *The Daily Telegraph* (30 Sept. 1967)

THE MINOTAUR (BALLET)

Berger, Arthur: *New York Herald Tribune* (28 Mar. 1947)
_____ *New York Herald Tribune* (19 May 1947)
Goldman, Richard Franko: RFG 40
Smith, Cecil: 'Sights and Sounds of Spring', *Theatre Arts* 31 no. 6 (June 1947), 34
Terry, Walter: *New York Herald Tribune* (6 Apr. 1947)

THE MINOTAUR (SUITE)

Watt, Douglas: *New Yorker* 32 no. 14 (26 May 1956), 130

A MIRROR ON WHICH TO DWELL

Clements, Andrew: 'UK Première for Carter', *Music and Musicians* 25 no. 4 (Dec. 1976), 4

DeRhen, Andrew: 'Speculum Musicae: Carter Première', *High Fidelity and Musical America* 26 no. 6 (June 1976), MA27

Dyer, Richard: 'Carter song-cycle performed', *Boston Globe* (11 May 1977), 53

Guzelimian, Ara: 'Elliott Carter Première at Bing Theatre', *Los Angeles Times* (23 Mar. 1978)

Hamilton, David: *The Nation* 222 (27 Mar. 1976), 382

Henahan, Donal: *New York Times* (26 Feb. 1976)

Heyworth, Peter: 'Peering into the Mirror', *The Observer* (12 May 1976), 28

Kerner, Leighton: 'Carter Reclaims the Voice for the Mind', *Village Voice* (8 Mar. 1976), 76

Mann, William: *The Times* (30 Mar. 1976)

Northcott, Bayan: 'Better Late . . .', *Sunday Telegraph* (2 June 1976)

Porter, Andrew: 'Elliott Carter Songs', *Financial Times* (13 Mar. 1976)

—— 'Reflections', *New Yorker* 52 no. 3 (8 Mar. 1976), 122, 125–6

Schiff, David: 'Elliott Carter: A Mirror on Which to Dwell', *New York Arts Journal* 2 no. 1 (Spring 1977), 41–3

Shawe-Taylor, Desmond: 'The Meeting of the Rivers', *The Times* (6 Nov. 1977)

MUSICIANS WRESTLE EVERYWHERE

Goldman, Richard Franko: RFG 35–6

Thomson, Virgil: *New York Herald Tribune* (16 June 1951)

NIGHT FANTASIES

Bowen, Meirion: 'Elliott Carter Première', *The Guardian* (4 June 1980)

Griffiths, Paul: *The Times* (4 June 1980)

Heyworth, Peter: 'Carter's Characters', *The Observer* (8 June 1980)

Murray, David: 'Bath Festival', *Financial Times* (5 June 1980)

Northcott, Bayan: 'Bath Night', *Sunday Telegraph* (8 June 1980)

Shawe-Taylor, Desmond: *Sunday Times* (8 June 1980)

PIANO CONCERTO

Boretz, Benjamin: *The Nation* 204 (Apr. 1967), 445–6

Cohn, Arthur: *The American Record Guide* 34 no. 10 (June 1968), 936–7, 945

Crichton, Ronald: *Financial Times* (26 Mar. 1970)

Emmerson, Simon: 'Carter and Davies', *Music and Musicians* 26 no. 12 (Aug. 1978), 32–3

Finn, Robert: *Cleveland Plain Dealer* (14 Dec. 1969)

Greenfield, Edward: *The Guardian* (26 Mar. 1970)

Hamilton, David: 'The New Craft of the Contemporary Concerto: Carter and Sessions', *High Fidelity* 18 no. 5 (May 1968), 67–8

Henahan, Donal: *New York Times* (24 Feb. 1975)

_____ 'Why Must New York Wait for New Music?', *New York Times* (9 Mar. 1975), II 21

Heyworth, Peter: *The Observer Review* (29 Mar. 1970)

_____ 'Secret Door', *The Observer Review* (5 Mar. 1978)

Kerner, Leighton: 'Carter's Fire-Eating Landmark', *Village Voice* (17 Mar. 1975)

_____ 'Concerto Wars', *Village Voice* (18 Dec. 1978)

Klein, Howard: *New York Times* (17 Mar. 1968)

_____ 'Little to Think About', *Daily Express* (26 Mar. 1970)

Mann, William: *The Times* (2 Mar. 1978), 8

Mason, Colin: *The Daily Telegraph* (26 Mar. 1970)

Meyer, John Arthur: 'The Idea of Conflict in the Concerto', *Studies in Music* (Australia), 8 (1974), 49–50

Murray, David: 'Carter's Piano Concerto', *Financial Times* (3 Mar. 1978)

Northcott, Bayan: 'Concerto in Conflict', *Sunday Telegraph* (5 Mar. 1978)

Saal, Hubert: *Newsweek* 69 no. 3 (16 Jan. 1967), 94

Steinberg, Michael: *Boston Globe* (7 Jan. 1967)

Stone, Kurt: 'Current Chronicle: New York', *Musical Quarterly* 55 no. 4 (Oct. 1969), 559–72

_____ 'Treat Worth the Travail', *Time* 89 no. 2 (13 Jan. 1967), 44

Walsh, Stephen: 'Elliott Carter's Piano Concerto', *The Listener* 81 no. 2087 (31 Mar. 1969), 357

_____ *The Times* (6 Mar. 1970)

PIANO SONATA

Below, Robert: 'Elliott Carter's Piano Sonata: an Important Contribution to Piano Literature', *Music Review* 34 nos. 3–4 (Aug.–Nov. 1973), 282–93

Berger, Arthur: *New York Herald Tribune* (3 May 1948)

_____ 'King David and Reforestation', *Saturday Review* 35 no. 13 (29 Mar. 1952), 48

_____ *New York Herald Tribune* (28 Oct. 1958)

Cohn, Arthur: *American Record Guide* 29 no. 11 (July 1963), 867–8

Goldman, Richard Franko: RFG 37–40, 71–2

Harmon, Carter: *New York Times* (13 Mar. 1948)

_____ *New York Times* (3 May 1948)

Keys, Ivor: *Music and Letters* 30 no. 1 (Jan. 1949), 89

Meyerstein, E. H. W.: *Music Review* 10 no. 1 (Feb. 1949), 45

Perkins, Francis D.: *New York Herald Tribune* (6 Mar. 1947)

Rosen, Charles: sleeve notes for his recording on EPIC LC 3850 + BC 1250

Steinfirst, Donald S.: *Pittsburgh Post Gazette* (18 Dec. 1947)

Strauss, Noel: *New York Times* (6 Mar. 1947)

Thomson, Virgil: *New York Herald Tribune* (13 Mar. 1948)

POCAHONTAS (BALLET)

Martin, John: *New York Times* (25 May 1939)

POCAHONTAS (SUITE)

Cohn, Arthur: *American Record Guide* 29 no. 11 (Jul. 1963), 867–8
Klein, Howard: *New York Times* (12 May 1963)
Rosen, Charles: sleeve notes for recording on EPIC LC 3850 + BC 1260

SONATA FOR FLUTE, OBOE, CELLO AND HARPSICHORD

Griffiths, Paul: *The Musical Times* 114 no. 1565 (Jul. 1973), 726
Moore, David W.: 'A Very Different Impression of Elliott Carter', *The American Record Guide* 36 no. 7 (Mar. 1970), 498
Morgan, Robert P.: *High Fidelity* 20 no. 2 (Feb. 1970), 84
Salzman, Eric: *New York Times* (23 Jul. 1961)
Thomson, Virgil: *New York Herald Tribune* (11 Nov. 1953)
Trimble, Lester: *Stereo Review* 24 no. 3 (Mar. 1970), 86–87

SONATA FOR VIOLONCELLO AND PIANO

Berger, Arthur: *New York Herald Tribune* (28 Feb. 1950)
——— 'King David and Reforestation', *Saturday Review* 35 no. 13 (29 Mar. 1952), 48
Bergsma, William: *Music Library Association Notes* 11 no. 3 (June 1954), 434–5
Biancolli, Louis: *New York Sun* (28 Feb. 1950)
Goldman, Richard Franko: RFG 41–43, 69–74
Kastendieck, Miles: *New York Journal American* (28 Feb. 1950)
Moore, David W.: 'A Very Different Impression of Elliott Carter', *The American Record Guide* 36 no. 7 (Mar. 1970), 498
Morgan, Robert P.: *High Fidelity* 20 no. 2 (Feb. 1970), 84
Rudiakov, Michael: 'Carter Sonata', sleeve notes for recording of Sonata by Michael Rudiakov and Ursula Oppens, Golden Crest RE 7081
Thomson, Virgil: *New York Herald Tribune* (20 Nov. 1950)

STRING QUARTET NO. 1

Cairns, David: 'Stepping Stones to Greatness', *The Times* (17 Oct. 1976)
Clements, Andrew: 'Elliott Carter and the Composers Quartet', *Music and Musicians* 24 no. 3 (Nov. 1975), 12, 14
Cogan, Robert, and Pozzi Escot: *Sonic Design* (Englewood Cliffs, N.J.: Prentice-Hall, 1976), 204–5
De la Grange, Henri Louis: *Arts* (Paris) (5 Nov. 1957)
Downes, Edward: *New York Times* (9 Dec. 1956)
Frankenstein, Alfred: *San Francisco Chronicle* (6 Jan 1956)

Glock, William: 'Music Festival in Rome', *Encounter* 2 no. 6 (June 1954), 60–3

Goldman, Richard Franko: RFG 43–4

Hamza, George: *Contributii la interpretarea cvartetului de coarde* (Bucharest: Editura Muzicala, 1977), 114–22

Harrison, Max: *The Times* (22 Jan. 1972)

Kerman, Joseph: 'American Music: The Columbia Series', *Hudson Review* 11 no. 3 (Autumn 1958), 420–5

Kolodin, Irving: *Saturday Review* 53 no. 18 (2 May 1970), 28

Lang, Paul Henry: *New York Herald Tribune* (24 Oct. 1958)

Mayer, Martin: *Esquire* 47 no. 2 (Feb. 1957), 17

Morgan, Robert P.: *High Fidelity* 21 no. 2 (Feb. 1971), 76–8

____ *Musical Newsletter* 4 no. 3 (Summer 1974), 3–11

Northcott, Bayan: 'Crosstalk', *New Statesman* 86 no. 2230 (14 Dec. 1973), 920–1

Rochberg, George: *Musical Quarterly* 43 no. 1 (Jan. 1957), 130–2

Schonberg, Harold: *New York Times* (27 Feb. 1953)

Shawe-Taylor, Desmond: 'A New Voice', *New Statesman and Nation* 50 no. 1290 (26 Nov. 1955), 702–3

Soblosky, Irving: *Chicago Daily News* (7 Feb. 1957)

Strongin, Theodore M.: *New York Herald Tribune* (27 Feb. 1953)

Thomson, Virgil: *New York Herald Tribune* (5 May 1953)

Yates, Peter: 'Chamber Music and the Spontaneous', *Arts and Architecture* 76 no. 8 (Aug. 1959), 4–5, 8–10

STRING QUARTET NO. 2

Cairns, David: 'Stepping Stones to Greatness', *The Times* (17 Oct. 1976)

Clements, Andrew: 'Elliott Carter and the Composers Quartet', *Music and Musicians* 24 no. 3 (Nov. 1975), 12, 14

____ 'Composers Quartet', *Music and Musicians* 25 no. 4 (Dec. 1976), 51–2

Cogan, Robert, and Pozzi Escot: *Sonic Design* (Englewood Cliffs N.J.: Prentice-Hall, 1976), 59–71, 205–7, 284–9

Goldman, Richard Franko: RFG 119–22

Hamilton, David: 'The Unique Imagination of Elliott Carter', *High Fidelity and Musical America* 24 no. 7 (Jul. 1974), 73–5

Harrison, Max: *The Times* (22 Jan. 1972)

Kliewer, Vernon L.: 'Melody: Linear Aspects of Twentieth-Century Music', *Aspects of Twentieth-Century Music* ed. Gary E. Wittlich (Englewood Cliffs N.J.: Prentice-Hall, 1975), 308–10

Kolodin, Irving: *Saturday Review* 53 no. 18 (2 May 1970), 28

Lang, Paul Henry: *New York Herald Tribune* (26 Mar. 1960)

Martin, William R., and Julius Drossin: *Music of the Twentieth Century* (Englewood Cliffs N.J.: Prentice-Hall, 1980), 241–7

Moevs, Robert; *Musical Quarterly* 61 no. 1 (Jan. 1975), 165–8

Morgan, Robert P.: *High Fidelity* 21 no. 2 (Feb. 1971), 76–8

____ *Musical Newsletter* 4 no. 3 (Summer 1974), 3–11

Northcott, Bayan: 'Crosstalk', *New Statesman* 86 no. 2230 (14 Dec. 1973), 920–1

Parmenter, Ross: *New York Times* (22 Dec. 1960)

Perkins, Francis D.: *New York Herald Tribune* (22 Dec. 1960)

Salzman, Eric: 'Carter's String Quartet No. 2 Earns Citation from New York Critics', *New York Times* (7 May 1961)

Schonberg, Harold: *New York Times* (25 Jan. 1962)

Steinberg, Michael: 'Elliott Carter's Second String Quartet', *Score* 27 (Jul. 1960), 22–6

_____ *Boston Globe* (4 Dec. 1968)

Taubman, Howard: *New York Times* (26 Mar. 1960)

STRING QUARTET NO. 3

Bender, William: *Time* 101 no. 6 (5 Feb. 1973), 59–60

Belt, Byron: *Newark Star-Ledger* (24 Jan. 1973)

Cairns, David: 'Stepping Stones to Greatness', *The Times* (17 Oct. 1976)

Clements, Andrew: 'Elliott Carter and the Composers Quartet', *Music and Musicians* 24 no. 3 (Nov. 1975), 12, 14

Cole, Hugo: *The Guardian* (25 Nov. 1975)

'Elliott Carter drittes Streichquartett', *Neue Zuericher Zeitung* (10 Feb. 1973)

Hamilton, David *The Nation* 216 no. 8 (19 Feb. 1973), 250–2

_____ 'The Unique Imagination of Elliott Carter', *High Fidelity and Musical America* 24 no. 7 (Jul. 1974), 73–75

Henahan, Donal: *New York Times* (25 Jan. 1973)

Johnson, Harriet: *New York Post* (25 Jan. 1973)

Jones, Patricia: 'Rutgers University: Elliott Carter Lectures', *Current Musicology* 20 (1975), 9–10

Kenyon, Nicholas: *Music and Musicians* 24 no. 2 (Oct. 1975), 50, 52, 54

Kerner, Leighton: *Village Voice* (1 Feb. 1973)

Kolodin, Irving: *Saturday Review of Education* 1 no. 2 (Mar. 1973), 80

Mayer, Martin: 'Recordings', *Esquire* 82 (Aug. 1974), 30

Moevs, Robert: *Musical Quarterly* 61 no. 1 (Jan. 1975), 157–65

Northcott, Bayan: 'Crosstalk', *New Statesman* 86 no. 2230 (14 Dec. 1973), 920–1

Porter, Andrew: 'Mutual Ordering', *New Yorker* 48 no. 50 (3 Feb. 1973), 82–7

Rockwell, John: *Music and Musicians* 21 no. 7 (Mar. 1973), 58–9

Schonberg, Harold: 'Carter, Cage, Reich . . .Speak to Me', *New York Times* (4 Feb. 1973)

Smith, Patrick J.: *High Fidelity and Musical America* 23 no. 5 (May 1973), MA16–MA17

Steinberg, Michael: *Boston Globe* (11 Feb. 1973)

_____ *Boston Globe* (19 Feb. 1973)

SYMPHONY NO. 1

Salzman, Eric: *New York Times* (23 Jul. 1961)
Steinberg, Michael: sleeve notes for Louisville Recording, LOU–611
White, John R. *Music Library Association Notes* 22 no. 1 (Fall 1965), 820–1

A SYMPHONY OF THREE ORCHESTRAS

Breuer, Robert: 'Neues bei den New Yorker Philharmonikern', *Oesterreichische Musikzeitschrift* 32 no. 5/6 (May-June 1977)
Doucelin, Jacques: 'Boulez tire l'Orchestre de l'Opéra de sa Fosse', *Le Monde* (Paris) (5 Oct. 1977), 28
Dyer, Richard: 'Multiple orchestras at the BSO's Opening', *Boston Globe* (27 Sept. 1978)
Freeman, J. W.: 'Da New York', *Nuova Rivista Musicale Italiana* 11 no. 2 (1977), 251–3
Finn, Robert: *Cleveland Plain Dealer* (15 Apr. 1978)
Gill, Dominic: *Financial Times* (31 Jul. 1979)
Hamilton, David: *The Nation* 224 (12 Mar. 1977), 318
Heyworth, Peter: 'Great Sea of Events', *The Observer* (25 Mar. 1979)
Hruby, Frank: *Cleveland Plain Dealer* (14 Apr. 1978)
Kerner, Leighton: 'Elliott Carter Restores the Symphony's Double Identity', *Village Voice* (7 Mar. 1977), 52+
Kolodin, Irving: 'Carter's Symphony . . .', *Saturday Review* 4 (2 Apr. 1977), 37–8
Loppert, Max: *Financial Times* (23 Mar. 1979)
Mayer, William: 'Modern American Music Makes a Breakthrough', *Horizon* 20 no. 1 (Sept. 1977), 52–8
Mila, Massimo: 'L'americano Carter per tripla orchestra', *La Stampa* (Turin) (2 Mar. 1980)
Northcott, Bayan: 'French Powerhouse', *Sunday Telegraph* (16 Oct. 1977)
—— 'Three's a Crowd', *Sunday Telegraph* (25 Mar. 1979)
Porter, Andrew: 'Great Bridge, Our Myth', *New Yorker* 53 no. 3 (7 Mar. 1977), 101–4
Schiffer, Brigitte: 'Paris', *Music and Musicians* 26 no. 6 (Feb. 1978), 53–4
Schonberg, Harold : *New York Times* (18 Feb. 1977)
Smith, Patrick J.: 'New York', *Musical Times* 118 no. 1610 (Apr. 1977), 329

SYRINGA

Acton, Charles: *Irish Times* (Dublin) (8 Jan. 1980)
Heyworth, Peter: 'Orphic Mysteries', *The Observer* (1 June 1979)
Kerner, Leighton: 'Elliott Carter Wrestles at 70', *Village Voice* (25 Dec. 1978), 87–8
Kramer, Lawrence: ' "Syringa", John Ashbery and Elliott Carter', *Beyond Amazement: New Essays on John Ashbery* ed. David Lehman (Ithaca, N.Y.: Cornell University Press, 1980), 255–71

Northcott, Bayan: 'America's Magna Carter', *Sunday Telegraph* (17 Dec. 1978)
____ 'Carter's "Syringa" ', *Tempo* 128 (Mar. 1979), 31–2
Porter, Andrew: 'Famous Orpheus', *New Yorker* (8 Jan. 1979), 56–8, 61–3
____ 'Carter's "Syringa" ', *Financial Times* (16 Jan. 1979)
Schiffer, Brigitte: 'Elliott Carter', *Music and Musicians* 27 no. 8 (Apr. 1979), 61–2

TO MUSIC

Woodward, Henry: *Music Library Association Notes* 13 no. 2 (Mar. 1956), 348

VARIATIONS FOR ORCHESTRA

Acton, Charles: *Irish Times* (Dublin) (8 Jan. 1980)
Finn, Robert: *Cleveland Plain Dealer* (7 Mar. 1965)
Frankenstein, Alfred: *San Francisco Chronicle* (1 Feb. 1963)
Goldman, Richard Franko: RFG 45–7
Heyworth, Peter: 'American Mainstreamer', *The Observer* (28 Aug. 1966)
____ *Observer Weekend Review* (28 Aug. 1966)
Kenyon, Nicholas: *Music and Musicians* 25 no. 9 (May 1977), 47
Lees, Eugene: *Louisville Times* (23 Apr. 1956)
Mahlke, Sybill: *Der Tages Spiegel* (Berlin) (28 Apr. 1979)
Mann, Williams: *The Times* (15 Mar. 1972)
Marsh, Robert C.: *Chicago Sun-Times* (15 Oct. 1971)
____ *Showcase/Chicago Sun-Times* (21 Nov. 1971)
____ *Chicago Sun-Times* (27 June 1977)
Rostand, Claude: *Figaro Littéraire* (16 Feb. 1967)
Salzman, Eric: 'From Minneapolis, Some Great Music', *New York Herald Tribune* (10 Feb. 1966)
Schloss, Edwin H.: *Philadelphia Inquirer* (7 Dec. 1962)
Shawe-Taylor, Desmond: *Sunday Times* (19 Mar. 1972)
Stadlen, Peter: *The Daily Telegraph* (6 Sept. 1971)
Steinberg, Michael: *Boston Globe* (20 Mar. 1964)
Stewart, Robert: 'Serial Aspects of Elliott Carter's Variations for Orchestra', *Music Review* 34 no. 1 (Feb. 1973), 62–5

VOYAGE

Bernas, Richard: *Classical Music Weekly* (Jul. 1978)
Heyworth, Peter: 'Voyage of Discovery', *The Observer* (6 June 1976)
Horowitz, Joseph: *New York Times* (23 Feb. 1980)
Schonberg, Harold: *New York Times* (22 May 1975)

WARBLE FOR LILAC TIME

Schonberg, Harold: *New York Times* (22 May 1975)

WOODWIND QUINTET

Berger, Arthur: *New York Herald Tribune* (24 Oct. 1949)
Daniel, Oliver: *Bulletin of the American Composers Alliance* 4 no. 2 (1954), 21
Harmon, Carter: *New York Times* (28 Feb. 1949)
Thomson, Virgil: *New York Herald Tribune* (28 Feb. 1949)

Discography

(compiled by John Shepard)

All recordings are long-playing stereophonic discs except where the record number has the suffix (m) which denotes monophonic.

BRASS QUINTET

American Brass Quintet (Raymond Mase and Louis Ranger, trumpets; Edward Birdwell, French horn; Herbert Rankin, tenor trombone; Robert Biddlecombe, bass trombone); produced by Thomas Frost; with *Eight Pieces for Four Timpani* and *A Fantasy about Purcell's Fantasia upon One Note*; **Odyssey Y 34137** [1976]

CANON FOR 3: IN MEMORIAM IGOR STRAVINSKY

Two instrumentations: (1) Gerard Schwarz, trumpet, straight mute; Louis Ranger, trumpet, solotone mute; Stanley Rosenzweig, trumpet, cup mute; and (2) Gerard Schwarz, flugelhorn; Louis Ranger, cornet; Stanley Rosenzweig, trumpet (open); recorded by Jerry Bruck; in the collection *New Music for Trumpet, Played by Gerard Schwarz*; **Desto DC-7133** [1973]

Thomas Stevens, Mario Guarneri, Roy Poper, trumpets; in the collection *Music for Trumpet*; **Crystal S 361** [1976]

CONCERTO FOR ORCHESTRA

New York Philharmonic Orchestra, Leonard Bernstein conductor; produced by Richard Killough; with William Schuman's *In Praise of Shahn*; **Columbia** (USA) **M-30112** [1970]; re-released with *Syringa*; **CRI SD 469** [1982]

THE DEFENSE OF CORINTH

Thomas G. Gutheil, narrator; Harvard Glee Club, Elliot Forbes, conductor; **Harvard Glee Club F-HGC 64** [1964]

Jan Opalach, narrator; Edward Green and Mark Sutton Smith, pianists; The Columbia University Men's Glee Club, Gregg Smith, conductor; recorded by David Hancock; with *Musicians Wrestle Everywhere* in the collection *America Sings (1920-1950)*; **Vox SVBX 5353** [1977]

355

DOUBLE CONCERTO FOR HARPSICHORD AND PIANO WITH TWO CHAMBER ORCHESTRAS

Ralph Kirkpatrick, harpsichord; Charles Rosen, piano; English Chamber Orchestra, Gustav Meier, conductor; produced by Jane Friedmann; with Leon Kirchner's *Concerto for Violin, Cello, Ten Winds and Percussion*; **Epic LC 3830** (m) and **BC 1157** [1962]; released in UK with Piano Sonata (Rosen); **EMI ALP 2025** (m) and **ASD 601**

Paul Jacobs, harpsichord; Charles Rosen, piano; English Chamber Orchestra, Frederik Prausnitz, conductor; produced by Andrew Kazdin; with *Variations for Orchestra*; **Columbia** (USA) **MS-7191** [1968]

Paul Jacobs, harpsichord; Gilbert Kalish, piano; Contemporary Chamber Ensemble, Arthur Weisberg, conductor; co-ordinated by Teresa Sterne; with *Duo for Violin and Piano*; **Nonesuch H-71314** [1975]

DUO FOR VIOLIN AND PIANO

Paul Zukofsky, violin; Gilbert Kalish, piano; co-ordinated by Teresa Sterne; with *Double Concerto*; **Nonesuch H-71314** [1975]

DUST OF SNOW
(see *Three Poems of Robert Frost*)

EIGHT ETUDES AND A FANTASY FOR WOODWIND QUARTET

Members of the New York Woodwind Quintet (Murray Panitz, flute; David Glazer, clarinet; Jerome Roth, oboe; Bernard Garfield, bassoon); with Quincey Porter's String Quartet No. 8; **CRI 118** (m) [1958]

Members of the New York Woodwind Quintet (Samuel Baron, flute; Ronald Roseman, oboe; David Glazer, clarinet; Arthur Weisberg, bassoon); with Gunther Schuller's Woodwind Quintet and Irving Fine's *Partita for Wind Quintet*; **Concert-Disc M 1229** (m) and **CS 229** [1963]

Members of the Dorian Quintet (Karl Kraber, flute; Charles Kuskin, oboe; William Lewis, clarinet; Jane Taylor, bassoon); with Woodwind Quintet and Hans Werner Henze's Quintett; **Candide 31016** [1969]

[*Eight Etudes* only] Paula Robinson, flute; Leonard Arner, oboe; Gervase de Peyer, clarinet; Loren Glickman, bassoon; in the collection *The Chamber Music Society of Lincoln Center*; **Classics Record Library SQM 80-5731** [1975]

EIGHT PIECES FOR FOUR TIMPANI

Morris Lang, timpani; produced by Thomas Frost; with Brass Quintet and *A Fantasy about Purcell's Fantasia upon One Note*; **Odyssey Y 34137** [1976]

[4 pieces only: *Recitative, Moto Perpetuo, Saëta, Improvisation*] Sylvio Gualda, timpani; with Nguyen Thien Dao's *May* and Iannis Xenakis's *Psappha*; **Erato 71106** [1978]

ELEGY FOR STRING ORCHESTRA

Los Angeles Chamber Orchestra, Gerard Schwarz, conductor; produced by Marc J. Aubort and Joanna Nickrenz; with Samuel Barber's *Serenade*, Op. 1, David Diamond's *Rounds* and Irving Fine's *Serious Song*; **Nonesuch 79002** [1980]

ELEGY FOR STRING QUARTET

Composers Quartet (Matthew Raimondi and Anahid Ajemian, violins; Jean Dane, viola; Michael Rudiakov, cello); in the collection *The Composers String Quartet Plays Literature of American Contemporary Composers*; **Golden Crest NEC-115** [1977]

THE HARMONY OF MORNING

The Gregg Smith Singers, Orpheus Ensemble, Gregg Smith, conductor; recorded by David Hancock; in the collection *America Sings, Vol. IV*; **Vox SVBX 5354** [1979]

HEART NOT SO HEAVY AS MINE

Hamline A Cappella Choir, Robert Holliday, conductor; in the collection *Choral Music of the 20th Century* in the *Music In America* series; **The Society for the Preservation of the American Musical Heritage MIA 116** [1961]

Canby Singers, Edward Tatnall Canby, conductor; production supervised by Teresa Sterne; with *Musicians Wrestle Everywhere* in the collection *The Dove Descending*; **Nonesuch H-1115** (m) and **H-71115** [1966]

HOLIDAY OVERTURE

American Composers Orchestra, Paul Dunkel, conductor; recorded by David Hancock; with *Suite from Pocahontas* and Symphony No. 1; **CRI SD 475** [1982]

THE LINE GANG
(see *Three Poems of Robert Frost*)

A MIRROR ON WHICH TO DWELL

[2 songs only: *Argument* and *Sandpiper*] Deborah Cook, soprano; Ensemble InterContemporain, Pierre Boulez, conductor; recorded commentary in French by Elliott Carter and Pierre Boulez; produced by Jean-Pierre Derrien; with Olivier Messiaen's *Mode de valeurs et d'intensités*; **Radio France/IRCAM cassette Le Temps Musical 3** [1978]

Susan Davenny Wyner, soprano; Speculum Musicae, Richard Fitz, conductor; produced by Andrew Kazdin; with *A Symphony of Three Orchestras*; **Columbia** (USA) **M 35171** [1980]

MUSICIANS WRESTLE EVERYWHERE

Canby Singers, Edward Tatnall Canby, conductor; production supervised by Teresa Sterne; with *Heart Not So Heavy as Mine* in the collection *The Dove Descending*; **Nonesuch H-1115** (m) and **H-71115** [1966]

The Gregg Smith Singers, Gregg Smith, conductor; recorded by David Hancock; with *The Defense of Corinth* in the collection *America Sings (1920-1950)*; **Vox SVBX 5353** [1977]

Tanglewood Festival Chorus, John Oliver, conductor; produced by Rainer Brock; with works of Charles Ives, Aaron Copland, and Jacob Druckman in the collection *American Choral Music of the Twentieth Century*; **Deutsche Grammophon 2530912** [1979]

NIGHT FANTASIES

Paul Jacobs, piano; with Piano Sonata; recorded by Max Wilcox to be released by **Nonesuch** [1983]

PASTORAL FOR CLARINET AND PIANO

John Russo, clarinet; Lydia Walton Ignacio, piano; in the collection *Pastorale*; **Orion 77275** [1977]

Else Ludewig-Verdehr, clarinet; David Liptak, piano; with Mario Castlenuovo-Tedesco's Sonata and Vincent Frohne's *Study*; **Grenadilla GS 1018** [1980]

PIANO CONCERTO

Jacob Lateiner, piano; Boston Symphony Orchestra, Erich Leinsdorf, conductor (recorded during performances at Symphony Hall, Boston, 7–8 Jan. 1967); produced by Howard Scott; with Michael Colgrass's *As Quiet As*; **RCA Victor LM-3001** (m) and **LSC-3001** [1968]

PIANO SONATA

Beveridge Webster, piano; with Sonata for Violoncello and Piano; **American Recording Society ARS-25** (m) [1951]; re-released by **Desto Records** as **D-419** (m) and **DST-6419** [1965]

Charles Rosen, piano; with *Suite from Pocahontas*; **Epic LC 3850** (m) and **BC 1250** [1963]. Released in UK with *Double Concerto*; **EMI ALP 2052** (m) and **ASD 601**

Beveridge Webster, piano; with Aaron Copland's *Piano Variations* and Roger Sessions's Second Sonata; **Dover 5265** (m) and **7265** [1966]

Noel Lee, piano; with Aaron Copland's *Piano Variations* and Roger Sessions's Second Sonata; **Valois MB 755** [1967]

Evelinde Trenkner, piano; produced by Giveon Cornfield; with works of Alfredo Casella, Arthur Honegger and Franz Liszt; **Orion ORS 79342** [1980]

Paul Jacobs, piano; with *Night Fantasies*; recorded by Max Wilcox to be released by **Nonesuch** [1983]

THE ROSE FAMILY
(see *Three Poems by Robert Frost*)

SONATA FOR FLUTE, OBOE, CELLO, AND HARPSICHORD

Anabel Brieff, flute; Josef Marx, oboe; Lorin Bernsohn, cello; Robert Conant, harpsichord; with Harold Shapero's String Quartet No. 1; **Columbia (USA) ML 5576** (m) and **MS 6176** [1960]

Samuel Baron, flute; Ronald Roseman, oboe; Alexander Kouguell, cello; Sylvia Marlowe, harpsichord; produced by Israel Horowitz; with works by Falla, Rorem, and Sauguet; **Decca DL 10108** (m) and **DL 710108** [1965]

Harvey Sollberger, flute; Charles Kuskin, oboe; Fred Sherry, cello; Paul Jacobs, harpsichord; co-ordinated by Teresa Sterne; with Sonata for Violoncello and Piano; **Nonesuch 71234** [1969]

Boston Symphony Chamber Players (Doriot Anthony Dwyer, flute; Ralph Gomberg, oboe; Jules Eskin, cello; Robert Levin, harpsichord); produced by Karl Faust and Tom Mowrey; with Charles Ives's *Largo* and Quincey Porter's Quintet for Oboe and String Quartet; **Deutsche Grammophon 2530 104** [1971]

New England Conservatory of Music Chamber Players (Jolie Troob, flute; Cheryl Priebe, oboe; Gloria Johns, cello; Christopher Kies, harpsichord); recorded by Robert Rachdorf; with works of Milton Babbitt, Henry Brant, and Igor Stravinsky; **Golden Crest NEC 109** [1976]

SONATA FOR VIOLONCELLO AND PIANO

Bernard Greenhouse, cello; Anthony Makas, piano; with Piano Sonata; **American Recording Society ARS-25**(m) [1951]; re-released by **Desto Records** as **D-419** (m) and **DST-6419** [1965]

Joel Krosnick, cello; Paul Jacobs, piano; co-ordinated by Teresa Sterne; with Sonata for Flute, Oboe, Cello, and Harpsichord; **Nonesuch 71234** [1969]

Michael Rudiakov, cello; Ursula Oppens, piano; with Bach's Suite in G, BWV 1007; **Golden Crest RE 7081** [1979]

DISCOGRAPHY
STRING QUARTET NO. 1

Walden Quartet of the University of Illinois (Homer Schmitt and Bernard Goodman, violins; John Garvey, viola; Robert Swenson, cello); **Columbia** (usa) **ML 5104** (m) [1956]

Composers Quartet (Matthew Raimondi and Anahid Ajemian, violins; Jean Dupouy, viola; Michael Rudiakov, cello); co-ordinated by Teresa Sterne; with String Quartet No. 2; **Nonesuch 71249** [1970]

STRING QUARTET NO. 2

Juilliard String Quartet (Robert Mann and Isadore Cohen, violins; Raphael Hillyer, viola; Claus Adam, cello); produced by Peter Dellheim; with William Schuman's String Quartet No. 3; **RCA Victor LM-2481** (m) and **LSC-2481** [1961]

Composers Quartet (Matthew Raimondi and Anahid Ajemian, violins; Jean Dupouy, viola; Michael Rudiakov, cello); co-ordinated by Teresa Sterne; with String Quartet No. 1; **Nonesuch 71249** [1970]

Juilliard String Quartet (Robert Mann and Earl Carlyss, violins; Raphael Hillyer, viola; Claus Adam, cello); produced by Richard Killough; with String Quartet No. 3; **Columbia** (usa) **M 32738** [1974]

STRING QUARTET NO. 3

Juilliard String Quartet (Duo I: Earl Carlyss, violin; Claus Adam, cello; Duo II: Robert Mann, violin; Samuel Rhodes, viola); produced by Jay David Saks; with String Quartet No. 2; **Columbia** (usa) **M 32738** [1974]

SUITE FROM POCAHONTAS

Zurich Radio Orchestra, Jacques Monod, conductor; with Piano Sonata; **Epic LC 3850** (m) and **BC 1250** [1963]

American Composers Orchestra, Paul Dunkel, conductor; recorded by David Hancock; with *Holiday Overture* and Symphony No. 1; **CRI SD 475** [1982]

SUITE FROM THE MINOTAUR

Eastman-Rochester Symphony Orchestra, Howard Hanson, conductor; produced by David Hall; with Colin McPhee's *Tabuh-Tabuhan*; **Mercury MG 50103** (m) [1956]; re-released with Henry Cowell's Symphony No. 4 and Wallingford Riegger's *New Dance;* **Mercury Golden Imports SRI 75111** (m) [1978]

SYMPHONY NO. 1

Louisville Orchestra, Robert Whitney, conductor; with Alexei Haieff's *Divertimento*; **Louisville LOU-611** (m) [1961]

American Composers Orchestra, Paul Dunkel, conductor; recorded by David Hancock; with *Holiday Overture* and *Suite from Pocahontas*; **CRI SD 475** [1982]

A SYMPHONY OF THREE ORCHESTRAS

New York Philharmonic Orchestra, Pierre Boulez, conductor; produced by Andrew Kazdin; with *A Mirror on Which to Dwell*; **Columbia** (USA) **M 35171** [1980]

SYRINGA

Jan de Gaetani, mezzo-soprano; Thomas Paul, bass; Speculum Musicae, Harvey Sollberger, conductor; recorded by David Hancock; with *Concerto for Orchestra*; **CRI SD 469** [1982]

TARANTELLA

Harvard Glee Club, Elliot Forbes, conductor; in the collection *Harvard in Song*; **Carillon 118** (m) [1961]

TELL ME WHERE IS FANCY BRED

Unidentified alto, unidentified guitarist; in Shakespeare's *The Merchant of Venice* (condensed) with Orson Welles and members of the Mercury Theatre; on side 14 of **Columbia** (USA) **Masterworks set MC-6** (m) (12 12-inch discs 78rpm) [1938]

Rosalind Rees, soprano; David Starobin, guitar; recorded by David Hancock; in the collection *20th Century Music for Voice and Guitar*; **Turnabout TV 34727** [1978]

THREE POEMS OF ROBERT FROST

Meriel Dickinson, mezzo-soprano; Peter Dickinson, piano; with *Voyage* in the collection *An American Anthology*; **Unicorn RHS 353** [1978]

[*Dust of Snow* and *The Rose Family* only] William Hess, tenor; Robert Fizdale, piano; with Theodore Chanler's *The Doves* and three *Epitaphs*; **Hargail HN-708** (m) (10-inch 78rpm) [1947]

TO MUSIC

University of Michigan Chamber Choir, Thomas Hillbish, conductor; produced by Andrew Raeburn; with Randall Thompson's *Americana* and Seymour Shifrin's *The Odes of Shang*; **New World Records NW 219** [1977]

VARIATIONS FOR ORCHESTRA

Louisville Orchestra, Robert Whitney, conductor; with Everett Helm's Second Piano Concerto; **Louisville LOU 58-3** (m) [1958]

New Philharmonia Orchestra, Frederik Prausnitz, conductor; produced by Andrew Kazdin; with *Double Concerto;* **Columbia** (USA) **MS-7191** [1968]

VOYAGE

Meriel Dickinson, mezzo-soprano; Peter Dickinson, piano; with *Three Poems of Robert Frost* in the collection *An American Anthology*; **Unicorn RHS 353** [1978]

WOODWIND QUINTET

New Art Wind Quintet (Andrew Lolya, flute; Melvin Kaplan, oboe; Irving Neidich, clarinet; Tina di Dario, bassoon; Elizabeth Bobo, French horn); in the collection *American Woodwind Symposium*; **Classic Editions CE 2003** (m) [1953]

Boston Symphony Chamber Players (Doriot Anthony Dwyer, flute; Ralph Gomberg, oboe; Gino Cioffi, clarinet; Sherman Walt, bassoon; James Stagliano, French horn); produced by Richard Mohr; with works by Mozart, Beethoven, Brahms, Copland, Fine, and Piston; **RCA Victor LM-6167** (m) and **LSC-6167** [1966]

Dorian Quintet (Karl Kraber, flute; Charles Kuskin, oboe; William Lewis, clarinet; Jane Taylor, bassoon; Barry Benjamin, French horn); with *Eight Etudes and a Fantasy* and Hans Werner Henze's Quintett; **Candide 31016** [1969]; re-released in the collection *The Avant-Garde Woodwind Quintet in the U.S.A.*; **Vox SVBX 5307** [1977]

List of Charts

363

Index of Carter's Works

General Index